1971

INFERNO

DANTE ALIGHIERI

Inferno

The Italian text
with translation and notes
by

ALLAN GILBERT

1 9 6 9
DUKE UNIVERSITY PRESS
Durham, N. C.

PRINTED IN THE UNITED STATES OF
AMERICA BY HERITAGE PRINTERS, INC.

To the Memory of Robert L. Flowers,
who in 1924, as Treasurer of Duke University,
approved the publication, by the infant Duke
University Press, of my *Dante's
Conception of Justice.*

Acknowledgments

I am grateful to Duke University, as represented by the Research Council, the Duke University Press, the William E. Perkins Library, and other officials, for forty-five years of continuous assistance with my Dante studies. My onetime pupil, Dr. Enzo Orvieto of the University of Cincinnati, has loaned me his photographs of Guido da Pisa's commentary on the *Inferno*. I am also indebted to Professor Joseph G. Fucilla and Professor Robert J. Clements.

CONTENTS

PREFACE

Though Dante has left nothing on translating his *Commedia*, he did speak on translation when considering Latin commentary on some of his *canzoni*. Paraphrase or translation into Latin would take those poems, he explains, where they could be carried only in their ideas, not in their musical beauty. Everybody, indeed, should realize that nothing harmonized according to the rules of poetry can be carried over from its own language into some other without destroying all its sweetness and harmony. This is the reason why Homer cannot be turned from Greek into Latin as can Greek scientific writers. And this is the reason why the verses of the Psalter are without the sweetness of poetical music and harmony, because they were translated from Hebrew into Greek, and from Greek into Latin, and in the first translation all such sweetness vanished (freely rendered from Dante's *Convivio* 1.7).

For amusingly evident reasons, this assertion is not often quoted by translators of Dante, especially by those translating, as they put it, "in the meter of the original." They seldom indicate the necessity of Milton's qualification: "as near as the language will permit." Such translators argue that since Dante wrote in verse, in that medium his effect can be carried over into another language. That is, their English verse renders the spirit of Dante's Italian verse. But this belief implies details concealed in the brief statement. When fully stated, it runs: Bad English verse renders the effect of good Italian verse. Some translators, with a misty perception of the difficulty, have abandoned *terza rima* —a difficult English meter. Longfellow, most practiced in verse-writing of the English translators, wisely abandoned rime. But even making the ridiculous assumption of a translator with Dante's metrical skill, we cannot expect from a versifier bound to another man's thought, lines equaling those in the original. So while the Italian asks to be read aloud, tough-eared is he who can be content to listen to a hundred lines of translator's verse. If ever verse renderings are tolerable by the ear, their effect is so unlike that of the original that Dante disappears to make room for the English versifier; the latter may offer—though he seldom does so—pretty enough poetry, but not Dante.

Translators into English *terza rima*—supposed equivalent to the meter of the original—or into some laudable simplification of it, have shown practically that their native verse is unlike Italian, in that they have not attempted the feminine rimes all but universal in the *Commedia*.[1] Yet their line-by-line or tercet-by-tercet reproductions show their failure to observe elementary differences between English and Italian. Any caricature of speech by an Italian first attempting English reveals the larger number of vowels he is accustomed to. Thus English *road*, with its synonyms *way, street, track, course, path*, appears as *via, strada, viale, corso, sentiero*, which force a writer toward the larger number of syllables in *avenue, highway, byway, thoroughfare*. Though Italian has syllable-saving economies of her own, such as elimination of subject pronouns and continual elision, the ten or thirty syllables per line or tercet offered in an English interpretation do not correspond with the eleven or thirty-three of the original. Eight or twenty-four—with some exceptions—more often are enough to render the idea. So the English versifier is driven to what Herrick called "farcing buckram." He adds words which dilute his archetype, or ideas which pervert it.

Prose versions have no immunity from the Dantesque condemnation of any attempt to carry poetry over into another language. Yet, avoiding the delusive pretenses of the verse rendering, they offer negative virtues. They do not raise a barrier against enjoyment by professing to offer the qualities of their model, when powerless to do so. They strive to give the sense of the exemplar, without attempting that carrying over of beauty which Dante knew to be unattainable. The translator who eschews meter admits Dante's understanding of poetical aesthetic, and defends an English rendering by asserting that a shadowy and inadequate view of a great work is better than total ignorance of it. Even this position may be assailed; the reader of translations easily chloroforms himself into thinking he has read the great works themselves.

The maker of a humble prose version has some advantages. Not being under the tyranny of ten syllables, he can more easily than the versifier be succinct where Dante is succinct, be plain where Dante is plain, is less tempted to devise figures of speech unknown to the poet. In those few but important passages where equivalent English syllables outnumber the Italian, he is under

1. In Longfellow's unrimed version the feminine ending is frequent.

no necessity for truncating the master's thought in order to fit it to the line or the tercet. The unmetrical worker, however, after he has fulfilled his primary duty to the sense of the archetype, must strive for language that does not contradict the spirit of the original, and is subject to all the demands of prose style.

If the close rendering possible to prose be allowed, how is it to be defined? Some recent versions, for example, offer *thou* for the Italian *tu*, the second person singular. Surely a reader should not forget that Dante wrote more than six centuries ago; but on the other hand he used the language of his day, though now and then the commentators even of his own century seem to have misunderstood him. Long ago *thou* was current, but now no Americans and few Englishmen hear it spoken except in church. Such ecclesiastical suggestion hinders appreciation of the *Commedia* as a comedy. I have throughout avoided archaism and sought for language immediately intelligible, avoiding un-English expressions without being false to the Italian. Whether I am to have credit for more than effort, readers can judge. As to the effect of the Italian, a translator can hope to move toward the quality of another language, but not far. My assumption has been that Dante always means something and that the simpler of two explanations is likely to be correct; doubtless I have sometimes made him appear too obvious.

The meaning of many passages is debated by scholars, as, for example by Professor Antonino Pagliaro in his recent *Ulisse, Ricerche Semantiche sulla Divina Commedia*. While—since a translator must choose—I follow what seem to me the most probable interpretations, I do not deny that other explanations deserve consideration; certainty is sometimes impossible. I do not wish to hint that I have divined the poet's intentions. I have, however, sometimes departed from the usual translations, and even from the views of important Italian editors. For such deviations, I have always sought justification, yet some of them doubtless should be modified or rejected.[2]

The *Commedia* combines two elements: a poem by the historical Dante; a narrative by a fictitious traveler named Dante. The most evident examples of the first are the invocations of the Muse, as *Inferno* 2.7–9. These and other passages in which the

2. Some such passages on which I have written notes are *Inf.* 2.10; 3.136; 4.72; 5.4, 19, 56, 79; 6.33; 9.1–3; 10.63; 11.70; 12.131; 13.21, 150; 14.69, 105; 18.114; 19.20, 24; 21.54, 69; 22.84; 27.17, 95, 129; 28.128; 29.27; 32.6, 17, 41, 47, 96; 34.1.

writer as such is prominent, I have indicated as by the Poet. The narrative is of two sorts. The traveler gives his own experiences and observations. These I have marked as by the Narrator. But this narrator also reports what was said by various characters, including himself. To emphasize this dramatic quality, I have put the name of the speaker before all such passages. Since the work is, however, not a drama or dialogue, bits of narrative often accompany what is reported as said.

I have endeavored to give my readers the benefit of recent scholarly work. Especially I have consulted various books printed too late for use by most of the translators of the *Inferno* into English. Natalino Sapegno's edition of the *Commedia* appeared in 1957, the revision of that by Carlo Steiner in 1958, and Chimenz' in 1962. Scartazzini's comprehensive edition was reprinted in 1965; the original of 1899 is not easily obtained. The text of the *Inferno* in Giorgio Petrocchi's *La Commedia secondo l'antica vulgata* is dated 1966. The first of the four volumes now issued of Salvatore Battaglia's *Grande Dizionario della Lingua Italiana* came out in 1961, and the first part of the Cambridge Italian Dictionary in 1962. The year 1954 saw the completion of Gerhard Rohlfs' *Historische Grammatik der Italienischen Sprache,* and 1960 that of Battaglia and Pernicone's *Grammatica Italiana.* Siebzehner-Vivanti's *Dizionario della Divina Commedia* is of 1958. The *Concordance to the Divine Comedy* edited by Wilkins and Bergen was issued in 1965. In 1966 appeared Robert C. Melzi's *Castelvetro's Annotations to the Inferno* and Antonino Pagliaro's *Ulisse, Ricerche semantiche sulla Divina Commedia.*

I have endeavored to keep in mind as I have worked that the only real *Commedia* is that which flowed in Italian from Dante's pen. A translator is successful in proportion as he sends readers to the original.

Drew University
Madison, New Jersey
May 1967

INTRODUCTION

I. THE NATURE OF THE POEM

1. Poetic greatness

Seven hundred years ago (1265) Dante was born. Today his work is better known in the English-speaking world than ever before. There have been ups and downs in Dantesque sympathies, but his mark has been left on most English poets, from Chaucer to T. S. Eliot. From Longinus to the present, the test of a poem's greatness has been its continuing power to please, to please in all eras all men, however different in occupations, habits, ideals and ages. As Emerson said, a classic is a work written a thousand years ago which seems to have been written today, a work written today which might have been composed a thousand years since. Such views rest on belief in human nature as unchanging in fundamentals, to be dated only in what is superficial. The work of art which vanishes in a few years is overconcerned with the passing scene and leaves untouched the things that abide; it does not bear the imprint of a maker's vigor and wisdom.

The present popularity of Dante (if that word can be applied to him) is reduced on observing that his poem has now become one of the things every educated man is supposed to know. But though we admit the part played by pedagogues, why did schoolmen select Dante rather than some other? When in the fluctuations of taste, Dante has at times been almost forgotten or has been regarded with amused contempt, as by Voltaire, why has he again come to general knowledge? Why has he not been placed among those pitiable authors known only to scholars, professional students of Romance literature? The answer must admit intrinsic greatness, or must assert that the verdict of history cannot be trusted.

2. Poetry and erudition

By writing about poetry little is accomplished. What matters is the goodness and beauty, as Dante puts it, that each reader sees or feels for himself. Even to readers of slight attainment, poems may reveal excellence undiscovered by professional students. To no man is an idea about a poem of value unless it is his own, derived from his personal application and meditation. This may be insisted upon even by one skeptical about human power to originate. Little aid can be given to any person who reads with pleasure, with what is called appreciation. I imply no disparagement of preparatory knowledge. Evidently the easiest reading would be that by a contemporary of Dante, at home in the age's language, natural science, theology and history. Yet the value of trying to gain such knowledge before reading the poetry can be too much insisted on.

An extreme case illustrates this. The Florentine author took for granted the astronomy of his day, namely that the earth is in the center of the universe; around it revolve the heavenly bodies, including the sun. On this system depends the sequence of the *Paradiso*. Now imagine the poem read by a person ignorant of astronomical history. He has only to take the *Paradiso* as it comes; Beatrice takes her pupil up and up, from star to star, until they reach the highest heaven. Any sensible man will assume that the poet is not trying to be abnormal; the sequence is surely not merely what Dante wished for poetical purposes—the main matter—but it also probably seemed not unusual to fourteenth-century readers. For the purposes of the poem, why not take the heavens in which the poet places his action as though they were the undiscovered lands visited by Gulliver?

To Dante perhaps more than to any other stellar poet, great learning has commonly been assigned. It appears in the *Chronicle* of his younger contemporary, Giovanni Villani, who reports that his countryman "was author of the *Commedia*, which he wrote in polished verse with long and subtle disquisitions, moral, natural, astrological, philosophical; and with fine and novel figures and comparisons and poetical passages, in a hundred chapters or cantos he dealt with his having been in Hell and Purgatory and Paradise,[1] as nobly as can be, as anyone of subtle intellect can see and understand through the said work" (9.135). Though Villani realized poetical power, this science and philosophy was to him—as generally to the early commentators—one proof of Dante's greatness. Indeed, the early writers on the *Commedia* were more concerned with the learned man than with the poet.

1. I follow the copy in my library printed in Florence in 1587 by the Giunti brothers. The text often followed says—incorrectly, I suppose—that he dealt with "the being and state of Hell," etc.

In modern times there has been some reaction. The celebrated Italian critic De Sanctis spoke out against the *Paradiso*, the part of the poem where learning is most evident. By one American Dantist, devoted to his subject, some such parts of the *Paradiso* are frankly called arid.

To the great Florentine his own learning presumably appeared admirable. He insists on the pleasure to be derived from the ideas expressed in poetry; it is greater than the pleasure derived from beauty of language (*Convivio* 2.11). This notion of poetical pleasure in idea has been neglected by modern students of aesthetics. Yet in his *Commedia* Dante perhaps gave too much space to good ideas, relatively little touched with beauty. Such a procedure fitted with his zeal in teaching. Moreover, as a studious man he was influenced—even overinfluenced—by the didactic notions of his era. To digress, as Dante admits that he does, we need not forget that the present literary art is powerfully influenced by didactic aims, both as to composition and critical estimate. To return, Dante himself is in part responsible for the insistence of modern scholars on his learning.

Influenced by it, they present the *Commedia* as an "encyclopedia" of the middle ages. Many of us can declare our pleasure in encyclopedias. Yet an encyclopedia is not a poem. Whatever the information, incidental or avowedly offered, in the three *cantiche*, they are not an assemblage of unrelated pieces of information in plain rather than poetical language. Villani, for all his interest in Dante's learning, does not go that far. Dante did insist on beauty in poetry. To call the work an encyclopedia is to say to the reader that he can look forward to the pleasure of learning facts rather than to that derived from imaginative fiction. Even the most arid exposition in the *Commedia* has at least a tinge of poetic quality.

3. Dante did not write for the learned only

Dante wrote nothing in explanation of his *Commedia*, unless a letter addressed to the Veronese nobleman, Can Grande della Scala, is genuine. Of debated authenticity, it is not a basis for proof.[1] It presents critical ideas normal in Dante's century.

In his *Convivio*, of undebated genuineness, Dante deals with

1. See my "Did Dante Dedicate the *Paradiso* to Can Grande della Scala?" *Italica*, XLIII (1966), 100–124.

the poetry of his lyrics. Poetic verity, he says, "is hidden under the cloak of the stories the poets tell,[2] and is a truth hidden under a pleasing lie" (2.1).[3] In his work *On the Vulgar Tongue*, that is, *On the Italian Language*, he says that poetry "is nothing other than fiction handled by means of rhetoric and music" (2.4). However important the ideas of poetry, they are not the sole reasons for reading:

> Oh men who cannot perceive the meaning of this *canzone*, do not for that reason reject it; but give your attention to its beauty, which is great both because of its construction, which grammarians deal with, and through the arrangement of what is said, which rhetoricians deal with, and through the versification of the various parts, which interests those who look for beauty of sound. In this poem, then, these things seem admirable to anybody who looks carefully. (*Convivio* 2.11)

Thus Dante concedes much to the ordinary reader, who interests him as much as do the learned. Indeed, with all his respect for erudition, Dante shows some distrust of university men, because "they are so inclined to greed for wealth that it takes them away from all loftiness of mind. . . . In censure of them I say that they should not be called devoted to learning, because they do not acquire learning for its worth, but only because through it they gain money or rank" (*Convivio* 1.9).

The poet then decides to comment on his *canzoni* in Italian rather than Latin, because many are ignorant of the learned language:

> It is obvious that anything written in Latin will benefit few, but anything in Italian will certainly be useful to many. Because goodness of mind, which desires this service, is found in those who through the wretched malpractice of the world have left education in Latin to those who have made that language from a ruling lady into a whore; and these noble persons are princes, barons, knights and many other noble persons, not men only but women, both of whom abound in this country, knowing Italian but not understanding Latin. (*Convivio* 1.9)

2. Literally, "these stories," explained by commentators as mythological stories and poetic fictions.
3. I accept the usual emended text.

Though our author is here speaking of his lesser works, application to the *Commedia* is evident. To write in Italian was to seek
as readers the many rather than the few. This is given reverse
demonstration by Boccaccio, who regretted that the older author
made the wonders of his poem accessible to men without Latin
education, for it was worthy of a learned audience. Dante, wails
Boccaccio, wrote in the language in which ignorant women converse.[4] Yet for an audience speaking that language our poet prepared the "beautiful falsehood" of the journey entirely through
the globe of earth and to highest heaven.

To the modern reader this deliberately popular character of the
Commedia is of high importance. Dante wrote not only for laymen but for Italian laymen, with no apparent thought of foreign
circulation. For example, only a person who has been in Bologna
can get the full force of the comparison of a giant with a leaning
tower in that city (*Inf.* 31.136). No notes can do it, as I can testify
from my own experience. Here the passage of time has also
worked against Dante, since the tower was in his day higher,
hence more impressive. Somewhat less difficult is *Inferno* 31.41,
full of meaning to anyone who has seen a towered fortress,
though best of all is to have seen Monteriggioni herself, even in
her present degenerate state, with only part of her towers, and
they lower than when Dante passed them on the road to Siena.
Yet the two lines are so impressive as to justify themselves to a
reader ignorant of the particular *castello* named. Indeed even in
America, a land without castles, as Ruskin remarked, the vivid-
ness of both figures brings something of the spirit of the medieval
fortress to our castleless territory.

We need not assert that Dante never wrote only for the learned.
How many ignorant of Latin in his day could connect anything
with some of the names in the canto of Limbo? Yet such a name
as Averroes doubtless conveyed some notion then, just as Dar-
win's name now conveys something, even to writer or reader who
has never opened one of his books.

At the end of Canto 11, we read: "The Fishes are wiggling on
the horizon, and the Great Dipper is right over Caurus." To most
readers in this day these lines mean nothing. In Dante's time,
many, we may suppose, told the time from the heavenly bodies
instead of clocks. Commentators say it means that more than a

---

4. See the *Epistle to Can Grande*, sec. 10, for a similar remark. This is
one of many instances in which the Epistle speaks the language of the time.

third of the time alloted to Hell on Virgil's timetable has gone by. At least a modern reader who does not bother with notes probably here gets the idea that time is pressing.

Just preceding is a passage showing the effects of age, though its idea would have caused no remark when written. Virgil explains why usury is a sin (11.94 ff.). Perhaps his explanation would have appeared subtle to Giovanni Villani, but usury was commonly known to be sinful. To most moderns—even those who know that in *The Merchant of Venice* Shakespeare deals with objections to moneylending—to think the taking of interest wrong seems silly. Could Dante have assumed that many readers would be glad of a clear presentation of its sinfulness? At least any modern reader willing to enter into Dante's fiction, even to observe the naturalness of the traveler's question to Virgil that brings on the exposition, can hardly find the passage difficult. Passages so smacking of the schoolmaster are less evident in the *Inferno* than in the other parts, especially the *Paradiso*.

In its relative freedom from didactic exposition, the *Inferno* is more immediately and generally satisfying than the other two *cantiche*, especially than the *Paradiso*. Even so devoted a Dantist as the late Professor Grandgent admitted that he took little pleasure in some of the didactic portions of the heavenly experience, and De Sanctis spoke still more severely. Yet even in the *Paradiso* formidable passages need not be unduly struggled with; the reader may make a sort of anthology of the passages he finds to his poetical taste, leaving others to be reconsidered when his information is greater. Our immediate concern, the *Inferno*, offers few passages so scholastic as to impede readers willing to take the work simply and naturally, as a poem should be taken.

II. THE TOPOGRAPHY OF THE *INFERNO*
OR
THE STAGE FOR THE FIRST ACT
OF THE COMEDY

As has been a thousand times observed, the general shape of Dante's Inferno is that of a huge inverted cone with its base near the surface of the globe of earth and its point at the center. Inside this cone are shelves or terraces extending around the circumference, each evidently of smaller diameter than that above. Since the whole is as unreal as a dream, we need not think strange Dante's failure to tell how the thin shell of earth's surface covering this enormous cavity is sustained. We no more ask about the probability of this underworld than we do of the region inside the earth visited by Aeneas, as related in *Aeneid* 6, or about the fairy world underground in an old English ballad, or under the waters of a lake in *Orlando Innamorato*. In contrast with these, Dante's Hell sometimes offers an exactness making it the scene of the most unreal, and at the same time the most real, of visits to the other world.

To the size of Hell, Dante pays little attention, as though there is nothing strange in arriving at the earth's center in twenty-four hours. Since the poet never indicates—as he does in his *Paradiso* —any miraculous progress, we have nothing to suppose other than that the travelers cover the distance of a day's walk, supplemented by their ride on Geryon. In Aeneas' journey in the lower world, no specification of time or distance appears; the effect is merely that of a walk long enough to offer such variation of topography as a single day might furnish. The Latin hero does not visit Tartarus, being merely told that it extends down into the darkness twice the distance from earth to the heavenly Olympus (*Aeneid* 6.577 ff.).

The early commentators on the *Commedia* took the topography of Hell for granted, but after two hundred years, a school of arithmetical or geometrical literalists arose, to concern themselves with the topography and measurements of Dante's pit, set forth in various diagrams, differing somewhat among themselves but all passionately defended by their makers. This type of study, catching in its current so great a man as the astronomer Galileo, continued into the last century. Its results appear in the diagrams in current editions of Dante.

They set out from the passage in which Master Adam says that the bolgia in which he is tortured has a circumference of eleven miles and is half a mile wide (*Inf.* 30.86 f.). To this is added Virgil's assertion that the ninth bolgia extends twenty-two miles (29.8), the traveler's estimate that the giants' bodies rise twenty-five feet above the edge of the pit of Circle Nine (31.65, 113), and the knowledge that the distance to the center of the earth from the surface was for Dante 3,250 miles. The chart-makers assume that Hell is an exact and symmetrical construction. To one of them, Circles One to Four are each half a mile wide, the drop from one to another is fourteen miles, and the distance down the sloping bank from one to another is seventeen miles. The first nine bolgias of Circle Eight are each three-fourths of a mile. Other measurements are exact to harmonize with these. Other systems show the same exactness and—as their makers believe—knowledge of Dante's intentions. Some have represented the bolgias of Malebolge as increasing in circumference eleven miles with each ascent, though this prevents uniform width for the ditches and the intervening banks. In order to get geometrical uniformity, a number of lines of bridges have been given to Malebolge, so that its plan is that of a wheel with spokes; though differing from each other, the various map-makers have pretended to know how many spokes Dante wished. Such perfection is a late development; Manetti, about 1500, provides but a single line of bridges. Thus the assumption of these plans is an exact and uniform Hell. Their wide circulation has led to belief in such exactness and uniformity by many who are more impressed with the plans than with the words of the poem. Sometimes, indeed, the diagram-makers seem to have read only passages containing figures, without regarding other indications in the incidental description.

Respect for those who have taken such charts seriously requires examination of Dante's topographical indications.

Passing through Hell Gate with no mention of descent, the travelers come into a space giving room for such a multitude following a banner that the narrator cannot believe that death has destroyed so many (3.57). The vistors go on to the river Acheron, crossing it by means not indicated, while the traveler Dante is in a swoon. Soon they descend into the dark world, reaching the First Circle (4.8, 13, 24; 12.39). Here again there is a large crowd (4.29). They move on to a walled town where the worthy of antiquity are seen. Afterward, they descend to Circle Two (5.1); no particulars of descent are given. In this Second Circle, there is evidently a multitude on a wind-swept field; Virgil is said to name more than a thousand (5.67). The traveler swoons, to find himself in the Third Circle on recovering. Since no descent is mentioned, one may wonder whether the word *circle* here is equivalent to *district*. No reference to circularity is made. Passing through the region of the gluttons, the travelers reach a downgrade where Plutus sits (6.114). They descend into the fourth *lacca* (7.16); this word has been debated; at least it can mean circle only to one who makes it a synonym for *cerchio*. Here the avaricious in one company and the prodigal in another move in opposite directions around a circle; they meet and turn back to meet again on the opposite side of their circular course (7.31 ff.). Though they form the largest crowd Dante has yet seen, their actions take place under his eye (7.25). If so, they are moving in a circle not enormously larger than a modern race track. From the circle of the misers and the wasters, the fourth, the travelers descend near the course of a falling stream (7.97–107), to the Fifth Circle, as editors call it, formed by the Stygian Marsh; the word *circle* is not applied to it individually, though it would be included in the plural of 8.129. This marsh is evidently on a level with the Sixth Circle, that of the heretics. To this also the word *circle* is not specifically applied (though generally in 10.4); cliffs in a circle do form its inner side (11.2).

Hell farther down is said to be made up of three small circles (11.17, 28, 57, 64), with circular subdivisions (11.30, 42, 49); in the eleventh canto Dante does not apply the word *circle* to the parts of Hell above Circle Six but indicates them by their qualities or their denizens (11.70 ff.).

As the travelers descend the slope to the Seventh Circle (12.28), the guide directs his charge to look; he sees a "wide watercourse bent into a bow, so as to encircle the whole plain." Is this what in American is called a moccasin bend in a river, or the great encirclement—all but complete—made by the Tiber below Otricoli, as Ariosto tells of it (*Orlando Furioso* 14.38)? A common interpretation is that this river or watercourse or ditch (*fossa, fosso*—12.52, 126) encircles all of Hell below it. One scrupulous commentator explains that though the returned traveler said he saw the plain encircled, he really saw only a small section of it. If we are to literalize, how much of a curve could he see in a ditch encircling, with conservative topographers, some 180 miles, or with the more liberal, several times that distance? And what plain does the river encircle? The forest of the suicides is close to it; will that do (12.139; 13.1; 14.10 f.)?

That forest, the second round of Circle Seven (11.41; 13.17), entered by the travelers as soon as they pass the river, is not described as either higher or lower than the river shore or than the burning sands of the third round. So extensive is this third round or *girone* that before the traveler has crossed it, his distance from the forest is so great that "I would not have seen where it was if I had turned around" (15.14 f.). The reader can choose whether Dante here wishes to indicate a considerable distance or whether he intends the reader to think of the obscure air not permitting clear vision; if the latter were intended, the obscurity might well have been mentioned. There are some other indications of an extensive field. The burning sands hold many groups of sinners (14.19). As the travelers move along the margin of the stream, their interview with Brunetto Latini, walking on the lower level beside them, occupies ninety-eight lines. When the shade of Brunetto leaves, he runs at speed to join a group now at some distance. By the time he departs, the travelers have come so far as to hear the roar of the waterfall as it plunges down into the Eighth Circle, Malebolge. As they move on farther, the noise becomes deafening (16.91 ff.).[1] How far back from the brink of the fall do they hear it?

In explaining the structure of Hell, Virgil tells his pupil that the cavity is round and that they have been moving around it always to the left (and descending), yet at the Seventh Circle they still have not completed a single spiral around the inside of the cone (14.124). Thus the diagrams are correct in their general presentation of Hell. Its size diminishes as the center of the earth is approached (11.17, 49, 64, etc.).

Circularity is thus of slight consequence for the reader of the first seventeen cantos of the *Inferno*. The immediate effect is that such spirits as are moving do so in large fields; we even have to remind ourselves that these fields are terraces on the downward slope of Hell. Though descent is mentioned, "Dante likes to pass lightly over the transitions from one step to another."[2] Movement downward into Circle Three is not specified, and the nature of the Fifth Circle, a lake, makes descent to the Sixth Circle on its shore impossible.

To a reader the important matter is what the poem now is, not how it became what it is. Reasons for a condition nevertheless

---

1. The poet later neglects his traveler's assertion that before they reach the head of the fall they can scarcely be heard. At the brink of the cliff the travelers converse (16.121); the visitor talks with the usurers; when Geryon is partly down, the riders "already" hear the noise of the water striking in the Eighth Circle (17.118).

Having allowed his compound river (14.116 ff.) to fall into the Eighth Circle, Dante conveniently and commendably forgets about it throughout the passage through Malebolge, letting it later appear, frozen, as Cocytus (14.119; 31.123; 32.23; 34.52). So far as I am aware, no maker of charts has endeavored to provide for the passage of the water through or under the ditches of Malebolge.

2. Charles H. Grandgent, in his edition of the *Commedia*, argument to Canto 6.

have some explanatory value, both for the individual poem and
for the poetic process. An inference, and that only, is that Dante
began a poem telling of a journey to Hell, somewhat like that related in *Aeneid 6*. The landscape, though beneath the earth's surface, did not differ from ours. Then as he worked, planning and
executing portions of the *Purgatorio* and the *Paradiso*, with their
strong circularity, the poet decided to alter what he had done on
the early *Inferno* to conform with them. With Malebolge, perhaps a new section, he made nearly half the *Inferno* correspond
in its circles with the Mount of Purgatory and with the astronomical heaven of the day. He did not, however, rework his
manuscript of what are now Cantos 3 to 17 to give them the
complete circularity of Cantos 18 to 31. He added passages referring to circles and descents, to give superficial uniformity, but
did not make important changes in verses written with no
thought of a regularly circular Hell.

So far, then, as the first six circles are non-circular open spaces,
diagrams of them as circles damage the reader, influencing him
to think of a neatly measured and uniform Hell, rather than one
with some vague variety and mystery. To suppose Dante intent
on topographical consistency is to misinterpret his purpose. Important though the topography is in securing the effect of bizarre
reality observed by the traveler, it still provides only background.
Of first importance are the traveler's interviews with the damned,
showing their mental and moral states and the visitor's reaction.
To this end the makeup of Hell is flexibly varied. An extreme
case illustrates this, the movement of the avaricious and the
prodigal in a circle, mentioned above. Dante says that he saw the
whole process of their collision and return for another and another. There can be no question of a circle extending dozens or
hundreds of miles. Yet is it possible that here Dante has deliberately so diminished the Fourth Circle of Hell as to bring it all
under the observer's eye? I suspect the passage written with no
thought of the circularity of Hell, and that the lavish and stingy
are merely in an open field, yet anyone who wishes to think
otherwise is at liberty to do so. As we have noticed, if the river
of blood is interpreted as a full circle around Hell (12.53), most
of it is beyond the eye reach. However that may be, the centaur needs to explain parts of the river too far distant for the
travelers to see them (12.129 ff.). If from Cantos 3 to 17 were
removed the word *circle* and Virgil's assertion that Hell is round,

how many readers—if independent of diagrams—would have a strong feeling of circular planning?

For Malebolge, the compound Eighth Circle, with its ten smaller circles, the reader's impression is different, though even here variety is not lacking. This part of Hell is introduced by a passage—the like of which is lacking for the earlier parts—asserting circularity. The belt of land between the central pit of Hell and the foot of the high rocky cliff rising to Circle Seven is described as round, and its bottom is divided into ten valleys. Just as when the various parts are shaped to protect the walls of a castle or a fortified town, there are a number of moats outside the walls, so appeared these valleys of Malebolge. And as at such fortresses little bridges extend from the thresholds of their gates, so from the base of the high cliff wall of Malebolge extend rock bridges which pass across the ditches and their confining banks as far as the central pit of Hell, where they end (18.7 ff.).

There is no explicit statement on the width of the moats or bolgias and the banks dividing them. The comparison with a castle or fortified town (not a large city such as Florence) implies no great width. The moat, now dry, of the Tower of London offers room for drawing up a squad of soldiers. The third and the sixth bolgias are called narrow (19.42; 23.84). The first moat is compared with the bridge near the Castle of St. Angelo in Rome, offering room for two lines of pedestrians. The adventure with the devils of the fifth bolgia implies a narrow ditch and bank. The devils with their fleshhooks or devils' pitchforks, perhaps five feet long, stretch them out in attempting from both sides to rescue their companions caught in the tar of the ditch (22.149). Virgil and his charge go along the bank with the devils who are watching to keep sinners from rising out of the boiling tar, yet they are so close to the next bolgia that when alarmed they can slide into it without delay. (It should, however, be observed that with laudable inconsistency Dante gives the effect of a bridge longer than is necessary for a narrow ditch when the devil carrying a sinner appears on it; he does not even appear to see the travelers on the same bridge [21.37].) The sixth bolgia so deserves the word *narrow* that the pathway at its bottom is blocked by one man lying there; those moving along the bolgia must step on him (23.119 f.). Narrowness seems the pattern for the first nine of the bolgias; the action in none of them requires much space.

On the circumference of the first eight bolgias, the poet is not specific. At the fourth, that of the soothsayers, the observer on the bridge sees the sinners coming along their "round valley" (20.7). The poet does not here mention the murky air of Malebolge, which he does specify when he thinks it effective for his narrative (24.71; 29.39); perhaps we are to take it for granted. How large in diameter can a ditch be and still seem round, not merely slightly curving, to an observer? So the extent of this bolgia is limited. The simile of the fireflies introducing the eighth bolgia (26.25 ff.) is one of landscape and valley, though still with its scale small enough for the little lights to be distinct; the comparison, moreover, is only in the number of lights below, not in other matters.

For the ninth and tenth bolgias there is a change. Even the tenth, like the ninth, seems to have no reason for much width, but suddenly Master Adam declares it half a mile wide (30.86). This may be attributed to the exaggeration of a man unable to move an inch in a hundred years, as Adam is unable, in harmony with the proverb, "A miss is as good as a mile." Or does it suggest Dante's slight concern with consistency that he can at pleasure widen a bolgia so that it bears no resemblance to the moats surrounding a castle and would require for crossing a rock bridge half a mile long? Does its description as "long" (29.53) mean that? Even the wonderful stone bridge over the Serchio above Lucca, the Ponte del Diavolo, is not that long. With the half-mile goes Adam's assertion that the circumference of the bolgia is eleven miles, and Virgil's that the preceding one extends twenty-two miles. If these figures are made mathematical, the bank separating the two bolgias is some mile and a half wide. Yet these measurements are not in themselves alone enough to destroy the impression that Hell is sufficiently limited to make a twenty-four-hour walk through it not an absurdity, at least in a dreamlike poem.

The roundness of Malebolge is employed in the narrative. The punishment of the panders and seducers is to be driven around and around by scourging demons (18.34, 64, 74). The backward journey of the soothsayers indicates their wickedness in trying to get ahead of what is granted to man (20.14). The hypocrites walk with difficulty in their heavy robes of lead and must punish the Jewish leaders concerned in the Crucifixion by trampling on them (23.120). This sixth bolgia has on its bottom the ruins of a fallen bridge of rock. How the hypocrites in their circular course (23.59) surmounted these ruins—since they can do little more than move on the level (23.71, 84)—Dante neglects to say. He has no reason to explain, for wise readers do not ask, but take the story as it is. As Mohammed and his companions walk around their circle of pain, at one point their wounds, which had closed in their progress, are renewed by a devil.

For some of the sinners in Malebolge, especially the flatterers and the grafters, the circular form of the bolgia is without consequence for their punishment. Yet for all of them the bridge offers opportunity for sight to the travelers, or emphasizes the darkness of the bolgia as the observers vainly peer down into the depths.

Notwithstanding all its apparent regularity of plan, Malebolge is a wild and irregular place. So broken are the rocks forming one of the huge jagged bridges that they furnish hiding places to the timid traveler (21.60, 89). One of them is so Alp-like that it would be a hard path for a goat (19.132). However limited the space, it is not expressed in the smooth regularity of a geometrical drawing.

From the last bolgia the travelers walk toward the center, soon reaching the giants. Evidently they do not go far, because the darkness greatly limits visibility (31.23). The giants are described with such particularity that the Ninth Circle is something like thirty-five feet lower than the Eighth. The width of the four parts of the last circle is not said to be great. The last part allows a distorted sight of Satan across it, even in the air darkened by fog or twilight (34.4). His bust, with his arms, rises above the ice. However huge his size, his mouth is not so elevated as to prevent the traveler from a clear look at the tortures of Judas, Brutus and Cassius.

There is, then, no part of Dante's Hell where he strives for effects of great space. His place of torment does not, like Milton's, have as merely one of its parts a "frozen continent"; no, only a frozen lake over which the travelers can walk in a few minutes. There is no passing "o'er many a frozen, many a fiery alp" (*Paradise Lost* 2.620). Dante the visitor merely gets out of breath in climbing up the side of one of the ditches (24.44), not so deep but that Virgil had been able to slide down its higher bank, carrying his pupil. The various parts of Hell are limited for the sake of the limited action occurring in them. We may say

limited for the sake of Dante's comedy, for the medieval notion
of comedy required it to deal with events in the lives of ordinary
men, not spectacular or heroic actions. There is no detail that
does not fit easily with the single day which the tour allotted to
the Inferno. Yet that day brings the travelers from the earth's
surface to its center. If a reader reflects on the disparity, he is
astonished, since no means for covering more than 3,000 miles
have been provided. The poetically minded reader, however, has
all he needs, finding no difficulty in the two different rates of
progress by the travelers: a walking pace, quickened to meet
schedule, and a marvelous transit from one world to the bottom
of the other. It offers no more difficulty than the two clocks, as
it were, by which Shakespeare could reconcile short and long
spaces of time in *King Lear*. Poetry resides in the individual
scenes rather than in the rationalized generality of the long
journey. Yet the charts of the Inferno emphasize the generality,
not the poetic detail. They eliminate the constant variety of
Dante's background, making all uniform, when unlikeness is the
source of charm. The mechanical drawing does not allow for the
inconsistencies of vivid and complex narrative. But that the charts
are far from accurate is the least of their vices. Nor need we be
seriously disturbed by their triviality. But since they have so
generally been presented to readers of the *Commedia* since 1500,
we must regret their prosaic character, the antithesis of poetry.
No attack on Dante could so damage appreciation as this well-
meant attempt to assist the reader's eye in places where Dante
has given words to the ear. So pernicious are those charts that a
reader who does nothing more than close his eyes to them has
moved far toward appreciation of Dante's *Commedia*.

All individual scenes are set in realistic landscapes, and all
specific settings are from this world of the living. The ditches of
Malebolge are the moats Dante's contemporaries saw protecting
castles (*Inf.* 18.10 ff.). The descent from the Sixth Circle, of the
heretics, is like that above the Adige near Trent (12.4 ff.). The
hill of Purgatory is as steep as San Leo near San Marino (*Purg.*
4.25). The situation of Dis on a shallow lake is not unlike that of
Mantua as Virgil describes her (*Inf.* 7.106–8.81; 20.67–90). Pic-
torially, the possibilities of *Inferno* and *Purgatorio* for illustration depend on the immediate landscape in which events are
enacted, not on the plan of the *cantiche*. Hence the superiority
as illustrators of Blake and even Doré. They normally do not

regard the apparatus of circles offered by the chart-makers and limit themselves to earthly landscapes. Botticelli, for all his skill, allows himself to be "cabined, cribbed, confined" within the charts. We cannot too often remind ourselves that Dante's travelers pass through real landscapes, not through childish mechanical drawings.

III. DANTE'S *COMMEDIA* AS A COMEDY

When after Dante's death, men began calling his work *divine*, they meant, so far as we can transfer the word to our language, no more than that it was a great poem. Nothing of the religious quality now residing in the term was asserted. Its verses were not divine otherwise than are the writings of any established poet, not otherwise than as Homer, Shakespeare, and Tasso are divine for us. The high seriousness now suggested by the word is superficially (and only so) at variance with the other part of the title, *comedy*, in that the modern world is strangely reluctant to hold comedy as great as tragedy. Though for Dante the word *divine*, applied by his admirers, has almost overwhelmed the word *commedia*, the latter only is Dante's own. Twice in the *Inferno* he calls the poem his comedy (16.128; 21.2).

For understanding comedy as we think of it, Dante did not have the best advantages. He never had seen, it appears, a text of either of the two Latin writers of comic drama, Plautus and Terence,[1] and the period of modern Italian comic drama, of Machiavelli and Ariosto, was two hundred years in the future. Yet his genius obtained the essence of the matter. In the *Derivationes* of Uguccione of Pisa he had read that "comedy deals with the actions of private persons, tragedy with those of kings and great men. Comedy is written in lowly language, tragedy in lofty language." Aware of the difference in subject fitting difference in style, he says in his *De Vulgari Eloquentia*, or *On the Italian Language*, that in tragedy, with loftiness of verse, splendor of structure and excellence of diction are joined weighty ideas. Tragic poetry offers *magnalia*, important matters, such as might in arms, love's fires and the course of the will. Among the Latin poets the highest tragic form is embodied in Virgil's *Aeneid*, in the *Commedia* called a tragedy (20.113). Dante did not give the

---

1. The only reference to Terence (and to Seneca also) which suggests reading is that in the letter to Can Grande della Scala. Until this letter is proved authentic, the reference is not in evidence.

subjects of comedy. If the two types are parallel, to the humble style of comedy would fit *parvalia*, matters of slight importance, the doings of private persons rather than those in high position.

This difference appears on comparing Dante's *Commedia* with Virgil's *Aeneid*. Aeneas is a prince, the leader of a fleet and army, the founder—however remote—of Rome, imperial and papal. Dante the hero of the *Commedia*, not to be identified with the historical Dante, has no claim to fame. He has ancestors of some importance, especially Cacciaguida of the *Paradiso*; he broke the font in San Giovanni; he knows the *Aeneid* by heart. But that traveler in the other world does not speak of high place in Florentine government, the chief non-literary claim of the historical Dante to worldly importance. A Florentine prior is one of six, and his term of office two months. Aeneas, though to some he has appeared too much directed by the gods for a vigorous character, is still of great personal courage, as appears in the battles of the *Aeneid*'s later books. The difference between him and the tourist Dante is clear in the latter's trembling expostulation: "I am not Aeneas . . . neither I myself nor any other man thinks me fit" for a journey to the other world (2.32). But Aeneas presses on with no doubt of his capacity: if Orpheus, if Hercules could visit the lower world, why not he? (For the comic quality of the timid and inquisitive traveler on whom Dante bestows his own name, see Chapter 4.)

Thus the *Inferno* is in harmony with the medieval notion of comedy. Yet the fourteenth century objected to the title. Obsessed by the notion, still not dead, that amusement and greatness do not fit together, Boccaccio and other medieval Italians struggled to raise the poem, as they thought, from the low level of comedy. They were the predecessors of those who, attempting to give the work dignity, with a misunderstanding that would have astonished Dante, have called his *Comedy* an epic. The fourteenth-century commentator Buti showed much good sense when he wrote that

> the author called the work a comedy. The word *comedy* signifies a poem about countrymen, and deals with persons of the middle classes, and in a middle style it should be written, and it must begin with adversity and end in happiness, as did the plots of Terence and Plautus. There is uncertainty whether this poem by our author ought to be called a comedy or not, but since he chose to call it a comedy, we ought to allow it to him (on *Inf.* 21.2).

Once Dante refers to his poem as a comedy when swearing by it to the truth of his incredible story of Geryon—one of the least believable of the traveler's experiences, suited for Baron Munchausen (16.128). For their airy voyages, poets usually have imagined some fairly probable means of transportation. Chaucer, for example, in his *House of Fame* represents himself as carried by an eagle. However comic in his conversation with his burden, that "foul" is still appropriate for the narrator's celestial journey. Dante's flying creature—even for a voyage as short as his—is the most unlikely animal possible, compared with a beaver, and swimming, not flying, through the air. The feigned observer's oath that he is truthful is intended to emphasize the absurdity of his fiction. Those who will believe such a story, especially when supported by deposition to its truth, are like Boccaccio's Calandrino. He was gulled by Maso with a tale of Bengodi. In that land is a mountain of grated Parmesan cheese, inhabited by men who do nothing else than make macaroni and ravioli and cook it in capon broth; then they throw it down the mountain, for every man to take what he will; and nearby is a river of Vernaccia, the best any man ever drank, and without the least mixture of water (*Decamerone* 8.3). For the moment Dante the returned traveler, telling of Geryon, is a Maso.

Geryon is wonderful partly because "his back and his breast and both his sides were gorgeous with rosettes and wheels in more colors in foreground and background than ever Turks and Tartars put into their fabric" (17.14 ff.). The aged Boccaccio commented on the beauty of this description, but in order to do so, he omitted from his remarks Dante's descriptive word for Geryon, *sozza*, *nasty*, though it appears in the text he quotes. Had he forgotten that in the *Decamerone* he described a character comic for his great pretenses, though he was incredibly ragged and filthy? "His jacket, enameled with filth around his neck and under his armpits, showed more spots and colors than ever did Tartar or Indian cloths" (6.10). Was such a comparison colloquial and proverbial, like the colors of the rainbow in English? At least the filthy Geryon is an animal counterpart of the comic Guccio the Filthy or the Pig. So Dante swears by his comedy when dealing with such matter as Boccaccio offers for amusement.

At the verge of the Second Circle of Hell sits Minos, the just judge. He is competent, never in error, and his decrees are at once executed (29.120). On him depends the justice of the whole Inferno. In Virgil's *Aeneid*, he is a dignified though briefly mentioned *quaesitor*; in Statius' *Thebaid* he is not comic.[2] Yet Dante —for all Minos' unerring justice—makes him grotesque. Having examined a sinner, the judge indicates the number of the circle in Hell proper for penalty by girding himself with his tail as many times as is required (5.11). This picture Dante liked so well that he alluded to it far on in the *cantica* (27.124). Whether Minos when condemning Guido da Montefeltro (27.125) wrapped around him a long tail in eight circles, or whether he made one encircling eight times with a short tail, we are not told. Which is more grotesque? The illustrators of Landino's Dante (Venice, 1507) preferred the long tail, capable of encompassing Minos as many as nine times. Through such a judge could Dante have signified the justice of an entirely serious Inferno?

If we remember Minos, we shall be prepared for comedy at any point in the Inferno, especially when we recall that medieval taste in comedy often appears to us less squeamish or more realistic or more brutal, or what you will—good or bad—than our own. Indeed some critics, far from common life, have even called Dante "the master of the disgusting."

Sacrilegious though it may appear to champions of Love's priority over marriage vows, there have been through the ages hardy souls who have caught a touch of bawdy comedy in Francesca's verbally decent putting of the aftermath of her reading with Paolo in the book about the love of Lancelot and King Arthur's wife: "That day we read in it no further" (5.138). In irreproachable language with unnecessary sexual suggestion is the description of the false prophetess Manto moving backward, so that "all of her hairy skin is on the other side" (20.54). Perhaps a predecessor of the passage on the "third leg" in Joyce's *Ulysses* is the following: "Then the serpent's hind feet, twisted together, became the member that man conceals, and from the miserable man's member two feet were made" (25.115). These details of transformation are not inevitable. If we follow the medieval commentator Guido da Pisa in supposing that the naked simoniacs, upside down in their holes, appear above ground to their buttocks, with what obscene comedy the popes are treated!

The flatterers outrage modern taste by being ducked in filth from human privies. Yet this amused the traveler who reports it.

2. See Canto 5, note 1.

One man was so filthy that "it wasn't plain whether he were lay-man or priest"; and the tourist remembers seeing him "when his hair was dry"—an expressive understatement. The sinner's em-barrassment is expressed by "cracking himself on the punkin" (18.112 ff.). This is language not higher than that middle rank above which medieval comedy did not aspire. In comic stories of the fourteenth century such smearing with filth is cause for laughter. Boccaccio tells of an arrogant but pleasure-greedy and gullible doctor thrown into stercoraceous ditches near Santa Maria della Scala. The storyteller does not spare insisting that he was plastered and replastered from head to foot in his struggles to escape, that he even got the nastiness into his mouth, and that his house stank for hours after he entered it (*Decamerone* 8.9). This story incidentally gives opportunity for proverbial jokes on Bologna such as Dante uses in the bolgia of the hypocrites (23.142). Sacchetti (*ca.* 1330–*ca.* 1400) offers a tale of a tavern-keeper who frightened some of his guests into taking refuge in such foulness while he disported himself with the wife of one of them (*Trecento novelle* 190; see also 24, 144).

The longest comic passage in the *Commedia* deals with the Malebranche or Badclaws (Cantos 21; 22; 23.1–57, 140–146). One recent commentator observes that here Dante "gives free rein to the comic spirit." Another grudgingly makes the episode a "concession to the popular spirit of the Middle Ages." A third recognizes the mood of these cantos as "disconcerting to the more solemn-minded of Dante's admirers." That so developed a pas-sage has been supposed unique and has not made readers alert for others in the comic spirit is one of the mysteries of poetic study. But search among commentators provides some restora-tion of faith in scholarly perception, for altogether a consider-able number of passages have been noted as amusing. The dis-covery of most of these and of others can be left to the taste and perception of the reader, for to all of us, only that is comic which we perceive as such. A few may be mentioned.

The interview of Guido da Montefeltro with Pope Boniface VIII—so brief as to require from the reader attention and imagi-nation, as often with Dante's brevity—exhibits one fox out-witting another. The experienced and practical Guido abandons the wisdom derived from his life of trickery before one whom he believes theoretically qualified, becoming a child before theo-logical authority. So the wily Guido becomes stupid, as do most subjects for comedy. Still further, the meeting of St. Francis and the devil who comes for Guido's soul offers an absurd and comic reversal of what we suppose their normal positions; the black cherub protests about the injustice with which the saint is about to treat him and supports himself with admirable concise theological argument. St. Francis, vanquished, makes no attempt at reply. The devil then emphasizes the comedy of the fox turned stupid, saying: "I see you were not planning on my being a logician" (27.122).

Even in the lowest pit of Hell, sinners gripped in its terrible ice are jocose on their surroundings. Camicion de' Pazzi says of his neighbors: "You can hunt through all Caina and you will not find a shade more deserving to be set in frozen pudding (or jelly)" (32.60). Bocca speaks of the sinners as "put in the cold," as though they were food to be preserved. Frate Alberigo, again with an allusion to the punishing ice, speaks of a shade as "spending the winter" (33.135).

Thus the further we read, the more completely we enter into the spirit of Dante's *Commedia*, we perceive that as he dealt with justice, with divine power, with the most lofty wisdom and the fundamental love, he used the method required by the title he gave, that of the comic poet's wisdom.

IV. THE TOURIST DANTE AS A COMIC FIGURE

Evident, but so easily forgotten that a reader must often remind himself of it, is that the name *Dante* applied to the central figure of the *Commedia* has not one meaning only, but two or more. Occurring but once in the poem (*Purg.* 30.55), the word *Dante* signifies Beatrice's lover, with reminiscence of the *Vita Nuova*. Thus he is author of that early work and of the *Commedia* itself, and yet is an imaginary character, a fictitious traveler in the other world.

However these characters may be confused, most passages can be analyzed. The author Dante, the poet who hopes his pen will bring him immortality, is a historical figure engaged in Florentine politics and banished as a dangerous enemy of the ruling faction. He is the poet who, like Virgil or Milton, calls on the Muse to aid him (*Inf.* 2.7 ff.), thus standing apart from his poem and looking at it as his achievement. At times this author breaks narrative continuity for a digression, as in his invective against

Pisa (*Inf.* 33.79 ff.) or his diatribe against Italian misgovernment (*Purg.* 6.76–151). Such passages by the historical poet in his own person are less conspicuous in the *Inferno* than in the other *cantiche*, in deference to the greater narrative development. Yet all these hardly dramatic verses by the historical Dante are veiled—sometimes lightly, sometimes more heavily—with the reality or the unreality of poetry.

Such passages by the poet in his own person shade into dramatic utterances by the returned traveler narrating his experiences. The fiction of the work is that a man who actually has seen Hell, Purgatory, and Heaven, on his return puts his reminiscences in verse. For example, at the beginning of the *Paradiso* he writes: "O good Apollo, for the last part of my work make me such a vessel of your poetic strength as you require for the gift of the laurel you so love" (*Par.* 1.13). The poet here views his product as an object. Yet in preceding lines he stands as dramatic traveler asserting poetic truth but prosaic falsehood: "In the heaven that takes the largest share of the divine light I was, and I saw things that one who descends from there is without power to relate" (*Par.* 1.4 ff.). Here his role is that of visitor returned from Heaven. Seventeen times, as poet-reminiscent, he addresses the reader (*Inf.* 8.94; 22.118; *Purg.* 10.106; *Par.* 5.109; etc.). At times Dante, playing his part as a traveler who will return to the world of the living, appears as though he were that pilgrim of whom he writes, standing in a great church, looking in wonder and thinking of the circle of listeners to whom he may speak of his travels, rather than write verses about them (*Par.* 31.43). Colloquial rather than for conventional verse is his declaration, as on his return to earth he remembers the shades frozen in the ice of the Ninth Circle, that "I shudder and always shall on seeing frozen brooks" (*Inf.* 32.71). But his word *dire* (literally, *say*) in the *Commedia* as in the *Vita Nuova*, usually signifies *write*. As the reminiscences in verse of the loquacious tourist back from his travels, the poem appears in the declaration: "By the measures of this *Commedia*, reader, as I hope they will not fail of lasting popularity, I swear to you" that I saw the incredible monster Geryon swimming through the air (16.127 ff.).

Through the eyes of this invented traveler named Dante, the other world is seen, and the tongue of that dramatic character describes it. When the imaginary traveler is close to the factual Dante, he hopes that his "sacred poem" will take him back to the

Florence which has exiled him. Going further, we find in the poem the melancholy Dante of the death mask, reproduced ten thousand times as a bust, and the Dante exhorting Henry VII to take on Florence the most terrible revenge (Epistles 6 and 7).

We have indications that the historical Dante was not invariably melancholy or bitter. In the years after his death, stories in the comic taste of the time were assigned to him, usually containing a witty saying by the poet.[1] Would these stories, however apocryphal, have been assigned to a morose Dante? Included in Dante's works is a series of sonnets exchanged between him and Forese Donati (*Purg.* 23.48 ff.), which, though not now wholly intelligible, seem jocose in intention. (Some students, however, have taken them as serious or even savage in tone, as befits the conventional saturnine Dante.) There is, then, some background for thinking Dante enough interested in humor to justify him in writing a poem which he called a comedy. We may even infer that he could pass the most difficult of the comic writer's tests, namely that he could sometimes see himself as a subject for comedy. Could a man with an overweening sense of his own dignity have given his own name to a traveler in the other world so disadvantageously represented as is Dante the tourist?

One of the qualities of that wayfarer is cowardice, a fussy and undignified cowardice. Retreating in terror before the three animals in his road, the man who has lost his way, on seeing Virgil, does not pause to consider whether the newcomer has the look of a valiant helper; nor does he ask guidance; rather he shrieks: "Pity me, whatever you are" (1.65). When, after consenting to follow Virgil, he draws back, he acts without dignity, as one who shilly-shallies (2.37). At the gate of Dis, he is terrified when Virgil briefly leaves him; he begs his guide to abandon the journey, though he knows that the Latin poet has already aided him, as he says with exaggeration, seven times (8.97), and that his teacher's reliability is divinely assured (2.96). To abandon the road through Hell would be no considered retreat, but a flight with no prudence behind it. The same sort of irrational timidity, both utter trust in his guide and fear that Virgil cannot aid him, appears in the adventure with the Malebranche (21.128), after he has left the hiding place where he has been squatting in fright (21.59, 89). The giants ringing the final abyss of Hell were

1. A number are given by Paget Toynbee, *Dante Alighieri* (5th ed.; London, 1914), pp. 176 ff.

enough to shake a courageous heart, but the reminiscing traveler does not put it with dignity, saying what amounts to "I was like to have died of fright" (31.109). And notwithstanding his experience of the trustworthy Virgil's protection, he "would have liked to take some other road" (31.141) than that indicated by his guide. In Purgatory something of the same fear continues, especially on the highest ledge, where he is with difficulty persuaded to enter the fire (*Purg.* 27.15 ff.). Even in Paradise he has moments of fear (e.g., *Par.* 26.1, 19).

The traveler is in the other world to get experience, chiefly by observing the spirits. Yet as future reporter he pushes beyond what is required, in his eagerness to know the identity of those he encounters. There is fascinating variety in the method of learning names, but no small number throughout the three *cantiche* come from the traveler's question: "Who are you?" Sometimes he recognizes characters; twice the accommodating Virgil asks for him. But the continual and almost mechanical repetition of the tourist in his desire to know becomes comic in its iteration and in its interest in personalities. As such a busybody—the word fits him—would be, he is first interested in persons of importance, asking Brunetto Latini about his companions who are "most known and of highest station" (15.102); twice he says the same thing to Virgil (20.103; 23.74), once adding that only such men concern him.

To the modern reader, even if an Italian, the poem hardly bears out such an interest; the zealous commentators of Dante's century could not give information about some of the persons named. The author can hardly have expected their names to be known to a large proportion of his early readers, even in Florence. Yet Dante hoped for a general Italian circulation extending into the future (as in *Inf.* 16.129), if the traveler here represents the poet. Perhaps the answer is that insistence on seeing men whom it was proper to treat with respect (as he puts it in *Vita Nuova* 35) fits in with the character of the comic traveler. Yet if these important men with whom the tourist loves to associate, as with the poets who were polite to him in Limbo (4.102), are not to be found, he is inquisitive about those not known to fame, just as he listened, when the Badclaws in the fifth bolgia addressed each other, until he knew the name of every one (22.37). The unknown sinners so carefully named, mingled with such as Ulysses and Mahomet, give an effect of universality in their sweep through all classes. Such equality of the lowest and the highest before Death was a frequent medieval theme, as in Gower's *Confessio Amantis* 2.3405 ff. Important for a work called a comedy, Dante's interest in naming all he saw appears in the amusing stories of his century. Boccaccio and still more Sacchetti are assiduous in so distinguishing the persons they deal with, high or low, who have had some notable experience, or who amuse us with their wit or their stupidity. Not only is the unfailing and even misplaced inquisitiveness of the traveler amusing in itself, but it is essential to the poet's narrative attempt to bring before us a gallery of characters, lowly or exalted, with their specific qualities.

The character named Dante is often absurdly amusing because treated like a child. Virgil tells him not to look at the Gorgon, but evidently realizes that his pupil's insatiable curiosity will master his fear and bring him into danger (*Inf.* 9.60). This curiosity almost made him stop to look back when running from the devil on the fifth bridge of Malebolge (*Inf.* 21.25 ff.). Often Virgil thinks he must carry him. The mentor keeps his charge from falling or fearing he will fall off Geryon's back, though the panic-stricken pupil is too agitated to ask support (17.92). Virgil lugs him down into the third bolgia and then out again (19.34, 43, 124); like a mother rescuing her child from a fire, the guide carries the traveler in rescuing him from the Badclaws; Virgil makes him a bundle (what loss of dignity!) with himself while Antaeus sets them down in the lowest Hell (31.134); the traveler clings around Virgil's neck as they descend Satan's body, and the teacher sets the pupil on the edge of a rock (34.70, 86). Those who have called the *Commedia* an epic have forgotten what an epic hero is. Socrates in a basket is not more ridiculous than Dante hanging to his guardian's neck. However miraculous Virgil's strength, these passages lead us to suppose the timid and inquisitive tourist a little weak man.

Sometimes in the great variety of the poem, perhaps because of long-extended composition, with slight opportunity to revise, the comic little traveler disappears for a time, to be replaced by one more self-reliant. In the lowest Hell, though still addressing Virgil as his teacher, he speaks like a person of vigor (32.82), continuing thus until behind Virgil he shelters himself from the wind (34.8). When in the Sixth Heaven, Beatrice relaxes her supervision, the traveler conducts himself with independence. In the *Inferno* he commonly has little to say for himself. When he learns that Pope Boniface is a simoniac in a "purse," he rebukes the enemy of the White party in Florence, but with a preceding apology: "I don't know whether I was too foolish [almost *too comic*] in answering him as I did" (19.88). The invective is gratuitous, after the Pope has fully acknowledged the propriety of his punishment. It passes over into an exclamation rather by historical poet than by dramatic tourist: "O Constantine, what great evil had as its mother, not your conversion, but that dower which the first rich father received from you" (19.115 ff.). Even here the speech receives Virgil's commendation, as he might applaud a bright boy who had spoken up in a way to merit pedagogical approval.

Before he wrote the *Commedia*, Dante achieved power to see himself as unheroic. However young he may have been when he wrote the *Vita Nuova* (usual estimates make him nearly thirty), he can hardly have shown nothing of the interest in Florentine government and the ability in it that sent him on government missions to San Gimignano and to the papal court. Yet in the little book nothing of the sort appears. He gives himself dignity as a writer of verse, but otherwise the story is of terrors, inadequacies and difficulties. He weeps, he trembles, he is an object of jest to ladies. Here is nothing of the strong man whom his political opponents could not allow in Florence. Perhaps in the comedy, in the work so named, of the inquisitive little tourist named Dante, we see a later and more mature development of the power, apparent in the fiction of the *Vita Nuova*, to regard himself without too much awe, which is required for full-blown comedy. Are the traits of the dramatic Dante in the *Commedia* exaggerated from the weaknesses of the historical poet, weaknesses that the poet himself could view with some objective amusement?

V. ALLEGORY

1. Vital allegory

In the latest as in the earliest writings on Dante's poetry, allegory is made important. The word, derived from the Greek, signifies saying one thing and meaning another. So under allegory may be classed attempts, as by symbolism, to find in poetry something more than its literal meaning, something other than the story that is told. At their best, such attempts have relation to art as the concrete universal. To illustrate simply, Dante's Ulysses (*Inf.* 26.55 ff.) tells the story of his last exploring voyage. Dante has made Ulysses the type of man with the exploring mind, from which we move easily to Aristotle's "all men by nature desire to know." We give Ulysses' name to any man eager to penetrate the unknown.

Such derivation of ideas from a story by analogy is nothing strange. The narratives of history are often instructive on what we may follow or avoid; indeed the prudent man draws conclusions from his own experience. Thus the experience offered in art and that factually occurring are in their results close together. Instruction issues from observed experience, one's own or that of others, and from the imitation of life and experience in art. Wherever there is experience, actual or simulated, man can reflect on it.

Art thus offers a basis for reflection. Yet it does not offer a secure footing for conclusions. History—only in its unapproachable ideal, indeed—offers facts. The novelist or the poet—using truths or probabilities that seem true—does something with facts, changing them until they fit into a good story, shifting them until they are suited to give the sort of pleasure proper to art. The historian presents and perhaps interprets a photograph. The poet offers a landscape, perhaps still recognizable as the photographer's scene, but differing from it in many ways; his most elementary departure would be the introduction of bits from other photographs.

Such reflections from art and experience are themselves an admirable and necessary allegory. They are much the same for all men. Inevitably from the story of Ulysses the spirit of exploration is derived. Dante does not need to mention that spirit.

2. Scholars' allegory

There is another sort of allegory which may be called the poor cousin of the allegory just sketched. It too exhibits permanent qualities of the human mind, but qualities not of the most admirable sort. This is the allegory excogitated by those who strive to explain poetry. It does not naturally follow from the literal meaning of a poem.

Its origins may be suggested. Artistic work requires long and intelligent application. Yet it may be held to serve no practical purpose; it is merely delightful. Can there be such labor with no serious achievement? On a lower level, men seldom feel such a difficulty. He is a miser indeed who will not make his house pleasing to himself, to his family and to men generally, even though he could get mere shelter for much less money. But after enormous labor by an artist, a man obviously gifted, can poetry be anything but man's most serious concern? The wisest poets have not found any difficulty here. Milton, however he exalted poetry, understood that it was for men at leisure. Government, even merchandise, must be dealt with before poetry is read. Yet an aesthetic of pleasure has been throughout the centuries abhorrent to most men, at least to most writing men believing their labors important, and we may expect it to continue so. This poetry produced with such labor must be good for something; what is it worth?

Teachers of poetry and writing scholars have a still further difficulty. Their business is to talk, with tongue or pen, yet often to say much about a poem is difficult. Nevertheless, teachers feel forced to speak. Can they merely say to their pupils: "Read and enjoy, if you can, or as you can"? And perhaps some pupils are not mature enough to do so. Moreover, what of the teacher's occupation if he is not to explain the poem? Throughout the ages, many teachers, including those more exalted teachers who have written about poetry, have been of prosaic minds. So have been many of Dante's commentators. At least when in their academic robes, teachers become serious-minded. Or sometimes parents demand morally improving instruction. Altogether, the teacher of poetry and the scholar are by their own occupation required to speak in season and out of season. The manufacture of allegory offers to the ingenious but prosaic mind an opportunity to speak at length with the appearance of wisdom, giving poetry the ethical quality demanded by puritanical minds.

3. The permanence of allegory

Allegorical interpretation began early. Plato's Socrates, telling in the *Phaedrus* the story of Oreithyia, the maiden carried off by Boreas, laughs at the allegorists of his day, who said that the truth of the story is that the girl was swept off the rock by a gust of the North Wind, personified as the winged god Boreas. A zealous allegorist was Philo Judaeus, flourishing about A.D. 25. To him the narratives of the Pentateuch, with the descriptions of the Jewish Tabernacle and other practical directions, were not sufficiently religious or instructive. So instead of admitting the truth, or perhaps not seeing it, he found in the books of Moses much solemn information. The cherubs of the Ark of the Covenant, for example, are the geographical hemispheres. St. Augustine was also an allegorist. He saw that the Book of Judges contained narratives not conducive to moral elevation. Hence he explained that the harlot's house visited by Samson was like Hell. So Samson, entering it, was like Christ entering Hell after the Crucifixion. Throughout the Middle Ages, allegorizing continued. Ovid's pleasing story of Europa and the bull became Christian teaching, as do Shakespeare's plays at present. In the seventeenth century, John Bunyan not only wrote genuine allegory, but indulged in commentator's allegory of the Bible in his *Solomon's Temple Spiritualized*. Modern scholars have continued the tradition with such discoveries as the "historical allegory" of the *Faerie Queene*, with Artegal as Lord Grey, etc.

Modern allegorical interpretation, like that of classical, medieval, and renaissance days, is an occupational disease. Candidates for Ph.D.'s in literature and teachers of poetry are under pressure to write printable matter derived from "original research." For such writing, allegory and related prosaic exegesis of literature, as symbolism, etc., are well adapted. Such scholar-made allegories are of no importance for those interested in poetry as such. The commentator's allegorical interpretation is not in the same world as the artist's allegory. In his *Pilgrim's Progress* and even in his *Holy War* or *Siege of Mansoul*, Bunyan is an artist in allegory. In *Solomon's Temple Spiritualized*, his explanation of the parts of the temple and its furnishings is without value, though the work still has literary interest as one type of fiction. But few moderns attempting allegorical commentary have Bunyan's rhetorical power.

4. Dante on allegory

Into the stream of allegorical interpretation came Dante, fond of study and with a longing to teach. As artists sometimes do, he had too much respect for the learned men of his time, though capable of objecting to their venality and other vices. From scholarship he gained the notion of allegorical interpretation of the Bible. To wit, a Biblical passage could be taken in four ways. First literally; then allegorically, in three ways: the allegorical (in a more limited sense), the moral, and the anagogical. In the letter addressed to the Veronese nobleman Can Grande della Scala, already mentioned as attributed to Dante, an interesting medieval document, the following Biblical verse is expounded: "In the going out of Israel from Egypt, of the family of Jacob from a barbarous people, Judea is made his sanctification, Israel his power." Literally, this is explained as referring to the departure of the Israelites from Egypt under Moses. Allegorically, it signifies our redemption accomplished by Christ. Morally, it means the conversion of the soul from the affliction and misery of sin to a state of grace. Anagogically, it applies to the departure of the holy soul from the slavery of this corruption to the liberty of eternal glory.

In Dante's *Convivio*, of unquestioned authorship, the same example appears, explained by the same method, but not with the same details. The theologians, says Dante, differ from the poets (meaning, it seems, writers on poetry) in allegorical explanation. This suggests St. Thomas' belief that poetry differs from Scripture in allowing but one allegorical explanation, instead of three. It is true that Dante once may allow all three for poetry (*Convivio* 2.1, end), but seemingly he never applied more than the first, either to his own poetry or to that of others. In *Convivio* 2.1 he illustrates allegory from Ovid's tale of Orpheus, who tamed the wild beasts and made the rocks and trees come to him. But the other two he illustrates from the Bible: the moral from the Gospel narrative of the Transfiguration, and the anagogical from Psalm 113 (114 in the English Bible), on the exodus of Israel from Egypt. The writer of the letter to Can Grande della Scala neglects the difference between allegorized Scripture and secular poetry, illustrating all four senses from Psalm 113 only. (Does this hint that Dante did not write the letter?)

In his *Convivio* (only a part of the work planned) Dante gives the meaning of three of his *canzoni*. Much of his exposition is devoted to the learned background of the poems. For example, a reference to the Third Heaven gives rise to pages explaining the celestial system of the age. This is hardly explication of the poem. Strictly allegorical interpretation is not long: the lady invoked is Philosophy; Heaven indicates learning in general. For the fourth book (the last published) he avowedly abandons allegory, expanding the ideas presented in the third *canzone*. Thus, to allegorical treatment of the *canzoni* are devoted only parts of eight chapters among the seventy-three composing the *Convivio*.

Moreover the author declares initially: "I plan to show the real meaning of these *canzoni*, because no one can learn it unless I explain it, because it is hidden under the figure of allegory" (1.2, end). Without the author's key, a reader would suppose a living lady dealt with in the *canzoni*, rather than the Lady Philosophy.

If from the letter to Can Grande we take the part applicable to the *Inferno*, we get the literal subject as "the state of souls after death, taken simply." Allegorically, "the subject is man, as by deserving and failing to deserve, in liberty of will, he is subject to justice which punishes." For the *Purgatorio* and the *Paradiso* (the special concern of the letter) the formula is not more elaborate.

In the poem itself a statement of the allegory of some of the punishments is at least approached. Alessio Interminei among the flatterers asserts: "Down here the flatteries with which my tongue was never sated have flowed over me" (18.125). His tongue has produced so many filthy flatteries that they make a pond almost deep enough to drown him. Flattery is a nasty vice. The filth of his punishment is the filth he chose when alive. Bertrand de Born complains: "Because I separated persons so joined, my brain—alas!—is separated from its beginning in this body. So is carried out in me the corresponding suffering" (28.139). This is a tooth for a tooth, and eye for an eye. But the punishment gives only a hint at his life, does not present it, for when alive he divided; here instead he is divided. In the bolgia of the simoniacs there is enough correspondence between punishment and deed to enable Pope Nicholas to say, with grim jocosity: "Up in the world money and here myself, I put in a purse" (19.72). But here too is suggestion rather than correspondence. We do not see the popes putting themselves or anything else in purses; they are put in by divine justice. In their ridiculous punishment there is nothing other than the Pope's joke to enable a reader to guess that simony is their fault.

On the fortunetellers, the narrator says that "they had to go backward because seeing ahead was taken from them" (20.14, 38). This is not far from explaining that in their endeavor, when alive, to see into the future, they completely failed. To the grafters, the devils say: Here you can play your game under cover (21.54). Concealment was necessary for their use of public office for private profit, but there are other sins requiring cover. As the narrative moves ahead, it appears that the sinners are eager to escape from their concealment under the boiling tar. In life, on the contrary, they sought concealment. Thus there is no attempt to give the allegory validity throughout.

Other penalties, though not commented on, are expressive of the sinners' lives. The misers and the spendthrifts are engaged in useless toil in which they oppose each other as in life their activities were opposed (7.26). The penalty of uselessly rolling weights seems devised for the misers rather than for their opponents. The first only toil for no good reason; we hardly think of wasters as working hard in their effort to get rid of their money. An expressive punishment is that of the Epicureans, who denied the immortality of the soul—a position which Dante severely condemns (*Convivio* 2.8). Since in effect they said that the grave ends all, after their deaths they are confined in fiery graves (10.13). No penalty is clearer than that of Phlegethon, the river of boiling blood. In that blood are those who were bloody in their lives: tyrants, conquerors, murderers (12.105). The hypocrites, their mantles gilded on the outside, suggest the Biblical hypocrites called whited sepulchers (23.64). Many have thought the ice of the lowest part of Hell suited to the traitors, as indicating that they are without warm human feeling (Canto 32 *et seq.*). Thus these various penalties give some suggestion—however faint—of the life of the sinner, without attempt at making the allegory apparent throughout.

The panders and seducers are driven on by demons (18.35 f.), but all of the wicked are incited by Satan. No special fitness is evident in the punishment of the thieves; it is suited for such snaky crimes as those of the confidence man more than for simpler stealing. Ulysses and his companions, within their flames, suffer a conventional hellish punishment not suggesting their foxy misdeeds (26.42; 27.75). Why should the falsifiers suffer sickness more than do other evil men (29.46)?

Like other artists who have dealt with Hell, Dante is not content with the fire with which theologians usually are satisfied. The artist's modification is often for the sake of fitness and variety. For example, Fra Angelico represents the gluttons as seated at a table with loathsome reptiles in their dishes. For his detailed account of Hell, with twenty-three groups of sinners to be made interesting, Dante required ingenuity, especially since he swung away from crude punishments, such as stretching the lustful on flaming beds. The river of blood is his most direct allegory. Mohammed's state is designed for poetical purposes rather than for the logic of an expositor who wishes allegory to go on all fours. The early commentators generally saw correctly that in presentation of the lives of the wicked on earth and their relation to divine judgment by means of the damned, lay important allegory. This is the only allegory applied to the poem by the author of the Epistle to Can Grande. But going further, the early commentators attempted to develop Dante's hints into complete series of correspondences, or allowed themselves to speculate wildly. For example, the venal popes pushed down into the crevices of the rocks under Pope Nicholas and his successors are by some of the expositors said to be searching for gold like miners. For this absurdity, Dante gives no basis. Yet insofar as the damned do give some suggestion of the wicked life on earth, there lies the prime allegory of the *Inferno*.

Of other possible allegory in the *Comedy*, no writing attributed to Dante gives any hint. Is Beatrice the symbol of the Bible and do her members scattered on the earth (*Purg.* 31.51) symbolize the Biblical texts dispersed over the world, as Buti thinks? Do the seven walls of the noble town in Limbo signify the seven virtues: faith, hope, charity, prudence, justice, temperance, fortitude? Medieval commentators—men not renowned for their poetic good taste—declared those walls thus symbolic, though without demonstrating that Dante even hinted such a thing. Is Virgil at the gate of the city of Dis an allegory of Reason? So thought the early commentator called the Anonymous Florentine. On the quenching of the flames at the sides of and above Phlegethon as that river flows through the burning sands (14.141) a modern annotator asks: "Does the quenching of the fire by boiling blood signify the appeasing of God's anger by human suffering?" If so, Dante has left no word to justify such a flight of fancy. Nor has he told us that the rope the traveler took from his waist and gave to Virgil (16.106) indicates self-confidence. So for the *Inferno* and for the whole poem there are many such allegorical explanations. To all of them we may apply Dante's words when about to indicate the allegory of the *Convivio*: "No one can see its true meaning if I myself do not explain it, because it is hidden under the figure of allegory" (1.2, end). Dante has not told us the true meaning of the allegories of the *Inferno*, if such there be. Are we to trust any commentator to give them correctly? Dante has not even indicated that many of the passages allegorized are figures of allegory at all, though now and then he has indicated hidden meaning without developing it, as in *Inferno* 9.62 and *Purgatorio* 8.19. Any reader is at liberty to allegorize for himself, but he can have no assurance that his solutions would have pleased the poet, or that they carry value for other men. The only person who knows, the author, has been silent.

We have observed that in the *Convivio* Dante gives less than a tenth of his space to allegorically hidden truth. Indeed, after some discussion of the beauty of his first *canzone*, he personifies the poem, letting it say: "Since you do not see my excellence [of idea], give your attention to my beauty." The author then speaks:

> O you who cannot grasp the idea of this *canzone*, do not therefore reject her; but give your attention to her beauty, which is great both in structure, which is a matter for grammarians, for the arrangement of the language, which pertains to the rhetoricians, and for the harmony of her parts, which pertains to musicians. These things about her can be seen as beautiful by anybody who looks closely (2.11, end).

Shall we hesitate, then, to look for the beauty of the *Inferno*, that is, to treat it as a poem, neglecting any hidden meanings?

INFERNO*

* With permission, the text of the Società Dantesca Italiana is here printed, with selected modifications from *La Commedia secondo l'antica vulgata*, a cura di Giorgio Petrocchi, under the auspices of the Società.

CANTO 1

Nel mezzo del cammin di nostra vita
mi ritrovai per una selva oscura,
chè la diritta via era smarrita.
Ahi quanto a dir qual era è cosa dura
esta selva selvaggia e aspra e forte
6 che nel pensier rinnova la paura!
Tant' è amara che poco è più morte;
ma per trattar del ben ch' io vi trovai,
dirò de l' altre cose ch' io v' ho scorte.
Io non so ben ridir com' io v' entrai,
tant' era pieno di sonno a quel punto
12 che la verace via abbandonai.
Ma poi ch' i' fui al piè d' un colle giunto,
là dove terminava quella valle
che m' avea di paura il cor compunto,
guardai in alto, e vidi le sue spalle
vestite già de' raggi del pianeta
18 che mena dritto altrui per ogni calle.
Allor fu la paura un poco queta
che nel lago del cor m' era durata
la notte ch' io passai con tanta pieta.
E come quei che con lena affannata
uscito fuor del pelago a la riva,
24 si volge a l' acqua perigliosa e guata,
così l' animo mio, ch' ancor fuggiva,
si volse a rietro a rimirar lo passo
che non lasciò già mai persona viva.
Poi ch'ei posato un poco il corpo lasso,
ripresi via per la piaggia deserta,
30 sì che 'l piè fermo sempre era 'l più basso.
Ed ecco, quasi al cominciar de l'erta,
una lonza leggiera e presta molto,
che di pel maculato era coverta;

CANTO 1

Prelude

[Lost in the dark forest: 1.1–30]

[NARRATOR] In the midst of my journey through this life of ours,[1] I was in a dark forest, because I had lost the right road.[2] Oh, how hard it is to tell of what sort this forest was—so wild, rugged, and difficult that as I remember it my fear returns![3] It so afflicts me that death is little less bitter. But that I may deal with the good which there I found, I shall write of all the things I saw. I cannot in any way report how I got into it— so overcome with sleep I was at the moment when I left the true road. But on reaching the foot of a hill at the edge of that lowland which had pierced my heart with fear, I looked up and saw its ridges already lighted by the rays of the planet[4] which leads us straight on every path. Then the fear in the bottom of my heart, which had lasted through the night[5] I passed so wretch-edly, was a little subdued. And like one who, gasping for breath, comes out of the sea upon the shore,[6] and turns to the fearful waters and stares, so my mind, still running away, turned backward to observe the peril from which never before has any person come out alive.[7] When I had a little rested my weary body, I started up the deserted slope, so that my firmly planted foot was always the lower one.

[The leopardess, the lion, the she-wolf: 1.31–60]

[NARRATOR] Then I saw, almost at the bottom of the slope, a graceful and very speedy leopardess with a

e non mi si partia dinanzi al volto,
anzi impediva tanto il mio cammino,
36   ch'i' fui per ritornar più volte volto.
Temp'era dal principio del mattino,
e 'l sol montava 'n su con quelle stelle
ch'eran con lui quando l'amor divino
mosse di prima quelle cose belle;
sì ch'a bene sperar m'era cagione
42   di quella fera a la gaetta pelle
l'ora del tempo e la dolce stagione;
ma non sì che paura non mi desse
la vista che m'apparve d'un leone.
Questi parea che contra me venesse
con la test'alta e con rabbiosa fame,
48   sì che parea che l'aere ne tremesse.
Ed una lupa, che di tutte brame
sembiava carca ne la sua magrezza,
e molte genti fé già viver grame,
questa mi porse tanto di gravezza
con la paura ch'uscia di sua vista,
54   ch'io perdei la speranza de l'altezza.
E qual è quei che volontieri acquista,
e giugne 'l tempo che perder lo face,
che 'n tutt'i suoi pensier piange e s'attrista;
tal mi fece la bestia sanza pace,
che, venendomi incontro, a poco a poco
60   mi ripigneva là dove 'l sol tace.
Mentre ch'i' rovinava in basso loco,
dinanzi a li occhi mi si fu offerto
chi per lungo silenzio parea fioco.
Quando vidi costui nel gran diserto,
«Miserere di me» gridai a lui,
66   «qual che tu sii, od ombra od omo certo!»
Rispuosemi: «Non omo, omo già fui,
e li parenti miei furon lombardi,
mantovani per patria ambedui.

spotted hide. She did not move from in front of me, but so hindered my journey that many times I turned to go back. The hour was daybreak, and the sun was coming up, along with the stars which were with him when Love Divine first set those beautiful things in motion, so that the hour of the day in its sweetness gave me cause for good hope about that animal with the pleasing hide[8]—yet not so much that a lion I saw did not frighten me. I thought I saw him coming upon me with head raised, and in raging hunger, so that the air seemed to tremble before him. And a wolf,[9] appearing gaunt as though afflicted with every sort of greed—and already she has made many live in misery—caused me such distress, with the fear her aspect roused, that I lost all hope of the summit. For though I was eager to go forward, a time had come when I was forced to fail, because that beast which never rests made me in all my thoughts lament and feel sad, for, coming toward me, bit by bit she drove me back where the sun is strengthless.

[*Virgil to the rescue: 1.61–99*]

[NARRATOR] As I was plunging down to low ground, to my eyes was presented one who, through long silence, I suppose, was hoarse.

[DANTE] When I saw him in that vast wilderness, "Pity me," I shouted to him, "whoever you are, whether a shade or really a man."[10]

[VIRGIL] He answered: "I am not a man. Long ago I was a man, and my parents were Lombards, both of

Nacqui sub Iulio, ancor che fosse tardi,
    e vissi a Roma sotto 'l buono Augusto
72   al tempo de li dei falsi e bugiardi.
Poeta fui, e cantai di quel giusto
    figliuol d'Anchise che venne da Troia,
    poi che il superbo Iliòn fu combusto.
Ma tu perchè ritorni a tanta noia?
    perchè non sali il dilettoso monte
78   ch' è principio e cagion di tutta gioia?»
«Or se' tu quel Virgilio e quella fonte
    che spandi di parlar sì largo fiume?»
    rispuos' io lui con vergognosa fronte.
«O degli altri poeti onore e lume,
    vagliami il lungo studio e 'l grande amore
84   che m' ha fatto cercar lo tuo volume.
Tu se' lo mio maestro e 'l mio autore;
    tu se' solo colui da cu' io tolsi
    lo bello stilo che m' ha fatto onore.
Vedi la bestia per cu' io mi volsi:
    aiutami da lei, famoso saggio,
90   ch' ella mi fa tremar le vene e i polsi.»
«A te convien tenere altro viaggio»
    rispuose poi che lagrimar mi vide,
    «se vuo' campar d' esto loco selvaggio:
chè questa bestia, per la qual tu gride,
    non lascia altrui passar per la sua via,
96   ma tanto lo 'mpedisce che l' uccide;
e ha natura sì malvagia e ria,
    che mai non empie la bramosa voglia,
    e dopo il pasto ha più fame che pria.
Molti son li animali a cui s' ammoglia,
    e più saranno ancora, infin che 'l Veltro
102   verrà, che la farà morir con doglia.
Questi non ciberà terra nè peltro,
    ma sapienza, amore e virtute,
    e sua nazion sarà tra feltro e feltro.

them Mantuan natives. I was born under Julius, though late in his reign, and I lived in Rome under the good Augustus, in the time of the false and deceptive gods. A poet I was, and I sang of that just son of Anchises who came from Troy after proud Ilium was burned. But why are you going back to such pain? Why do you not climb the pleasant mountain which originates and causes every joy?"[11]

[DANTE] "Are you that Virgil, that spring which pours out language in so noble a river?" I modestly replied. "Oh, honor and light of all the poets, I rely for aid on my years of devotion, and on the great love that has made me pore over your book. You are my teacher and my maker. You are the only one from whom I took the lovely style that has brought me honor.[12] You see the animal for which I turned back. Help me against her, famous bard, because she makes my veins and arteries tremble."

[VIRGIL] "You will have to go by another road," he replied, seeing my tears, "if you are to escape from this wild place, because the animal about which you are shouting, does not let any one go along her road, but obstructs him until she kills him. And her nature is so malicious and evil that never does she satisfy her greedy desire, but after a meal she hungers more than before."[13]

*[Virgil prophesies Italy's deliverance from
bad government: 1.100–111]*

[VIRGIL] "Many are the animals with which she mates, and more there will be still, until the Veltro comes,[14] who will put her to a painful death. He will not feed on land or wealth, but on wisdom, love and courage; and his birthplace will be between Feltro and Feltro.

Di quella umile Italia fia salute
  per cui morì la vergine Cammilla,
108   Eurialo e Turno e Niso di ferute.
Questi la caccerà per ogni villa,
  fin che l'avrà rimessa ne lo 'nferno,
  là onde invidia prima dipartilla.
Ond'io per lo tuo me' penso e discerno
  che tu mi segui, e io sarò tua guida,
114   e trarrotti di qui per luogo etterno,
ov'udirai le disperate strida,
  vedrai li antichi spiriti dolenti,
  che la seconda morte ciascun grida;
e vederai color che son contenti
  nel foco, perché speran di venire
120   quando che sia a le beate genti.
A le qua' poi se tu vorrai salire,
  anima fia a ciò più di me degna:
  con lei ti lascerò nel mio partire;
ché quello imperador che là su regna,
  perch'io fu' ribellante a la sua legge,
126   non vuol che 'n sua città per me si vegna.
In tutte parti impera e quivi regge;
  quivi è la sua città e l'alto seggio:
  oh felice colui cu' ivi elegge!»
E io a lui: «Poeta, io ti richeggio
  per quello Dio che tu non conoscesti,
132   acciò ch'io fugga questo male e peggio,
che tu mi meni là dov'or dicesti,
  sì ch'io veggia la porta di san Pietro
  e color cui tu fai cotanto mesti.»
Allor si mosse, e io li tenni retro.

Of that 'low-lying Italy'[15] he will be the salvation for which the virgin Camilla, Euryalus and Turnus and Nisus died of their wounds. He will pursue the wolf through every town until he has driven her back into Hell, from which envy first brought her."

[*The journey through the world of
the dead: 1.112–136*]

[VIRGIL] "So I believe and conclude it best for you to follow me, and I will be your guide, and from here will take you to the everlasting place, where you will hear shrieks of desperation, where you will see the famous spirits in such pain that each one calls for the second death. And you will see those who are happy in the fire because they hope, when their time comes, to join the blessed. To these, when at last you ascend, a worthier spirit than I am will be your guide.[16] With her I shall leave you when we part, because that Emperor who reigns up there, since I did not comply with his laws, does not allow me to enter his city. Everywhere he is in power, but there he reigns; there is his city and his capital. Happy the man whom he chooses for it!"

[DANTE] I replied: "Poet, in the name of that God whom you do not acknowledge, I beg you, in order that I may escape this ill and worse, to lead me where you say, that I may see St. Peter's gate, and those who you say are so wretched."

[NARRATOR] Then he started and I followed him.[17]

CANTO 2

Lo giorno se n'andava, e l'aere bruno
toglieva gli animai che sono in terra
da le fatiche loro; e io sol uno
m'apparecchiava a sostener la guerra
sì del cammino e sì de la pietate,
6   che ritrarrà la mente che non erra.
O Muse, o alto ingegno, or m'aiutate;
o mente che scrivesti ciò ch'io vidi,
qui si parrà la tua nobilitate.
Io cominciai: «Poeta che mi guidi,
guarda la mia virtù s'ell'è possente,
12   prima ch'a l'alto passo tu mi fidi.
Tu dici che di Silvio il parente,
corruttibile ancora, ad immortale
secolo andò, e fu sensibilmente.
Però se l' avversario d' ogni male
cortese i fu, pensando l' alto effetto
18   ch' uscir dovea di lui, e 'l chi e 'l quale
non pare indegno ad omo d' intelletto;
ch' ei fu de l' alma Roma e di suo impero
ne l' empireo ciel per padre eletto:
la quale e 'l quale, a voler dir lo vero,
fu stabilita per lo loco santo
24   u' siede il successor del maggior Piero.
Per questa andata onde li dai tu vanto,
intese cose che furon cagione
di sua vittoria e del papale ammanto.
Andovvi poi lo Vas d' elezione,
per recarne conforto a quella fede
30   ch' è principio a la via di salvazione.
Ma io, perchè venirvi? o chi 'l concede?
Io non Enea, io non Paolo sono:
me degno a ciò nè io nè altri crede.

CANTO 2

PRELUDE, *cont.*

[The traveler hesitates to undertake the journey: 2.1–42]

[NARRATOR] The day was getting on and darkness was taking from their labors the creatures on earth;[1] and I only of living men was preparing to bear the strain both of the journey and of compassion, which memory, never erring, will bring back.

[POET] *O Muses, O lofty genius, now aid me! O memory, you who write what I saw, here will be shown your magnificence.*[2]

[DANTE] I said:[3] "Poet, you who are to guide me, estimate my valor, to learn if it is mighty, before you intrust me to the difficult test. You write that Silvius' father,[4] while still mortal, went to the everlasting realm and was in possession of his senses. Though if to him the Enemy of All Evil was generous, contemplating the noble result to come from him, both the who and the what to a thoughtful man do not seem strange, because in the Empyrean Heaven he had been chosen as the father of fostering Rome and her empire, for both of these were founded (if I am to speak the truth) in the holy place where sits the successor of great Peter. On this visit for which you glorify him, he learned matters which caused his victory and the papal mantle. Later the Chosen Vessel[5] went there, to bring back exhortation to that faith which starts us on salvation's road. But I, why should I go there? Or who grants it? I am not Aeneas;[6] Paul I am not. That I am worthy of it, nei-

Per che, se del venire io m' abbandono,
    temo che la venuta non sia folle:
36   se' savio; intendi me' ch' io non ragiono.»
E qual è quei che disvuol ciò che volle
    e per novi pensier cangia proposta,
    sì che dal cominciar tutto si tolle,
tal mi fec' io in quella oscura costa,
    perchè, pensando, consumai la 'mpresa
42   che fu nel cominciar cotanto tosta.
«S' i' ho ben la parola tua intesa»
    rispuose del magnanimo quell' ombra,
    «l' anima tua è da viltate offesa;
la qual molte fiate l' omo ingombra
    sì che d' onrata impresa lo rivolve,
48   come falso veder bestia quand' ombra.
Da questa tema acciò che tu ti solve,
    dirotti perch' io venni e quel ch' io 'ntesi
    nel primo punto che di te mi dolve.
Io era tra color che son sospesi,
    e donna mi chiamò beata e bella,
54   tal che di comandare io la richiesi.
Lucevan li occhi suoi più che la stella;
    e cominciommi a dir soave e piana,
    con angelica voce, in sua favella:
'O anima cortese mantovana,
    di cui la fama ancor nel mondo dura,
60   e durerà quanto il mondo lontana,
l'amico mio, e non de la ventura,
    ne la diserta piaggia è impedito
    sì nel cammin, che volt'è per paura;
e temo che non sia già sì smarrito,
    ch'io mi sia tardi al soccorso levata,
66   per quel ch'i' ho di lui nel cielo udito.
Or movi, e con la tua parola ornata
    e con ciò ch'ha mestieri al suo campare,
    l'aiuta sì ch'i' ne sia consolata.

ther I myself nor any other believes. Hence, if, surrendering myself, I go, I fear my going will be foolish. You are prudent; you comprehend better than I explain."
[NARRATOR] One of those men who unwish what they wish, and change their plans on further thought, thus withdrawing from all action, I myself became on that dark slope, because by thinking I destroyed the enterprise so hastily begun.

[*Virgil tells of Beatrice's intercession
for Dante: 2.43–93*]

[VIRGIL] "If I have clearly understood what you have said," answered that magnanimous poet's shade, "your spirit is conquered by cowardice, which often so impedes a man that he turns away from a noble enterprise, just as false seeing makes a horse do when it shies. So that you may rid yourself of this fear, I shall tell you why I came, and what I learned in the first moment when I grieved for you. I was among those who are in suspense.[7] A blessed and beautiful lady addressed me,[8] and I begged her to command me. Her eyes shone brighter than stars, and she said, in tones soft and low, speaking with angelic utterance:[9]
[BEATRICE *quoted*] " 'O courteous Mantuan spirit, whose renown still lasts in the world, and will last as long as the world itself, my friend—but not the friend of Chance[10]—on the deserted slope is so obstructed as in dismay to have turned back upon his path, and I fear he is already so bewildered that too late I have risen for his assistance, according to what I have heard of him in Heaven. Now set out, and with your beauteous language and with what else is needed for his escape, so

I' son Beatrice che ti faccio andare;
vegno del loco ove tornar disio;
72   amor mi mosse, che mi fa parlare.
Quando sarò dinanzi al signor mio,
di te mi loderò sovente a lui'.
Tacette allora, e poi comincia' io:
'O donna di virtù sola per cui
l'umana spezie eccede ogni contento
78   di quel ciel c'ha minor li cerchi sui,
tanto m'aggrada il tuo comandamento,
che l'ubidir, se già fosse, m'è tardi;
più non t'è uo' ch'aprirmi il tuo talento.
Ma dimmi la cagion che non ti guardi
de lo scender qua giuso in questo centro
84   de l'ampio loco ove tornar tu ardi'.
'Da che tu vuo' saper cotanto a dentro,
dirotti brievemente' mi rispuose,
'perch'io non temo di venir qua entro.
Temer si dee di sole quelle cose
c'hanno potenza di fare altrui male;
90   de l'altre no, chè non son paurose.
Io son fatta da Dio, sua mercé, tale,
che la vostra miseria non mi tange,
nè fiamma d'esto incendio non m'assale.
Donna è gentil nel ciel che si compiange
di questo impedimento ov'io ti mando,
96   sì che duro giudicio là su frange.
Questa chiese Lucia in suo dimando
e disse: Or ha bisogno il tuo fedele
di te, ed io a te lo raccomando.
Lucia, nimica di ciascun crudele,
si mosse, e venne al loco dov'i' era,
102   che mi sedea con l'antica Rachele.
Disse: Beatrice, loda di Dio vera,
chè non soccorri quei che t'amò tanto,
ch'uscì per te de la volgare schiera?

aid him as to comfort me. I who send you am Beatrice.
I come from a place to which I long to return. Love
caused me to act, and it makes me speak. When I am in
the presence of my Lord, I often shall tell him of my
gratitude to you."[11]
[VIRGIL] "Then she was silent, and at once I said: 'O
lady of excellence through which alone the human race
surpasses all contained within that heaven whose circles
are smallest,[12] so much your bidding pleases me that
my obeying—if already done—is too slow. You need
do no more than reveal to me your wish. But tell me the
reason why you did not avoid coming down to this center[13] from the spacious place to which you long to return.'
[BEATRICE *quoted*] " 'About what you so greatly desire
to know—why I do not fear to come here—' she replied, 'I shall tell you briefly. We ought to fear only
things having power to do us harm; other things not,
because they are not worth fearing. God has so made
me—thanks be to him—that your misery does not affect me, nor does any flame of this burning place attack me.' "[14]

[The Virgin Mary and St. Lucia in Heaven
assist the traveler: 2.94–126]

[BEATRICE *quoted*] " 'There is in Heaven a noble Lady[15]
so grieved by this blockage because of which I am sending you that the stern decree up there she breaks.'
[THE VIRGIN *quoted*] " 'She uttered her command to
Lucia,[16] saying: "Now your faithful servant has need
of you, and I put his case before you."
[BEATRICE *quoted*] " 'Lucia, enemy of all harshness, rose
and came to the place where I was sitting with the
noble Rachel.'
[LUCIA *quoted*] " 'She said: "Beatrice, true praise of
God, why do you not rescue the man who so greatly

non odi tu la pieta del suo pianto?
non vedi tu la morte che 'l combatte
108   su la fiumana ove 'l mar non ha vanto?
Al mondo non fur mai persone ratte
a far lor pro o a fuggir lor danno,
com'io, dopo cotai parole fatte,
venni qua giù del mio beato scanno,
fidandomi nel tuo parlare onesto,
114   ch'onora te e quei ch'udito l'hanno'.
Poscia che m'ebbe ragionato questo,
li occhi lucenti lacrimando volse;
per che mi fece del venir più presto:
e venni a te così com'ella volse;
dinanzi a quella fiera ti levai
120   che del bel monte il corto andar ti tolse.
Dunque che è? perchè, perchè ristai?
perchè tanta viltà nel cuore allette?
perchè ardire e franchezza non hai,
poscia che tai tre donne benedette
curan di te nella corte del cielo,
126   e 'l mio parlar tanto ben t'impromette?»
Quali fioretti, dal notturno gelo
chinati e chiusi, poi che 'l sol li 'mbianca
si drizzan tutti aperti in loro stelo,
tal mi fec'io di mia virtute stanca,
e tanto buono ardire al cor mi corse,
132   ch'i' cominciai come persona franca:
«Oh pietosa colei che mi soccorse!
e te cortese ch'ubidisti tosto
a le vere parole che ti porse!
Tu m'hai con disiderio il cor disposto
sì al venir con le parole tue,
138   ch'i' son tornato nel primo proposto.
Or va, ch' un sol volere è d' ambedue:
tu duca, tu segnore, e tu maestro.»
Così li dissi; e poi che mosso fue,
intrai per lo cammino alto e silvestro.

loved you that for you he left the common herd? Do
you not hear his piteous lament? Do you not see Death
attacking him by the river where the sea does not tri-
umph?"[17]

[BEATRICE *quoted*] " 'In this world never were persons
so speedy to seek their advantage or to escape harm as
I, after this speech, was to come down from my blessed
seat, confiding in your noble diction, which elevates
you and those who have heard it.'

[VIRGIL] "When she had thus spoken to me, her shin-
ing eyes filled with tears, so that she made my coming
still quicker; and I came to you as she directed. I got
you out of danger from that wild beast which denied
you the short road to the fair mountain.[18] What then?
Why, why do you wait? Why nourish such cowardice
in your heart? Why are you not eager and sure when
three such holy ladies are concerned for you in the court
of Heaven, and my words promise you such great
good?"

[*Dante decides to visit the world of the dead
with Virgil: 2.127–142*]

[NARRATOR] Just as little flowers bent and closed by
the chill of night, when the sun shines upon them,
straighten themselves, fully open upon their stems, so
my wearied vigor acted.

[DANTE] So much good courage rushed into my heart
that I said fearlessly: "Oh, piteous was she who res-
cued me! And courteous are you who quickly followed
the true instructions she gave you. By your speeches
you have roused my heart with such desire for the
journey that I have returned to my first purpose. Now
go, for we two have a single will. You are leader, you
are ruler, you are teacher."

[NARRATOR] So I spoke to him, and as soon as he
moved, I took that difficult and rugged road.[19]

CANTO 3

«Per me si va ne la città dolente,
    per me si va ne l' etterno dolore,
    per me si va tra la perduta gente.
Giustizia mosse il mio alto fattore;
    fecemi la divina potestate,
6   la somma sapienza e 'l primo amore.
Dinanzi a me non fuor cose create
    se non etterne, e io etterno duro.
    Lasciate ogni speranza, voi ch' entrate.»
Queste parole di colore oscuro
    vid' io scritte al sommo d' una porta;
12   per ch' io: «Maestro, il senso lor m' è duro.»
Ed elli a me, come persona accorta:
    «Qui si convien lasciare ogni sospetto;
    ogni viltà convien che qui sia morta.
Noi siam venuti al loco ov' io t' ho detto
    che tu vedrai le genti dolorose
18   c' hanno perduto il ben de l' intelletto.»
E poi che la sua mano a la mia pose
    con lieto volto, ond' io mi confortai,
    mi mise dentro a le segrete cose.
Quivi sospiri, pianti e alti guai
    risonavan per l' aere sanza stelle,
24   per ch' io al cominciar ne lagrimai.
Diverse lingue, orribili favelle,
    parole di dolore, accenti d' ira,
    voci alte e fioche, e suon di man con elle
facevano un tumulto, il qual s' aggira
    sempre in quell' aura sanza tempo tinta,
30   come la rena quando turbo spira.
E io ch' avea d' error la testa cinta,
    dissi: «Maestro, che è quel ch' i' odo?
    e che gent' è che par nel duol sì vinta?»

CANTO 3

[Hell Gate: 3.1–18]

[NARRATOR] THROUGH ME YOU GO INTO THE CITY OF PAIN; THROUGH ME YOU GO INTO EVERLASTING WOE; THROUGH ME YOU GO AMONG THE LOST. JUSTICE IMPELLED MY LOFTY MAKER. I WAS MADE BY POWER DIVINE, BY HIGHEST WISDOM AND BY PRIMAL LOVE. BEFORE ME WERE NO CREATED THINGS EXCEPT THOSE EVERLASTING, AND I CONTINUE EVERLASTINGLY. GIVE UP ALL HOPE, YOU WHO COME IN.

These words, in dark color, I saw written above a gate. [DANTE] Hence I said: "Teacher, for me their meaning is too hard."

[VIRGIL] And he replied, as a man of understanding: "Here every fear you must let go; here all cowardice must lie dead. We have come to the place I told you of, where you will see the sorrowing people who have lost the intellect's vigor."[1]

[The neutrals: 3.19–69]

[NARRATOR] When he laid his hand on mine with a happy face that encouraged me, I went among things kept secret.[2] There sighs, laments and loud shrieks echoed through the starless air, so that at first I wept. Frightening talk, horrid speeches,[3] words of pain, tones of anger, shouts loud and hoarse, and along with them noise made by hands, produced turbulence circling ever about in that air timelessly dark, like sand when a whirlwind is blowing.

[DANTE] And I, my head gripped by uncertainty, said: "Teacher, what am I hearing? And what people are these so vanquished by pain?"

Ed elli a me: «Questo misero modo
tengon l' anime triste di coloro
36   che visser sanza infamia e sanza lodo.
Mischiate sono a quel cattivo coro
de li angeli che non furon ribelli
nè fur fedeli a Dio, ma per sè fuoro.
Caccianli i ciel per non esser men belli,
nè lo profondo inferno li riceve,
42   ch' alcuna gloria i rei avrebber d' elli.»
E io: «Maestro, che è tanto greve
a lor che lamentar li fa sì forte?»
Rispuose: «Dicerolti molto breve.
Questi non hanno speranza di morte,
e la lor cieca vita è tanto bassa,
48   che 'nvidiosi son d' ogni altra sorte.
Fama di loro il mondo esser non lassa;
misericordia e giustizia li sdegna:
non ragioniam di lor, ma guarda e passa.»
E io, che riguardai, vidi una insegna
che girando correva tanto ratta,
54   che d' ogni posa mi parea indegna;
e dietro le venia sì lunga tratta
di gente, ch' io non averei creduto
che morte tanta n' avesse disfatta.
Poscia ch' io v' ebbi alcun riconosciuto,
vidi e conobbi l' ombra di colui
60   che fece per viltà il gran rifiuto.
Incontanente intesi e certo fui
che questa era la setta de' cattivi,
a Dio spiacenti ed a' nemici sui.
Questi sciaurati, che mai non fur vivi,
erano ignudi e stimolati molto
66   da mosconi e da vespe ch' eran ivi.
Elle rigavan lor di sangue il volto,
che, mischiato di lagrime, ai lor piedi
da fastidiosi vermi era ricolto.

[VIRGIL] He replied: "This is the wretched state of the worthless souls of men who lived without ill repute and without praise. They are mingled with that cowardly band of angels who were not rebellious[4] and not faithful to God, but were for themselves. The heavens reject them, in order not to be less beautiful, and the bottomless pit does not accept them, because the damned would find them cause for pride."[5]

[DANTE] I replied: "Teacher, what is so grievous to them, making them wail so loud?"

[VIRGIL] He answered: "I shall tell you very briefly. These souls have no hope of death, and their obscure existence is so degraded that they envy every other lot. Fame the world does not allow them. Mercy and Justice are ashamed of them. Let us not talk about them; just look and pass on."

[NARRATOR] And I, as I looked, saw a banner so speedily circling about that I inferred it had no claim to any rest.[6] And behind it came a procession of people so long that I should not have supposed death had destroyed so many. After I had recognized some of them, I saw the shade of him who through cowardice made the great rejection.[7] Instantly I understood and was sure that this was the company of incapables, who please neither God nor his enemies. These wretches, who never lived like men, were naked[8] and badly stung by the wasps and horseflies there. These insects streaked their faces with blood which, mixed with tears, was taken up by repulsive worms at their feet.

E poi ch' a riguardare oltre mi diedi,
   vidi genti a la riva d' un gran fiume;
72   per ch' io dissi: «Maestro, or mi concedi
ch' i' sappia quali sono, e qual costume
   le fa di trapassar parer sì pronte,
   com' io discerno per lo fioco lume.»
Ed elli a me: «Le cose ti fier conte,
   quando noi fermerem li nostri passi
78   su la trista riviera d'Acheronte.»
Allor con li occhi vergognosi e bassi,
   temendo no 'l mio dir li fosse grave,
   infino al fiume del parlar mi trassi.
Ed ecco verso noi venir per nave
   un vecchio, bianco per antico pelo,
84   gridando: «Guai a voi, anime prave!
non isperate mai veder lo cielo:
   i' vegno per menarvi a l'altra riva
   ne le tenebre etterne, in caldo e 'n gelo.
E tu che se' costì, anima viva,
   partiti da cotesti che son morti.»
90   Ma poi che vide ch'io non mi partiva,
disse: «Per altra via, per altri porti
   verrai a piaggia, non qui, per passare:
   più lieve legno convien che ti porti.»
E 'l duca lui: «Caron, non ti crucciare:
   vuolsi così colà dove si puote
96   ciò che si vuole, e più non dimandare.»
Quinci fuor quete le lanose gote
   al nocchier de la livida palude,
   che 'ntorno a li occhi avea di fiamme rote.
Ma quell'anime, ch'eran lasse e nude,
   cangiar colore e dibattieno i denti,
102   ratto che 'nteser le parole crude.
Bestemmiavano Dio e lor parenti,
   l'umana spezie e 'l luogo e 'l tempo e 'l seme
   di lor semenza e di lor nascimenti.

[*Crowds on the banks of the river
Acheron: 3.70–136*]

[DANTE] As soon as I looked into the distance, I saw crowds on a great river's bank. So I said: "Teacher, now be so kind as to tell me who they are, and what usage makes them so eager to cross the river, as I make out in the dim light."[9]

[VIRGIL] And he replied: "These things will be clear to you when we pause on Acheron's sad shore."

[NARRATOR] Then with eyes bashfully downcast, fearing my talk would annoy him, I kept from speaking until we reached the river.

[CHARON] And just then in a boat came toward us an old man, white with the hair of old age, shouting: "Woe to you, wicked souls! Do not hope ever to see the sky. I come to take you to the other bank, to everlasting darkness, to heat and cold. And you there, living soul,[10] move away from the dead." And when he saw that I did not move away, he said: "By another road, on other boats, you will reach shore, not by passing here. A swifter bark must carry you."[11]

[VIRGIL] And my guide said to him: "Charon, do not get vexed. Thus it is decreed in that place where anything decreed is carried out. So ask no more."

[NARRATOR] This quieted the woolly cheeks of the dark swamp's boatman, who around his eyes had circles of flame. But the souls there, who were weary and naked, changed color and gnashed their teeth as soon as they heard his harsh words. They cursed God and their parents, the human race and the place and the time, their

Poi si ritrasser tutte quante insieme,
  forte piangendo, a la riva malvagia
108   ch'attende ciascun uom che Dio non teme.
Caron dimonio, con occhi di bragia,
  loro accennando, tutti li raccoglie;
  batte col remo qualunque s'adagia.
Come d'autunno si levan le foglie
  l'una appresso de l'altra, fin che 'l ramo
114   vede a la terra tutte le sue spoglie,
similemente il mal seme d'Adamo
  gittansi di quel lito ad una ad una
  per cenni, come augel per suo richiamo.
Così sen vanno su per l' onda bruna,
  e avanti che sien di là discese,
120   anche di qua nuova schiera s' auna.
«Figliuol mio,» disse il maestro cortese,
  «quelli che muoion ne l' ira di Dio
  tutti convegnon qui d' ogni paese;
e pronti sono a trapassar lo rio,
  chè la divina giustizia li sprona,
126   sì che la tema si volve in disio.
Quinci non passa mai anima buona;
  e però, se Caron di te si lagna,
  ben puoi sapere omai che 'l suo dir suona.»
Finito questo, la buia campagna
  tremò sì forte, che de lo spavento
132   la mente di sudore ancor mi bagna.
La terra lagrimosa diede vento,
  che balenò una luce vermiglia
  la qual mi vinse ciascun sentimento;
e caddi come l' uom che 'l sonno piglia.

ancestry and their own births. Then, loudly weeping, they all rushed to one spot on the evil shore awaiting every man who fears not God. Charon the devil, with eyes like coals, giving a signal, gathers them all together; he strikes with his oar whoever is slow. As in autumn the leaves fall one after another, till the branch sees all its ornaments on the earth, so the evil race of Adam throw themselves upon that shore one after another, drawn by signals as a bird by a lure.[12] Thus they go away, over the dark waters, and before they land on the other side, here again a fresh crowd gathers.

[VIRGIL] "My son," said my courteous teacher, "those who die in the wrath of God all assemble here from every country. And they are eager to cross the river because heavenly justice spurs them on, so that their fear is changed to longing. Here a good soul never crosses. Hence if Charon is angry at you, you can now understand what his talk means."

[NARRATOR] As Virgil ended, the dark plain shook so hard that even now the recollection of my fear soaks me with sweat. The weeping earth sent forth a wind in which flashed a scarlet light that conquered all my senses, and I fell, overcome by sleep.[13]

CANTO 4

Ruppemi l' alto sonno nella testa
un greve truono, sì ch' io mi riscossi
come persona ch' è per forza desta;
e l' occhio riposato intorno mossi,
dritto levato, e fiso riguardai
6   per conoscer lo loco dov' io fossi.
Vero è che 'n su la proda mi trovai
de la valle d' abisso dolorosa
che truono accoglie d' infiniti guai.
Oscura e profonda era e nebulosa,
tanto che, per ficcar lo viso a fondo,
12   io non vi discernea alcuna cosa.
«Or discendiam qua giù nel cieco mondo»
cominciò il poeta tutto smorto:
«io sarò primo, e tu sarai secondo.»
E io, che del color mi fui accorto,
dissi: «Come verrò, se tu paventi,
18   che suoli al mio dubbiare esser conforto?»
Ed elli a me: «L'angoscia de le genti
che son qua giù, nel viso mi dipigne
quella pietà che tu per tema senti.
Andiam, ché la via lunga ne sospigne.»
Così si mise e così mi fé intrare
24   nel primo cerchio che l'abisso cigne.
Quivi, secondo che per ascoltare,
non avea pianto mai che di sospiri
che l'aura etterna facevan tremare.
Ciò avvenia di duol sanza martiri
ch'avean le turbe, ch'eran molte e grandi,
30   d'infanti e di femmine e di viri.
Lo buon maestro a me: «Tu non dimandi
che spiriti son questi che tu vedi?
Or vo' che sappi, innanzi che più andi,

CANTO 4

THE VESTIBULE OF HELL, *cont.*

[Preparation for the First Circle of Hell: 4.1–22]

[NARRATOR] A loud thunderclap broke the sleep weighing my head down. So I awoke, roused by its violence. I looked around, with sight refreshed, having risen to my feet, and steadily gazed, to learn the place where I was. In truth, I was on the edge of the sad abysmal valley which gathers thunder from countless laments. It was so dark and deep and cloudy that, straining my eyes into its depths, I made out nothing there.

[VIRGIL] "Now let us go down into the world where little can be seen," said my poet, very pale. "I shall be first and you will be second."

[DANTE] And I, who observed his color, said: "How shall I go if you are disturbed, who are wont in my fears to be my support?"

[VIRGIL] He replied: "The suffering of the people down below gives my face that color of pity[1] which you mistake for fear. Let us go, for the long road urges us on."[2]

CIRCLE ONE

[Limbo, for virtuous pre-Christians: 4.23–66]

[NARRATOR] So he went into, and so he had me enter, the first circle that surrounds the pit. There, according to my hearing, no lamentation was uttered except by sighing, which caused the never-ending breeze to tremble. This resulted from the grief, without torture, of the crowds; these were many and large, of infants and women and men.

[VIRGIL] My good teacher said to me: "You do not ask what spirits are these you see. Now let me tell you, be-

ch'ei non peccaro; e s'elli hanno mercedi,
non basta, perché non ebber battesmo,
36   ch'è porta de la fede che tu credi.
E se furon dinanzi al cristianesmo,
non adorar debitamente a Dio:
e di questi cotai son io medesmo.
Per tai difetti, non per altro rio,
semo perduti, e sol di tanto offesi,
42   che sanza speme vivemo in disio.»
Gran duol mi prese al cor quando lo 'ntesi,
però che gente di molto valore
conobbi che 'n quel limbo eran sospesi.
«Dimmi, maestro mio, dimmi, segnore,»
comincia' io per volere esser certo
48   di quella fede che vince ogni errore:
«uscicci mai alcuno, o per suo merto
o per altrui, che poi fosse beato?»
E quei, che 'ntese il mio parlar coperto,
rispuose: «Io era nuovo in questo stato,
quando ci vidi venire un possente,
54   con segno di vittoria coronato.
Trasseci l'ombra del primo parente,
d'Abel suo figlio e quella di Noè,
di Moisè legista e obediente;
Abraàm patriarca e Davìd re,
Israèl con lo padre e co' suoi nati
60   e con Rachele, per cui tanto fé;
e altri molti, e feceli beati;
e vo' che sappi che, dinanzi ad essi,
spiriti umani non eran salvati.»
Non lasciavam l'andar perch'ei dicessi,
ma passavam la selva tuttavia,
66   la selva, dico, di spiriti spessi.
Non era lunga ancor la nostra via
di qua dal sonno, quand'io vidi un foco
ch'emisperio di tenebre vincia.

fore you go farther, that they did not sin. Yet though they have merits, that is not enough, since baptism they did not have, which is the door of that religion you believe in. And if they were earlier than Christianity, they did not worship God suitably. I myself am one of these. For these defects—not through other sin—we are lost, and only so far punished that, without hope, we continue to desire."

[NARRATOR] Great pain struck to my heart when I heard that, because I knew that in that limbo people of great worth were in suspense.

[DANTE] "Tell me, Teacher, tell me, Sir," I said in my wish to be certain with that assurance which conquers every doubt, "has any soul ever gone out from here, either through his own merit or through some other's, and then been saved?"

[VIRGIL] He, understanding my masked speech, replied: "I was new in this condition, when I saw a powerful visitor come here, with symbol of victory crowned.[3] He took from Hell the shades of our first parent, of Abel his son, of Noah, of Moses the lawgiver and obedient man, Abraham the patriarch and King David, Israel with his father and with his sons and with Rachel, for whom he labored so much, and many others, and gave them salvation. I assure you that before these no human spirits were redeemed."

[NARRATOR] We did not stop walking to let him speak, but all the time were passing the forest, the forest, I mean, of close-standing spirits.

[*The great classical poets in Limbo: 4.67–101*]

[NARRATOR] We had not yet gone far beyond the spot where I swooned, when I saw a fire which overcame a

Di lungi v'eravamo ancora un poco,
   ma non sì ch'io non discernessi in parte
72   ch'orrevol gente possedea quel loco.
«O tu ch'onori scienzia ed arte,
   questi chi son, c'hanno cotanta onranza,
   che dal modo de li altri li diparte?»
E quelli a me: «L'onrata nominanza
   che di lor suona su ne la tua vita,
78   grazia acquista nel ciel che sì li avanza.»
Intanto voce fu per me udita:
   «Onorate l'altissimo poeta:
   l'ombra sua torna, ch'era dipartita.»
Poi che la voce fu restata e queta,
   vidi quattro grand'ombre a noi venire:
84   sembianza avean né trista né lieta.
Lo buon maestro cominciò a dire:
   «Mira colui con quella spada in mano,
   che vien dinanzi ai tre sì come sire.
Quelli è Omero poeta sovrano;
   l'altro è Orazio satiro che vene;
90   Ovidio è il terzo, e l'ultimo Lucano.
Però che ciascun meco si convene
   nel nome che sonò la voce sola,
   fannomi onore, e di ciò fanno bene.»
Così vidi adunar la bella scuola
   di quel signor de l'altissimo canto
96   che sovra gli altri com'aquila vola.
Da ch'ebber ragionato insieme alquanto,
   volsersi a me con salutevol cenno;
   e 'l mio maestro sorrise di tanto.
E più d'onore ancor assai mi fenno,
   ch'ei sì mi fecer de la loro schiera,
102   sì ch'io fui sesto tra cotanto senno.
Così andammo infino a la lumera,
   parlando cose che 'l tacere è bello,
   sì com' era 'l parlar colà dov' era.

hemisphere of night. We still were somewhat distant, but not so far but what I could perceive—uncertainly— that the place contained[4] people to be honored.

[DANTE] "O you who are an honor to knowledge and to art, who are those receiving such great respect that it separates them from the state of the others?"

[VIRGIL] He replied: "Their honored reputation, which resounds up there in your world, gains favor with Heaven, which so distinguishes them."

[A VOICE] Meanwhile I heard a voice saying: "Do honor to the lofty poet. His shade is returning, which has been gone."[5]

[NARRATOR] When the voice had stopped and was still, I saw coming toward us four noble shades. They appeared neither sad nor happy.

[VIRGIL] My good teacher said: "Look at the one with that sword in his hand, who walks in front of the three like their lord. That is Homer, the king of poets. He who is second is Horace the satirist; Ovid is the third, and the last is Lucan. Since each one shares with me in the name spoken by the single voice, they do me honor, and in this they are right."[6]

[NARRATOR] Thus I saw assembled the fair company of that master of the noblest song, which flies above the others like an eagle.[7] When they had spoken together a little, they approached me with signs of salutation, and my guide smiled at it. And still more honor besides they did me, because they took me into their group, so that I was the sixth in the midst of so much intellect.

[*Other great pre-Christians in Limbo: 4.103–151*]

[NARRATOR] So we went on as far as the light, speaking of things about which silence is good, just as to speak of

Giugnemmo al piè d' un nobile castello,
sette volte cerchiato d' alte mura,
108   difeso intorno d' un bel fiumicello.
Questo passammo come terra dura;
per sette porte intrai con questi savi:
venimmo in prato di fresca verdura.
Genti v' eran con occhi tardi e gravi,
di grande autorità ne' lor sembianti:
114   parlavan rado, con voci soavi.
Traemmoci così da l' un de' canti,
in luogo aperto, luminoso e alto,
sì che veder si potean tutti quanti.
Colà diritto, sopra 'l verde smalto,
mi fuor mostrati li spiriti magni,
120   che del vedere in me stesso n' esalto.
I' vidi Elettra con molti compagni,
tra' quai conobbi Ettor ed Enea,
Cesare armato con li occhi grifagni.
Vidi Cammilla e la Pantasilea
da l' altra parte; vidi 'l re Latino
126   che con Lavina sua figlia sedea.
Vidi quel Bruto che cacciò Tarquino,
Lucrezia, Iulia, Marzia e Corniglia;
e solo in parte vidi il Saladino.
Poi ch' innalzai un poco più le ciglia,
vidi 'l maestro di color che sanno
132   seder tra filosofica famiglia.
Tutti lo miran, tutti onor li fanno:
quivi vid' io Socrate e Platone,
che 'nnanzi a li altri più presso li stanno;
Democrito che 'l mondo a caso pone,
Diogenès, Anassagora e Tale,
138   Empedoclès, Eraclito e Zenone;
e vidi il buono accoglitor del quale,
Diascoride dico; e vidi Orfeo,
Tullio e Lino e Seneca morale;

them there was good. We came close to a splendid fortress, seven times encircled with high walls, and protected all around by a beautiful streamlet. This we passed over as though it were hard earth.[8] Through seven gates I went in with those poets. We came to a meadow with fresh green grass.

People were there with eyes calm and serious, appearing to have great dignity. They spoke seldom, in low voices. We went to one side, to a clear space, well lighted and high, so that we could see them all. Right there on the greensward to me were shown the great spirits, so that at heart I exult in the sight. I saw Electra with many companions, among whom I recognized Hector and Aeneas, and Caesar in armor, with his griffin's eyes.[9] I saw Camilla and Penthesilea. On the other side I saw King Latinus, sitting with his daughter Lavinia. I saw the Brutus who drove out Tarquin, Lucretia, Julia, Marcia, and Cornelia; and alone, on one side, I saw Saladin. Then when I raised my eyes a little more, I saw the teacher of those who understand, sitting amid his philosophic following. All gazed on him; all did him honor. There I saw Socrates and Plato, who in front of the rest were nearest him; Democritus, who attributed the world to chance, Diogenes, Anaxagoras and Thales, Empedocles, Heraclitus and Zeno. And I saw the good collector of qualities—I mean Dioscorides; and I saw

Euclide geometra e Tolomeo,
    Ipocrate, Avicenna e Galieno,
144   Averroìs, che 'l gran comento feo.
Io non posso ritrar di tutti a pieno,
    però che sì mi caccia il lungo tema,
    che molte volte al fatto il dir vien meno.
La sesta compagnia in due si scema:
    per altra via mi mena il savio duca,
150   fuor de la queta, ne l' aura che trema;
e vegno in parte ove non è che luca.

Orpheus, Cicero and Linus and moral Seneca, Euclid the geometer and Ptolemy, Hippocrates, Avicenna and Galen, Averroes who wrote the great commentary. I cannot list them all complete, because my far-reaching subject so hurries me on that often what I write falls short of the reality.

The group of six diminishes to two. Into another path my prudent guide leads me, out of the quiet into the trembling air, and I come to a place where nothing shines.

CANTO 5

Così discesi del cerchio primaio
   giù nel secondo, che men luogo cinghia,
   e tanto più dolor, che punge a guaio.
Stavvi Minòs orribilmente, e ringhia:
   essamina le colpe ne l' entrata;
6   giudica e manda secondo ch' avvinghia.
Dico che quando l' anima mal nata
   li vien dinanzi, tutta si confessa;
   e quel conoscitor de le peccata
vede qual luogo d' inferno è da essa:
   cignesi con la coda tante volte
12   quantunque gradi vuol che giù sia messa.
Sempre dinanzi a lui ne stanno molte:
   vanno a vicenda ciascuna al giudizio;
   dicono e odono, e poi son giù volte.
«O tu che vieni al doloroso ospizio,»
   disse Minòs a me quando mi vide,
18   lasciando l' atto di cotanto offizio,
«guarda com' entri e di cui tu ti fide:
   non t' inganni l' ampiezza de l' entrare!»
   E 'l duca mio a lui: «Perchè pur gride?
Non impedir lo suo fatale andare:
   vuolsi così colà dove si puote
24   ciò che si vuole, e più non dimandare.»
Ora incomincian le dolenti note
   a farmisi sentire; or son venuto
   là dove molto pianto mi percuote.
Io venni in luogo d' ogni luce muto,
   che mugghia come fa mar per tempesta,
30   se da contrari venti è combattuto.
La bufera infernal, che mai non resta,
   mena li spirti con la sua rapina:
   voltando e percotendo li molesta.

CANTO 5

CIRCLE TWO

[Minos, the grotesque judge of the Inferno: 5.1–24]

[NARRATOR] So I went down from the first circle to the second, which rings about a smaller space and, by so much, more pain, which pricks to lamentation. There the horrible[1] Minos sits and snarls. He examines sins at the entrance; he judges and dispatches according as he entwines. I mean that when the wretched soul comes before him, it confesses everything; and that expert in sins knows what part of Hell befits it. He coils his tail around himself as many times as count the grades he decrees to have it sent down. Always before him stand many of them; they come, each in his turn, to judgment. They tell and hear, and then they take the downward road.[2]

[MINOS] "O you who come to the house of pain," said Minos to me when he saw me, turning from the duties of his high position, "watch how you go[3] and whom you trust; be not deceived by the spacious entrance."

[VIRGIL] But my guide said to him: "Why should you shout? Hinder not his journey, which has been approved by fate. It is decreed up there where what is decreed can be done; so ask no more."[4]

[Sexual sinners: 5.25–72]

[NARRATOR] Now again I hear sounds of pain: I now have come where loud lamentation distresses me. I have entered a place deprived of all light,[5] which roars as does the sea in a storm, when contrary winds are fighting. The everlasting tempest, never resting, carries the spirits along with its violence; with whirling and beat-

Quando giungon davanti a la ruina,
    quivi le strida, il compianto, il lamento;
36   bestemmian quivi la virtù divina.
Intesi ch'a così fatto tormento
    enno dannati i peccator carnali,
    che la ragion sommettono al talento.
E come li stornei ne portan l'ali
    nel freddo tempo a schiera larga e piena,
42   così quel fiato li spiriti mali
di qua, di là, di giù, di su li mena;
    nulla speranza li conforta mai,
    non che di posa, ma di minor pena.
E come i gru van cantando lor lai,
    faccendo in aere di sé lunga riga,
48   così vidi venir, traendo guai,
ombre portate da la detta briga:
    per ch'i' dissi: «Maestro, chi son quelle
    genti che l'aura nera sì gastiga?»
«La prima di color di cui novelle
    tu vuo' saper» mi disse quelli allotta,
54   «fu imperadrice di molte favelle.
A vizio di lussuria fu sì rotta,
    che libito fé licito in sua legge
    per torre il biasmo in che era condotta.
Ell'è Semiramìs, di cui si legge
    che succedette a Nino e fu sua sposa;
60   tenne la terra che 'l Soldan corregge.
L'altra è colei che s'ancise amorosa,
    e ruppe fede al cener di Sicheo;
    poi è Cleopatràs lussuriosa.
Elena vedi, per cui tanto reo
    tempo si volse, e vedi il grande Achille
66   che con amore al fine combatteo.
Vedi Parìs, Tristano»; e più di mille
    ombre mostrommi, e nominommi, a dito
    ch'amor di nostra vita dipartille.

ing it tortures them. When they are exposed to its rav-
age, then shrieks, cries, lamentation; here they curse
the power of Heaven. I learned that to this torment
were damned the fleshly sinners, who submit their
reason to their appetite. And as their wings carry off
the starlings in cold weather, in a large and crowded
flock, so that breath drives the evil spirits to this side,
to that, up and down. Hope never comforts them, even
of slighter pain, much less of quiet. And as the cranes
sing their song, forming their long line in the air, so I
saw wailing shades carried by those conflicting winds.
[DANTE] So I said: "Teacher, who are these whom the
black wind so punishes?"
[VIRGIL] "The first of those whose stories you wish to
hear," he told me then, "was empress of many nations.
By the vice of lust she was so spoiled that by her law
she gave allowance to whim,[6] to get rid of the censure
she had incurred. She is Semiramis, of whom we read
that she succeeded King Ninus and was his wife. She
held the land the Sultan rules. The next is she who
killed herself for love, and broke faith with Sichaeus'
ashes. Next is the lustful Cleopatra. There is Helen, for
whom so many evil years were spent; and there is the
great Achilles, who through love brought his fighting
to an end.[7] There is Paris, Tristram." And more than
a thousand shades he pointed at and named to me,
which love from our life took away. After I had heard

Poscia ch'io ebbi il mio dottore udito
nomar le donne antiche e' cavalieri,
72   pietà mi giunse, e fui quasi smarrito.
I' cominciai: «Poeta, volontieri
parlerei a quei due che 'nsieme vanno,
e paion sì al vento esser leggieri.»
Ed elli a me: «Vedrai quando saranno
più presso a noi; e tu allor li prega
78   per quello amor che i mena, ed ei verranno.»
Sì tosto come il vento a noi li piega,
mossi la voce: «O anime affannate,
venite a noi parlar, s'altri nol niega!»
Quali colombe dal disio chiamate,
con l'ali alzate e ferme al dolce nido
84   vegnon per l'aere dal voler portate;
cotali uscir de la schiera ov'è Dido,
a noi venendo per l'aere maligno,
sì forte fu l'affettuoso grido.
«O animal grazioso e benigno
che visitando vai per l'aere perso
90   noi che tignemmo il mondo di sanguigno,
se fosse amico il re de l'universo,
noi pregheremmo lui de la tua pace,
poi c'hai pietà del nostro mal perverso.
Di quel che udire e che parlar vi piace,
noi udiremo e parleremo a vui,
96   mentre che 'l vento, come fa, ci tace.
Siede la terra dove nata fui
su la marina dove 'l Po discende
per aver pace co' seguaci sui.
Amor, ch'al cor gentil ratto s'apprende,
prese costui de la bella persona
102   che mi fu tolta; e 'l modo ancor m'offende.
Amor, ch'a nullo amato amar perdona,
mi prese del costui piacer sì forte,
che, come vedi, ancor non m'abbandona.

my teacher name those ladies and knights renowned,
I felt compassion and was almost frightened.

[*Francesca and Paolo, the murdered adulterers:*
5.73–142]

[DANTE] I said: "Poet, I should like to speak with those
two who keep together, and seem so yielding before the
wind."

[VIRGIL] He answered me: "Watch until they are closer
to us, and then you may ask, in the name of that love
which controls them, and they will come."

[DANTE] As soon as the wind swerved them toward us,[8]
I shouted: "O wearied spirits, come to speak with us,
if He does not forbid it."

[NARRATOR] Like doves drawn by their longing, when
with wings raised and steady they come to their sweet
nest,[9] carried through the air by their wish, so these
left the group where Dido is, coming to us through the
malignant air; so effective was my heartfelt shout.

[FRANCESCA] "O creature gracious and humane, who in
the murky air are visiting us who stained the world
with blood, if the king of the universe were our friend,
we would pray him for peace to you, since you feel
compassion for our horrid suffering.[10] Tell what you
wish to hear and to speak of, for we shall hear and
speak while the wind, as now, is still. The city where
I was born lies on the shore to which the Po comes to
get peace with his pursuers. Love, which quickly lays
hold of the noble heart, caught this one here with the
beautiful body which was snatched from me; and the
way Love did it still afflicts me.[11] Love, which excuses
no one from loving, seized me with such force by means
of my delight in him that still, as you see, it does not

Amor condusse noi ad una morte:
Caina attende chi a vita ci spense.»
108   Queste parole da lor ci fur porte.
Quand'io intesi quell'anime offense,
chinai 'l viso, e tanto il tenni basso,
fin che 'l poeta mi disse: «Che pense?»
Quando rispuosi, cominciai: «Oh lasso,
quanti dolci pensier, quanto disio
114   menò costoro al doloroso passo!»
Poi mi rivolsi a loro e parla' io,
e cominciai: «Francesca, i tuoi martiri
a lacrimar mi fanno tristo e pio.
Ma dimmi: al tempo de' dolci sospiri,
a che e come concedette amore
120   che conosceste i dubbiosi desiri?»
E quella a me: «Nessun maggior dolore
che ricordarsi del tempo felice
ne la miseria; e ciò sa 'l tuo dottore.
Ma s' a conoscer la prima radice
del nostro amor tu hai cotanto affetto,
126   dirò come colui che piange e dice.
Noi leggiavamo un giorno per diletto
di Lancialotto come amor lo strinse:
soli eravamo e sanza alcun sospetto.
Per più fiate li occhi ci sospinse
quella lettura, e scolorocci il viso;
132   ma solo un punto fu quel che ci vinse.
Quando leggemmo il disiato riso
esser baciato da cotanto amante,
questi, che mai da me non fia diviso,
la bocca mi baciò tutto tremante.
Galeotto fu il libro e chi lo scrisse:
138   quel giorno più non vi leggemmo avante.»
Mentre che l' uno spirto questo disse,
l' altro piangea, sì che di pietade
io venni men così com' io morisse;
e caddi come corpo morto cade.

leave me. Love brought us to one death. Caina is ready
for him who blotted out our lives." These words they
spoke to us.

[VIRGIL] When I had listened to these afflicted souls, I
lowered my face and kept it downcast until the poet
said to me: "What are you thinking about?"

[DANTE] On answering, I said: "Oh woe! How many
sweet thoughts, what great longing brought these to
their sad condition!" Then I turned to them and spoke,
saying: "Francesca, your sufferings make me weep for
sadness and pity. But tell me: at the moment of your
sweet sighs, through what and how did Love grant
you knowledge of your wavering desires?"

[FRANCESCA] She replied: "There is no greater pain than
to remember a happy time in misery. That your instructor knows. But if you are so eager to learn the first root
of our love, I shall tell you as, weeping, I speak. One day
for pleasure we were reading of Lancelot, how love
bound him tight. Alone we were and without the least
suspicion. Many times that reading brought our eyes
together and took the color from our faces, but it was
one passage only that conquered us. When we read
that the worshipped lips were kissed by one who loved
so much, this man, who never from me will be divided,
kissed my mouth all trembling. Galeotto was the book
and he who wrote it.[12] That day we read no further in
it.

[NARRATOR] While one spirit said this, the other was
weeping so that with compassion I was faint, as though
I should die; and I fell as a dead body falls.

CANTO 6

Al tornar de la mente, che si chiuse
   dinanzi a la pietà de' due cognati,
   che di trestizia tutto mi confuse,
novi tormenti e novi tormentati
   mi veggio intorno, come ch' io mi mova
6   e ch' io mi volga e come che io guati.
Io sono al terzo cerchio, de la piova
   etterna, maladetta, fredda e greve:
   regola e qualità mai non l' è nova.
Grandine grossa, acqua tinta e neve
   per l'aere tenebroso si riversa;
12   pute la terra che questo riceve.
Cerbero, fiera crudele e diversa,
   con tre gole caninamente latra
   sopra la gente che quivi è sommersa.
Li occhi ha vermigli, la barba unta e atra,
   e 'l ventre largo, e unghiate le mani;
18   graffia li spirti ed iscoia ed isquatra.
Urlar li fa la pioggia come cani:
   de l'un de' lati fanno a l'altro schermo;
   volgonsi spesso i miseri profani.
Quando ci scorse Cerbero, il gran vermo,
   le bocche aperse e mostrocci le sanne;
24   non avea membro che tenesse fermo.
Lo duca mio distese le sue spanne,
   prese la terra, e con piene le pugna
   la gittò dentro a le bramose canne.
Qual è quel cane ch'abbaiando agugna,
   e si racqueta poi che 'l pasto morde,
30   chè solo a divorarlo intende e pugna,
cotai si fecer quelle facce lorde
   de lo demonio Cerbero, che 'ntrona
   l'anime sì ch'esser vorrebber sorde.

CANTO 6

Circle Three

[Cerberus: 6.1–33]

[NARRATOR] At the return of my senses, which had failed in my pity for the brother-in-law and sister-in-law, which wholly bewildered me with sadness, I see around me new sufferings and new sufferers, wherever I move and turn and wherever I gaze. I am in the third circle, that of everlasting rain, cursed, cold and heavy. Never is it different in its law or nature. Huge hailstones, turbid water and snow stream down through the darkened air; stinking is the earth on which these fall. Cerberus, a beast cruel and horrid, with his three throats barks like a dog over the crowd exposed to that storm. His eyes are bright red, his beard greasy and black, his belly huge, and his hands like birds' claws;[1] he scratches the spirits, tears off their skins and rends them. The rain makes them snarl like dogs. With one side they protect the other; again and again those wretched spirits roll over. When Cerberus, the filthy monster, saw us, he opened his mouths and showed his tushes; not one of his limbs was quiet. My guide spread his fingers, seized some earth, and when his fists were full, threw it into the greedy throats.[2] Like a dog that shows his hunger by baying and gets quiet when he bites some food, since he heeds only gulping it down, and struggles, so acted those filthy snouts of the demon Cerberus, who so thunders at the souls that they are made deaf.[3]

Noi passavam su per l'ombre che adona
la greve pioggia, e ponavam le piante
36   sopra lor vanità che par persona.
Elle giacean per terra tutte quante,
fuor d'una ch'a seder si levò, ratto
ch'ella ci vide passarsi davante.
«O tu che se' per questo inferno tratto,»
mi disse, «riconoscimi, se sai:
42   tu fosti, prima ch'io disfatto, fatto.»
E io a lui: «L'angoscia che tu hai
forse ti tira fuor de la mia mente,
sì che non par ch'i' ti vedessi mai.
Ma dimmi chi tu se' che 'n sì dolente
loco se' messo e hai sì fatta pena,
48   che s'altra è maggio, nulla è sì spiacente.»
Ed elli a me: «La tua città, ch'è piena
d'invidia sì che già trabocca il sacco,
seco mi tenne in la vita serena.
Voi cittadini mi chiamaste Ciacco:
per la dannosa colpa de la gola,
54   come tu vedi, a la pioggia mi fiacco.
E io anima trista non son sola,
chè tutte queste a simil pena stanno
per simil colpa.» E più non fè parola.
Io li rispuosi: «Ciacco, il tuo affanno
mi pesa sì, ch' a lagrimar m' invita;
60   ma dimmi, se tu sai, a che verranno
li cittadin de la città partita;
s' alcun v' è giusto; e dimmi la cagione
per che l' ha tanta discordia assalita.»
Ed elli a me: «Dopo lunga tencione
verranno al sangue, e la parte selvaggia
66   caccerà l' altra con molta offensione.
Poi appresso convien che questa caggia
infra tre soli, e che l' altra sormonti
con la forza di tal che testè piaggia.

[*The gluttons. Ciacco condemns Florentine
quarrels: 6.34–99*]

[NARRATOR] We walked upon the shades which the
heavy rain beats down; we put our feet on their empti-
ness, which looked like bodies.⁴ Each and all were lying
on the ground, except one who sat up as he saw us
passing near him.

[CIACCO] "O you who are guided through this Inferno,"
he said to me, "bring me to mind if you can. You were
made before I was unmade!"

[DANTE] And I said to him: "Your suffering really takes
you out of my memory, so that I cannot suppose I ever
saw you. But tell me who you are, who are put in so
painful a place and suffer such punishment that, if
others are more severe, none is so disgusting."

[CIACCO] And he to me: "Of your city, which is so full
of envy that actually it is spilling from the sack, I was
an inmate in the happy life. You citizens called me
Ciacco. For the damning sin of gluttony, I am beaten
down, as you see, by the rain. And I am not the only
wretched soul, for all these endure like pain for like
vice." And he said not another word.

[DANTE] I answered him: "Ciacco, your distress so
weighs upon me that it summons my tears. But tell
me, if you can, what the citizens of the divided city⁵
will come to; whether any man there is just; and tell
me the reason why such dissension has attacked her."

[CIACCO] And he to me: "After long dispute they will
come to blood, and the rustic party will rout the other
with great harrassment. Then in turn in less than three
years, this is fated to fall, and the other to rise through
the power of him who now dissimulates.⁶ For a long

Alte terrà lungo tempo le fronti,
tenendo l' altra sotto gravi pesi,
72   come che di ciò pianga o che n' adonti.
Giusti son due, e non vi sono intesi;
superbia, invidia e avarizia sono
le tre faville c' hanno i cuori accesi.»
Qui puose fine al lacrimabil suono.
E io a lui: «Ancor vo' che m' insegni,
78   e che di più parlar mi facci dono.
Farinata e il Tegghiaio, che fuor sì degni,
Iacopo Rusticucci, Arrigo e 'l Mosca
e li altri ch' a ben far puoser li 'ngegni,
dimmi ove sono e fa ch' io li conosca;
chè gran disio mi stringe di savere
84   se 'l ciel li addolcia, o lo 'nferno li attosca.»
E quelli: «Ei son tra l' anime più nere:
diverse colpe giù li grava al fondo;
se tanto scendi, là i potrai vedere.
Ma quando tu sarai nel dolce mondo,
priegoti ch' a la mente altrui mi rechi:
90   più non ti dico e più non ti rispondo.»
Li diritti occhi torse allora in biechi:
guardommi un poco, e poi chinò la testa:
cadde con essa a par de li altri ciechi.
E 'l duca disse a me: «Più non si desta
di qua dal suon de l'angelica tromba.
96   Quando verrà la nimica podesta,
ciascun rivederà la trista tomba,
ripiglierà sua carne e sua figura,
udirà quel che in etterno rimbomba.»
Sì trapassammo per sozza mistura
de l'ombre e de la pioggia, a passi lenti,
102   toccando un poco la vita futura.
Per ch'io dissi: «Maestro, esti tormenti
cresceranno ei dopo la gran sentenza,
o fier minori, o saran sì cocenti?»

time it will hold its forehead high, keeping the other
under heavy weights, however much it may weep and
show anger. Two men are just,[7] and are not listened to
there. Pride, envy, and avarice are the three sparks that
have set hearts afire."

[DANTE] Here he ended his tear-exciting speech, and I
replied: "I hope you will keep on informing me and
favor me with further talk. Farinata and Tegghiaio, who
were so deserving, Jacopo Rusticucci, Arrigo and Mosca
and others who used their gifts in doing good, tell me
where they are and teach me how to know them, because a strong desire constrains me to learn if Heaven
caresses them or Hell poisons them."

[CIACCO] He answered: "They are among the blacker
souls.[8] Horrible[9] sins crush them down to the depths; if
you go down so far, you will see them. But when you
are in the sweet world, I pray that you will recall me to
men's memory. More I do not say to you, and more I
do not answer."

[NARRATOR] His eyes, which had looked straight, he
turned askance. He gazed at me a bit, then bowed his
head; he let it fall till he was level with the rest of those
unseeing men.

[VIRGIL] And my guide said to me: "He will not lift
himself up again until the angelic trumpet's blast. When
the hostile power comes, every man will revisit his
mournful tomb, will reassume his body and his human
form, and will hear what everlastingly resounds."[10]

*[Virgil speaks on the future of the
damned: 6.100–115]*

[DANTE] We moved on through the filthy mixture of
shadows and of rain, with slow steps, speaking a little
on the future life. So I said: "Teacher, as to these tor-
ments, will they increase after the Last Judgment, or
will they lessen, or will they torture to just the same extent?"

Ed elli a me: «Ritorna a tua scienza,
che vuol, quanto la cosa è più perfetta,
108   più senta il bene, e così la doglienza.
Tutto che questa gente maladetta
in vera perfezion già mai non vada,
di là più che di qua essere aspetta.»
Noi aggirammo a tondo quella strada,
parlando più assai ch'io non ridico;
114   venimmo al punto dove si digrada:
quivi trovammo Pluto, il gran nemico.

[VIRGIL] And he answered: "Go back to your philosophy, which teaches that, as a thing is more perfect, it
more experiences good and likewise pain. Even though
this cursed multitude can never go on to true perfection,
they expect to be more so afterward than now."[11]

[NARRATOR] We followed a circular course, with much
more conversation than I repeat, until we reached a
downward slope. There we found Plutus, the mighty
foe.

CANTO 7

«Papé Satàn, papé Satàn aleppe!»
  cominciò Pluto con la voce chioccia;
  e quel savio gentil, che tutto seppe,
disse per confortarmi: «Non ti noccia
  la tua paura; ché, poder ch'elli abbia,
6   non ci torrà lo scender questa roccia.»
Poi si rivolse a quella infiata labbia,
  e disse: «Taci, maladetto lupo:
  consuma dentro te con la tua rabbia.
Non è sanza cagion l'andare al cupo:
  vuolsi ne l'alto là dove Michele
12   fé la vendetta del superbo strupo.»
Quali dal vento le gonfiate vele
  caggiono avvolte, poi che l'alber fiacca,
  tal cadde a terra la fiera crudele.
Così scendemmo ne la quarta lacca,
  pigliando più de la dolente ripa
18   che 'l mal de l' universo tutto insacca.
Ahi giustizia di Dio! tante chi stipa
  nove travaglie e pene, quant' io viddi?
  e perchè nostra colpa sì ne scipa?
Come fa l' onda là sovra Cariddi,
  che si frange con quella in cui s' intoppa,
24   così convien che qui la gente riddi.
Qui vidi gente più ch' altrove troppa,
  e d' una parte e d' altra, con grand' urli,
  voltando pesi per forza di poppa.
Percoteansi incontro; e poscia pur lì
  si rivolgea ciascun, voltando a retro,
30   gridando: «Perchè tieni?» e «Perchè burli?»

CANTO 7

CIRCLE FOUR

[Plutus the Money God: 7.1–15]

[PLUTUS] "Pape Satan, pape Satan, aleppe," said Plutus in a raucous voice.

[VIRGIL] And that kindly poet, who understood completely,[1] said to comfort me: "Don't feel afraid, because, whatever his power, he will not keep us from going down this cliff." Then he turned to that angry face and said: "Be still, cursed wolf! Destroy your inwards with your rage. Not without cause is our journey to the depths. It is dictated on high, in the place where Michael punished arrogant revolt."

[NARRATOR] As sails swollen by the wind sometimes fall, when the mast cracks, so fell to the earth that cruel beast.

*[The avaricious and the prodigal in Circle Four:
7.16–66]*

[NARRATOR] So down we went into the fourth hollow,[2] thus traversing more of the gloomy bank that holds as in a sack all the evil of the universe.[3]

[POET] *O justice of God! You who bring together all the strange sufferings and pains that I saw! Now why does our sin make such havoc of us?*

[NARRATOR] Like the wave there at Charybdis, shattered by that with which it collides, so the multitude here must dance. Here I saw crowds much larger than anywhere else, and from one side and the other, with loud screeches, they were rolling weights with push of breast.

[THE MISERS AND THE WASTERS] They crashed together, and then each turned around, right there, rolling back and yelling: "Why do you save?" and "Why do you throw away?"

Così tornavan per lo cerchio tetro
   da ogni mano a l' opposito punto,
   gridandosi anche loro ontoso metro;
poi si volgea ciascun, quand' era giunto,
   per lo suo mezzo cerchio a l' altra giostra.
36   E io, ch' avea lo cor quasi compunto,
dissi: «Maestro mio, or mi dimostra
   che gente è questa, e se tutti fuor cherci
   questi chercuti a la sinistra nostra.»
Ed elli a me: «Tutti quanti fuor guerci
   sì de la mente in la vita primaia,
42   che con misura nullo spendio ferci.
Assai la voce lor chiaro l' abbaia,
   quando vegnono a' due punti del cerchio
   dove colpa contraria li dispaia.
Questi fuor cherci, che non han coperchio
   piloso al capo, e papi e cardinali,
48   in cui usa avarizia il suo soperchio.»
E io: «Maestro, tra questi cotali
   dovre' io ben riconoscere alcuni
   che furo immondi di cotesti mali.»
Ed elli a me: «Vano pensiero aduni:
   la sconoscente vita che i fè sozzi
54   ad ogni conoscenza or li fa bruni.
In etterno verranno a li due cozzi:
   questi resurgeranno del sepulcro
   col pugno chiuso, e questi coi crin mozzi.
Mal dare e mal tener lo mondo pulcro
   ha tolto loro, e posti a questa zuffa:
60   qual ella sia, parole non ci appulcro.
Or puoi veder, figliuol, la corta buffa
   de' ben che son commessi a la Fortuna,
   per che l' umana gente si rabuffa:
chè tutto l' oro ch' è sotto la luna
   e che già fu, di quest' anime stanche
66   non poterebbe farne posare una.»

[NARRATOR] So they moved in their gloomy circle from either side to the opposite spot, still yelling their insulting verse. Then each, when he had reached it, turned back on his half-circle for the next encounter.

[DANTE] And I, my heart almost pierced through, said: "Teacher, explain to me now what crowd this is, and whether those tonsured fellows on the left all were clergymen."

[VIRGIL] And he: "In the first life they were all so mentally twisted that with moderation never they spent money. Clearly enough their speech barks it out when they come to the two points in the circle where the contrary fault makes them part. Those who do not have a hairy covering on their heads were clergymen and popes and cardinals, in whom stinginess works her utmost."

[DANTE] And I said: "Teacher, among these I ought to recognize some who were filthy with such sins."

[VIRGIL] He answered: "You have worked out a silly conclusion. The unrecognizing life that made them sottish now darkens them beyond all recognition.⁴ Everlastingly will they go to the two buttings. Those in one group will rise from their graves with fists clenched; the others with hair shaved. Evil giving and evil keeping have taken from them the beautiful world and set them at this contest. On what it is, I shall not prettify words. Now you can see, my son, the brief vanity of the good things under Fortune's control, for which the human race distracts itself. For all the gold under the moon, and all that has been, among these wearied souls, could not make one stand still."

«Maestro,» diss' io lui, «or mi dì anche:
  questa Fortuna di che tu mi tocche,
  che è, che i ben del mondo ha sì tra branche?»
Ed elli a me: «Oh creature sciocche,
  quanta ignoranza è quella che v' offende!
72   Or vo' che tu mia sentenza ne 'mbocche.
Colui lo cui saver tutto trascende,
  fece li cieli e diè lor chi conduce,
  sì ch' ogni parte ad ogni parte splende,
distribuendo igualmente la luce:
  similemente a li splendor mondani
78   ordinò general ministra e duce
che permutasse a tempo li ben vani
  di gente in gente e d' uno in altro sangue,
  oltre la difension di senni umani;
per ch' una gente impera ed altra langue,
  seguendo lo giudicio di costei,
84   che è occulto come in erba l' angue.
Vostro saver non ha contasto a lei:
  questa provede, giudica, e persegue
  suo regno come il loro li altri dei.
Le sue permutazion non hanno triegue:
  necessità la fa esser veloce;
90   sì spesso vien chi vicenda consegue.
Quest' è colei ch' è tanto posta in croce
  pur da color che le dovrien dar lode,
  dandole biasmo a torto e mala voce:
ma ella s' è beata e ciò non ode;
  con l' altre prime creature lieta
96   volve sua spera e beata si gode.
Or discendiamo omai a maggior pieta;
  già ogni stella cade che saliva
  quand' io mi mossi, e 'l troppo star si vieta.»
Noi ricidemmo il cerchio a l'altra riva
  sovr'una fonte che bolle e riversa
102   per un fossato che da lei deriva.

[Fortune, the ruler of material things: 7.67–96]

[DANTE] "My teacher," I said to him, "now tell me further: This Fortune you mention to me, what is she, who so has the good things of the world in her clutches?" [VIRGIL] And he answered me: "O silly creatures, what great ignorance is this which harms you! Now be sure that you take in my statement about her. He whose wisdom transcends all things, made the heavens and gave them their directors, so that every part shines upon every other part, distributing light uniformly. Likewise for earth's splendors, he set up a universal manager and ruler, who from time to time should shift the valueless good things from nation to nation and from one race to another, beyond stoppage by human prudence. Hence one nation rules and another is feeble, according to Fortune's decree, which is hidden, like a snake in the grass. Your knowledge cannot strive with her; she arranges, judges, and administers her kingdom as the other gods do theirs. Her shiftings have no pause; necessity makes her swift. Hence frequently we experience changes. This is she who so often is crucified[5] even by those who ought to praise her—wrongly blaming and speaking ill of her. But she is blessed and does not hear it. With the other first-created beings, she happily turns her sphere, and rejoices in blessedness."

CIRCLE FIVE

[The Stygian Swamp, for wrathful sinners: 7.97–130]

[VIRGIL] "Now let us go down to greater pity. Already every star is falling which was rising when I set out, and too much stopping is forbidden."[6]
[NARRATOR] We cut across the circle to the other edge by a spring which bubbles up and empties into a chan-

L'acqua era buia assai più che persa;
e noi, in compagnia de l'onde bige,
entrammo giù per una via diversa.
In la palude va c'ha nome Stige
questo tristo ruscel, quand'è disceso
108　al piè de le maligne piagge grige.
E io, che di mirare stava inteso,
vidi genti fangose in quel pantano,
ignude tutte, con sembiante offeso.
Questi si percotean non pur con mano,
ma con la testa e col petto e coi piedi,
114　troncandosi co' denti a brano a brano.
Lo buon maestro disse: «Figlio, or vedi
l'anime di color cui vinse l'ira;
e anche vo' che tu per certo credi
che sotto l'acqua ha gente che sospira,
e fanno pullular quest'acqua al summo,
120　come l'occhio ti dice, u' che s'aggira.
Fitti nel limo, dicon: 'Tristi fummo
ne l'aere dolce che dal sol s'allegra,
portando dentro accidioso fummo:
or ci attristiam nella belletta negra.'
Quest'inno si gorgoglian ne la strozza,
126　ché dir nol posson con parola integra.»
Così girammo de la lorda pozza
grand'arco tra la ripa secca e 'l mézzo,
con li occhi volti a chi del fango ingozza:
venimmo al piè d'una torre al da sezzo.

nel leading from it. The water was much darker than purple. Along with the muddy ripples, we went down by a difficult route. Into the swamp named Styx, flows this melancholy brook, when it has fallen to the base of the untoward gray slopes. And I, intent on looking,[7] saw muddy people in that marsh, naked all of them, and appearing angered. They were striking one another not with their hands alone, but with their heads and their feet, and tearing each other to pieces with their teeth, bit by bit.

[VIRGIL] My good teacher said: "My son, now see the souls of those whom anger overcomes. And you are also to believe for certain that there are people under the water who gasp and make this water bubble on the surface, as your eye tells you wherever it turns.

[THE ANGRY *quoted*] "Stuck in the slime, they are saying: 'Melancholy we were in the sweet air made cheerful by the sun, having within us slothful smoke. Now melancholy we are in the black oozy mire.'

[VIRGIL] "This hymn they gurgle in their throats, because in clear speech they cannot utter it."

[NARRATOR] Thus we circled about the filthy pool in a large curve between the dry bank and the wetness, with our eyes turned on those gobbling down the mud. At last we came to a tower's base.

CANTO 8

Io dico, seguitando, ch'assai prima
  che noi fussimo al piè de l'alta torre,
  li occhi nostri n'andar suso a la cima
per due fiammette che i vedemmo porre,
  e un'altra da lungi render cenno,
6   tanto ch'a pena il potea l'occhio tòrre.
E io mi volsi al mar di tutto 'l senno:
  dissi: «Questo che dice? e che risponde
  quell' altro foco? e chi son quei che 'l fenno?»
Ed elli a me: «Su per le sucide onde
  già scorgere puoi quello che s' aspetta,
12   se 'l fummo del pantan nol ti nasconde.»
Corda non pinse mai da sè saetta
  che sì corresse via per l' aere snella,
  com' io vidi una nave piccioletta
venir per l' acqua verso noi in quella,
  sotto il governo d' un sol galeoto,
18   che gridava: «Or se' giunta, anima fella!»
«Flegiàs, Flegiàs, tu gridi a voto»
  disse lo mio signore «a questa volta:
  più non ci avrai che sol passando il loto.»
Qual è colui che grande inganno ascolta
  che li sia fatto, e poi se ne rammarca,
24   fecesi Flegiàs ne l' ira accolta.
Lo duca mio discese ne la barca,
  e poi mi fece intrare appresso lui;
  e sol quand' io fui dentro parve carca.
Tosto che 'l duca e io nel legno fui,
  segando se ne va l' antica prora
30   de l' acqua più che non suol con altrui.

CANTO 8

CIRCLE FIVE, *cont.*

*[Phlegyas, the Boatman of the Stygian
Swamp: 8.1–30]*

[NARRATOR] To continue, I say that long before we were
at the base of that high tower, our eyes were turned toward its summit because of two little flames we saw put
there, and another giving a signal so far away that the
eye could hardly get it.
[DANTE] Turning to the sea of all understanding, I said:
"What does this mean? And what is the answer from
that other fire? And who are making it?"
[VIRGIL] And he said to me: "Over the filthy waves you
now can see what we are waiting for, if the mist of the
marsh does not hide it from you."
[NARRATOR] A bowstring never drove an arrow which
flew through the air so fast as did a little boat I saw at
that moment coming toward us on the water, managed
by a single boatman.
[PHLEGYAS] He was yelling: "Now you have got here,
wicked soul."[1]
[VIRGIL] "Phlegyas, Phlegyas, this time you are yelling
in vain," said my director, "You will have us only just
long enough to cross the slush."
[NARRATOR] On being told of the great deception practiced on him, and then being irritated by it, Phlegyas
showed in his actions the wrath he felt. My guide
stepped into the skiff and then, close to him, had me
get in; and only when I was aboard did it seem loaded.
As soon as my guide and I were in the boat, her aged
prow cut more water than when having other freight.

Mentre noi corravam la morta gora,
    dinanzi mi si fece un pien di fango,
    e disse: «Chi se' tu che vieni anzi ora?»
E io a lui: «S' i' vegno, non rimango;
    ma tu chi se', che sì se' fatto brutto?»
36   Rispuose: «Vedi che son un che piango.»
E io a lui: «Con piangere e con lutto,
    spirito maladetto, ti rimani;
    ch' i' ti conosco, ancor sie lordo tutto.»
Allora stese al legno ambo le mani;
    per che 'l maestro accorto lo sospinse,
42   dicendo: «Via costà con li altri cani!»
Lo collo poi con le braccia mi cinse;
    baciommi il volto, e disse: «Alma sdegnosa,
    benedetta colei che in te s' incinse!
Quei fu al mondo persona orgogliosa;
    bontà non è che sua memoria fregi:
48   così s' è l' ombra sua qui furiosa.
Quanti si tengon or là su gran regi
    che qui staranno come porci in brago,
    di sé lasciando orribili dispregi!»
E io: «Maestro, molto sarei vago
    di vederlo attuffare in questa broda
54   prima che noi uscissimo del lago.»
Ed elli a me: «Avante che la proda
    ti si lasci veder, tu sarai sazio:
    di tal disio convien che tu goda.»
Dopo ciò poco vid'io quello strazio
    far di costui a le fangose genti,
60   che Dio ancor ne lodo e ne ringrazio.
Tutti gridavano: «A Filippo Argenti!»;
    e 'l fiorentino spirito bizzarro
    in se medesmo si volvea co' denti.

*[Filippo Argenti and others punished for anger
in the swamp: 8.31–63]*

[FILIPPO] While we were running over that stagnant water, a mud-covered figure appeared to me, saying: "Who are you who have come before your time?"
[DANTE] And I to him: "If I come, I do not stay. But who are you, who are so filthy?"
[FILIPPO] He answered: "You see that I am one who weeps."
[DANTE] And I to him: "With weeping and with sorrow, cursed spirit, stay here, for I recognize you, covered with filth as you are."
[VIRGIL] Then with both hands he reached for the boat, but my ready teacher pushed him back, saying: "Away there with the other dogs." Then he threw both arms around my neck, kissed me on the face, and said: "Soul quick to anger, blessed she who bore you! In the world he was a proud person; no goodness adorns his memory. Likewise his shade is raving here. How many are considered great kings up in the world who here will be like swine in the mire, leaving behind their ugly reputations!"
[DANTE] And I: "Teacher, I should be greatly pleased to see him plunged in this broth before we leave the lake."
[VIRGIL] And he to me: "Before we see the beach, you will be contented; it is proper that such a wish be gratified."
[NARRATOR] A little later I saw the muddy people inflict on him such torment that still I praise and thank God for it.
[THE ANGRY] All shrieked: "Go at Filippo Argenti!"
[NARRATOR] And the angered Florentine spirit attacked himself with his own teeth.[2]

Quivi il lasciammo, che più non ne narro;
　　ma ne l'orecchie mi percosse un duolo,
66　per ch'io avante l'occhio intento sbarro.
Lo buon maestro disse: «Omai, figliuolo,
　　s'appressa la città c'ha nome Dite,
　　coi gravi cittadin, col grande stuolo.»
E io: «Maestro, già le sue meschite
　　là entro certe ne la valle cerno,
72　vermiglie come se di foco uscite
fossero.» Ed ei mi disse: «Il foco etterno
　　ch'entro l'affoca le dimostra rosse,
　　come tu vedi in questo basso inferno.»
Noi pur giugnemmo dentro a l'alte fosse
　　che vallan quella terra sconsolata:
78　le mura mi parean che ferro fosse.
Non sanza prima far grande aggirata,
　　venimmo in parte dove il nocchier forte
　　«Usciteci» gridò: «qui è l'entrata.»
Io vidi più di mille in su le porte
　　da ciel piovuti, che stizzosamente
84　dicean: «Chi è costui che sanza morte
va per lo regno de la morta gente?»
　　E 'l savio mio maestro fece segno
　　di voler lor parlar secretamente.
Allor chiusero un poco il gran disdegno,
　　e disser: «Vien tu solo, e quei sen vada,
90　che sì ardito intro per questo regno.
Sol si ritorni per la folle strada:
　　pruovi, se sa; ché tu qui rimarrai
　　che li hai scorta sì buia contrada.»
Pensa, lettor, se io mi sconfortai
　　nel suon de le parole maladette,
96　ché non credetti ritornarci mai.
«O caro duca mio, che più di sette
　　volte m'hai sicurtà renduta e tratto
　　d'alto periglio che 'ncontra mi stette,

[*The gate of the city of Dis, with
guardian devils: 8.64–130*]

[NARRATOR] There we left him, and I shall tell no more
of him. But my ears were pierced with lamentation that
made me turn my eyes intently ahead.

[VIRGIL] My good teacher said: "Now my son, the city
named Dis is near, with its worthy citizens and its large
army."[3]

[DANTE] I replied: "Teacher, already I clearly make out
its mosques inside it, within the wall—red, as though
they had come from the fire."

[VIRGIL] He said to me: "The everlasting fire that blazes
within them makes them seem scarlet, as you see in this
low inferno."

[NARRATOR] We got within the deep moats that surround that comfortless city. Its walls seemed of iron.

[PHLEGYAS] Not without first making a wide circuit did
we get to a place where the boatman loudly yelled:
"Get out; here is the entrance."

[DEMONS] I saw above the gates more than a thousand
fallen from Heaven, who snappishly said: "Who is this
fellow, who without death is in the kingdom of the
dead?"

[NARRATOR] My wise teacher made a sign that he
wished to speak with them in private.

[DEMONS] Then they a little lessened their great scorn
and said: "You come alone, and let him leave, who so
rashly has come into this kingdom. Let him go back
alone on his foolish path. Let him show whether he can,
because here you will remain, who have guided him
through so dark a region."

[NARRATOR] Imagine, reader, if I were disheartened by
the import of their accursed speeches, because I did not
believe I ever should get back here.

[DANTE] "O my dear guide, who more than seven times

non mi lasciar» diss'io «così disfatto;
   e se 'l passar più oltre ci è negato,
102   ritroviam l'orme nostre insieme ratto.»
E quel signor che lì m'avea menato,
   mi disse: «Non temer; che 'l nostro passo
   non ci può torre alcun: da tal n'è dato.
Ma qui m'attendi, e lo spirito lasso
   conforta e ciba di speranza buona,
108   ch'i' non ti lascerò nel mondo basso.»
Così sen va, e quivi m'abbandona
   lo dolce padre, e io rimango in forse,
   che no e sì nel capo mi tenciona.
Udir non potti quello ch'a lor porse;
   ma ei non stette là con essi guari,
114   che ciascun dentro a pruova si ricorse.
Chiuser le porte que' nostri avversari
   nel petto al mio segnor, che fuor rimase,
   e rivolsesi a me con passi rari.
Li occhi a la terra e le ciglia avea rase
   d'ogni baldanza, e dicea ne' sospiri:
120   «Chi m'ha negate le dolenti case!»
E a me disse: «Tu, perch'io m'adiri,
   non sbigottir, ch'io vincerò la prova,
   qual ch'a la difension dentro s'aggiri.
Questa lor tracotanza non è nova;
   ché già l'usaro a men secreta porta,
126   la qual sanza serrame ancor si trova.
Sopr'essa vedestù la scritta morta:
   e già di qua da lei discende l'erta,
   passando per li cerchi sanza scorta,
tal che per lui ne fia la terra aperta.»

have given me safety, and taken me from great danger
threatening me, do not leave me," I said, "in such distress, and if they refuse us further passage, let us quickly retrace our steps together."

[VIRGIL] And that lord who had led me there said: "Never fear, for no one can deprive us of passage; by such a
one it is given to us. But wait for me here; comfort your
tired spirit and feed it with good hope, for I shall not
leave you in the underworld."

[NARRATOR] So my kind father goes away and leaves
me there, and I remain in suspense, so that "Yes" and
"No" struggle in my head. I could not hear what he offered them, but he did not stand there with them long
before each one rushed inside as though trying to be
first. These opponents of ours closed the gates in the
face of my master, who remained outside and came
back to me with slow steps. His looks were downcast
and his eyes had lost all confidence, and sighing, he said:

[VIRGIL] "See them forbid me the mansions of pain!"
But to me he said: "You, though I am worried,[4] should
not fear, for I shall win the contest, whatever defense
may be devised inside. This their wilfulness is not new
—which once they used at a less secret gate, which
still is without its lock. Above that you saw the inscription declaring death. And below it, already there
is coming down the slope, passing through the circles
without escort, a being so strong that he will open the
city to us."[5]

CANTO 9

Quel color che viltà di fuor mi pinse,
   veggendo il duca mio tornare in volta,
   più tosto dentro il suo novo ristrinse.
Attento si fermò com' uom ch' ascolta;
   chè l' occhio nol potea menare a lunga
6   per l' aere nero e per la nebbia folta.
«Pur a noi converrà vincer la punga»
   cominciò el, «se non.... Tal ne s' offerse:
   oh quanto tarda a me ch' altri qui giunga!»
I' vidi ben sì com' ei ricoperse
   lo cominciar con l' altro che poi venne,
12   che fur parole a le prime diverse;
ma nondimen paura il suo dir dienne,
   perch' io traeva la parola tronca
   forse a peggior sentenzia che non tenne.
«In questo fondo de la trista conca
   discende mai alcun del primo grado,
18   che sol per pena ha la speranza cionca?»
Questa question fec' io; e quei «Di rado
   incontra» mi rispuose «che di nui
   faccia il cammino alcun per qual io vado.
Ver è ch' altra fiata qua giù fui,
   congiurato da quella Eritòn cruda
24   che richiamava l' ombre a' corpi sui.
Di poco era di me la carne nuda,
   ch' ella mi fece intrar dentr' a quel muro,
   per trarne un spirto del cerchio di Giuda.
Quell' è il più basso loco e 'l più oscuro,
   e 'l piú lontan dal ciel che tutto gira:
30   ben so il cammin; però ti fa sicuro.
Questa palude che 'l gran puzzo spira,
   cinge dintorno la città dolente,
   u' non potemo intrare omai sanz' ira.»

CANTO 9

INTERLUDE BETWEEN CIRCLES FIVE AND SIX

[Dante's terror at the city gate of Dis: 9.1–63]

[NARRATOR] The hue cowardice painted on me as I saw my guide return, at once his last words dispelled.[1] He stood still as though listening, because the eye could not see far in the dark air and the thick fog.

[VIRGIL] "Certainly we are going to win the fight,"[2] he said, "unless . . . .[3] Such was promised to us.[4] Oh, how slow he seems in getting here!"

[NARRATOR] I saw clearly how he covered his beginning with something else coming after—words unlike the first ones. But nevertheless what he said frightened me, perhaps because I pushed the broken-off speech to a meaning worse than it really had.

[DANTE] "Into this depth of the mournful shell does anybody ever come from the first terrace, which for punishment has only hope denied?" This question I asked.

[VIRGIL] And he answered: "Seldom it happens that any of us goes on the journey I am taking. It is true that I was down here once before, conjured by that savage Erictho,[5] who could summon shades back to their bodies. Only a little while my flesh had lacked me,[6] when she made me go inside that wall to take a spirit away from the circle of Judas. That is the lowest place and the darkest and the farthest from the heaven which turns everything around. Well I know the road; so feel safe. This swamp which gives off the great stench encircles the city of sorrow, which we cannot now enter without anger."

E altro disse, ma non l' ho a mente;
  però che l' occhio m' avea tutto tratto
36 ver l' alta torre a la cima rovente,
dove in un punto furon dritte ratto
  tre furie infernal di sangue tinte,
  che membra femminine avieno e atto,
e con idre verdissime eran cinte;
  serpentelli e ceraste avean per crine,
42 onde le fiere tempie erano avvinte.
E quei, che ben conobbe le meschine
  de la regina de l'etterno pianto,
  «Guarda» mi disse «le feroci Erine.
Quest'è Megera dal sinistro canto;
  quella che piange dal destro è Aletto;
48 Tesifone è nel mezzo»; e tacque a tanto.
Con l'unghie si fendea ciascuna il petto;
  battiensi a palme; e gridavan sì alto,
  ch'i' mi strinsi al poeta per sospetto.
«Vegna Medusa: sì 'l farem di smalto»
  dicevan tutte riguardando in giuso:
54 «mal non vengiammo in Teseo l'assalto.»
«Volgiti in dietro e tien lo viso chiuso;
  ché se il Gorgòn si mostra e tu 'l vedessi,
  nulla sarebbe del tornar mai suso.»
Così disse 'l maestro; ed elli stessi
  mi volse, e non si tenne a le mie mani,
60 che con le sue ancor non mi chiudessi.
O voi ch'avete li 'ntelletti sani,
  mirate la dottrina che s'asconde
  sotto il velame de li versi strani.
E già venia su per le torbid' onde
  un fracasso d'un suon, pien di spavento,
66 per che tremavano amendue le sponde,
non altrimenti fatto che d'un vento
  impetuoso per li avversi ardori,
  che fier la selva e sanz'alcun rattento

[NARRATOR] And he said something further, but I do not remember it, for I was directing my eye wholly upon the burning summit of the high tower, where in an instant suddenly stood three hellish furies stained with blood. Their limbs and their bearing were female; and with dark green hydras they were girdled; serpents and cerastes instead of hair were wound about their dreadful temples.

[VIRGIL] He, who well knew the servants of the queen of endless lamentation, said to me: "Look at the savage Furies. The one on the left is Megara; Alecto is she who weeps on the right; Tesiphone is in the middle." With that he was silent.

[NARRATOR] With her claws each one tore her breast. They struck their palms together and shrieked so loud that I clung to the poet in my fear.

[FURIES] "Let Medusa come, so we can turn him into stone," they all said, looking down. "Wrongly we did not avenge on Theseus his attack."7

[VIRGIL] "Turn around and keep your face covered, because if the Gorgon appears and you see her, no going back up can ever be." So spoke my teacher; and himself he turned me around, and he did not rely on my hands so much that with his own as well he did not cover it for me.

[POET] *O you whose minds are sound, examine the teaching hidden under the cloak of the difficult verses.*

[*A supernatural being to the rescue: 9.64–105*]

[NARRATOR]   And now over the muddy waves was coming a medley of sounds full of terror, at which both shores trembled, as though caused by a wind violent with opposing blasts, which strikes the forest and, un-

li rami schianta, abbatte e porta fori;
  dinanzi polveroso va superbo,
72 e fa fuggir le fiere e li pastori.
Gli occhi mi sciolse e disse: «Or drizza il nerbo
  del viso su per quella schiuma antica
  per indi ove quel fummo è più acerbo.»
Come le rane innanzi a la nemica
  biscia per l'acqua si dileguan tutte,
78 fin ch'a la terra ciascuna s'abbica,
vid'io più di mille anime distrutte
  fuggir così dinanzi ad un ch'al passo
  passava Stige con le piante asciutte.
Dal volto rimovea quell' aere grasso,
  menando la sinistra innanzi spesso;
84 e sol di quell' angoscia parea lasso.
Ben m' accorsi ch' egli era da ciel messo,
  e volsimi al maestro; e quei fè segno
  ch' i' stessi queto ed inchinassi ad esso.
Ahi quanto mi parea pien di disdegno!
  Venne a la porta, e con una verghetta
90 l' aperse, che non v' ebbe alcun ritegno.
«O cacciati del ciel, gente dispetta.»
  cominciò elli in su l' orribil soglia,
  «ond' esta oltracotanza in voi s' alletta?
Perchè recalcitrate a quella voglia
  a cui non può il fin mai esser mozzo,
96 e che più volte v' ha cresciuta doglia?
Che giova ne le fata dar di cozzo?
  Cerbero vostro, se ben vi ricorda,
  ne porta ancor pelato il mento e 'l gozzo.»
Poi si rivolse per la strada lorda,
  e non fè motto a noi, ma fè sembiante
102 d' omo cui altra cura stringa e morda
che quella di colui che li è davante;
  e noi movemmo i piedi inver la terra,
  sicuri appresso le parole sante.

bridled, shatters the branches, throws them down and carries them away; in its pride it drives the dust before it, and puts to flight the wild beasts and the shepherds. [VIRGIL] My eyes he set free, and said: "Now look hard across the filthy scum to the place where the smoke is more pungent."[8]

[NARRATOR] As the frogs fleeing before the threatening snake all rush through the water, until each one is bunched up on the bottom, so I saw more than a thousand damned souls fleeing before one who, in passing, passed[9] the Styx with dry soles. From his face he brushed away that greasy air, flourishing his left hand often before him; and by that annoyance only did he seem affected. Clearly I understood that he was sent from Heaven,[10] so I turned to my teacher, who gave me a sign to be quiet and bow to him. How very disdainful he seemed to me! He came to the gate and opened it with his wand, meeting no resistance there.

[MESSENGER] "O accursed throng, hurled from Heaven," he said at the horrid threshold, "on what is nourished this arrogance of yours? Why do you kick against that will whose purpose can never be cut short, and which often has increased your pain? What do you gain by butting against the fates? Your Cerberus, as you perhaps remember, through so doing still lacks hair on his chin and throat."[11]

[NARRATOR] Then he took that filthy path again; and he said not a word to us, but acted as though pushed and annoyed by further care than that of the person before him. And we set foot within the city, confident after his holy words.

Dentro li entrammo sanz' alcuna guerra;
  e io, ch' avea di riguardar disio
108   la condizion che tal fortezza serra,
com' io fui dentro, l' occhio intorno invio;
  e veggio ad ogne man grande campagna,
  piena di duolo e di tormento rio.
Sì come ad Arli, ove Rodano stagna,
  sì com' a Pola, presso del Carnaro
114   ch' Italia chiude e suoi termini bagna,
fanno i sepulcri tutt' il loco varo,
  così facevan quivi d' ogni parte,
  salvo che 'l modo v' era più amaro;
chè tra li avelli fiamme erano sparte,
  per le quali eran sì del tutto accesi,
120   che ferro più non chiede verun' arte.
Tutti li lor coperchi eran sospesi,
  e fuor n' uscivan sì duri lamenti,
  che ben parean di miseri e d' offesi.
E io: «Maestro, quai son quelle genti
  che, seppellite dentro da quell' arche,
126   si fan sentir con li sospir dolenti?»
Ed elli a me: «Qui son li eresiarche
  coi lor seguaci, d' ogni setta, e molto
  più che non credi son le tombe carche.
Simile qui con simile è sepolto,
  e i monimenti son più e men caldi.»
132   E poi ch' a la man destra si fu volto,
passammo tra i martìri e gli alti spaldi.

CIRCLE SIX

[*The city of Dis, with the heretics'*
tombs: 9.106–133]

[NARRATOR] In we went without opposition, and I, eager
to see the sort of thing inclosed in that fortress, when I
was inside, cast my eyes about. On all sides I saw a great
plain given over to suffering and grievous torment. As
at Arles, where the Rhone enters the sea,[12] as at Pola
near the Carnaro, which bounds Italy and washes her
borders, the tombs make all the place uneven, so they
did here everywhere, except that here the method was
more painful, for within the monuments, flames were
disposed,[13] by which they were so thoroughly heated
that hotter iron no handicraft requires. All their covers
were lifted, and from them were coming such deep
lamentations that plainly they were those of the wretched and afflicted.

[DANTE] And I said: "Teacher, what sort of people are
these who, buried in these vaults, make themselves
heard with such sorrowful groans?"

[VIRGIL] And he answered me: "Here are the arch-
heretics, with their disciples, of every sect, and the
tombs are much more crowded than you would believe.
Like here with like is buried, so the sepulchers are more
hot and less so."

[NARRATOR] And after we had turned to the right, we
passed between the sufferings[14] and the lofty battle-
ments.

CANTO 10

Ora sen va per un secreto calle,
   tra 'l muro de la terra e li martiri,
   lo mio maestro, e io dopo le spalle.
«O virtù somma, che per li empi giri
   mi volvi» cominciai, «com' a te piace,
6   parlami e sodisfammi a' miei disiri.
La gente che per li sepolcri giace
   potrebbesi veder? già son levati
   tutt' i coperchi, e nessun guardia face.»
Ed elli a me: «Tutti saran serrati
   quando di Iosafàt qui torneranno
12   coi corpi che là su hanno lasciati.
Suo cimitero da questa parte hanno
   con Epicuro tutt' i suoi seguaci,
   che l' anima col corpo morta fanno.
Però a la dimanda che mi faci
   quinc' entro satisfatto sarà tosto,
18   e al disio ancor che tu mi taci.»
E io: «Buon duca, non tegno riposto
   a te mio cuor se non per dicer poco,
   e tu m' hai non pur mo a ciò disposto.»
«O Tosco che per la città del foco
   vivo ten vai così parlando onesto,
24   piacciati di restare in questo loco.
La tua loquela ti fa manifesto
   di quella nobil patria natio
   a la qual forse fui troppo molesto.»
Subitamente questo suono uscio
   d'una de l'arche; però m'accostai,
30   temendo, un poco più al duca mio.
Ed el mi disse: «Volgiti: che fai?
   Vedi là Farinata che s'è dritto:
   da la cintola in su tutto 'l vedrai.»

CANTO 10

CIRCLE SIX, cont.

[The traveler asks to see the heretics: 10.1–21]

[NARRATOR] Now my teacher takes a narrow path between the city wall and the sufferings, and I behind him. [DANTE] "O lofty genius, you who lead me through the wicked circles as you please," I said, "speak to me and satisfy my wishes. The people who lie in the graves—can I see them? All the covers are raised, you see, and no one is on guard."

[VIRGIL] He answered: "They all will be fastened when the souls get back from Jehosaphat with the bodies they have left up there.[1] In this spot, with Epicurus, all his disciples, who assert that the soul dies with the body, have their burial place. But to the question you ask me, satisfaction will quickly be given right here, and also to the wish that you keep still about."

[DANTE] And I said: "Good guide, I am not concealing my heart from you except by saying little, and not merely now have you inclined me to that."[2]

[Farinata degli Uberti, the magnanimous patriot, and Cavalcante Cavalcanti: 10.22–114]

[FARINATA DEGLI UBERTI] "Tuscan, you who are going alive through the city of fire, speaking so nobly, have the goodness to pause here. Your speech proclaims you a native of that splendid city to which, as I admit, I did much damage."[3]

[NARRATOR] Suddenly this speech came from one of the vaults. Hence, in fear, I drew a little closer to my guide. [VIRGIL] And he said to me: "Turn around! What are you at? Look at Farinata, who is standing up. From his belt upward you can see him."[4]

I' avea già il mio viso nel suo fitto;
ed el s'ergea col petto e con la fronte
36   com'avesse l'inferno in gran dispitto.
E l'animose man del duca e pronte
mi pinser tra le sepulture a lui,
dicendo: «Le parole tue sien conte.»
Com'io al piè de la sua tomba fui,
guardommi un poco, e poi, quasi sdegnoso,
42   mi dimandò: «Chi fuor li maggior tui?»
Io ch'era d'ubidir disideroso,
non gliel celai, ma tutto gliel' apersi;
ond'ei levò le ciglia un poco in soso;
poi disse: «Fieramente furo avversi
a me e a miei primi e a mia parte,
48   sì che per due fiate li dispersi.»
«S'ei fur cacciati, ei tornar d'ogni parte»
rispuosi lui «l'una e l'altra fiata;
ma i vostri non appreser ben quell'arte.»
Allor surse a la vista scoperchiata
un'ombra lungo questa infino al mento:
54   credo che s'era in ginocchie levata.
Dintorno mi guardò, come talento
avesse di veder s'altri era meco;
e poi che il sospecciar fu tutto spento,
piangendo disse: «Se per questo cieco
carcere vai per altezza d'ingegno,
60   mio figlio ov'è? perché non è ei teco?»
E io a lui: «Da me stesso non vegno:
colui ch'attende là, per qui mi mena,
forse cui Guido vostro ebbe a disdegno.»
Le sue parole e 'l modo de la pena
m'avean di costui già letto il nome;
66   però fu la risposta così piena.
Di subito drizzato gridò: «Come
dicesti? elli ebbe? non viv'elli ancora?
non fiere li occhi suoi il dolce lome?»

[NARRATOR] By then I had fixed my eyes on his; and he held chest and brow high, as though feeling utter contempt for Hell.

[VIRGIL] Then the hand of my guide, spirited and ready, pushed me toward him among the graves, saying: "Make your words fitting."

[FARINATA] When I was at the foot of his grave, he looked at me a little and, almost scornful, asked: "Who were your ancestors?"

[NARRATOR] I, eager to obey, did not conceal them from him but laid them all before him.

[FARINATA] At this he lifted his eyebrows a little, then said: "Savagely they opposed me and my forefathers and my party, so that twice I scattered them."

[DANTE] "If they were put to flight, they returned from all directions," I answered him, "both the first time and the second; but yours failed to gain skill in returning."

[NARRATOR] Then beside the first, another shade rose to view, uncovered down to the chin; I believe it had raised itself on its knees. All around me it looked, as though trying to see if someone was with me.

[CAVALCANTE] And when its hope was exhausted, weeping it said: "If through this dark prison you are going because of your lofty genius, my son[5]—where is he? Why is he not with you?"

[DANTE] And I said to him: "I do not come by myself. That man who is waiting there, whom your Guido disdained, you know, is leading me through here."[6]

[NARRATOR] His words and the nature of his penalty had already told me the speaker's name;[7] hence my answer was so full.

[CAVALCANTE] Suddenly rising to his full height, he cried: "Why do you say *disdained*?[8] Is he not still alive? Does the sweet light not fall upon his eyes?"

Quando s'accorse d'alcuna dimora
ch'io facea dinanzi a la risposta,
72   supin ricadde e più non parve fora.
Ma quell'altro magnanimo a cui posta
restato m'era, non mutò aspetto,
né mosse collo, né piegò sua costa;
e sé continuando al primo detto,
«S'egli han quell'arte» disse «male appresa,
78   ciò mi tormenta più che questo letto.
Ma non cinquanta volte fia raccesa
la faccia de la donna che qui regge,
che tu saprai quanto quell'arte pesa.
E se tu mai nel dolce mondo regge,
dimmi: perché quel popolo è sì empio
84   incontr'a' miei in ciascuna sua legge?»
Ond'io a lui: «Lo strazio e 'l grande scempio
che fece l'Arbia colorata in rosso,
tali orazion fa far nel nostro tempio.»
Poi ch'ebbe sospirando il capo mosso,
«A ciò non fu' io sol» disse, «né certo
90   sanza cagion con li altri sarei mosso.
Ma fu' io solo, là dove sofferto
fu per ciascun di torre via Fiorenza,
colui che la difesi a viso aperto.»
«Deh, se riposi mai vostra semenza»
prega' io lui, «solvetemi quel nodo
96   che qui ha inviluppata mia sentenza.
El par che voi veggiate, se ben odo,
dinanzi quel che 'l tempo seco adduce,
e nel presente tenete altro modo.»
«Noi veggiam, come quei c'ha mala luce,
le cose» disse «che ne son lontano;
102   cotanto ancor ne splende il sommo duce.
Quando s'appressano o son, tutto è vano
nostro intelletto; e s'altri non ci apporta,
nulla sapem di vostro stato umano.

[NARRATOR] When he observed that I delayed a little in answering, he fell backward and no more appeared outside. But that great-souled man I had spoken with, for whose sake I had paused, did not change his expression or move his neck or bend his back.

[FARINATA] "And if," he said, going on with his earlier words, "and if they have gained little skill in that, it afflicts me more than this bed. But not fifty times will the face of the mistress who reigns here be lighted again before you will find out how hard it is to acquire such skill. And as you hope to return sometime to the pleasant world, I beg you to tell me why that city is in all her laws so pitiless against me."

[DANTE] So I said to him: "The rout and the great slaughter which colored the Arbia's waters red,[9] causes such prayers in our church."[10]

[FARINATA] When with a sigh he had moved his head, he said: "In that not alone was I, and surely without cause I would not have acted with the others. But alone I was in that meeting where every one agreed on getting rid of Florence, when I defended her boldly."

[DANTE] "Oh, as you hope your descendants may some day live in quiet," I begged him, "untie this knot for me, which here has bound up my judgment. If I hear correctly, you see in advance what time brings with it, but as to the present you are in a different state."

[FARINATA] "As does a man with bad eyesight," he said, "we see distant things. To that extent the Almighty Guide enlightens us. When they come close or happen, our minds are wholly empty, and if someone does not inform us, we know nothing of your human state. Thus

Però comprender puoi che tutta morta
fia nostra conoscenza da quel punto
108   che del futuro fia chiusa la porta.»
Allor, come di mia colpa compunto,
dissi: «Or direte dunque a quel caduto
che 'l suo nato è co' vivi ancor congiunto;
e s' i' fui, dianzi, a la risposta muto,
fate i saper che 'l fei perché pensava
114   già nell' error che m' avete soluto.»
E già il maestro mio mi richiamava;
per ch' i' pregai lo spirito più avaccio
che mi dicesse chi con lu' istava.
Dissemi: «Qui con più di mille giaccio:
qua dentro è 'l secondo Federico,
120   e 'l Cardinale; e de li altri mi taccio.»
Indi s' ascose; ed io inver l' antico
poeta volsi i passi, ripensando
a quel parlar che mi parea nemico.
Elli si mosse; e poi, così andando,
mi disse: «Perchè se' tu sì smarrito?»
126   E io li sodisfeci al suo dimando.
«La mente tua conservi quel che udito
hai contra te» mi comandò quel saggio.
«E ora attendi qui» e drizzò 'l dito:
«quando sarai dinanzi al dolce raggio
di quella il cui bell' occhio tutto vede,
132   da lei saprai di tua vita il viaggio.»
Appresso mosse a man sinistra il piede:
lasciammo il muro e gimmo inver lo mezzo
per un sentier ch' a una valle fiede
che 'nfin là su facea spiacer suo lezzo.

you can understand that wholly dead will be our knowledge at the moment when the door of the future is
closed."

[DANTE] Then in sorrow for my fault, I said: "Tell, then,
that fallen one that his son is still among the living. And
if I was silent before my answer, let him know that I
acted so because my thinking was then under the error
you have freed me from."

[From Beatrice the traveler will learn of
his future: 10.115–136]

[NARRATOR] Already my teacher was calling me,[11] so in
great haste I begged the spirit to tell me who was with
him.

[FARINATA] He said to me: "Here I lie with more than a
thousand. In this tomb are the second Frederick and the
Cardinal;[12] about the others I keep silent."

[NARRATOR] Then he disappeared, and I stepped over
to the noble poet, thinking about that speech which
seemed adverse to me.[13]

[VIRGIL] He moved on, and then, still walking along, he
said to me: "Why are you so upset?" And I answered
his question. "Keep in your memory what you have
heard against yourself," that poet charged me. "And
now pay attention to this," and he raised his finger,
"When you are in the pleasant light of that lady whose
fair eye sees all of it,[14] from her you will learn about the
voyage of your life."

[NARRATOR] Then he walked to the left. We moved
away from the wall, and went toward the middle along
a path ending at a valley which, even up there, dis-
pleased us with its stench.

CANTO 11

In su l' estremità d' un' alta ripa
　che facevan gran pietre rotte in cerchio,
　venimmo sopra più crudele stipa;
e quivi per l' orribile soperchio
　del puzzo che 'l profondo abisso gitta,
6　　ci raccostammo, in dietro, ad un coperchio
d' un grand' avello, ov' io vidi una scritta
　che dicea: «Anastasio papa guardo,
　lo qual trasse Fotin de la via dritta.»
«Lo nostro scender conviene esser tardo,
　sì che s' ausi un poco in prima il senso
12　　al tristo fiato; e poi no i fia riguardo.»
Così 'l maestro; e io «Alcun compenso»
　dissi lui «trova, che 'l tempo non passi
　perduto.» Ed elli: «Vedi ch' a ciò penso.»
«Figliuol mio, dentro da cotesti sassi»
　cominciò poi a dir «son tre cerchietti
18　　di grado in grado, come que' che lassi.
Tutti son pien di spirti maladetti;
　ma perchè poi ti basti pur la vista,
　intendi come e perchè son costretti.
D' ogni malizia, ch' odio in cielo acquista,
　ingiuria è 'l fine, ed ogni fin cotale
24　　o con forza o con frode altrui contrista.
Ma perchè frode è de l' uom proprio male,
　più spiace a Dio; e però stan di sutto
　li frodolenti e più dolor li assale.

CANTO 11

INTERLUDE, AN OUTLINE GUIDE TO HELL

[The stench from the Seventh Circle,
far below: 11.1–15]

[NARRATOR] On the edge of a high bank formed by a circle of huge broken rocks, we were above a still more cruel prison-cage.¹ And there, because of the hideous violence of the stench that the deep abyss threw up, we took refuge behind the cover of a great sepulcher, where I saw an inscription saying:

[INSCRIPTION] "I guard Pope Anastasius, whom Photinus led away from the right path."

[VIRGIL] "We must delay our descent a little, so that before going down, we may get our senses used a bit to the disgusting stink; then we shall not mind it." So my teacher.

[DANTE] And I said to him: "Find some device so that our time will not be lost."

[VIRGIL] And he: "Notice that I have it in mind."

[The arrangement in Hell of the vices
there punished: 11.16–27]

[VIRGIL] "My son, within these cliffs,"² he said, "are three small circles, one below another, like those you are leaving. They all are full of cursed spirits. But so that later merely seeing will be enough for you, you need to learn how and why they are imprisoned.

"Of all ill will which is hated by Heaven, injury is the result, and every such result wrongs others either by force or by fraud. But because fraud is exclusively man's evil,³ it is more displeasing to God. Therefore the fraudulent are underneath and more pain attacks them."

De' violenti il primo cerchio è tutto;
  ma perchè si fa forza a tre persone,
30   in tre gironi è distinto e costrutto.
A Dio, a sè, al prossimo si pòne
  far forza, dico in loro ed in lor cose,
  come udirai con aperta ragione.
Morte per forza e ferute dogliose
  nel prossimo si danno, e nel suo avere
36   ruine, incendii e tollette dannose;
onde omicide e ciascun che mal fiere,
  guastatori e predon, tutti tormenta
  lo giron primo per diverse schiere.
Puote omo avere in sè man violenta
  e ne' suoi beni; e però nel secondo
42   giron convien che sanza pro si penta
qualunque priva sè del vostro mondo,
  biscazza e fonde la sua facultade,
  e piange là dove esser de' giocondo.
Puossi far forza ne la deitade,
  col cuor negando e bestemmiando quella,
48   e spregiando natura e sua bontade;
e però lo minor giron suggella
  del segno suo Soddoma e Caorsa
  e chi, spregiando Dio col cor, favella.
La frode, ond' ogni coscienza è morsa,
  può l' omo usare in colui che 'n lui fida
54   ed in quel che fidanza non imborsa.
Questo modo di retro par ch'incida
  pur lo vinco d'amor che fa natura;
  onde nel cerchio secondo s'annida
ipocrisia, lusinghe e chi affattura,
  falsità, ladroneccio e simonia,
60   ruffian, baratti, e simile lordura.

[The first circle below (Seventh Circle of Hell)
for the violent: 11.28–51]

[VIRGIL] "The first circle below is entirely for the violent, yet because force is used against three persons,
that circle is arranged and constructed in three rounds.
Against God, against oneself, against one's neighbor
—that is, upon them and upon what pertains to them—
force can be used, as I shall tell you with clear reasoning. With force, death and painful wounds can be
inflicted on one's neighbor, and on his possessions, destruction, fire, and harmful theft. Hence homicides and
every man who strikes wickedly, destroyers and robbers
are all tormented in the first round in different com-
panies.

"A man can use violent hands upon himself and upon
his own goods. Therefore in the second round are fitly
placed all those who are punished with useless regret
because they have deprived themselves of your world,
have gambled away and squandered their property, and
wept when they should have been happy.

"Force can be used against the deity by denying him
in one's heart and cursing him, and despising nature
and her goodness. Therefore the smallest round seals
with its mark both Sodom and Cahors,[4] and him who,
despising God in his heart, speaks it out."

[The second circle below (Eighth Circle of Hell)
for the fraudulent: 11.52–60]

[VIRGIL] "Fraud, by which all consciousness is bitten,[5]
man can use against someone who trusts him, and
against someone whose wallet contains no trust.[6] This
latter form cuts merely the chain of love which nature
forms.[7] Hence in the second circle below are the nests of
hypocrisy, flatterers, and fortunetellers, falsifying,
theft, and simony, pimps, grafters and similar filth."

Per l'altro modo quell'amor s'oblia
che fa natura, e quel ch'è poi aggiunto,
di che la fede spezial si cria;
onde nel cerchio minore, ov'è 'l punto
de l'universo in su che Dite siede,
66   qualunque trade in etterno è consunto.»
E io: «Maestro, assai chiara procede
la tua ragione, ed assai ben distingue
questo baratro e 'l popol ch'e' possiede.
Ma dimmi: quei de la palude pingue,
che mena il vento, e che batte la pioggia,
72   e che s'incontran con sì aspre lingue,
perchè non dentro da la città roggia
sono ei puniti, se Dio li ha in ira?
e se non li ha, perchè sono a tal foggia?»
Ed elli a me «Perché tanto delira»
disse «lo 'ngegno tuo da quel che suole?
78   o ver la mente dove altrove mira?
Non ti rimembra di quelle parole
con le quai la tua Etica pertratta
le tre disposizion che 'l ciel non vuole,
incontinenza, malizia e la matta
bestialitade? e come incontinenza
84   men Dio offende e men biasimo accatta?
Se tu riguardi ben questa sentenza,
e rechiti a la mente chi son quelli
che su di fuor sostegnon penitenza,
tu vedrai ben perché da questi felli
sien dipartiti, e perché men crucciata
90   la divina vendetta li martelli.»

[The third circle below (Ninth Circle of Hell)
for traitors: 11.61–66]

[VIRGIL] "In the other kind of fraud, the love produced by nature is forgotten, and whatever is later added to it, from which individual trust is formed. Hence in the smallest circle, in which is the center of the universe where Dis⁸ stands, the betrayer is everlastingly tormented."

[A doubt about the upper circles dispelled by
citing Aristotle's Ethics: 11.67–93]

[DANTE] I said: "Teacher, your discourse moves very clearly and analyzes very well this pit and the people it contains. But tell me: those in the teeming swamp,⁹ and those whom the wind sweeps along, and whom the rain strikes, and who oppose one another with such rough tongues,¹⁰ why are they not punished inside the fiery city,¹¹ if God is angry at them? If he is not angry, why are they in such a state?"

[VIRGIL] And he replied to me: "Why does your intelligence turn so far from what is usual with it? Or what other teaching is your mind accepting? Do you not remember the words in which your *Ethics*¹² deals with the three moral habits which Heaven forbids: incontinence, malice, and insane bestiality,¹³ and that incontinence less angers God and less brings on itself condemnation? If you well consider this opinion, and bring before your mind who they are who outside these lower circles¹⁴ endure punishment, you will fully understand why they are separated from these wicked souls,¹⁵ and why punishment divine less wrathfully hammers them."

«O sol che sani ogni vista turbata,
  tu mi contenti sì quando tu solvi,
  che, non men che saver, dubbiar m'aggrata.
Ancora un poco in dietro ti rivolvi»
  diss'io, «là dove di' ch'usura offende
96   la divina bontade, e 'l groppo solvi.»
«Filosofia» mi disse «a chi la 'ntende,
  nota non pure in una sola parte,
  come natura lo suo corso prende
da divino intelletto e da sua arte;
  e se tu ben la tua Fisica note,
102   tu troverai, non dopo molte carte,
che l' arte vostra quella, quanto puote,
  segue, come 'l maestro fa il discente;
  sì che vostr' arte a Dio quasi è nepote.
Da queste due, se tu ti rechi a mente
  lo Genesì dal principio, convene
108   prender sua vita ed avanzar la gente:
e perchè l' usuriere altra via tene,
  per sè natura e per la sua seguace
  dispregia, poi ch' in altro pon la spene.
Ma seguimi oramai che 'l gir mi piace;
  chè i Pesci guizzan su per l' orizzonta,
114   e 'l Carro tutto sovra 'l Coro giace,
e 'l balzo via là oltra si dismonta.»

[*Why usury is sinful: 11.94–115*]

[DANTE] "O sun, you who heal every ailing eye, you so satisfy me, when you explain, that not less than knowing, inquiring delights me. Yet turn back a little," I said, "to the place where you said that usury angers divine goodness, and untie the knot."

[VIRGIL] "Philosophy," he said, "for one who understands it, observes not merely in a single passage that Nature's process moves from the divine intelligence and its creative force. And if with care you look at your *Physics*,[16] you will find, not many pages along, that your creative action, so far as it can, follows, as the pupil does the teacher, so that your art is, as it were, God's grandchild. From these two, if you summon to mind the early part of Genesis,[17] man must get his living and prosper. And because the usurer employs another method, he shows contempt for Nature herself and for her follower, for elsewhere he puts his hope.

"But now that I am ready to go, follow me, for the Fishes are wiggling on the horizon, and the Northern Wagoner is wholly above the Northwest Wind, and the cliff can be descended much farther on."

CANTO 12

Era lo loco ov' a scender la riva
  venimmo, alpestro e, per quel ch' iv' er' anco,
  tal, ch' ogni vista ne sarebbe schiva.
Qual è quella ruina che nel fianco
  di qua da Trento l'Adice percosse,
6   o per tremoto o per sostegno manco,
che da cima del monte, onde si mosse,
  al piano è sì la roccia discoscesa,
  ch' alcuna via darebbe a chi su fosse;
cotal di quel burrato era la scesa;
  e 'n su la punta de la rotta lacca
12   l' infamia di Creti era distesa
che fu concetta ne la falsa vacca;
  e quando vide noi, se stesso morse,
  sì come quei cui l' ira dentro fiacca.
Lo savio mio inver lui gridò: «Forse
  tu credi che qui sia il duca d'Atene,
18   che su nel mondo la morte ti porse?
Partiti, bestia: ché questi non vene
  ammaestrato da la tua sorella,
  ma vassi per veder le vostre pene.»
Qual è quel toro che si slaccia in quella
  c'ha ricevuto già 'l colpo mortale,
24   che gir non sa, ma qua e là saltella,
vid'io lo Minotauro far cotale;
  e quello accorto gridò: «Corri al varco;
  mentre ch'è in furia, è buon che tu ti cale.»
Così prendemmo via giù per lo scarco
  di quelle pietre, che spesso moviensi
30   sotto i miei piedi per lo novo carco.

CANTO 12

Circle Seven, First Round

[The descent to the Seventh Circle: 12.1–10]

[NARRATOR] The place where we expected to go down the slope was like a mountain side and, because of what besides was there,[1] such that any eye would turn from it. Like that landslide which on this side of Trent struck the shore of the Adige, whether through an earthquake or through weak support (in which from the summit of the mountain, where it started, the rock has so come down to the bottom that it offers no path to one above),[2] was the slope of that cliff.

[The Minotaur, an ineffective guardian: 12.11–27]

[NARRATOR] Then on the edge of the broken cliff was lying the infamy of Crete, which was conceived in the counterfeit cow. And when he saw us, he bit himself, since wrath mastered his mind.[3]

[VIRGIL] My wise guide shouted at him: "You seem to believe the Duke of Athens is here, who up in the world struck you dead.[4] Move out of our way, ignoramus, for this man has not been instructed by your sister, but is traveling to see your punishments."

[NARRATOR] The bull that gets loose just at the instant when it receives its mortal blow cannot walk, but leaps to one side and to the other; so I saw the Minotaur do.

[VIRGIL] And that alert guide shouted: "Run to the opening;[5] while he is in his fit, you have your chance to go down."

[Descent to the Seventh Circle: 12.28–45]

[NARRATOR] So we made our way down that tumbled slope of stones, which often moved under my feet because of the weight new to it.[6]

Io gia pensando; e quei disse: «Tu pensi
  forse in questa ruina, ch'è guardata
  da quell'ira bestial ch'io ora spensi.
Or vo' che sappi che l'altra fiata
  ch'i' discesi qua giù nel basso inferno,
36   questa roccia non era ancor cascata.
Ma certo poco pria, se ben discerno,
  che venisse colui che la gran preda
  levò a Dite del cerchio superno,
da tutte parti l'alta valle feda
  tremò sì, ch'i' pensai che l'universo
42   sentisse amor, per lo qual è chi creda
più volte il mondo in caòs converso;
  ed in quel punto questa vecchia roccia
  qui e altrove tal fece riverso.
Ma ficca gli occhi a valle, ché s'approccia
  la riviera del sangue in la qual bolle
48   qual che per violenza in altrui noccia.»
Oh cieca cupidigia e ira folle,
  che sì ci sproni ne la vita corta,
  e ne l'etterna poi sì mal c'immolle!
Io vidi un'ampia fossa in arco torta,
  come quella che tutto il piano abbraccia,
54   secondo ch'avea detto la mia scorta;
e tra 'l piè de la ripa ed essa, in traccia
  corrien centauri, armati di saette,
  come solien nel mondo andare a caccia.
Veggendoci calar, ciascun ristette,
  e de la schiera tre si dipartiro
60   con archi e asticciuole prima elette;
e l' un gridò da lungi: «A qual martiro
  venite voi che scendete la costa?
  Ditel costinci; se non, l' arco tiro.»
Lo mio maestro disse: «La risposta
  farem noi a Chiron costà di presso:
66   mal fu la voglia tua sempre sì tosta.»

[VIRGIL] I was thoughtful; and he said: "Perhaps you are thinking about this landslide guarded by the crazy anger[7] that I just now disposed of. So I shall explain that the other time when I went down here into lower Hell, this cliff had not yet fallen. But certainly, if I well understand, a little before He came, who took from Dis the great spoil of the first circle,[8] everywhere the deep and terrible valley trembled, so that I judged the universe felt love, by which, as some believe, the world many times is brought to chaos. And at that moment this solid cliff,[9] here and elsewhere, fell in this way."

[Phlegethon, the river of boiling blood,
guarded by centaurs: 12.46–99]

[VIRGIL] "But cast your eyes downward, for we are approaching the river of blood in which boils anyone who with violence harms others."

[POET] *O blind greed and foolish wrath, which so spur us on in the brief life, and in the everlasting then so terribly immerse us!*[10]

[NARRATOR] I saw a wide river bent like a bow, thus inclosing the whole plain, as my escort had told me. And between the base of the slope and the river were running a troop of centaurs, armed with arrows, as they were in the world when they went hunting. Seeing us climbing down, all of them stopped, and three left the company with bows and arrows ready for use.

[NESSUS] One of them shouted from a distance: "To what penalty do you come, you who are moving down the slope?[11] Tell us from where you are; if you do not, I will draw my bow."

[VIRGIL] My teacher said: "We shall reply to Chiron over there when we get near. It was bad that your de-

Poi mi tentò e disse: «Quegli è Nesso,
che morì per la bella Deianira
e fè di sè la vendetta elli stesso.
E quel di mezzo, che al petto si mira,
è il gran Chiron, il qual nodrì Achille;
72   quell' altro è Folo, che fu sì pien d' ira.
Dintorno al fosso vanno a mille a mille,
saettando qual anima si svelle
del sangue più che sua colpa sortille.»
Noi ci appressammo a quelle fiere snelle:
Chiron prese uno strale, e con la cocca
78   fece la barba in dietro a le mascelle.
Quando s' ebbe scoperta la gran bocca,
disse a' compagni: « Siete voi accorti
che quel di retro move ciò ch' el tocca?
Così non soglion fare i piè de' morti.»
E 'l mio buon duca, che già li era al petto,
84   dove le due nature son consorti,
rispuose: «Ben è vivo, e sì soletto
mostrar li mi convien la valle buia:
necessità 'l ci 'nduce, e non diletto.
Tal si partì da cantare alleluia
che mi commise quest' officio novo:
90   non è ladron, nè io anima fuia.
Ma per quella virtù per cu' io movo
li passi miei per sì selvaggia strada,
danne un de' tuoi, a cui noi siamo a provo,
e che ne mostri là dove si guada,
e che porti costui in su la groppa,
96   chè non è spirto che per l' aere vada.»
Chiron si volse in su la destra poppa,
e disse a Nesso: «Torna, e sì li guida,
e fa cansar s' altra schiera v' intoppa.»
Or ci movemmo con la scorta fida
lungo la proda del bollor vermiglio,
102   dove i bolliti facean alte strida.

sire was always so hasty." Then he nudged me, saying:
"That is Nessus, who died for the fair Deianira; and he
himself took revenge for himself. And the one in the
middle, who looks down at his breast, is the great Chiron, who brought up Achilles. That other is Pholus, who
showed such great anger. Along the river are thousands
and thousands of them, shooting any soul which pushes
out of the blood more than its sin prescribes for it."

[NARRATOR] We came near those swift animals. Chiron
took an arrow, and with the nock pushed his beard
backward on his jaws.

[CHIRON] When he had uncovered his huge mouth, he
said to his companions: "Are you aware that the one
behind moves what he touches? The feet of the dead
never do that."

[VIRGIL] And my good guide, who already was at his
breast, where the two natures are united, answered:
"He really is alive, and it is my duty to show him, all by
himself, the dark valley. Necessity brings him here, not
pleasure. A certain person left off singing hallelujahs to
assign me this strange function. He is not a robber, nor
am I a thievish soul. But in the name of that Power
through whom I am passing along so wild a road, give
us one of your company to whom we may keep close,
who will show us where we may ford the river, and who
will carry this man on his back, for he is not a spirit that
moves through the air."

[CHIRON] Chiron turned sharply to the right and said to
Nessus: "About face and guide them, and make any
other troop that meets you turn aside."

[Tyrants in the boiling stream: 12.100–139]

[NARRATOR] Now we went with our faithful[12] escort
along the bank of the scarlet boiling, where those boiled
were raising loud shrieks.

Io vidi gente sotto infino al ciglio;
e 'l gran Centauro disse: «E' son tiranni
che dier nel sangue e ne l'aver di piglio.
Quivi si piangon li spietati danni;
quivi è Alessandro, e Dionisio fero,
108   che fé Cicilia aver dolorosi anni.
E quella fronte c'ha 'l pel così nero,
è Azzolino; e quell'altro ch'è biondo,
è Opizzo da Esti, il qual per vero
fu spento dal figliastro su nel mondo.»
Allor mi volsi al poeta, e quei disse:
114   «Questi ti sia or primo, e io secondo.»
Poco più oltre il Centauro s'affisse
sovr'una gente che 'nfino a la gola
parea che di quel bulicame uscisse.
Mostrocci un'ombra da l'un canto sola,
dicendo: «Colui fesse in grembo a Dio
120   lo cor che 'n su Tamici ancor si cola.»
Poi vidi gente che di fuor del rio
tenean la testa ed ancor tutto il casso;
e di costoro assai riconobb'io.
Così a più a più si facea basso
quel sangue, sì che cocea pur li piedi;
126   e quindi fu del fosso il nostro passo.
«Sì come tu da questa parte vedi
lo bulicame che sempre si scema»
disse 'l Centauro, «voglio che tu credi
che da quest'altra a più a più giù prema
lo fondo suo, infin ch'el si raggiunge
132   ove la tirannia conven che gema.
La divina giustizia di qua punge
quell'Attila che fu flagello in terra,
e Pirro e Sesto; ed in etterno munge
le lagrime, che col bollor diserra,
a Rinier da Corneto, a Rinier Pazzo,
138   che fecero a le strade tanta guerra.»
Poi si rivolse, e ripassossi 'l guazzo.

[NESSUS] I saw people in the stream up to their eye-brows, and the great centaur said: "They are tyrants who seized upon life and property. Here they lament their pitiless wrongdoings. Here is Alexander and the savage Dionysius, who to Sicily caused sorrowful years. And that forehead[13] with such black hair is Ez-zolino; and that blonde one is Obizzo da Este, who indeed was slain by his wicked son up in the world."

[VIRGIL] At this speech I turned to the poet, but he said: "Let Nessus now be first with you, and let me be second."

[NARRATOR] A little farther on, the centaur paused near a group rising out of the boiling stream down to their necks.

[NESSUS] He showed us a shade alone to one side, say-ing: "In God's bosom, this man pierced the heart still honored along the Thames."

[NARRATOR] Then I saw some who were keeping out of the river their heads and their whole chests; many of these I recognized. Thus more and more was that blood lowered, until it cooked only the feet. And there was our crossing of the channel.

[NESSUS] "Just as on this side the boiling stream gets always shallower," said the centaur, "I assure you that on this other side its depth pushes down and down, un-til a place is reached where tyrannical violence fitly groans.[14] Justice divine over there punishes Attila, who was a scourge on earth, and Pyrrhus and Sextus; and everlastingly it milks the tears loosened by boiling from Rinieri da Corneto, from Rinieri de' Pazzi, who on the highways made so many attacks."

[NARRATOR] Then he wheeled and recrossed the stream.

CANTO 13

Non era ancor di là Nesso arrivato,
   quando noi ci mettemmo per un bosco
   che da nessun sentiero era segnato.
Non fronda verde, ma di color fosco;
   non rami schietti, ma nodosi e 'nvolti;
6   non pomi v' eran, ma stecchi con tosco:
non han sì aspri sterpi nè sì folti
   quelle fiere selvagge che in odio hanno
   tra Cecina e Corneto i luoghi colti.
Quivi le brutte Arpie lor nidi fanno,
   che cacciar de le Strofade i Troiani
12   con tristo annunzio di futuro danno.
Ali hanno late, e colli e visi umani,
   piè con artigli, e pennuto il gran ventre;
   fanno lamenti in su li alberi strani.
E 'l buon maestro «Prima che più entre,
   sappi che se' nel secondo girone,»
18   mi cominciò a dire, «e sarai mentre
che tu verrai ne l' orribil sabbione:
   però riguarda ben; sì vederai
   cose che torrien fede al mio sermone.»
Io sentia d' ogni parte trarre guai,
   e non vedea persona che 'l facesse;
24   per ch' io tutto smarrito m' arrestai.
Cred' io ch' ei credette ch' io credesse
   che tante voci uscisser tra quei bronchi
   da gente che per noi si nascondesse.
Però disse 'l maestro: «Se tu tronchi
   qualche fraschetta d' una d' este piante,
30   li pensier c' hai si faran tutti monchi.»
Allor porsi la mano un poco avante,
   e colsi un ramicel da un gran pruno;
   e 'l tronco suo gridò: «Perchè mi schiante?»

CANTO 13

CIRCLE SEVEN, ROUND TWO

[The bleeding trees of the suicides: 13.1–54]

[NARRATOR] Not yet had Nessus reached the other bank when we entered a wood not crossed by a single path. Not green foliage but blackish in color; not smooth twigs but knotty and contorted; not there grew fruits but venomous thorns. Not bushes so prickly nor so thick shelter the forest animals that between Cecina and Corneto hate the cultivated spots. There make their nests the nasty harpies, which drove the Trojans from the Strophades with melancholy proclamation of coming ill. Spreading wings they have, and human necks and faces, and feet with claws; feathers cover their huge bellies. They utter lamentations in the horrid trees.

[VIRGIL] My good teacher said to me: "Before you go farther, let me tell you that you are in the second round, and will be until you come upon the frightful sand. Therefore look closely. In that way you will see things which will raise belief in my narrative."[1]

[NARRATOR] I heard groans uttered on every side but saw no one who could be uttering them. Hence, quite bewildered, I paused. I believe he believed that I believed that so many sounds among those bushes came from people hiding from us.

[VIRGIL] Therefore my teacher said: "If you break some shoots from one of these trees, your present notions will be entirely cut away."

[NARRATOR] Then I stretched out my hand a bit and pulled a little twig from a big thorn tree.

[PETER OF VINEA] And its trunk shouted: "Why do you

Da che fatto fu poi di sangue bruno,
   ricominciò a dir: «Perchè mi scerpi?
36   non hai tu spirto di pietà alcuno?
Uomini fummo, e or siam fatti sterpi:
   ben dovrebb' esser la tua man più pia,
   se state fossimo anime di serpi.»
Come d'un stizzo verde ch'arso sia
   da l'un de' capi, che da l'altro geme
42   e cigola per vento che va via;
sì de la scheggia rotta usciva inseme
   parole e sangue; ond'io lasciai la cima
   cadere, e stetti come l' uom che teme.
«S'egli avesse potuto creder prima»
   rispuose il savio mio, «anima lesa,
48   ciò c'ha veduto pur con la mia rima,
non averebbe in te la man distesa;
   ma la cosa incredibile mi fece
   indurlo ad ovra ch'a me stesso pesa.
Ma dilli chi tu fosti, sì che 'n vece
   d'alcun'ammenda tua fama rinfreschi
54   nel mondo su, dove tornar li lece.»
E 'l tronco: «Sì col dolce dir m'adeschi,
   ch'i' non posso tacere; e voi non gravi
   perch'io un poco a ragionar m'inveschi.
Io son colui che tenni ambo le chiavi
   del cor di Federigo, e che le volsi,
60   serrando e diserrando, sì soavi,
che dal secreto suo quasi ogn'uom tolsi:
   fede portai al glorioso offizio,
   tanto ch'i' ne perde' li sonni e' polsi.
La meretrice che mai da l'ospizio
   di Cesare non torse gli occhi putti,
66   morte comune, de le corti vizio,
infiammò contra me li animi tutti;
   e li 'nfiammati infiammar sì Augusto,
   che' lieti onor tornaro in tristi lutti.

break me?" When it had grown dark with blood, it said further: "Why do you rend me? Don't you have any sense of pity? We were men and now we are thorn trees. Your hand should be more piteous if we were the souls of serpents."

[NARRATOR] As from a green stick of firewood which is burned at one end, and at the other groans and sputters with the air that leaves it, so from the broken twig came out together words and blood. So I let the shoot fall, and stood in terror.

[VIRGIL] "If he had been able to believe earlier, O injured spirit," answered my poet, "what he has heard of only through my verse,[2] he would not have laid a hand on you; but the thing not believed made me push him to an act that weighs upon myself. But tell him who you were, so that by way of compensation he may brighten your fame in the world above, to which he is allowed to return."

[Peter of Vinea, minister to the Emperor
Frederick II: 13.55–78]

[PETER OF VINEA] The tree replied: "So with sweet speech you entice me that I cannot keep silent, and I hope it will not annoy you if I stick to my talking a little.[3] I am he who held both the keys of Frederick's heart, and turned them so gently in locking and unlocking that I removed from his confidence almost every other man. I was faithful to my splendid position, so much so that by it I lost peace and my life.[4] The harlot who never from the court of Caesar removed her whorish eyes, the general death and vice of courts, kindled all spirits against me; and those who were kindled so kindled Augustus that my happy honors changed to sad woes.

L'animo mio, per disdegnoso gusto,
    credendo col morir fuggir disdegno,
72   ingiusto fece me contra me giusto.
Per le nove radici d'esto legno
    vi giuro che già mai non ruppi fede
    al mio signor, che fu d'onor sì degno.
E se di voi alcun nel mondo riede,
    conforti la memoria mia, che giace
78   ancor del colpo che 'nvidia le diede.»
Un poco attese, e poi «Da ch'el si tace»
    disse 'l poeta a me, «non perder l'ora;
    ma parla, e chiedi a lui, se più ti piace.»
Ond' io a lui: «Domandal tu ancora
    di quel che credi ch' a me satisfaccia;
84   ch' i' non potrei, tanta pietà m' accora!»
Perciò ricominciò: «Se l' uom ti faccia
    liberamente ciò che 'l tuo dir priega,
    spirito incarcerato, ancor ti piaccia
di dirne come l' anima si lega
    in questi nocchi; e dinne, se tu puoi,
90   s' alcuna mai di tai membra si spiega.»
Allor soffiò il tronco forte, e poi
    si convertì quel vento in cotal voce:
    «Brievemente sarà risposto a voi.
Quando si parte l' anima feroce
    dal corpo ond' ella stessa s' è disvelta,
96   Minòs la manda a la settima foce.
Cade in la selva, e non l' è parte scelta;
    ma là dove fortuna la balestra,
    quivi germoglia come gran di spelta.
Surge in vermena ed in pianta silvestra:
    l'Arpie, pascendo poi de le sue foglie,
102   fanno dolore, e al dolor fenestra.
Come l' altre verrem per nostre spoglie,
    ma non però ch' alcuna sen rivesta;
    chè non è giusto aver ciò ch' om si toglie.

My spirit, with scornful passion, thinking with death to escape scorn, unjust made me to my just self. By the marvelous roots of this tree I swear to you that never in any way did I break faith with my master, who was so deserving of honor. And if either of you returns to the world, succor my reputation, which is perishing from the blow that Envy gave it."

[*The suicides in Circle Seven, round two: 13.79–108*]

[VIRGIL] After waiting a bit, the poet said to me: "Since he is silent, do not lose your chance, but speak to him and ask, if you wish more."
[DANTE] So I said to him: "You ask him further about what you think will suit me, because I cannot—such compassion wrings my heart."
[VIRGIL] Then he continued: "As you hope the man will be so generous as to do for you what your words ask, imprisoned spirit, have the goodness to tell how the soul is bound in these knotty trunks, and tell us, if you can, whether from these limbs any soul ever frees itself."
[PETER OF VINEA] At once the tree gave a vigorous puff, and then that wind changed into this speech: "I shall answer you briefly. When the violent spirit leaves the body from which she has uprooted herself, Minos dispatches her to the seventh gorge. She falls in the forest, and the spot is not selected for her, but where Fortune slings her, there she germinates like a grain of corn. She rises in a sprout and a forest tree. The harpies, then eating her leaves, give her pain, and to the pain a window.[5] Like the others, we shall go for our bodies.[6] Nevertheless, none of our souls will reclothe herself with one, because it is not just to have what a man takes

Qui le strascineremo, e per la mesta
selva saranno i nostri corpi appesi,
108   ciascuno al prun de l' ombra sua molesta.»
Noi eravamo ancora al tronco attesi,
credendo ch' altro ne volesse dire,
quando noi fummo d' un romor sorpresi,
similemente a colui che venire
sente il porco e la caccia a la sua posta,
114   ch' ode le bestie, e le frasche stormire.
Ed ecco due da la sinistra costa,
nudi e graffiati, fuggendo sì forte,
che de la selva rompieno ogne rosta.
Quel dinanzi: «Or accorri, accorri, morte!»
E l' altro, cui pareva tardar troppo,
120   gridava: «Lano, sì non furo accorte
le gambe tue a le giostre dal Toppo!»
E poi che forse li fallia la lena,
di sè e d' un cespuglio fece un groppo.
Di rietro a loro era la selva piena
di nere cagne, bramose e correnti
126   come veltri ch'uscisser di catena.
In quel che s'appiattò miser li denti,
e quel dilaceraro a brano a brano;
poi sen portar quelle membra dolenti.
Presemi allor la mia scorta per mano,
e menommi al cespuglio che piangea
132   per le rotture sanguinenti invano.
«O Giacomo» dicea «da santo Andrea,
che t'è giovato di me fare schermo?
che colpa ho io de la tua vita rea?»
Quando 'l maestro fu sovr'esso fermo,
disse: «Chi fosti, che per tante punte
138   soffi con sangue doloroso sermo?»
Ed elli a noi: «O anime che giunte
siete a veder lo strazio disonesto
c'ha le mie fronde sì da me disgiunte,

from himself. Here we shall drag them, and in the gloomy forest our bodies will be hung up, each on the thorn tree of its harmful spirit."

[Spendthrifts and another suicide in the forest of Circle Seven: 13.109–151]

[NARRATOR] We still were attentive to the tree, believing it intended to say more, when we were startled by a noise, just as anyone at his station when he hears the boar and the hunt coming, who listens to the animals and the crashing of branches. And we saw two men on the left side, naked and scratched, running so hard as to break through every thicket in the forest.

[LANO] The one in front yelled: "Now run to aid us, run to aid us, Death!"

[JACOPO DA SANTO ANDREA] And the other, who saw that he was far too slow, cried out: "Lano, your legs were not so speedy at the jousts of the Toppo."⁷

[NARRATOR] And, since indeed his wind gave out, he made of himself and of a bush one tangle. Behind them the forest was full of black dogs, eager, and running like greyhounds getting off the leash. Into him who had cowered, they set their teeth, and tore him into little bits; then they carried away those miserable limbs. After that my guide took me by the hand and led me to the bush, which through its bleeding breaks was weeping uselessly.

[A FLORENTINE SUICIDE] It was saying: "O Jacopo da Santo Andrea, how did it help you to make me your shield; how can I be blamed for your guilty life?"

[VIRGIL] When my teacher was standing over it, he said: "Who were you, who by so many wounds breathe out painful speech and blood?"

[A FLORENTINE SUICIDE] He answered us: "O souls who here see the vile mangling which has so taken my

raccoglietele al piè del tristo cesto.
      I' fui de la città che nel Batista
144   mutò il primo padrone; ond'e' per questo
sempre con l'arte sua la farà trista;
      e se non fosse che 'n sul passo d'Arno
      rimane ancor di lui alcuna vista,
que' cittadin che poi la rifondarno
      sovra l' cener che d'Attila rimase,
150   avrebber fatto lavorare indarno.
Io fei giubbetto a me de le mie case.»

twigs away, collect them under my wretched bush. I lived in the city which for the Baptist gave up her first protector;[8] the latter therefore always with his art will make her miserable. And if it were not that at the crossing of Arno there still is some slight likeness of him, those citizens who rebuilt the city on the ashes left by Attila would have labored uselessly.[9]

"I made myself a gibbet from my own mansion."

CANTO 14

Poi che la carità del natio loco
  mi strinse, raunai le fronde sparte,
  e rende' le a colui, ch'era già fioco.
Indi venimmo al fine ove si parte
  lo secondo giron dal terzo, e dove
6   si vede di giustizia orribil arte.
A ben manifestar le cose nove,
  dico che arrivammo ad una landa
  che dal suo letto ogni pianta rimove.
La dolorosa selva l' è ghirlanda
  intorno, come 'l fosso tristo ad essa:
12   quivi fermammo i passi a randa a randa.
Lo spazzo era una rena arida e spessa,
  non d' altra foggia fatta che colei
  che fu da' piè di Caton già soppressa.
O vendetta di Dio, quanto tu dei
  esser temuta da ciascun che legge
18   ciò che fu manifesto a li occhi miei!
D' anime nude vidi molte gregge
  che piangean tutte assai miseramente,
  e parea posta lor diversa legge.
Supin giacea in terra alcuna gente;
  alcuna si sedea tutta raccolta,
24   e altra andava continuamente.
Quella che giva intorno era più molta,
  e quella men cha giacea al tormento,
  ma più al duolo avea la lingua sciolta.
Sovra tutto 'l sabbion, d' un cader lento,
  piovean di foco dilatate falde,
30   come di neve in alpe sanza vento.
Quali Alessandro in quelle parti calde
  d'India vide sopra 'l suo stuolo
  fiamme cadere infino a terra salde;

CANTO 14

CIRCLE SEVEN, ROUND THREE

*[The violent against God, on the burning
sand: 14.1–42]*

[NARRATOR] Since love for my native place coerced me,
I gathered those scattered twigs and gave them to him,
who now was hoarse.

Then we came to the border where the second round
is divided from the third, and where justice shows horrible skill. To set forth properly those wonderful things,
I say that we reached a plain whose soil rejects all trees.
The melancholy forest bounds it, just as the wretched
river bounds the forest.[1] There we halted at the edge.
Its surface was sand, dry and deep, like that long ago
trod by Cato's feet.

[POET] *O punishment by God, how much you should
be feared by every man who reads of what met my eyes!*

[NARRATOR] Many bands of naked souls I saw, all weeping most wretchedly. And plainly different rules were
imposed on them: some on their backs lay on the
ground; some were sitting all hunched up; some were
always moving. The group that moved about was very
large, and smaller was that which lay in torment, but
their tongues were freer to lament. Everywhere upon
the sand, dropping slowly, rained swollen flakes of fire
like snow on a windless mountain. Just as Alexander, in
India's hot regions, saw flames falling on his army and
to the earth in full strength (for which he made his bri-

per ch' ei provide a scalpitar lo suolo
con le sue schiere, acciò che lo vapore
36   mei si stingeva mentre ch' era solo;
tale scendeva l' etternale ardore;
onde la rena s' accendea, com' esca
sotto focile, a doppiar lo dolore.
Sanza riposo mai era la tresca
de le misere mani, or quindi or quinci
42   escotendo da sè l' arsura fresca.
I' cominciai: «Maestro, tu che vinci
tutte le cose, fuor che' demon duri
ch'a l' entrar de la porta incontra uscinci,
chi è quel grande che non par che curi
lo 'ncendio e giace dispettoso e torto,
48   sì che la pioggia non par che 'l marturi?»
E quel medesmo che si fu accorto
ch' io domandava il mio duca di lui,
gridò: «Qual io fui vivo, tal son morto.
Se Giove stanchi 'l suo fabbro da cui
crucciato prese la folgore aguta
54   onde l'ultimo dì percosso fui;
o s'elli stanchi li altri a muta a muta
in Mongibello a la focina negra,
chiamando 'Buon Vulcano, aiuta aiuta!',
sì com'el fece a la pugna di Flegra,
e me saetti con tutta sua forza;
60   non ne potrebbe aver vendetta allegra.»
Allora il duca mio parlò di forza
tanto, ch'i' non l'avea sì forte udito:
«O Capaneo, in ciò che non s'ammorza
la tua superbia, se' tu più punito:
nullo martiro, fuor che la tua rabbia,
66   sarebbe al tuo furor dolor compito.»
Poi si rivolse a me con miglior labbia
dicendo: «Quei fu l'un de' sette regi
ch'assiser Tebe; ed ebbe e par ch'egli abbia

gades tramp on the soil, so that the flame would be more easily quenched while separate), so was falling the everlasting heat. It set the sand on fire like tinder under flint and steel, to double their pain. Without rest, ever, was the waving of their wretched hands, now here, now there, shaking off the fiery flakes last fallen.

[The proud Capaneus defies Jove: 14.43–75]

[DANTE] I said: "Teacher, you who have mastered everything except the strong demons who came out against us when we entered the gate, who is that grand figure who seems not to heed the burning, and lies scornful and irate, so that the downpour does not torture him?"[2] [CAPANEUS] And that very one, who was alert to my asking my guide about him, shouted: "What I was alive, such I am when dead. If Jove should tire out his blacksmith, from whom, in his rage, he took the sharp thunderbolt which on my last day struck me, or if he should tire out the others one after another at the black forge in Mongibello—shouting: 'Good Vulcan, help, help!' as he did in the fight at Phlegra—and if he should shoot me with all his strength, still he could get from it no delightful revenge."
[VIRGIL] Then my guide spoke with such vigor that I had not before heard him so forceful: "O Capaneus, in that your pride is not extinguished, you are punished the more. No torture other than your own fury could be pain matching your rage."
[VIRGIL] Then he turned to me with a milder expression, saying: "He was one of the seven kings who laid siege

Dio in disdegno, e poco par che 'l pregi;
ma, com'io dissi lui, li suoi dispetti
72   sono al suo petto assai debiti fregi.
Or mi vien dietro, e guarda che non metti,
ancor, li piedi ne la rena arsiccia;
ma sempre al bosco tien li piedi stretti.»
Tacendo divenimmo là 've spiccia
fuor de la selva un picciol fiumicello,
78   lo cui rossore ancor mi raccapriccia.
Quale del Bulicame esce ruscello
che parton poi tra lor le peccatrici,
tal per la rena giù sen giva quello.
Lo fondo suo ed ambo le pendici
fatt' era 'n pietra, e' margini da lato;
84   per ch'io m'accorsi che 'l passo era lici.
«Tra tutto l'altro ch'i' t'ho dimostrato,
poscia che noi entrammo per la porta
lo cui sogliare a nessuno è negato,
cosa non fu da li tuoi occhi scorta
notabile come 'l presente rio,
90   che sovra sé tutte fiammelle ammorta.»
Queste parole fuor del duca mio;
per ch'io 'l pregai che mi largisse il pasto
di cui largito m'avea il disio.
«In mezzo mar siede un paese guasto»
diss' elli allora, «che s' appella Creta,
96   sotto 'l cui rege fu già il mondo casto.
Una montagna v' è che già fu lieta
d' acqua e di fronde, che si chiamò Ida:
or è diserta come cosa vieta.
Rea la scelse già per cuna fida
del suo figliuolo, e per celarlo meglio,
102   quando piangea, vi facea far le grida.
Dentro dal monte sta dritto un gran veglio,
che tien volte le spalle inver Damiata
e Roma guarda come suo speglio.

to Thebes, and he held God in contempt and still does, and little does he value him.³ But as I said, his signs of contempt are ornaments well suited to his breast.

"Now follow me, and be careful not to put your feet at all on the burning sand, but keep your feet always close to the woodland."

[*The rivers of Hell; the Cretan statue: 14.76–120*]

[NARRATOR] In silence we came to a place where a little creek flows out of the forest; its redness still makes my hair stand on end. As from Bulicame comes out a little stream that the sinful women then share among them, so this was running off through the sand. Its bottom and both its sloping sides were of rock, as were the banks along it. So I understood that the passageway was there.

[VIRGIL] "Among all the things I have showed you since we came through the gate whose threshold is refused to no one, your eyes have beheld nothing so much worth seeing as the stream here, which puts out all the little flames above itself."

[NARRATOR] These were my guide's words. Because of them, I begged him to make me a gift of food, since he had given me longing for it.

[VIRGIL] He then went on: "In the midst of the sea lies a country laid waste, which is named Crete, under whose king long ago the world was chaste. A mountain stands there, which in the past was pleasant with water and with leaves, named Ida. Now it is in solitude and forgotten.⁴ Rhea chose it in ancient days as the trusty cradle of her son, and to hide him better, when he cried she caused loud clangor there. On⁵ the mountain stands erect a huge old man, who keeps his back toward Damiata and looks at Rome as his mirror. His head is wrought

La sua testa è di fino oro formata,
  e puro argento son le braccia e il petto,
108   poi è di rame infino a la forcata;
da indi in giuso è tutto ferro eletto,
  salvo che 'l destro piede è terra cotta;
  e sta 'n su quel, più che 'n su l' altro, eretto.
Ciascuna parte, fuor che l' oro, è rotta
  d' una fessura che lagrime goccia,
114   le quali, accolte, foran quella grotta.
Lor corso in questa valle si diroccia:
  fanno Acheronte, Stige e Flegetonta;
  poi sen van giù per questa stretta doccia
infin, là ove più non si dismonta,
  fanno Cocito; e qual sia quello stagno,
120   tu lo vedrai; però qui non si conta.»
E io a lui: «Se 'l presente rigagno
  si diriva così dal nostro mondo,
  perchè ci appar pur a questo vivagno?»
Ed elli a me: «Tu sai che 'l luogo è tondo;
  e tutto che tu sie venuto molto,
126   pur a sinistra, giù calando al fondo,
non se' ancor per tutto il cerchio volto;
  per che, se cosa n' apparisce nova,
  non de' addur maraviglia al tuo volto.»
E io ancor: «Maestro, ove si trova
  Flegetonta e Letè? chè de l' un taci,
132   e l' altro di' che si fa d' esta piova.»
«In tutte tue question certo mi piaci»
  rispuose; «ma 'l bollor de l' acqua rossa
  dovea ben solver l' una che tu faci.
Letè vedrai, ma fuor di questa fossa,
  là dove vanno l'anime a lavarsi
138   quando la colpa pentuta è rimossa.»
Poi disse: «Omai è tempo da scostarsi
  dal bosco; fa che di rietro a me vegne:
  li margini fan via, che non son arsi,
  e sopra loro ogni vapor si spegne.»

of fine gold, and pure silver are his arms and his chest; then he is copper down to his crotch; below that, he is all selected iron, except that his right foot is terra cotta, and he stands up on that rather than on the other. Every part, except the gold, is flawed by a crack from which tears drip; these, when they have gathered together, pierce that mountain.[6] They flow down the rocks into this valley; they form Acheron, Styx and Phlegethon. Then they go on down in this narrow channel until, when there is no more descent, they form Cocytus. And what that lake is you will see; so here I do not tell about it."

[The shape of Hell; more on the rivers: 14.121–142]

[DANTE] And I said to him: "If this little stream before us flows in this way from our world, why do we see it just at this margin?"[7]

[VIRGIL] And he answered: "You know that the place is round; and even though you have come far, always to the left, going down toward the bottom, not yet have you moved around the full circle. Hence if anything new appears to you, it should not bring to your face any sign of wonder."

[DANTE] And I kept on: "Teacher, where are Phlegethon and Lethe, because of the latter you say nothing, and the other you say is formed from this rain."[8]

[VIRGIL] "With all your questions you surely please me," he answered, "but the red water's boiling should answer the first you ask. Lethe you will see, but outside this pit, in the place where the souls go to be washed when sin repented is taken away."[9]

Then he said: "Now it is time to leave this wood. Come behind me. The banks of the stream give passage, since they are not fiery hot, and above them every flame disappears."

CANTO 15

Ora cen porta l'un de' duri margini;
  e 'l fummo del ruscel di sopra aduggia,
  sì che dal foco salva l'acqua e li argini.
Quali Fiamminghi tra Guizzante e Bruggia,
  temendo il fiotto che 'nver lor s'avventa,
6   fanno lo schermo perché 'l mar si fuggia;
e quali Padovan lungo la Brenta,
  per difender lor ville e lor castelli,
  anzi che Chiarentana il caldo senta;
a tale imagine eran fatti quelli,
  tutto che né sì alti né sì grossi,
12   qual che si fosse, lo maestro felli.
Già eravam da la selva rimossi
  tanto, ch'i' non avrei visto dov'era,
  perch'io in dietro rivolto mi fossi,
quando incontrammo d'anime una schiera
  che venian lungo l'argine, e ciascuna
18   ci riguardava come suol da sera
guardare uno altro sotto nuova luna;
  e sì ver noi aguzzavan le ciglia
  come 'l vecchio sartor fa ne la cruna.
Così adocchiato da cotal famiglia,
  fui conosciuto da un che mi prese
24   per lo lembo e gridò: «Qual maraviglia!»
E io, quando 'l suo braccio a me distese,
  ficcai li occhi per lo cotto aspetto,
  sì che 'l viso abbruciato non difese
la conoscenza sua al mio intelletto;
  e chinando la mia a la sua faccia,
30   rispuosi: «Siete voi qui, ser Brunetto?»
E quelli: «O figliuol mio, non ti dispiaccia
  se Brunetto Latino un poco teco
  ritorna in dietro e lascia andar la traccia.»

CANTO 15

CIRCLE SEVEN, ROUND THREE

[From the dike the sodomites are seen: 15.1–21]

[NARRATOR] Now one of the solid margins carries us on, and the steam from the brook rises to protect the water and the dikes from the fire. Just as the Flemings between Wissant and Bruges, fearing the tide that moves upon them, provide defense to repel the sea, and as the Paduans do along the Brenta, to protect their farms and towns, before Chiarentana feels heat—in that way these were made, though not so high nor so thick did their builder make them, whoever he was. We already were so far from the forest that I would not have seen where it was even though I had turned around,[1] when we met a troop of shades moving alongside the dike, and each one stared at us as in the evening one man stares at another under a new moon. So upon us they strained their eyes, as does an old tailor upon his needle's eye.

[Brunetto Latini, author: 15.22–60]

[BRUNETTO LATINI] So eyed by such a group, I was recognized by one of them, who seized me by the hem of my gown and exclaimed: "How strange!"
[DANTE] And I, when he stretched out his arm to me, so fixed my eyes on his cooked face that his scorched visage did not bar my mind against recognition, so, lowering my face toward his,[2] I answered: "Are you here, Ser Brunetto?"
[BRUNETTO] And he replied: "O my son, do not be vexed if Brunetto Latini walks back a little with you and lets his flock pass on."

I' dissi lui: «Quanto posso, ven preco;
e se volete che con voi m' asseggia,
36   faròl, se piace a costui che vo seco.»
«O figliuol,» disse, «qual di questa greggia
s' arresta punto, giace poi cent' anni
sanz' arrostarsi quando 'l foco il feggia.
Però va oltre: i' ti verrò a' panni;
e poi rigiugnerò la mia masnada,
42   che va piangendo i suoi etterni danni.»
I' non osava scender de la strada
per andar par di lui; ma 'l capo chino
tenea com' uom che reverente vada.
El cominciò «Qual fortuna o destino
anzi l' ultimo dì qua giù ti mena?
48   e chi è questi che mostra 'l cammino?»
«Là su di sopra in la vita serena»
rispuos' io lui «mi smarri' in una valle,
avanti che l' età mia fosse piena.
Pur ier mattina le volsi le spalle:
questi m' apparve, tornand' io in quella,
54   e reducemi a ca per questo calle.»
Ed elli a me: «Se tu segui tua stella,
non puoi fallire a glorioso porto,
se ben m' accorsi ne la vita bella;
e s' io non fossi sì per tempo morto,
veggendo il cielo a te così benigno,
60   dato t' avrei a l' opera conforto.
Ma quello ingrato popolo maligno
che discese di Fiesole ab antico,
e tiene ancor del monte e del macigno,
ti si farà, per tuo ben far, nemico:
ed è ragion, chè tra li lazzi sorbi
66   si disconvien fruttare il dolce fico.
Vecchia fama nel mondo li chiama orbi;
gent' è avara, invidiosa e superba:
dai lor costumi fa che tu ti forbi.

[DANTE] I said to him: "To my utmost I beg you to do so, and if you want me to sit down with you, I shall do so, if it suits this one here whom I am with."

[BRUNETTO] "O son," he said, "whoever of this herd pauses at all, then lies motionless a hundred years without brushing himself when the fire strikes him. So move on; I shall come along beside you, and then join my group, which is bewailing its everlasting punishments."

[NARRATOR] I dared not go down from my path to walk on a level with him, but I kept my head lowered, showing my respect.

[BRUNETTO] Then he said: "What fortune or fate³ brings you here before your final day? And who is this man who is showing you the road?"

[DANTE] "Up there above in the quiet life," I replied to him, "I was lost on a lowland, before my years were complete.⁴ Only yesterday morning I turned my back on it. This man appeared to me as I was retreating to that lowland, and is leading me to my dwelling by this path."

[BRUNETTO] And he said to me: "If you follow your star, you cannot come short of a haven of glory, if I judged rightly in the pleasant life. And if I had not died so early, I should, because I saw the heavens so propitious to you, have encouraged you in your work."

[Brunetto Latini on the wickedness of Florence and on Dante's personal troubles: 15.61–99]

[BRUNETTO] "But that ungrateful malicious people, which long ago came down from Fiesole, and still smacks of mountain and rock, will become your enemy because of your good works; and that is fitting, since the sweet fig is not wont to bear fruit among the bitter sorbs. Old report in the world calls them blind; it is a people greedy, envious, and proud. From their manners,

La tua fortuna tanto onor ti serba,
 che l' una parte e l' altra avranno fame
72 di te; ma lungi fia dal becco l' erba.
Faccian le bestie fiesolane strame
 di lor medesme, e non tocchin la pianta,
 s'alcuna surge ancora in lor letame
in cui riviva la sementa santa
 di que' Roman che vi rimaser quando
78 fu fatto il nido di malizia tanta.»
«Se fosse tutto pieno il mio dimando»
 rispuosi lui, «voi non sareste ancora
 de l'umana natura posto in bando;
ché 'n la mente m'è fitta, e or m'accora,
 la cara e buona imagine paterna
84 di voi quando nel mondo ad ora ad ora
m'insegnavate come l'uom s'etterna:
 e quant'io l'abbia in grado, mentr'io vivo
 convien che ne la mia lingua si scerna.
Ciò che narrate di mio corso scrivo,
 e serbolo a chiosar con altro testo
90 a donna che saprà, s'a lei arrivo.
Tanto vogl'io che vi sia manifesto,
 pur che mia coscienza non mi garra,
 ch'a la Fortuna, come vuol, son presto.
Non è nuova a li orecchi miei tale arra:
 però giri Fortuna la sua rota
96 come le piace, e 'l villan la sua marra.»
Lo mio maestro allora in su la gota
 destra si volse in dietro, e riguardommi;
 poi disse: «Bene ascolta chi la nota.»
Né per tanto di men parlando vommi
 con ser Brunetto, e dimando chi sono
102 li suoi compagni più noti e più sommi.
Ed elli a me: «Saper d'alcuno è buono;
 de li altri fia laudabile tacerci,
 chè 'l tempo saria corto a tanto suono.

keep yourself unspotted. Your fortune saves for you such high honor that both parties will hunger for you, but far from the goat will be the grass. Let the beasts of Fiesole feed themselves on stable litter,[5] and not touch the plant, if any such grows in their dungheap, in which is revived the holy seed of those Romans left there when the nest of such great malice was made."[6]

[DANTE] "If my desire were fulfilled," I answered him, "not yet would you be banished from man's nature;[7] because in my memory is fixed, and now pierces my heart, your dear and good paternal appearance when, in the world, time after time you taught me how man gains eternal fame; and my gratitude for it must as long as I live be evident in my speech. What you tell of my course I am writing down,[8] and I keep it to be commented on, with another text, by a lady who will know how,[9] when I reach her. I wish it to be evident to you that—so long as my conscience does not distress me—for Fortune, however she decrees, I am prepared. Such a prediction is not new to my ears. So let Fortune turn her wheel as she likes, and the farmer use his hoe."

[VIRGIL] At once my teacher, swinging to the right, turned around and looked at me, then said: "He listens well who notes it down."

[Other sodomites, and Brunetto Latini's departure: 15.100–124]

[NARRATOR] Nonetheless I keep on talking with Ser Brunetto, and ask who among his companions are more famous and important.[10]

[BRUNETTO] He replies: "To learn of some of them is proper; about the others, to keep silent will be praiseworthy, because our time will be too short for so much

In somma sappi che tutti fur cherci
  e litterati grandi e di gran fama,
108   d'un peccato medesmo al mondo lerci.
Priscian sen va con quella turba grama,
  e Francesco d'Accorso anche; e vedervi,
  s'avessi avuto di tal tigna brama,
colui potei che dal servo de' servi
  fu trasmutato d'Arno in Bacchiglione,
114   dove lasciò li mal protesi nervi.
Di più direi; ma 'l venire e 'l sermone
  più lungo esser non può, però ch'i' veggio
  là surger novo fummo del sabbione.
Gente vien con la quale esser non deggio:
  sieti raccomandato il mio Tesoro
120   nel qual io vivo ancora, e più non cheggio.»
Poi si rivolse, e parve di coloro
  che corrono a Verona il drappo verde
  per la campagna; e parve di costoro
quelli che vince, non colui che perde.

talk. In general, they all were clerics and men of great learning and high reputation, and in the world all foul with one and the same offense. Priscian is with that wretched company, and Francesco d'Accorso too. And if you have any wish for such filth, you can see him there who by the Servant of Servants was transferred from the Arno to the Bacchiglione, where he left the sinews he had vilely used. I should like to say more, but my coming and my speech cannot be longer, because I see new dust there rising from the sand. People are coming with whom I ought not to be. Let me commend to you my *Treasure*,[11] in which I still live, and I ask no more."
[NARRATOR] Then he turned, and he looked like one of those who in the field at Verona run for the green cloth; and he looked like the one who wins, and not the one who loses.

CANTO 16

Già era in loco onde s'udia 'l rimbombo
de l'acqua che cadea ne l'altro giro,
simile a quel che l'arnie fanno rombo;
quando tre ombre insieme si partiro,
correndo, d'una torma che passava
6   sotto la pioggia de l'aspro martiro.
Venian ver noi, e ciascuna gridava:
«Sostati tu ch'a l'abito ne sembri
esser alcun di nostra terra prava.»
Ahimè, che piaghe vidi ne' lor membri,
ricenti e vecchie, da le fiamme incese!
12   Ancor men duol pur ch'i' me ne rimembri.
A le lor grida il mio dottor s'attese;
volse 'l viso ver me, e disse: «Aspetta:
a costor si vuol essere cortese.
E se non fosse il foco che saetta
la natura del loco, i' dicerei
18   che meglio stesse a te che a lor la fretta.»
Ricominciar, come noi restammo, ei
l'antico verso; e quando a noi fuor giunti,
fenno una rota di sè tutti e trei.
Qual sogliono i campion far nudi e unti,
avvisando lor presa e lor vantaggio,
24   prima che sien tra lor battuti e punti,
così rotando, ciascuno il visaggio
drizzava a me, sì che 'ntra loro il collo
faceva e i piè continuo viaggio.
E «Se miseria d' esto loco sollo
rende in dispetto noi e nostri prieghi»
30   cominciò l' uno «e 'l tinto aspetto e brollo,
la fama nostra il tuo animo pieghi
a dirne chi tu se', che i vivi piedi
così sicuro per lo 'nferno freghi.

CANTO 16

CIRCLE SEVEN, ROUND THREE, *cont.*

[Three worthy Florentines: 16.1–63]

[NARRATOR] Already I had reached a place where I heard the boom of water falling into the circle beyond, like the humming made by beehives. Just then three shades together left, on the run, a group that was moving along under the rain of their harsh punishment.

[THREE FLORENTINE SODOMITES] They came toward us, and each one was shouting: "Halt, you who by your dress we take to be from our wicked city."

[NARRATOR] Alas, what wounds, new and old, I saw on their bodies, burned by the flames! I still feel pain when only I remember it. To their shouts my teacher listened.

[VIRGIL] He turned his face to me, saying: "Wait, to these you must be courteous. Indeed if it were not for the fire that the nature of the place shoots out, I should say that haste was more suited to you than to them."[1]

[NARRATOR] They repeated, as we stopped, their previous shout.[2] And when they reached us, the three formed themselves into one wheel. Like athletes stripped and oiled, intent on getting an advantageous grip, before they strike and punch each other, as they so wheeled around, each one kept his face turned toward me, so that their necks as well as their feet were constantly moving.[3]

[JACOPO RUSTICUCCI] And one said:[4] "Even if the misery of this place with its shifting sand, and our appearance, burned and stripped, bring contempt on us and on our requests, yet permit our fame to divert your rancor enough to let you tell us who you are, who so boldly set down[5] your living feet in Hell. This man, in whose

Questi, l' orme di cui pestar mi vedi,
    tutto che nudo e dipelato vada,
36   fu di grado maggior che tu non credi.
Nepote fu de la buona Gualdrada;
    Guido Guerra ebbe nome, ed in sua vita
    fece col senno assai e con la spada.
L' altro, ch' appresso me la rena trita,
    è Tegghiaio Aldobrandi, la cui voce
42   nel mondo su dovria esser gradita.
E io, che posto son con loro in croce,
    Iacopo Rusticucci fui; e certo
    la fiera moglie più ch' altro mi nuoce.»
S' i' fossi stato dal foco coperto,
    gittato mi sarei tra lor di sotto,
48   e credo che 'l dottor l' avria sofferto;
ma perch' io mi sarei bruciato e cotto,
    vinse paura la mia buona voglia
    che di loro abbracciar mi facea ghiotto.
Poi cominciai: «Non dispetto, ma doglia
    la vostra condizion dentro mi fisse,
54   tanta che tardi tutta si dispoglia,
tosto che questo mio segnor mi disse
    parole per le quali i' mi pensai
    che qual voi siete, tal gente venisse.
Di vostra terra sono, e sempre mai
    l' ovra di voi e li onorati nomi
60   con affezion ritrassi e ascoltai.
Lascio lo fele e vo per dolci pomi
    promessi a me per lo verace duca;
    ma infino al centro pria convien ch' i' tomi.»
«Se lungamente l' anima conduca
    le membra tue» rispuose quelli ancora,
66   «e se la fama tua dopo te luca,
cortesia e valor dì se dimora
    ne la nostra città sì come suole,
    o se del tutto se n' è gita fora;

tracks I am treading, though he is naked and singed, was of higher rank than you think; he was the grandson of the good Gualdrada; Guido Guerra was his name, and in life he accomplished much with his brain and with his sword. The other, who treads the sand behind me, is Tegghiaio Aldobrandi, whose reputation in the world above should be pleasing. And I, who am in torment with them, was Jacopo Rusticucci; and certainly my savage wife more than any other injures me."

[NARRATOR] If I had been protected from the fire, I should have thrown myself down among them, and I believe my instructor would have allowed it. But because I should be burned and roasted, fear conquered my affection, which made me eager to embrace them.

[DANTE] Then I said: "Not contempt but sorrow, your condition impressed upon me—sorrow so great that it will be slow to vanish wholly—as soon as my master here spoke words that led me to suppose that your sort of persons was coming. From your city I am, and always your deeds and your honored names I have spoken and heard of with devotion. I turn from gall and seek sweet fruits promised me by my truthful guide. But first down to the center I must fall."[6]

[Morals in Florence: 16.64–90]

[TEGGHIAIO ALDOBRANDI] "As you hope that your soul will long control your limbs," he further replied, "and that your fame will shine after you, tell us whether, in our city, courtesy and courage dwell, as once they did, or whether they have wholly gone; because Guglielmo

ché Guiglielmo Borsiere, il qual si duole
con noi per poco, e va là coi compagni,
72　assai ne cruccia con le sue parole.»
«La gente nova e i subiti guadagni
orgoglio e dismisura han generata,
Fiorenza, in te, sì che tu già ten piagni.»
Così gridai con la faccia levata;
e i tre, che ciò inteser per risposta,
78　guardar l'un l'altro com'al ver si guata.
«Se l'altre volte sì poco ti costa»
rispuoser tutti «il satisfare altrui,
felice te se sì parli a tua posta!
Però, se campi d'esti luoghi bui
e torni a riveder le belle stelle,
84　quando ti gioverà dicere 'I' fui',
fa che di noi a la gente favelle.»
Indi rupper la rota, ed a fuggirsi
ali sembiar le gambe loro snelle.
Un amen non saria potuto dirsi
tosto così, com'e' furo spariti;
90　per che al maestro parve di partirsi.
Io lo seguiva, e poco eravam iti,
che 'l suon de l'acqua n'era sì vicino,
che per parlar saremmo a pena uditi.
Come quel fiume c'ha proprio cammino
prima da monte Veso inver levante,
96　da la sinistra costa d'Apennino,
che si chiama Acquaqueta suso, avante
che si divalli giù nel basso letto,
e a Forlì di quel nome è vacante,
rimbomba là sovra San Benedetto
de l'Alpe, per cadere ad una scesa
102　dove dovria per mille esser recetto;
così, giù d'una ripa discoscesa,
trovammo risonar quell'acqua tinta,
sì che 'n poc'ora avria l'orecchia offesa.

Borsiere, who of late is suffering with us, and is over there with our companions, greatly disturbed us with his words."

[DANTE] "Men newly rich and speedy profits have begotten in you, Florence, pride and extravagance, so that now you are weeping for it." So I shouted with raised face.

[NARRATOR] And the three, who took this as an answer, stared at each other as men stare at truth.

[THREE FLORENTINE SODOMITES] "If at other times to satisfy others costs you so little," they all replied, "happy are you if so you speak when you wish. Hence, as you hope to escape from these dark regions and return to see the beautiful stars again, when you are taking pleasure in saying 'I was,' mention us to people."

[NARRATOR] Then they broke their wheel, and for getting away, their swift legs seemed wings. "Amen" could not be said so quickly as they disappeared. So then my teacher had us move on.

[*The cliff limiting Circle Seven, above
Malebolge: 16.91–114*]

[NARRATOR] I followed him, and not far did we go before the noise of the water was so close to us that, when speaking, we scarcely could be heard. Just as that river which is the first to have its own channel from Mount Veso to the east,[7] on the left slope of the Apennines— which is named Acquaqueta above, before going down into its lower bed, but at Forlì has already lost that name—roars above San Benedetto of the Alps by falling with one descent at a spot where there would be space for a thousand, so down from a rugged cliff that dark water we heard booming so that in a short time it would

Io avea una corda intorno cinta,
e con essa pensai alcuna volta
108   prender la lonza a la pelle dipinta.
Poscia che l'ebbi tutta da me sciolta,
sì come 'l duca m'avea comandato,
porsila a lui aggroppata e ravvolta.
Ond' ei si volse inver lo destro lato,
e alquanto di lunge da la sponda
114   la gittò giuso in quell' alto burrato.
«E' pur convien che novità risponda»
dicea fra me medesmo «al novo cenno
che 'l maestro con l' occhio sì seconda.»
Ahi quanto cauti gli uomini esser dienno
presso a color che non veggion pur l' ovra,
120   ma per entro i pensier miran col senno!
El disse a me: «Tosto verrà di sovra
ciò ch' io attendo e che il tuo pensier sogna:
tosto convien ch' al tuo viso si scovra.»
Sempre a quel ver c' ha faccia di menzogna
de' l' uom chiuder le labbra fin ch' el pote,
126   però che sanza colpa fa vergogna:
ma qui tacer nol posso; e per le note
di questa comedìa, lettor, ti giuro,
s' elle non sien di lunga grazia vote,
ch' i' vidi per quell' aere grosso e scuro
venir notando una figura in suso,
132   maravigliosa ad ogni cor sicuro,
sì come torna colui che va giuso
talora a solver l' ancora ch' aggrappa
o scoglio o altro che nel mare è chiuso,
che 'n su si stende, e da piè si rattrappa.

have injured our ears. I had a rope wound around me, with which once I planned to catch the leopardess with the spotted hide.[8] As soon as I had quite unfastened it, as my guide instructed me, I gave it to him bunched up and coiled. Then he turned to the right and threw it down, rather far from the edge, into that deep pit.

[*Geryon, the incredible flying
monster: 16.115–136*]

[DANTE] "Some strange thing will have to answer," I said to myself, "to this strange signal that my teacher so follows with his eye."

[POET] *Ah, how cautious men ought to be with those who see not merely acts, but also wisely look into their thoughts!*

[VIRGIL] He said to me: "Quickly what I am waiting for, and you are imagining, will come up; quickly it must be offered to your sight."

[NARRATOR] Always to the truth which has a lie's appearance, a man ought to shut his lips with all his might, since without fault he incurs disgrace. But in this matter I cannot keep silence. So by the words of this *Comedy*, reader, as I hope they will not fail of long-continued favor, I swear to you that I saw through that thick and murky air a form come swimming up, terrifying to the firmest heart, just as a man comes up again who goes down perhaps to loosen an anchor, which has caught on a rock or something or other hidden in the sea, for he stretches upward and gathers up himself from below.

CANTO 17

«Ecco la fiera con la coda aguzza,
    che passa i monti, e rompe i muri e l' armi;
    ecco colei che tutto 'l mondo appuzza!»
Sì cominciò lo mio duca a parlarmi;
    e accennolle che venisse a proda
6   vicino al fin de' passeggiati marmi.
E quella sozza imagine di froda
    sen venne, e arrivò la testa e 'l busto,
    ma 'n su la riva non trasse la coda.
La faccia sua era faccia d' uom giusto,
    tanto benigna avea di fuor la pelle,
12   e d' un serpente tutto l' altro fusto:
due branche avea pilose infin l' ascelle;
    lo dosso e 'l petto e ambedue le coste
    dipinti avea di nodi e di rotelle.
Con più color, sommesse e sopraposte
    non fer mai drappi Tartari nè Turchi,
18   nè fuor tai tele per Aragne imposte.
Come tal volta stanno a riva i burchi,
    che parte sono in acqua e parte in terra,
    e come là tra li Tedeschi lurchi
lo bivero s' assetta a far sua guerra,
    così la fiera pessima si stava
24   su l' orlo che, di pietra, il sabbion serra.
Nel vano tutta sua coda guizzava,
    torcendo in su la venenosa forca,
    ch' a guisa di scorpion la punta armava.
Lo duca disse: «Or convien che si torca
    la nostra via un poco insino a quella
30   bestia malvagia che colà si corca.»
Però scendemmo a la destra mammella,
    e diece passi femmo in su lo stremo,
    per ben cessar la rena e la fiammella.

CANTO 17

CIRCLE SEVEN, ROUND THREE, *cont.*
DESCENT TO CIRCLE EIGHT

[Geryon, the Image of Fraud: 17.1–30]

[VIRGIL] "Now see the monster with the sharp tail, which crosses the mountains and breaks walls and armies; now see what makes the whole world stink."
[NARRATOR] Thus my guide spoke to me, and he beckoned to it to come ashore near the end of the marble passageways.[1] So that filthy image of fraud[2] came forward and placed its head and its chest, but did not drag its tail upon the bank. Its face was the face of a just man—so far its outside showed good will—but all the rest of its body was that of a serpent. Its two paws were hairy to the armpits.[3] Its back and its breast and both its sides were ornamented with knots and rosettes. More colors never were woven and embroidered[4] in Turkish or Tartar fabrics,[5] nor were such webs ever laid out by Arachne. As sometimes skiffs are beached, so as to be partly in the water and partly on the land, and as up among the sottish Germans the beaver places itself to hunt, so the frightful beast rested on the border of rock that surrounds the sand. In the empty air its long tail was vibrating, twisting upward the poisonous fork which is a weapon for its point, like a scorpion's.
[VIRGIL] My guide said: "Now we need to bend our way a bit to that obnoxious beast which has come to rest over there."

[Usurers in the Seventh Circle: 17.31–75]

[NARRATOR] Then we went down on the right side and took ten steps along the edge, in order wholly to avoid

E quando noi a lei venuti semo,
    poco più oltre veggio in su la rena
36   gente seder propinqua al luogo scemo.
Quivi 'l maestro «Acciò che tutta piena
    esperienza d' esto giron porti»
    mi disse, «va, e vedi la lor mena.
Li tuoi ragionamenti sian là corti:
    mentre che torni, parlerò con questa,
42   che ne conceda i suoi omeri forti.»
Così ancor su per la strema testa
    di quel settimo cerchio tutto solo
    andai, dove sedea la gente mesta.
Per gli occhi fora scoppiava lor duolo;
    di qua, di là soccorrien con le mani
48   quando a' vapori, e quando al caldo suolo:
non altrimenti fan di state i cani
    or col ceffo, or col piè, quando son morsi
    o da pulci o da mosche o da tafani.
Poi che nel viso a certi li occhi porsi,
    ne' quali il doloroso foco casca,
54   non ne conobbi alcun; ma io m' accorsi
che dal collo a ciascun pendea una tasca
    ch'avea certo colore e certo segno,
    e quindi par che 'l loro occhio si pasca.
E com'io riguardando tra lor vegno,
    in una borsa gialla vidi azzurro
60   che d'un leone avea faccia e contegno.
Poi, procedendo di mio sguardo il curro,
    vidine un'altra come sangue rossa,
    mostrando un'oca bianca più che burro.
E un che d'una scrofa azzurra e grossa
    segnato avea lo suo sacchetto bianco,
66   mi disse: «Che fai tu in questa fossa?
Or te ne va; e perché se' vivo anco,
    sappi che 'l mio vicin Vitaliano
    sederà qui dal mio sinistro fianco.

the sand and the flame. And when we had reached the beast, a little farther on I saw people sitting on the sand near the Circle's border.[6]

[VIRGIL] Here my teacher said to me: "So that you may get complete experience of this round, go and see their condition. Let your talk there be brief. Until you return, I shall speak with this creature, to get it to lend us its strong back."

[NARRATOR] So still along the outmost edge of that seventh circle, I went all alone to the place where the sad people were sitting. Through their eyes their suffering was bursting out. On this side, on that, they defended themselves with their hands, sometimes against the burning air, sometimes against the hot earth. Not differently act dogs in summer, now with their noses, now with their paws, when they are bitten by fleas or flies or horseflies. After I had stared at the faces of a number of those on whom the painful fire was falling, I did not recognize one, but I observed that from the neck of each was hanging a pouch, which had a special color and a special mark, and on those their eyes were feeding. And as I was observing there, on a yellow bag I saw in blue what had the form and likeness of a lion. Then letting my gaze run on, I saw another bag red as blood, displaying a goose whiter than butter.

[A PADUAN USURER] And one soul, whose little white sack was painted with a blue and pregnant sow, said to me: "What are you doing in this ditch? Now be off. And because you are still alive, let me tell you that my neighbor Vitaliano will sit here on my left side. I am a Paduan

Con questi fiorentin son padovano:
spesse fiate m'intronan gli orecchi,
72   gridando: 'Vegna il cavalier sovrano,
che recherà la tasca coi tre becchi!'»
Qui distorse la bocca e di fuor trasse
la lingua come bue che 'l naso lecchi.
E io, temendo no 'l più star crucciasse
lui che di poco star m'avea ammonito,
78   torna'mi indietro da l'anime lasse.
Trova' il duca mio ch'era salito
già su la groppa del fiero animale,
e disse a me: «Or sie forte e ardito.
Omai si scende per sì fatte scale:
monta dinanzi, ch'i' voglio esser mezzo,
84   sì che la coda non possa far male.»
Qual è colui che sì presso ha 'l riprezzo
de la quartana, c'ha già l'unghie smorte,
e triema tutto pur guardando il rezzo,
tal divenn'io a le parole porte;
ma vergogna mi fé le sue minacce,
90   che innanzi a buon segnor fa servo forte.
I' m'assettai in su quelle spallacce:
sì volli dir, ma la voce non venne
com'io credetti: «Fa che tu m'abbracce.»
Ma esso, ch'altra volta mi sovvenne
ad altro forse, tosto ch'io montai
96   con le braccia m'avvinse e mi sostenne;
e disse: «Gerion, moviti omai:
le rote larghe, e lo scender sia poco:
pensa la nova soma che tu hai.»
Come la navicella esce di loco
in dietro in dietro, sì quindi si tolse;
102   e poi ch'al tutto si sentì a gioco,
là 'v'era il petto, la coda rivolse,
e quella tesa, come anguilla, mosse,
e con le branche l'aere a sé raccolse.

among these Florentines. Often they thunder in my ears with their shout: 'Welcome to the ruling knight, who will bring the pouch with the three goats.' "

[NARRATOR] Then he twisted his mouth and stuck his tongue out, like an ox licking its nose. And I, fearing that longer stay might irritate him who had enjoined short stay, went back to him from those afflicted souls.

[*The aerial ride on Geryon's back: 17.76–136*]

[NARRATOR] I found my guide already had climbed on the croup of the dreadful animal.

[VIRGIL] To me he said: "Now be strong and brave. This time we go down by stairs of this sort. Get on in front, because I am going to be middleman, so that the tail can do no harm."

[NARRATOR] When a man is so near the shivering fit of the quartan fever that his nails are already white, he trembles all over if he merely looks at the shade. So I did when he spoke those words, but shame threatened me, which in a good master's presence makes a servant strong. I seated myself on that great back.

[DANTE] I tried to say, but speech did not come as I intended: "Put your arms around me."

[NARRATOR] But he who had supported me at other times and in other trouble, as soon as I was mounted, threw his arms around me and held me on.

[VIRGIL] Then he said: "Geryon, now start, but make your circles big and your descent slow. Remember the strange load you are carrying."

[NARRATOR] Just as a little boat leaves its berth by backing and backing, it got away from there. Then when it saw that it had free play, it turned its tail where its breast had been, and stretching it out, moved it as would an eel, and with its paws the beast pulled the air to it-

Maggior paura non credo che fosse
quando Fetòn abbandonò li freni,
108   per che 'l ciel, come pare ancor, si cosse;
né quando Icaro misero le reni
sentì spennar per la scaldata cera,
gridando il padre a lui 'Mala via tieni!';
che fu la mia, quando vidi ch'i' era
ne l'aere d'ogni parte, e vidi spenta
114   ogni veduta fuor che de la fera.
Ella sen va notando lenta lenta:
rota e discende, ma non me n'accorgo
se non ch'al viso e di sotto mi venta.
Io sentia già da la man destra il gorgo
far sotto noi un orribile scroscio,
120   per che con gli occhi 'n giù la testa sporgo.
Allor fu' io più timido a lo scoscio,
però ch'i' vidi fuochi e senti' pianti;
ond'io tremando tutto mi raccoscio.
E vidi poi, ché nol vedea davanti,
lo scendere e 'l girar per li gran mali
126   che s'appressavan da diversi canti.
Come 'l falcon ch'è stato assai su l'ali,
che sanza veder logoro o uccello
fa dire al falconiere 'Ohmè, tu cali!',
discende lasso onde si move snello,
per cento rote, e da lunge si pone
132   dal suo maestro, disdegnoso e fello;
così ne puose al fondo Gerione
al piè al piè de la stagliata rocca
e, discarcate le nostre persone,
si dileguò come da corda cocca.

self. Greater fear I believe there was not, when Phaethon dropped the reins—so that, as we still see, the sky
was burned—and not, when the wretched Icarus felt
his loins losing their feathers as the wax melted—while
his father screamed at him: 'You are on the wrong
course'—than my fear was when I saw myself in the
air on every side, and saw nothing visible except the
animal. He swims on slowly, slowly, wheels and sinks
lower, but I do not realize it, except that air strikes my
face and comes from below. Already I was hearing the
torrent on my right making a frightful hubbub below
us.[7] So I stuck out my head to use my eyes. Then I was
more timid about our alighting, because I saw fires and
heard laments, so that all atremble I gripped with my
thighs. And then I saw—for I did not see it before—
that we were descending and circling, because of the
great evils which were getting closer on every hand.
Sometimes a falcon that has been long on the wing,
without seeing bird or lure, makes the falconer say:
"Too bad; you are dropping down." And it comes
wearily down to the ground from which it went up with
speed, with a hundred circles, and alights far from its
keeper, angry and dangerous. So Geryon put us on the
bottom, right at the base of the smooth rock and, having unloaded us, sped away like an arrow from the bowstring.[8]

CANTO 18

Luogo è in inferno detto Malebolge,
tutto di pietra di color ferrigno,
come la cerchia che dintorno il volge.
Nel dritto mezzo del campo maligno
vaneggia un pozzo assai largo e profondo,
6   di cui suo loco dicerò l' ordigno.
Quel cinghio che rimane adunque è tondo
tra 'l pozzo e 'l piè de l' alta ripa dura,
e ha distinto in dieci valli il fondo.
Quale, dove per guardia de le mura
più e più fossi cingon li castelli,
12   la parte dove son rende figura,
tale imagine quivi facean quelli;
e come a tai fortezze da' lor sogli
a la ripa di fuor son ponticelli,
così da imo de la roccia scogli
movien che ricidien gli argini e' fossi
18   infino al pozzo che i tronca e raccogli.
In questo luogo, de la schiena scossi
di Gerion, trovammoci; e 'l poeta
tenne a sinistra, e io dietro mi mossi.
A la man destra vidi nova pieta,
novo tormento e novi frustatori,
24   di che la prima bolgia era repleta.
Nel fondo erano ignudi i peccatori:
dal mezzo in qua ci venien verso 'l volto,
di là con noi, ma con passi maggiori,
come i Roman per l'essercito molto,
l' anno del giubileo, su per lo ponte
30   hanno a passar la gente modo colto,
che da l' un lato tutti hanno la fronte
verso 'l castello e vanno a Santo Pietro;
da l' altra sponda vanno verso il monte.

CANTO 18

CIRCLE EIGHT

[The topography of Malebolge: 18.1–21]

[NARRATOR] There is a place in Hell named Malebolge, all of rock and iron-colored, like the circle inclosing it. Right in the middle of its malignant space, yawns a well exceedingly wide and deep, the nature of which I shall tell in its place. The belt that is left, then, between the well and the base of the hard high cliff, is round, and its bottom is divided into ten ravines. Just as where —for the protection of their walls—a number of moats surround castles, the place where they are is shaped, such an appearance those here offer. And as such fortresses have little bridges from their thresholds to the bank beyond, so from the foot of the cliff, rock bridges extend, which cross the banks and ravines as far as the well, which cuts them off and ends them.[1] In this place, shaken from Geryon's back, we stood. The poet kept to the left, and I went behind him.

CIRCLE EIGHT, BOLGIA ONE

[Panders: 18.22–66]

[NARRATOR] On the right I saw strange objects for pity, strange punishment and strange scourgers, of which the first bolgia was full. On its bottom were the naked sinners. On our side of the middle, they came along facing us. On the other side they moved with us, but with longer steps.[2] In the same way the Romans, for the great throngs in the jubilee year, have devised a plan for moving the people over the bridge, so that on one side, all have their faces toward the Castle and are going to St. Peter's; on the other side, they are going toward

Di qua, di là, su per lo sasso tetro
vidi demon cornuti con gran ferze,
36   che li battien crudelmente di retro.
Ahi come facean lor levar le berze
a le prime percosse! già nessuno
le seconde aspettava nè le terze.
Mentr' io andava, li occhi miei in uno
furo scontrati; e io sì tosto dissi:
42   «Già di veder costui non son digiuno.»
Però a figurarlo i piedi affissi:
e 'l dolce duca meco si ristette,
e assentio ch' alquanto indietro gissi.
E quel frustato celar si credette
bassando il viso; ma poco li valse,
48   ch' io dissi: «O tu che l' occhio a terra gette,
se le fazion che porti non son false,
Venedico se' tu Caccianemico;
ma che ti mena a sì pungenti salse?»
Ed elli a me: «Mal volontier lo dico;
ma sforzami la tua chiara favella,
54   che mi fa sovvenir del mondo antico.
I' fui colui che la Ghisolabella
condussi a far la voglia del Marchese,
come che suoni la sconcia novella.
E non pur io qui piango bolognese;
anzi n' è questo luogo tanto pieno,
60   che tante lingue non son ora apprese
a dicer 'sipa' tra Savena e Reno;
e se di ciò vuoi fede o testimonio,
recati a mente il nostro avaro seno.»
Così parlando il percosse un demonio
de la sua scuriada, e disse: «Via,
66   ruffian! qui non son femmine da conio.»
I' mi raggiunsi con la scorta mia;
poscia con pochi passi divenimmo
là 'v' uno scoglio de la ripa uscia.

the Mount. On both sides I saw, on the black rock, horned devils with great whips, who were cruelly beating them from behind. Oh, how they made them raise their heels at the first strokes! By no means did one of them wait for the second and the third.

[DANTE] As I was going along, my eyes happened to light on one of them, which made me quickly say: "I haven't failed to see this man in the past."

[NARRATOR] Hence I stood still to look closely, and my good guide stopped with me and assented to my turning back somewhat. And that scourged fellow hoped to keep himself unknown by lowering his face, yet little it helped him.

[DANTE] For I said: "O you who drop your eyes to the ground, if your features do not deceive me, you are Venedico Caccianemico. But what brings you to such pricking sauces?"

[VENEDICO] And he answered: "Unwillingly I tell it, but your informed speech compels me, which makes me remember the former world. I it was who brought the fair Gisola to do the will of the Marquis, just as the disgraceful story says. And I am not weeping here as the only Bolognese; on the contrary, this place is so full of them that now so many tongues are not heard saying *sipa* between Savena and Reno. And if of this you wish proof or testimony, call to mind our avaricious hearts."

[DEMON] As he was saying this, a demon hit him with his scourge, saying: "Move on, pander. There are no women here to be tricked."

[Seducers in the first bolgia: 18.67–99]

[NARRATOR] I joined my director. Then in a few steps we reached the place where a rock bridge projected from

Assai leggeramente quel salimmo;
   e volti a destra su per la sua scheggia,
72   da quelle cerchie etterne ci partimmo.
Quando noi fummo là dov' el vaneggia
   di sotto per dar passo a li sferzati,
   lo duca disse: «Attienti, e fa che feggia
lo viso in te di quest' altri mal nati,
   ai quali ancor non vedesti la faccia
78   però che son con noi insieme andati.»
Del vecchio ponte guardavam la traccia
   che venia verso noi da l' altra banda,
   e che la ferza similmente scaccia.
E 'l buon maestro, sanza mia dimanda,
   mi disse: «Guarda quel grande che vene,
84   e per dolor non par lagrima spanda.
Quanto aspetto reale ancor ritene!
   quelli è Iason, che per cuore e per senno
   li Colchi del monton privati fene.
Ello passò per l'isola di Lenno,
   poi che l'ardite femmine spietate
90   tutti li maschi loro a morte dienno.
Ivi con segni e con parole ornate
   Isifile ingannò, la giovinetta
   che prima avea tutte l'altre ingannate.
Lasciolla quivi, gravida, soletta;
   tal colpa a tal martiro lui condanna;
96   e anche di Medea si fa vendetta.
Con lui sen va chi da tal parte inganna:
   e questo basti de la prima valle
   sapere, e di color che 'n sé assanna.»
Già eravam là 've lo stretto calle
   con l'argine secondo s'incrocicchia,
102   e fa di quello ad un altr'arco spalle.
Quindi sentimmo gente che si nicchia
   ne l'altra bolgia e che col muso scuffa,
   e se medesma con le palme picchia.

the bank. Easily enough we climbed it, and turning to the right along its rough surface, we left those eternal circles.[3]

[VIRGIL] When we reached the spot where it opened underneath to give passage to the scourged, my guide said: "Watch, and be sure the features of these other wretches are plain to you, for you have not seen their faces, since they have been moving along with us."

[NARRATOR] From the solid bridge we looked at the line coming toward us on the other side, whom the whip in the same way hurried along.

[VIRGIL] And my good teacher, without my asking, said to me: "Look at that great man who is coming, who does not shed a single tear for pain. What a kingly appearance he still keeps! That is Jason who, through courage and through brains, took the ram from the Colchians. He visited the island of Lemnos after the daring and pitiless women put all their men to death. There with tokens and fine talk he deceived Hypsipyle, the girl who before had deceived all the others. He left her there pregnant, alone. Such a sin to such suffering condemns him. And he also is punished for Medea. With him are they who in such a matter deceive. And this is all you need to know about the first ravine, and about those in it whom its fangs are rending."

CIRCLE EIGHT, BOLGIA TWO

[*Flatterers: 18.100–136*]

[NARRATOR] Already we were at the spot where the narrow path makes a cross with the second embankment, which serves as a footing for another arch. There we heard people in the next bolgia who were whining and snuffling with their noses, and striking themselves with

Le ripe eran grommate d'una muffa,
  per l'alito di giù che vi s'appasta,
108   che con li occhi e col naso facea zuffa.
Lo fondo è cupo sì, che non ci basta
  luogo a veder sanza montare al dosso
  de l'arco ove lo scoglio più sovrasta.
Quivi venimmo; e quindi giù nel fosso
  vidi gente attuffata in uno sterco
114   che da li uman privadi parea mosso.
E mentre ch'io là giù con l'occhio cerco,
  vidi un col capo sì di merda lordo,
  che non parea s'era laico o cherco.
Quei mi sgridò: «Perché se' tu sì 'ngordo
  di riguardar più me che li altri brutti?»
120   E io a lui: «Perché se ben ricordo,
già t'ho veduto coi capelli asciutti,
  e se' Alessio Interminei da Lucca:
  però t'adocchio più che li altri tutti.»
Ed elli allor battendosi la zucca:
  «Qua giù m'hanno sommerso le lusinghe
126   ond'io non ebbi mai la lingua stucca.»
Appresso ciò lo duca «Fa che pinghe»
  mi disse «il viso un poco più avante,
  sì che la faccia ben con l'occhio attinghe
di quella sozza e scapigliata fante
  che là si graffia con l'unghie merdose,
132   e or s'accoscia, e ora è in piedi stante.
Taide è, la puttana che rispuose
  al drudo suo quando disse 'Ho io grazie
  grandi appo te?': 'Anzi maravigliose!'.
E quinci sian le nostre viste sazie.»

their palms. The banks were incrusted with mold because of the vapor from below which stuck there, which
attacked the eyes and the nose. The bottom was so far
down that we could get a place from which to see it
only by climbing to the summit of the arch, where the
rock bridge is highest.⁴ There we went, and thence I
saw, down in the ravine, people stuck in ordure taken
from human privies.⁵ And while I was using my eyes
to investigate what was down there, I saw one whose
head was so nasty with shit that I could not make out
whether he were layman or cleric.

[ALESSIO INTERMINEI] He shouted to me: "Why are you
so much more greedy for looking at me than at the
other nasty folks?"

[DANTE] I answered him: "Because, if I remember correctly, I have seen you before, when your hair was dry;
and you are Alessio Interminei from Lucca. Hence I am
eyeing you more than any of the others."

[ALESSIO] And he then, giving himself a crack on his
punkin:⁶ "The flatteries of which my tongue was never
tired have thrown me down here."

[VIRGIL] Then my guide said to me: "Push your gaze
a little farther on, so that your eyes will light on the face
of that filthy and tousled wench who is so scratching
herself with her shit-covered nails, and sometimes
squats down, sometimes stands on her feet. Thais is she,
the slut who to her whoremaster—when he said: 'Am
I in high favor with you?'—replied: 'More than that;
incredibly.'⁷

"But in this place haven't we feasted our eyes
enough?"

CANTO 19

O Simon mago, o miseri seguaci
   che le cose di Dio, che di bontate
   deon essere spose, e voi rapaci
per oro e per argento avolterate;
   or convien che per voi suoni la tromba,
6   però che ne la terza bolgia state.
Già eravamo, a la seguente tomba,
   montati de lo scoglio in quella parte
   ch'a punto sovra mezzo il fosso piomba.
O somma sapienza, quante è l'arte
   che mostri in cielo, in terra e nel mal mondo,
12   e quanto giusto tua virtù comparte!
Io vidi per le coste e per lo fondo
   piena la pietra livida di fori,
   d'un largo tutti e ciascun era tondo.
Non mi parean men ampi né maggiori
   che que' che son nel mio bel San Giovanni,
18   fatti per luogo de' battezzatori;
l'un de li quali, ancor non è molt'anni,
   rupp'io per un che dentro v'annegava:
   e questo sia suggel ch'ogn'uomo sganni.
Fuor de la bocca a ciascun soperchiava
   d'un peccator li piedi e de le gambe
24   infino al grosso, e l'altro dentro stava.
Le piante erano a tutti accese intrambe;
   per che sì forte guizzavan le giunte,
   che spezzate averien ritorte e strambe.
Qual suole il fiammeggiar de le cose unte
   muoversi pur su per la strema buccia,
30   tal era lì dai calcagni a le punte.
«Chi è colui, maestro, che si cruccia
   guizzando più che gli altri suoi consorti»
   diss' io, «e cui più roggia fiamma succia?»

CANTO 19

[Simoniacs: 19.1–45]

[POET] *O Simon the sorcerer, O his wretched disciples, who the things of God—which should be the wives of goodness—prostitute in your greed for gold and silver, now for you the trumpet must sound, for you are in the third bolgia.*

[NARRATOR] By now we had, at the next grave,[1] climbed up the rock bridge to the part exactly overhanging the middle of the ditch.

[POET] *O Supreme Wisdom, what great art you show in the sky, on earth and in the world of evil, and how justly your power makes distribution!*

[NARRATOR] I saw along the sides and in the bottom of the bolgia the dark rock full of pits, all of one size, and each one round. To me they did not appear less roomy or larger than those now in my fair San Giovanni at the baptizing place. One of these, not many years ago, I broke for the sake of a person who was drowning in it. And I trust this will be a seal to free all men from error.[2]

From the mouth of each pit were sticking up a sinner's feet, and his legs up to his body, and the rest was inside.[3] Both the soles of all of them were on fire. They brandished their legs so vigorously that they would have broken withes and grass ropes. As the flaming of anything oiled moves only on the very surface, so there from the heels to the toes.

[DANTE] "Who is that, Teacher, who in his torture brandishes more than any of his companions," I asked, "and who is licked by a redder flame?"

Ed elli a me: «Se tu vuo' ch' i' ti porti
là giù per quella ripa che più giace,
36   da lui saprai di sè e de' suoi torti»
E io: «Tanto m' è bel, quanto a te piace:
tu se' segnore, e sai ch' i' non mi parto
dal tuo volere, e sai quel che si tace.»
Allor venimmo in su l' argine quarto:
volgemmo e discendemmo a mano stanca
42   là giù nel fondo foracchiato e arto.
Lo buon maestro ancor de la sua anca
non mi dipuose, sì mi giunse al rotto
di quel che sì piangeva con la zanca.
«O qual che se' che 'l di su tien di sotto,
anima trista come pal commessa,»
48   comincia' io a dir, «se puoi, fa motto.»
Io stava come 'l frate che confessa
lo perfido assessin, che poi ch' è fitto,
richiama lui, per che la morte cessa.
Ed el gridò: «Se' tu già costì ritto,
se' tu già costì ritto, Bonifazio?
54   Di parecchi anni mi mentì lo scritto.
Se' tu sì tosto di quell' aver sazio
per lo quel non temesti torre a 'nganno
la bella donna, e poi di farne strazio?»
Tal mi fec' io, quai son color che stanno,
per non intender ciò ch' è lor risposto,
60   quasi scornati, e risponder non sanno.
Allor Virgilio disse: «Digli tosto:
'Non son colui, non son colui che credi'»;
e io rispuosi come a me fu imposto.
Per che lo spirto tutti storse i piedi;
poi, sospirando e con voce di pianto,
66   mi disse: «Dunque che a me richiedi?
Se di saper ch'i' sia ti cal cotanto,
che tu abbi però la ripa corsa,
sappi ch'i' fui vestito del gran manto;

[VIRGIL] And he said to me: "If you will let me carry you down there, from the bank which lies lower, you can learn from him about himself and his evil deeds."

[DANTE] And I: "I like everything that pleases you. You are my master, and you know that I do not turn away from what you direct, and you know what I keep to myself."

[NARRATOR] Then we reached the fourth bank. We turned to the left and went down to the bottom, full of pits and narrow. My good teacher did not take me off his hip until he brought me to the hole of him who was lamenting with his shanks.

[*Nicholas V, a pope avaricious and simoniacal: 19.46–87*]

[DANTE] "Oh, whoever you are who hold down what should be up, miserable shade, thrust down like a post, if you can, speak a word," I said.

[NARRATOR] I was standing like the friar who hears the confession of some treacherous assassin who, when placed, calls him back, in order to postpone death.

[POPE NICHOLAS] And he yelled: "Are you already right there, are you already right there, Boniface? The writing deceived me by some years.[4] Are you so soon sated with those things because of which you did not fear to wed the Fair Lady by trickery, and to plunder her?"

[NARRATOR] In this position, not comprehending his reply, I felt as if mocked, and could not answer.

[VIRGIL] Then Virgil said: "Tell him quickly, 'I am not he, I am not he you think I am.'"

[NARRATOR] I replied as he directed.

[POPE NICHOLAS] Thereupon the spirit violently twisted its feet; then sighing and with tearful voice, it said: "Then what do you want from me? If you are so eager to know who I am that for it you have come down from the bank, I may as well tell you that I was clothed with

e veramente fui figliuol de l'orsa,
cupido sì per avanzar li orsatti,
72   che su l'avere, e qui me misi in borsa.
Di sotto al capo mio son li altri tratti
che precedetter me simoneggiando,
per le fessure de la pietra piatti.
Là giù cascherò io altressì quando
verrà colui ch'i' credea che tu fossi
78   allor ch'i' feci 'l subito dimando.
Ma più è 'l tempo già che i piè mi cossi
e ch'io son stato così sottosopra,
ch'el non starà piantato coi piè rossi:
ché dopo lui verrà di più laida opra
di ver ponente un pastor sanza legge,
84   tal che convien che lui e me ricopra.
Nuovo Iason sarà, di cui si legge
ne' Maccabei; e come a quel fu molle
suo re, così fia lui chi Francia regge.»
I' non so s'i' mi fui qui troppo folle,
ch'i' pur rispuosi lui a questo metro:
90   «Deh, or mi dì: quanto tesoro volle
Nostro Segnore in prima da san Pietro
ch'ei ponesse le chiavi in sua balìa?
Certo non chiese se non 'Viemmi retro'.
Né Pier né li altri tolsero a Mattia
oro od argento, quando fu sortito
96   al luogo che perdé l'anima ria.
Però ti sta, ché tu se' ben punito;
e guarda ben la mal tolta moneta
ch'esser ti fece contra Carlo ardito.
E se non fosse ch'ancor lo mi vieta
la reverenza de le somme chiavi
102   che tu tenesti ne la vita lieta,
io userei parole ancor più gravi;
ché la vostra avarizia il mondo attrista,
calcando i buoni e sollevando i pravi.

the great mantle. And truly I was a son of the she-bear, so eager to get the little bears ahead that, up above, money, and down here, myself, I put in purse. Under my head are pushed down the others who came before me in simony, hidden in the crannies of the rock. Down there I too shall drop when he comes who I thought you were, when I made my sudden query. But already my feet have been cooking and I have been upside down for a longer time than he will be planted with red feet; for after him will come from the west a lawless shepherd of still more wicked deeds, such that deservedly he will cover over him and me. A new Jason, of whom you read in Maccabees, he will be;⁵ and as to Jason his king was mild, so to him will be the ruler of France."

[Pope Nicholas' avarice rebuked: 19.88–123]

[DANTE] I am not sure whether I was then too rash, yet I did answer him with this speech: "Now tell me, how much treasure did Our Lord want from St. Peter before he put the keys in his power? Indeed he asked only: 'Follow me.' Not Peter nor the others took from Matthias gold or silver when by lot he gained the post the wicked soul lost.⁶ So stay here, because you are properly punished; and keep safe the ill-got money that made you fiery against Charles.⁷ And if my respect for the great keys you bore, up in the happy world, did not forbid it, I would use words still more severe; because the greed of you popes makes the world wicked, treading down the good and raising up the bad. The Evangelist

Di voi pastor s'accorse il Vangelista,
   quando colei che siede sopra l'acque
108   puttaneggiar coi regi a lui fu vista;
quella che con le sette teste nacque,
   e da le diece corna ebbe argomento,
   fin che virtute al suo marito piacque.
Fatto v' avete Dio d' oro e d' argento:
   e che altro è da voi a l' idolatre,
114   se non ch' elli uno, e voi ne orate cento?
Ahi, Costantin, di quanto mal fu matre,
   non la tua conversion, ma quella dote
   che da te prese il primo ricco patre!»
E mentr' io li cantava cotai note,
   o ira o coscienza che 'l mordesse,
120   forte spingava con ambo le piote.
I' credo ben ch' al mio duca piacesse,
   con sì contenta labbia sempre attese
   lo suon de le parole vere espresse.
Però con ambo le braccia mi prese;
   e poi che tutto su mi s' ebbe al petto,
126   rimontò per la via onde discese.
Nè si stancò d' avermi a sè distretto,
   sì men portò sovra 'l colmo de l' arco
   che dal quarto al quinto argine è tragetto.
Quivi soavemente spuose il carco,
   soave per lo scoglio sconcio ed erto
132   che sarebbe a le capre duro varco.
Indi un altro vallon mi fu scoperto.

had in mind you shepherds when he saw the woman who sat upon the waters committing whoredom with the kings—she who was born with seven heads and felt strong in her ten horns,[8] so long as virtue pleased her husband. Of gold and silver you have made God. So how do you differ from the idolater except that he prays to one and you pray to a hundred?"

[POET] *O Constantine, what great evil had as its mother not your conversion, but that dowry which the first rich father got from you!*[9]

[NARRATOR] While I was singing these notes, whether wrath or conscience bit him, he kicked hard with both feet. I feel sure my guide was pleased, because with a contented expression he listened throughout to the true words I spoke.

[Virgil carries his pupil up the bank of bolgia three: 19.124–133]

[NARRATOR] Then in both arms he took me, and when he had me well placed on his breast, he climbed up by the way he had gone down; and he did not get tired, though he kept me in his embrace until he had carried me to the summit of the arch that crosses from the fourth to the fifth bank.[10] There carefully he set down his burden, carefully on the rough steep rock bridge, which would be a difficult path for goats. From there, another ravine was open to my view.

CANTO 20

Di nova pena mi conven far versi
e dar matera al ventesimo canto
de la prima canzon, ch' è de' sommersi.
Io era già disposto tutto quanto
a riguardar ne lo scoperto fondo,
6   che si bagnava d' angoscioso pianto;
e vidi gente per lo vallon tondo
venir, tacendo e lagrimando, al passo
che fanno le letane in questo mondo.
Come 'l viso mi scese in lor più basso,
mirabilmente apparve esser travolto
12   ciascun tra 'l mento e 'l principio del casso;
chè da le reni era tornato il volto,
ed in dietro venir li convenia,
perchè 'l veder dinanzi era lor tolto.
Forse per forza già di parlasia
si travolse così alcun del tutto;
18   ma io nol vidi, nè credo che sia.
Se Dio ti lasci, lettor, prender frutto
di tua lezione, or pensa per te stesso
com' io potea tener lo viso asciutto,
quando la nostra imagine di presso
vidi sì torta, che 'l pianto de li occhi
24   le natiche bagnava per lo fesso.
Certo io piangea, poggiato a un de' rocchi
del duro scoglio, sì che la mia scorta
mi disse: «Ancor se' tu de li altri sciocchi?
Qui vive la pietà quand' è ben morta:
chi è più scellerato che colui
30   che al giudicio divin passion comporta?
Drizza la testa, drizza, e vedi a cui
s' aperse a gli occhi de' Teban la terra;
per ch' ei gridavan tutti: 'Dove rui,

CANTO 20

CIRCLE EIGHT, BOLGIA FOUR

[Fortunetellers and rascally prophets: 20.1–51]

[POET] *On further punishment I must make verses and must give matter to the first* canzone's *twentieth canto, which is about the submerged.*

[NARRATOR] I was now all intent on peering into the depth revealed, which tears of suffering were drenching. I saw people coming along the curving gorge, silent and shedding tears, at the pace used in this world by religious processions. When my gaze moved lower down on them, I saw that every one was marvelously twisted between his chin and the top of his chest, for their faces were turned to their loins, and backward they had to move, because they were deprived of seeing ahead. Perhaps in the past, paralysis's force has twisted someone so completely, but I never saw it and do not believe it can be. As I hope, reader, God will let you profit from your reading, now imagine, by putting yourself in my place, whether I could keep my face dry when I saw near at hand our image so contorted that the tears from the eyes were wetting the buttocks at the divide. Assuredly I was weeping, supported by one of the crags of the hard rock bridge.

[VIRGIL] Hence my director said to me: "Are even you a fool like the rest? Compassion lives here when it is good and dead. Who is more sinful than he who shows emotion opposed to divine decree? Raise your head, raise it, and see him for whom the earth opened before the Thebans' eyes, so that all of them shouted: 'Where

Anfiarao? perchè lasci la guerra?'
E non restò di ruinare a valle
36   fino a Minòs che ciascheduno afferra.
Mira c' ha fatto petto de la spalle:
perchè volle veder troppo davante,
di retro guarda e fa retroso calle.
Vedi Tiresia, che mutò sembiante
quando di maschio femmina divenne,
42   cangiandosi le membra tutte quante;
e prima, poi, ribatter li convenne
li duo serpenti avvolti, con la verga,
che riavesse le maschili penne.
Aronta è quei ch' al ventre li s' atterga,
che né monti di Luni, dove ronca
48   lo Carrarese che di sotto alberga,
ebbe tra' bianchi marmi la spelonca
per sua dimora; onde a guardar le stelle
e 'l mar non li era la veduta tronca.
E quella che ricuopre le mammelle,
che tu non vedi, con le treccie sciolte,
54   e ha di là ogni pilosa pelle,
Manto fu, che cercò per terre molte;
poscia si puose là dove nacqu'io;
onde un poco mi piace che m'ascolte.
Poscia che 'l padre suo di vita uscio,
e venne serva la città di Baco,
60   questa gran tempo per lo mondo gio.
Suso in Italia bella giace un laco,
a piè de l'Alpe che serra Lamagna
sovra Tiralli, c'ha nome Benaco.
Per mille fonti, credo, e più si bagna,
tra Garda e Val Camonica e Pennino
66   de l'acqua che nel detto laco stagna.
Luogo è nel mezzo là dove 'l Trentino
pastore e quel di Brescia e 'l Veronese
segnar poria, se fesse quel cammino.

are you falling to, Amphiarus? Why are you abandoning the war?' But he continued his plunging fall down to Minos, who siezes everyone.[1] See how his back has become his breast. Because he tried to see too far ahead, he looks behind and takes a backward path.[2] See Tiresias, who altered his appearance when he became female instead of male, changing all parts of his body. And later he had to strike once more with his staff the two serpents twined together before he could get again his masculine feathers.[3] Aruns is the one at his belly who follows at his back.[4] In the mountains of Luni, where the Carrarese, who lives below, works in the quarry,[5] a cave amidst white marble was his dwelling, where his view of the stars and of the sea was not impeded."

[Manto, founder of Virgil's city of
Mantua: 20.52–102]

[VIRGIL] "And she who is covering her breasts, which you do not see, with her loose tresses, and all of whose hairy skin is on the side turned away from us, was Manto, who visited in many lands; at last she settled where I was born. About that I wish you to listen to me a little. After her father departed this life, and the city of Bacchus was brought to slavery, she for a long time wandered through the world. Up in fair Italy lies a lake, at the foot of the mountain that bounds Germany beyond Tiralli,[6] which is named Benaco. By a thousand springs, I believe, and more, the region between Garda and Val Camonica and Pennino[7] is washed with the water that enters the lake just mentioned. There is a spot in the middle where the bishop of Trent and that of Brescia and the Veronese would be able to give a blessing, if they should take that road. Peschiera, a fair

Siede Peschiera, bello e forte arnese
da fronteggiar Bresciani e Bergamaschi,
72   ove la riva intorno più discese.
Ivi convien che tutto quanto caschi
ciò che 'n grembo a Benaco star non pò,
e fassi fiume giù per verdi paschi.
Tosto che l'acqua a correr mette co,
non più Benaco, ma Mencio si chiama
78   fino a Governol, dove cade in Po.
Non molto ha corso, ch'el trova una lama,
ne la qual si distende e la 'mpaluda;
e suol di state talor esser grama.
Quindi passando la vergine cruda
vide terra, nel mezzo del pantano,
84   sanza coltura e d'abitanti nuda.
Lì, per fuggire ogni consorzio umano,
ristette con suoi servi a far sue arti,
e visse, e vi lasciò suo corpo vano.
Li uomini poi che 'ntorno erano sparti
s'accolsero a quel luogo, ch'era forte
90   per lo pantan ch'avea da tutte parti.
Fer la città sovra quell'ossa morte;
e per colei che il luogo prima elesse,
Mantua l'appellar sanz'altra sorte.
Già fuor le genti sue dentro più spesse,
prima che la mattia da Casalodi
96   da Pinamonte inganno ricevesse.
Però t'assenno che se tu mai odi
originar la mia terra altrimenti,
la verità nulla menzogna frodi.»
E io: «Maestro, i tuoi ragionamenti
mi son sì certi e prendon sì mia fede,
102   che li altri mi sarien carboni spenti.
Ma dimmi, de la gente che procede,
se tu ne vedi alcun degno di nota;
ché solo a ciò la mia mente rifiede.»

and strong fortress confronting the Brescians and the Bergamasks, lies where the surrounding shore is lowest. There everything has to come down that cannot remain in Benaco's bosom, and a river is formed down in the green meadows. As soon as that water begins to run, no more is it called Benaco, but Mincio, as far as Governolo, where it empties into Po. Not far has it flowed when it finds a low spot where it spreads out to form a swamp, and sometimes in summer that is unhealthful. Traveling there, the cruel virgin saw a piece of land in the middle of the marsh, uncultivated and without inhabitants. There, to escape all human company, she halted with her servants to carry on her labors, and there she lived and there she left her empty body.[8] Later the men who were scattered about gathered in that place, which was strong because of the marsh on every side. They built their city over Manto's bones. And after her who first chose the spot, they called it Mantua, without any magic rites. Once the people within that city were more numerous, before the madness of Casalodi was deceived by Pinamonte. Thus I instruct you so that, if ever you are told that my city began in some other way, no lie may disguise itself as truth."[9]

[DANTE] And I: "Teacher, for me your discourses are so trustworthy and so engage my belief, that others will be like burned-out coals."

[*Other soothsayers in Circle Eight, bolgia four:*
20.103–130]

[DANTE] "But tell me if, among those who are passing, you see any worthy of note, because on that only does my memory seize."[10]

Allor mi disse: «Quel che da la gota
porge la barba in su le spalle brune,
108   fu, quando Grecia fu di maschi vota
sì ch'a pena rimaser per le cune,
augure, e diede 'l punto con Calcanta
in Aulide a tagliar la prima fune.
Euripilo ebbe nome, e così 'l canta
l'alta mia tragedìa in alcun loco:
114   ben lo sai tu che la sai tutta quanta.
Quell'altro che ne' fianchi è così poco,
Michele Scotto fu, che veramente
de le magiche frode seppe il gioco.
Vedi Guido Bonatti; vedi Asdente,
ch'avere inteso al cuoio ed a lo spago
120   ora vorrebbe, ma tardi si pente.
Vedi le triste che lasciaron l'ago,
la spuola e 'l fuso, e fecersi 'ndivine;
fecer malie con erbe e con imago.
Ma vienne omai; ché già tiene 'l confine
d'amendue li emisperi e tocca l'onda
126   sotto Sobilia Caino e le spine,
e già iernotte fu la luna tonda:
ben ten dee ricordar, ché non ti nocque
alcuna volta per la selva fonda.»
Sì mi parlava, e andavamo introcque.

[VIRGIL] Then he said to me: "That man whose beard falls from his cheeks upon his brown back was—when Greece was so empty of men that they hardly were left in the cradles—an augur, and with Calchas at Aulis he set the moment for cutting the first cable. Eurypylus was his name, as my noble tragedy somewhere sings. You, who know every bit of it, know the passage well. That other, so lean at the waist, was Michael Scot, who really knew the tricks of swindling by magic. There is Guido Bonatti; there is Asdente, who now wishes he had kept to his leather and waxed end, but too late he repents. There are wretched women who left their needles, their shuttles, and their spindles, and became fortunetellers; they wrought magic with herbs and with waxen effigies.

"But come now, for Cain and his thorns are really at the meeting of the two hemispheres and touch the waves near Seville,[11] and last night the moon was already full. You should remember that well, for at no time did it harm you in the thick forest." So he was speaking to me, and meanwhile we were walking on.

CANTO 21

Così di ponte in ponte, altro parlando
 che la mia comedìa cantar non cura,
 venimmo; e tenavamo il colmo, quando
restammo per veder l' altra fessura
 di Malebolge e li altri pianti vani;
6 e vidila mirabilmente oscura.
Quale nell' arzanà de' Viniziani
 bolle l' inverno la tenace pece
 a rimpalmare i legni lor non sani,
chè navicar non ponno; in quella vece
 chi fa suo legno novo e chi ristoppa
12 le coste a quel che più viaggi fece;
chi ribatte da proda e chi da poppa;
 altri fa remi e altri volge sarte;
 chi terzeruolo e artimon rintoppa;
tal, non per foco, ma per divin' arte,
 bollia là giuso una pegola spessa,
18 che 'nviscava la ripa d' ogni parte.
I' vedea lei, ma non vedea in essa
 mai che le bolle che 'l bollor levava,
 e gonfiar tutta, e riseder compressa.
Mentr' io là giù fisamente mirava,
 lo duca mio, dicendo 'Guarda, guarda!',
24 mi trasse a sè del loco dov' io stava.
Allor mi volsi come l' om cui tarda
 di veder quel che li convien fuggire,
 e cui paura subita sgagliarda,
che, per veder, non indugia 'l partire;
 e vidi dietro a noi un diavol nero
30 correndo su per lo scoglio venire.
Ahi quant' elli era ne l' aspetto fero!
 e quanto mi parea ne l' atto acerbo,
 con l' ali aperte e sovra i piè leggiero!

CANTO 21

CIRCLE EIGHT, BOLGIA FIVE

[Boiling tar to punish graft: 21.1–21]

[NARRATOR] So from bridge to bridge we came, speaking of things my comedy does not trouble to sing of; and on reaching the summit,[1] we paused, to look at the next gully of Malebolge and listen to the next useless laments. And I saw that it was strangely dark.

In the Venetians' arsenal in the winter, the glutinous tar boils for putting a fresh coat on their unsound vessels, since they cannot go to sea. So instead one rebuilds his ship; and another caulks the sides of one that has made many voyages; one man hammers at a bow and another at a stern; some are making oars and some are twisting cordage; another is patching a foresail and a mainsail. In the same way, not through fire but through wisdom divine, down in that bolgia was boiling a thick pitch, which made the bank sticky everywhere. I saw it, but did not see anything in it except the bubbles the boiling raised; and it all swelled and fell back compacted.

[A soul brought from Lucca by a devil: 21.22–57]

[VIRGIL] While I was staring intently down there, my guide, by saying: "Look out, look out," brought me to him from the place where I was standing.
[NARRATOR] Then I turned, delaying in order to see what I needed to flee from. But then, sudden fear so took my courage that I did not, in order to look, slow down my getting away.[2] What I saw was a black devil behind us, running over the bridge. Oh how savage he looked! And in his movements, how frightening I thought him, with spread wings and light of foot! On his shoulder,

L' omero suo, ch' era aguto e superbo,
 carcava un peccator con ambo l' anche,
36 e quei tenea de' piè ghermito il nerbo.
Del nostro ponte disse: «O Malebranche,
 ecco un de li anzian di santa Zita!
 Mettetel sotto, ch' i' torno per anche
a quella terra che n'è ben fornita:
 ogn' uom v' è barattier, fuor che Bonturo;
42 del no, per li denar, vi si fa *ita*.»
Là giù il buttò, e per lo scoglio duro
 si volse; e mai non fu mastino sciolto
 con tanta fretta a seguitar lo furo.
Quel s' attuffò, e tornò su convolto;
 ma i demon che del ponte avean coperchio,
48 gridar: «Qui non ha luogo il Santo Volto:
qui si nuota altrimenti che nel Serchio!
 Però, se tu non vuoi di nostri graffi,
 non far sopra la pegola soverchio.»
Poi l' addentar con più di cento raffi,
 disser: «Coverto convien che qui balli,
54 sì che, se puoi, nascosamente accaffi.»
Non altrimenti i cuoci a' lor vassalli
 fanno attuffare in mezzo la caldaia
 la carne con li uncin, perchè non galli.
Lo buon maestro «Acciò che non si paia
 che tu ci sia» mi disse, «giù t' acquatta
60 dopo uno scheggio, ch' alcun schermo t' aia;
e per nulla offension che mi sia fatta,
 non temer tu, ch' i' ho le cose conte,
 e altra volta fui a tal baratta.»
Poscia passò di là dal co del ponte;
 e com' el giunse in su la ripa sesta,
66 mestier li fu d' aver sicura fronte.
Con quel furore e con quella tempesta
 ch' escono i cani a dosso al poverello
 che di subito chiede ove s' arresta,

which was sharp and high, with both haunches a sinner rested; and the devil's claws were holding his tendons of Achilles.

[A DEVIL] From the bridge where we were, that devil called: "O Badclaws, here is one of the elders of Santa Zita. Shove him under the pitch, for I am going back for more to that city so well stocked with them. Every man is a grafter there, except Bonturo. There for money they make 'no' into 'yes.' "

[NARRATOR] He chucked him into the ditch and went back over the rough rock bridge; and never was mastiff let loose so speedy in chasing a thief. The sinner plunged under and came to the surface bedaubed.[3]

[THE BADCLAWS] But the demons, whom the bridge was hiding, yelled: "Here the Holy Face can't help you. Here you don't swim as you did in the Serchio. So if you don't want to feel our scratches, don't try to rise above the pitch." Then they bit into him with more than a hundred fleshhooks,[4] saying: "Here you have to dance under cover, to let you be secret, if you can, at your game of odd and even."[5]

[NARRATOR] In just that way, cooks make their helpers push the meat down into the middle of the kettle with their hooks, to keep it from floating.

[*Virgil negotiates with the Badclaws: 21.58–105*]

[VIRGIL] My good teacher said: "To hold back the devils from seeing you are here, squat down behind a rock that gives you cover; and no matter what attack they make on me, do not be afraid, because I understand these things and have been in such a fracas before."

[NARRATOR] Then he went beyond the end of the bridge, and when he reached the sixth bank, he needed a confident bearing. With the violence and the fury of dogs rushing upon a poor little man, who on a sudden calls

uosciron quei di sotto al ponticello,
   e volser contra lui tutt' i runcigli;
72   ma el gridò: «Nessun di voi sia fello!
Innanzi che l' uncin vostro mi pigli,
   traggasi avante l' un di voi che m' oda,
   e poi d' arruncigliarmi si consigli.»
Tutti gridaron: «Vada Malacoda!»
   Per ch' un si mosse, e li altri stetter fermi,
78   e venne a lui dicendo: «Che li approda?»
«Credi tu, Malacoda, qui vedermi
   esser venuto» disse 'l mio maestro
   «sicuro già da tutti vostri schermi,
sanza voler divino e fato destro?
   Lascian' andar, chè nel cielo è voluto
84   ch' i' mostri altrui questo cammin silvestro.»
Allor li fu l'orgoglio sì caduto,
   che si lasciò cascar l'uncino a' piedi,
   e disse a li altri: «Omai non sia feruto.»
E 'l duca mio a me: «O tu che siedi
   tra li scheggion del ponte quatto quatto,
90   sicuramente omai a me tu riedi.»
Per ch'io mi mossi, ed a lui venni ratto;
   e i diavoli si fecer tutti avanti,
   sì ch'io temetti ch'ei tenesser patto:
così vid'io già temer li fanti
   ch'uscivan patteggiati di Caprona,
96   veggendo sé tra nemici cotanti.
I' m'accostai con tutta la persona
   lungo 'l mio duca, e non torceva li occhi
   da la sembianza lor ch'era non buona.
Ei chinavan li raffi e «Vuo' che 'l tocchi»
   diceva l'un con l'altro «in sul groppone?»
102   E rispondien: «Sì, fa che gliele accocchi!»
Ma quel demonio che tenea sermone
   col duca mio, si volse tutto presto,
   e disse: «Posa, posa, Scarmiglione!»

out where he stops,[6] the devils came out from under the bridge and directed their fleshhooks right at him.

[VIRGIL] But he shouted: "Don't any of you be savage. Before your hooks get me, one of you step forward to hear me, and then think about giving me a clawing."

[THE BADCLAWS] They all shouted: "You go, Badtail."

[BADTAIL] At that, one started—but the others stood still—and came up to him saying: "What good does it do him?"

[VIRGIL] "Do you suppose, Badtail," said my teacher, "that I have come here, safe up to now from all your weapons,[7] without the divine command and favoring fate? Let us go on, because Heaven has ordered me to show someone this barbarous road."[8]

[BADTAIL] Then the devil's arrogance fell, and he let his hook drop to his feet, saying to the others: "Now we can't hit him."

[VIRGIL] And my guide called out to me: "O you, who are squatting so low among the rocks of the bridge, now you can safely come to me."

[NARRATOR] On that, I started and got to him with speed, but the devils all moved toward me, making me fear they would not keep their bargain. In the very same way I saw the infantry afraid, which, under terms, came out from Caprona, seeing themselves among so many enemies.[9] I squeezed myself as close to my leader as I could, and did not shift my eyes from their expression, which was not good.

[THE BADCLAWS] They were lowering their hooks,[10] and one was saying to another: "Shall I touch him on the rump?" And the answer was: "Yes, notch it for him."

[BADTAIL] But that demon who was talking with my guide instantly turned and said: "Stop, stop, Bigcomber."

Poi disse a noi: «Più oltre andar per questo
iscoglio non si può, però che giace
108   tutto spezzato al fondo l'arco sesto.
E se l'andare avante pur vi piace,
andatevene su per questa grotta;
presso è un altro scoglio che via face.
Ier, più oltre cinqu'ore che quest'otta,
mille dugento con sessanta sei
114   anni compié che qui la via fu rotta.
Io mando verso là di questi miei
a riguardar s'alcun se ne sciorina:
gite con lor, che non saranno rei.»
«Tra'ti avante, Alichino, e Calcabrina»
cominciò elli a dire, «e tu, Cagnazzo;
120   e Barbariccia guidi la decina.
Libicocco vegn'oltre e Draghignazzo,
Ciriatto sannuto e Graffiacane
e Farfarello e Rubicante pazzo.
Cercate intorno le boglienti pane;
costor sian salvi infino a l'altro scheggio
126   che tutto intero va sopra le tane.»
«Ohmè, maestro, che è quel ch'i' veggio?»
diss'io. «Deh, sanza scorta andianci soli,
se tu sa' ir; ch'i' per me non la cheggio.
Se tu se' sì accorto come suoli,
non vedi tu ch' e' digrignan li denti,
132   e con le ciglia ne minaccian duoli?»
Ed elli a me: «Non vo' che tu paventi:
lasciali digrignar pur a lor senno,
ch' e' fanno ciò per li lessi dolenti.»
Per l' argine sinistro volta dienno;
ma prima avea ciascun la lingua stretta
138   coi denti verso lor duca per cenno;
ed elli avea del cul fatto trombetta.

[The broken bridge and the escort of
devils: 21.106–139]

[BADTAIL] Then he said to us: "You cannot go farther by this bridge because its sixth arch lies smashed in pieces at the bottom. Yet if you still wish to go on, continue along this bank. Nearby is another rock bridge which gives passage. Yesterday, five hours later than this hour, it was a thousand two hundred and sixty-six years[11] since passage here was interrupted. I am sending to the other some of these rascals of mine, to see if any sinner is drying himself. Go with them; they won't hurt you.

"Move forward," he said at once, "Wildhunter and Brinerubber and you, Uglydog; Curlybeard is to command the ten. Hotblast can go too, and Uglydragon, Boartusk, Dogscratcher and Devilmaycare and crazy Redskin. Inspect all along the boiling glue. These men are to be safe as far as the next craggy bridge, which all complete goes over the dens."

[DANTE] "Oh, oh, Teacher, what's this I see?" I said. "Oh, let's go alone, without any escort, since you know the road; for my part I'm not asking for any. If you are as wide awake as usual, you see how they are grinding their teeth, and their eyes are threatening trouble for us."

[VIRGIL] But he said to me: "You needn't be afraid. Let them grind their teeth as they like, because they are doing it for the boiled wretches."

[NARRATOR] Along the embankment to the left they started; but first each one had stuck his tongue between his teeth, as a salute to their leader, and he of his ass had made a trumpet.[12]

CANTO 22

Io vidi già cavalier muover campo,
  e cominciare stormo e far lor mostra,
  e tal volta partir per loro scampo;
corridor vidi per la terra vostra,
  o Aretini, e vidi gir gualdane,
6   fedir torneamenti e correr giostra;
quando con trombe, e quando con campane,
  con tamburi e con cenni di castella,
  e con cose nostrali e con istrane;
nè già con sì diversa cennamella
  cavalier vidi muover nè pedoni,
12   nè nave a segno di terra o di stella.
Noi andavam con li diece demoni:
  ahi fiera compagnia! ma ne la chiesa
  coi santi, ed in taverna co' ghiottoni.
Pur a la pegola era la mia intesa,
  per veder de la bolgia ogni contegno
18   e de la gente ch' entro v' era incesa.
Come i dalfini, quando fanno segno
  a' marinar con l' arco de la schiena,
  che s' argomentin di campar lor legno,
talor così ad alleggiar la pena
  mostrav' alcun de' peccatori il dosso,
24   e nascondea in men che non balena.
E come a l' orlo de l' acqua d' un fosso
  stanno i ranocchi pur col muso fuori,
  sì che celano i piedi e l' altro grosso,
sì stavan d'ogne parte i peccatori;
  ma come s'appressava Barbariccia,
30   così si ritraén sotto i bollori.
I' vidi, e anco il cor me n'accapriccia,
  uno aspettar così, com'elli 'ncontra
  ch'una rana rimane ed altra spiccia;

CANTO 22

CIRCLE EIGHT, BOLGIA FIVE, *cont.*

[Mock-heroic devils: 21.1–15]

[NARRATOR] In my time I have seen horsemen under-
taking a march, and engaging in combat, and passing
in review, and sometimes retreating to save themselves.
I have seen plunderers in your land, O Aretines! and I
have seen foragers moving, and tournaments held and
jousts ridden, sometimes with bugles, sometimes with
bells, with drums and with signals from a castle, and
according to customs both native and foreign, but never
with so fantastic a buglehorn have I seen horsemen
move, or infantry, or a ship at sign from land or star.
We were walking with the ten demons. O odious company! but in the church with holy men and in the tavern
with sots.[1]

*[The Navarrese caught by the
Badclaws: 22.16–96]*

[NARRATOR] I was wholly intent upon the pitch, so as to
see all the bolgia's qualities and those of the crowd
burned in it. Like dolphins, when with the arch of their
backs they signal to sailors that they should take measures for saving their ship, so sometimes, to lighten
their sufferings, some of the sinners showed their backs
and hid themselves quicker than lightning. And as at
the edge of the water in a ditch, frogs lie with just their
muzzles sticking out, so that they hide their feet and the
rest of their bodies, thus on either side lay the sinners.
But when Curlybeard came near, they drew back like
frogs under the boiling glue. I saw—and still my heart
goes pit-pat from it—one of them waiting so, just as
one frog happens to stay and another goes away. And

e Graffiacan, che li era più di contra,
li arruncigliò le 'mpegolate chiome,
36   e trassel su, che mi parve una lontra.
I' sapea già di tutti quanti il nome,
sì li notai quando fuorono eletti,
e poi che si chiamaro, attesi come.
«O Rubicante, fa che tu li metti
li unghioni a dosso, sì che tu lo scuoi!»
42   gridavan tutti insieme i maladetti.
E io: « Maestro mio, fa, se tu puoi,
che tu sappi chi è lo sciagurato
venuto a man de li avversari suoi.»
Lo duca mio li s'accostò a lato;
domandollo ond'ei fosse, ed ei rispuose:
48   «I' fui del regno di Navarra nato.
Mia madre a servo d'un segnor mi puose,
che m'avea generato d'un ribaldo,
distruggitor di sé e di sue cose.
Poi fui famiglia del buon re Tebaldo:
quivi mi misi a far baratteria;
54   di ch'io rendo ragione in questo caldo.»
E Ciriatto, a cui di bocca uscia
d'ogni parte una sanna come a porco,
li fé sentir come l'una sdrucia.
Tra male gatte era venuto il sorco;
ma Barbariccia il chiuse con le braccia,
60   e disse: «State in là, mentr'io lo 'nforco.»
E al maestro mio volse la faccia:
«Domanda» disse «ancor, se più disii
saper da lui, prima ch'altri 'l disfaccia.»
Lo duca dunque: «Or dì: de li altri rii
conosci tu alcun che sia latino
66   sotto la pece?» E quelli: «I' mi partii,
poco è, da un che fu di là vicino:
così foss'io ancor con lui coperto,
ch'i' non temerei unghia né uncino!»

Dogscratcher, who was nearest him, hooked his tarry hair and dragged him out, looking to me like an otter. I now knew the name of every single one—I observed them so when they were chosen, and whenever they called each other by name, I noticed what they said.
[THE BADCLAWS] "O Redskin, set your claws to his back until you skin him," all together shrieked the accursed.
[DANTE] And I said: "Teacher, if you can, learn who this wretch is, who has got into his enemies' hands."
[NARRATOR] My guide went up to him; he asked where he was from.
[THE NAVARRESE] And the sinner answered: "I was born in the kingdom of Navarre. My mother, who had borne me to a ne'er-do-well, a waster of himself and his goods, made me the servant of a lord. Then I was page to the good King Thibault. There I took to swindling, for which I am paying the penalty in this heat."
[NARRATOR] And Boartusk, from whose mouth stuck out on either side a tusk like a boar's, made him feel how one of them rends. Among bad cats the mouse had got.
[CURLYBEARD] But Curlybeard held him tight in his arms, and said: "Stay over there, as long as I have him between my prongs." And to my teacher he turned his face, saying: "Keep on asking, if you want to learn more from him, before one of us tears him up."
[VIRGIL] My guide then said: "Now tell me, among all the sinners, do you know any Italian who is under the tar?"
[THE NAVARRESE] So he: "I left just now one from nearby. How I wish I still were covered along with him, not fearing claw or fleshhook!"

E Libicocco «Troppo avem sofferto»
  disse; e preseli 'l braccio col runciglio,
72 sì che, stracciando, ne portò un lacerto.
Draghignazzo anco i volle dar di piglio
  giuso a le gambe; onde 'l decurio loro
  si volse intorno intorno con mal piglio.
Quand'elli un poco rappaciati fuoro,
  a lui, ch'ancor mirava sua ferita,
78 domandò 'l duca mio sanza dimoro:
«Chi fu colui da cui mala partita
  di' che facesti per venire a proda?»
  Ed ei rispuose: «Fu frate Gomita,
quel di Gallura, vasel d'ogne froda,
  ch'ebbe i nemici di suo donno in mano,
84 e fé sì lor che ciascun se ne loda.
Danar si tolse, e lasciolli di piano,
  sì come dice; e ne li altri offici anche
  barattier fu non picciol, ma sovrano.
Usa con esso donno Michel Zanche
  di Logodoro; e a dir di Sardigna
90 le lingue lor non si sentono stanche.
Ohmè, vedete l'altro che digrigna:
  i' direi anche, ma i' temo ch'ello
  non s'apparecchi a grattarmi la tigna.»
E 'l gran proposto, volto a Farfarello
  che stralunava li occhi per fedire,
96 disse: «Fatti 'n costà, malvagio uccello.»
«Se voi volete vedere o udire»
  ricominciò lo spaurato appresso
  «Toschi o Lombardi, io ne farò venire;
ma stien i Malebranche un poco in cesso,
  sì ch'ei non teman delle lor vendette;
102 e io, seggendo in questo luogo stesso,
per un ch'io son, ne farò venir sette
  quand'io suffolerò, com'è nostro uso
  di fare allor che fori alcun si mette.»

[HOTBLAST] Then said Hotblast: "We have stood too much."

[NARRATOR] And he caught the man's arm with his hook so that, ripping, he brought away a sinew. Uglydragon also tried to grab him down on the legs. That made their sergeant whirl around with an ugly look.

[VIRGIL] When they were a bit calmed down, without delay my guide asked him, who still was gazing at his wound: "Who was he from whom you say you unluckily parted when you came to the bank?"

[THE NAVARRESE] He replied: "He was Frate Gomita, from Gallura, a vessel^2 of all things fraudulent; he had the enemies of his lord in his power, and so treated them that every one of them thanks him for it.^{3} Their money he took for himself, and let them off exonerated, as he tells us. And in his other offices too he was a grafter not lowly but supreme. One of his friends is Master Michael Zanche of Logodoro; and in talking about Sardinia, their tongues never tire. Oh me! see that other snarling! I should say more, but I'm afraid he's getting ready to scratch me where I itch."

[CURLYBEARD] And their grand commander, turning to Devilmaycare, who was eyeing him for a place to smite, said: "Get away there, horrid bird."

[*The Navarrese outwits the Badclaws: 22.97–151*]

[THE NAVARRESE] "If you wish to see or listen to Tuscans or Lombards," he went on in his terror, "I shall make some come. But the Badclaws must stand off a bit, so the comers will not fear their attacks, and I, sitting in this very spot, for one of me will make seven of them come. I shall whistle, as we always do when one of us gets out."

Cagnazzo a cotal motto levò il muso,
 crollando il capo, e disse: «Odi malizia
108 ch'elli ha pensata per gittarsi giuso!»
Ond'ei ch'avea lacciuoli a gran divizia,
 rispuose: «Malizioso son io troppo,
 quand'io procuro a' miei maggior tristizia.»
Alichin non si tenne, e, di rintoppo
 a li altri, disse a lui: «Se tu ti cali,
114 io non ti verrò dietro di gualoppo,
ma batterò sovra la pece l' ali:
 lascisi 'l collo, e sia la ripa scudo,
 a veder se tu sol più di noi vali.»
O tu che leggi udirai nuovo ludo:
 ciascun da l' altra costa li occhi volse;
120 quel prima ch' a ciò fare era più crudo.
Lo Navarrese ben suo tempo colse;
 fermò le piante a terra, ed in un punto
 saltò e dal proposto lor si sciolse.
Di che ciascun di colpa fu compunto,
 ma quei più che cagion fu del difetto;
126 però si mosse e gridò: «Tu se' giunto!»
Ma poco i valse; chè l' ali al sospetto
 non potero avanzar: quelli andò sotto,
 e quei drizzò volando suso il petto:
non altrimenti l'anitra di botto,
 quando 'l falcon s' appressa, giù s' attuffa,
132 ed ei ritorna su crucciato e rotto.
Irato Calcabrina de la buffa,
 volando dietro li tenne, invaghito
 che quei campasse per aver la zuffa;
e come 'l barattier fu disparito,
 così volse li artigli al suo compagno,
138 e fu con lui sopra 'l fosso ghermito.
Ma l' altro fu bene sparvier grifagno
 ad artigliar ben lui, ed amendue
 cadder nel mezzo del bogliente stagno.

[UGLYDOG] Uglydog at this speech raised his snout, shaking his head, and said: "Listen to the clever trick he has thought up for throwing himself under."

[THE NAVARRESE] To which he, who had devices in great plenty,[4] answered: "I am very clever when I gain my friends more grief."

[WILDHUNTER] Wildhunter did not hold back but, opposed to the others, said to him: "If you dive, I will come after you not at a gallop, but over the pitch will flap my wings.[5] We will leave the summit and let the bank conceal us,[6] to see if you by yourself can do more than we can."

[NARRATOR] O you who read! you will hear of strange sport. Each one turned his eyes to the other margin— he first who was most against doing so. The Navarrese chose his time well, planted his feet firm on the earth, and at the same instant leaped and freed himself from their purpose.[7]

[WILDHUNTER] All of them were stung with blame, but chiefly he who had caused the failure. So he came on yelling: "You are caught."

[NARRATOR] But little good it did him, because wings could not get ahead of fear. The sinner went under, and Wildhunter in his flight turned his chest up. No otherwise the duck in an instant, when the falcon is on her, dives under the water, and he rises up vexed and with ruffled plumage. Angered by the mockery,[8] Brinerubber came flying behind, eager for the sinner to escape, so he could have a scuffle. And since the grafter was out of sight, he turned his claws on his companion, and was at grips with him above the moat. But the other really was a sparrow hawk to claw him well, and they both fell into the middle of the boiling pond. The heat was a

Lo caldo sghermitor subito fue;
  ma però di levarsi era neente,
144   sì avieno inviscate l' ali sue.
Barbariccia con li altri suoi dolente,
  quattro ne fè volar da l' altra costa
  con tutt' i raffi, e assai prestamente
di qua, di là discesero a la posta:
  porser li uncini verso li 'mpaniati,
150   ch' eran già cotti dentro da la crosta;
e noi lasciammo lor così 'mpacciati.

rapid ungrappler, but still they couldn't get out—their wings were so gluey. Curlybeard, annoyed like all his troop, had four of them fly to the opposite bank, taking their hooks,[9] and very promptly on both sides they went to their stations. They stretched out their hooks to those who were stuck in the pitch,[10] who already were cooked below the crust. And we left them thus in turmoil.

CANTO 23

Taciti, soli, sanza compagnia
  n' andavam l' un dinanzi e l' altro dopo,
  come frati minor vanno per via.
Volt' era in su la favola d' Isopo
  lo mio pensier per la presente rissa,
6   dov' el parlò de la rana e del topo;
chè più non si pareggia 'mo' e 'issa',
  che l' un con l' altro fa, se ben s' accoppia
  principio e fine con la mente fissa.
E come l' un pensier de l' altro scoppia,
  così nacque di quello un altro poi,
12   che la prima paura mi fè doppia.
Io pensava così: «Questi per noi
  sono scherniti con danno e con beffa
  sì fatta, ch' assai credo che lor noi.
Se l' ira sovra 'l mal voler fa gueffa,
  ei ne verranno dietro più crudeli
18   che 'l cane a quella lievre ch' elli acceffa.»
Già mi sentia tutti arricciar li peli
  de la paura, e stava indietro intento,
  quand' io dissi: «Maestro, se non celi
te e me tostamente, i' ho pavento
  de' Malebranche: noi li avem già dietro:
24   io l' imagino sì, che già li sento.»
E quei: «S' i' fossi di piombato vetro,
  l' imagine di fuor tua non trarrei
  più tosto a me, che quella dentro impetro.
Pur mo venieno i tuo' pensier tra' miei,
  con simile atto e con simile faccia,
30   sì che d' intrambi un sol consiglio fei.
S' elli è che sì la destra costa giaccia,
  che noi possiam ne l' altra bolgia scendere,
  noi fuggirem l' imaginata caccia.»

CANTO 23

CIRCLE EIGHT, BOLGIA FIVE, *cont.*

[The travelers escape from the Badclaws: 23.1–57]

[NARRATOR] Silent, solitary, without company, we were walking one ahead and the other behind, like Minor Friars on a road. By the quarrel going on, my thought was turned to Aesop's fable, where he spoke of the frog and the mouse;[1] because *mo* and *issa* are not nearer alike than the one story and the other, if we properly couple beginning and end with attentive mind.[2] And as one thought bursts out from another, so another sprang from that to double my first fear. I was reasoning like this: "Because of us, they have been tricked with such injury and disgrace that I believe it greatly vexes them. If rage is added to their dislike, they will come after us more cruelly than the dog after the rabbit that he snaps up."

[DANTE] Now I was feeling all my hair standing straight up with fear, and was watching to the rear, when I said: "Teacher, unless you speedily hide yourself and me, I am in terror of the Badclaws. They are really behind us. I imagine them so strongly that I am sure I hear them."

[VIRGIL] And he replied: "If I were made of leaded glass,[3] I should not catch the look of your outside more quickly than I get hold of what is within you. Now your idea mixes itself with mine, acting like it and showing the same face, so that on the two, I have based one plan. If it happens that the right-hand slope so lies that we can get down into the next bolgia, we shall escape the pursuit we imagine."

Già non compiè di tal consiglio rendere,
   ch' io li vidi venir con l' ali tese
36   non molto lungi, per volerne prendere.
Lo duca mio di subito mi prese,
   come la madre ch' al romore è desta,
   e vede presso a sè le fiamme accese,
che prende il figlio e fugge e non s'arresta,
   avendo più di lui che di sé cura,
42   tanto che solo una camicia vesta;
e giù dal collo de la ripa dura
   supin si diede a la pendente roccia,
   che l'un de' lati a l'altra bolgia tura.
Non corse mai sì tosto acqua per doccia
   a volger ruota di molin terragno,
48   quand'ella più verso le pale approccia,
come 'l maestro mio per quel vivagno,
   portandosene me sovra 'l suo petto,
   come suo figlio, non come compagno.
A pena fuoro i piè suoi giunti al letto
   del fondo giù, ch'e' furono in sul colle
54   sovresso noi; ma non li era sospetto;
ché l'alta provedenza che lor volle
   porre ministri de la fossa quinta,
   poder di partirs' indi a tutti tolle.
Là giu trovammo una gente dipinta
   che giva intorno assai con lenti passi,
60   piangendo e nel sembiante stanca e vinta.
Elli avean cappe con cappucci bassi
   dinanzi a li occhi, fatte de la taglia
   che in Clugnì per li monaci fassi.
Di fuor dorate son sì ch'elli abbaglia;
   ma dentro tutte piombo, e gravi tanto,
66   che Federigo le mettea di paglia.
Oh in etterno faticoso manto!
   Noi ci volgemmo ancor pur a man manca
   con loro insieme, intenti al tristo pianto;

[NARRATOR] Not fully did he disclose his plan, before I saw them coming with spread wings not far away, trying to catch us. My guide quickly seized me, like a mother awakened by noise who sees flames rising near her; she seizes her child and runs and does not pause— more anxious for him than for herself—even to put on a shirt. And from the edge of the hard ridge, down the sloping bank that forms one wall of the next bolgia, on his back he slid. Water never ran so fast down a chute to turn the wheel of a mill on land, when it is nearest the paddles, as did my teacher down that cliff, carrying me on his breast like his child, not his companion. Scarcely had his feet touched the bottom of the gorge below, when they were on the summit above us, but he was not afraid, because the high Providence which appointed them servants at the fifth ravine, took from all of them power to leave it.[4]

CIRCLE EIGHT, BOLGIA SIX

[Hypocrites: 23.58–108]

[NARRATOR] Down there we found a resplendent crowd[5] moving around the circle with very sluggish steps, weeping and in appearance weary and overcome. They were wearing gowns with hoods low over their eyes, shaped after the cut of those made for the monks at Cluny. Outside they are gilded so that they dazzle, but inside they are all of lead, so heavy that Frederick might have put on straw ones.[6] Oh, what a wearisome mantle for eternity!

We turned, as always, to the left with them, listening to their sad lament, but because of the weight, that

ma per lo peso quella gente stanca
venia sì pian, che noi eravam nuovi
72   di compagnia ad ogni mover d'anca.
Per ch'io al duca mio: «Fa che tu trovi
alcun ch'al fatto o al nome si conosca,
e li occhi, sì andando, intorno muovi.»
E un che 'ntese la parola tosca,
di retro a noi gridò: «Tenete i piedi,
78   voi che correte sì per l'aura fosca!
Forse ch'avrai da me quel che tu chiedi.»
Onde 'l duca si volse e disse: «Aspetta,
e poi secondo il suo passo procedi.»
Ristetti, e vidi due mostrar gran fretta
de l'animo, col viso, d'esser meco;
84   ma tardavali 'l carco e la via stretta.
Quando fuor giunti, assai con l'occhio bieco
mi rimiraron sanza far parola;
poi si volsero in sé, e dicean seco:
«Costui par vivo a l'atto de la gola;
e se son morti, per qual privilegio
90   vanno scoperti de la grave stola?»
Poi disser me: «O Tosco, ch'al collegio
de l'ipocriti tristi se' venuto,
dir chi tu se' non avere in dispregio.»
E io a loro: «I' fui nato e cresciuto
sovra 'l bel fiume d'Arno a la gran villa,
96   e son col corpo ch'i' ho sempre avuto.
Ma voi chi siete, a cui tanto distilla
quant'i' veggio dolor giù per le guance?
e che pena è in voi che sì sfavilla?»
E l'un rispuose a me: «Le cappe rance
son di piombo sì grosse, che li pesi
102   fan così cigolar le lor bilance.
Frati Godenti fummo, e bolognesi;
io Catalano e questi Loderingo
nomati, e da tua terra insieme presi,

weary crowd went on so slowly that we had new companionship at every movement of our thighs.

[Dante] So I said to my guide: "Find any among them known by deed or fame,[7] and as we go in this way, use your eyes."

[catalano] And one who understood my Tuscan speech shouted behind us: "Stay your steps, you who are running so through the dark air! I promise you will get from me what you are asking for."

[virgil] At this my guide turned and said: "Wait, and then go at his pace."

[narrator] I stopped and saw two showing in their faces great haste of spirit to be with me, but they were delayed by their burdens and the narrow road.[8]

[catalano and loderingo] When they had come up, they looked at me a long time with squinting eyes, without saying a word, then turned to each other and said: "This man seems alive by the motion of his throat. And if they both are dead, by what exemption are they not covered with the heavy mantle?"

Then they said to me: "O Tuscan, who have come to the meeting place of the wretched hypocrites, do not disdain to tell us who you are."

[dante] And I told them: "I was born and grew up on the fair stream of Arno, in the great town, and I still have the body I always have had. But who are you, down whose cheeks are flowing all the tears I see, and what is your penalty that so sparkles?"[9]

[catalano] And one of them answered: "The yellow gowns are so heavy with lead that the weights make their balances squeak in this way.[10] We were Frati Godenti and Bolognese. I am named Catalano, and he Loderingo; and by your city we were chosen together,

come suole esser tolto un uom solingo
per conservar sua pace; e fummo tali,
108   ch'ancor si pare intorno dal Gardingo.»
Io cominciai: «O frati, i vostri mali . . .»;
ma più non dissi, ch'a l'occhio mi corse
un, crucifisso in terra con tre pali.
Quando mi vide, tutto si distorse,
soffiando ne la barba con sospiri;
114   e 'l frate Catalan, ch'a ciò s'accorse,
mi disse: «Quel confitto che tu miri,
consigliò i Farisei che convenia
porre un uom per lo popolo a' martiri.
Attraversato è, nudo, ne la via,
come tu vedi, ed è mestier ch'el senta
120   qualunque passa, come pesa, pria.
E a tal modo il socero si stenta
in questa fossa, e li altri dal concilio
che fu per li Giudei mala sementa.»
Allor vid' io maravigliar Virgilio
sovra colui ch' era disteso in croce
126   tanto vilmente ne l' etterno essilio.
Poscia drizzò al frate cotal voce:
«Non vi dispiaccia, se vi lece, dirci
s' a la man destra giace alcuna foce
onde noi amendue possiamo uscirci,
sanza costringer de li angeli neri
132   che vegnan d' esto fondo a dipartirci.»
Rispuose adunque: «Più che tu non speri,
s' appressa un sasso che da la gran cerchia
si move e varca tutt' i vallon feri,
salvo che 'n questo è rotto e nol coperchia:
montar potrete su per la ruina,
138   che giace in costa e nel fondo soperchia.»

as a single man is usually chosen, to maintain her peace.[11] And of what sort we were, you can still see round about the Gardingo."[12]

[Caiaphas and Annas, who condemned Jesus to the Cross: 23.109–126]

[DANTE] I said: "O brothers, your wicked deeds. . . ."
[NARRATOR] But I said no more, because to my eye came one crucified on the ground with three stakes. When he saw me, he writhed in disdain, blowing into his beard with heavy breathings.
[CATALANO] And Frate Catalano, who noticed this, said to me: "This one pinned down, whom you are looking at, advised the Pharisees that one man must be made to suffer for the people. Crosswise he is, naked, on the path, as you see, so he must feel about whoever goes past, how much he weighs, before [the passer gets by].[13] In the same way his father-in-law is tortured in this ravine, and the others of the Council which was for the Jews a bad sowing."[14]
[NARRATOR] Then I saw Virgil wondering about the man ignobly so stretched out like a cross in his eternal exile.[15]

[Badtail's lie about the bridge. Departure from bolgia six: 23.127–148]

[VIRGIL] Then he spoke as follows to the frate: "If you please, and if you are permitted, tell us if on the right hand there is some passage by which we two can get away, without forcing some black angels[16] to come to take us out of this hole."[17]
[CATALANO] He then answered: "Nearer than you expect is a rock that extends from the great circle and crosses all the wild valleys, except that for this one it is broken down and does not stand above it. You can climb up on the ruins, which lie against the side and are piled high on the bottom."

Lo duca stette un poco a testa china;
    poi disse: «Mal contava la bisogna
    colui che i peccator di qua uncina.»
E 'l frate: «Io udi' già dire a Bologna
    del diavol vizi assai, tra' quali udi'
144   ch' elli è bugiardo, e padre di menzogna.»
Appresso il duca a gran passi sen gì,
    turbato un poco d' ira nel sembiante;
    ond' io da li 'ncarcati mi parti'
dietro a le poste de le care piante.

[VIRGIL] My guide stood a bit with his head bent; then he said: "That devil who hooks the sinners just over there[18] spoke falsely on the matter."

[CATALANO] And the frate: "When I was at Bologna, they taught us that the devil has many vices; among these, they taught us that he is a deceiver and the father of lying."

[NARRATOR] Then with long steps my guide walked off —his face a little disturbed with anger. So I left the laden sinners, in the tracks of his loved feet.

CANTO 24

In quella parte del giovanetto anno
  che 'l sole i crin sotto l'Aquario tempra
  e già le notti al mezzo dì sen vanno,
quando la brina in su la terra assempra
  l' imagine di sua sorella bianca,
6   ma poco dura a la sua penna tempra;
lo villanello a cui la roba manca,
  si leva, e guarda, e vede la campagna
  biancheggiar tutta; ond' ei si batte l' anca,
ritorna in casa, e qua e là si lagna,
  come 'l tapin che non sa che si faccia;
12   poi riede, e la speranza ringavagna,
veggendo il mondo aver cangiata faccia
  in poco d'ora, e prende suo vincastro,
  e fuor le pecorelle a pascer caccia.
Così mi fece sbigottir lo mastro
  quand'io li vidi sì turbar la fronte,
18   e così tosto al mal giunse lo 'mpiastro;
ché, come noi venimmo al guasto ponte,
  lo duca a me si volse con quel piglio
  dolce ch'io vidi prima a piè del monte.
Le braccia aperse, dopo alcun consiglio
  eletto seco, riguardando prima
24   ben la ruina, e diedemi di piglio.
E come quei ch'adopera ed estima,
  che sempre par che 'nnanzi si proveggia,
  così, levando me su ver la cima
d'un ronchione, avvisava un'altra scheggia
  dicendo: «Sovra quella poi t'aggrappa;
30   ma tenta pria s'è tal ch'ella ti reggia.»
Non era via da vestito di cappa,
  ché noi a pena, ei lieve e io sospinto,
  potavam su montar di chiappa in chiappa.

CANTO 24

Circle Eight, Bolgia Six, *cont.*

*[The simile of the shepherd and the
hoarfrost: 24.1–15]*

[POET] *In that part of the youthful year when the Sun
warms his hair under Aquarius, and the nights already
are approaching half of the day, if the hoarfrost on the
ground copies the likeness of her white sister—though
only a little while does the mark of her pen last—the
simple countryman, poverty stricken, gets up in the
morning and looks and sees the countryside all white;
then he strikes his thigh, goes back into his house, and
moves about lamenting—a wretch who does not know
what to do; then he goes out and puts hope in his basket
again,*[1] *since he sees that the world in a short time has
changed her face; and he takes his crook and drives his
little sheep out to pasture.*[2]

[A hard climb up the ruins of the bridge: 24.16–60]

[NARRATOR] In the same way my teacher made me
tremble when I saw his brow so wrinkled, but with
equal speed he put the plaster on the cut, because when
we reached the ruined bridge, my guide turned to me
with that sweet expression that earlier I saw at the foot
of the mountain.[3] He extended his arms, having first
looked at the heap of rocks and decided on his plan, and
took hold of me.

[VIRGIL] And acting with consideration and always
looking ahead, whenever he raised me to the top of a
mass of rocks, he had his eye on another crag, saying:
"Next get a grip on that one, but test it first to make
sure it will hold you."

[NARRATOR] It was not a path for one clothed in a gown,[4]
because, though he was agile,[5] and I was pushed,
scarcely could we climb from foothold to foothold. And

E se non fosse che da quel precinto
più che da l'altro era la costa corta,
36   non so di lui, ma io sarei ben vinto.
Ma perché Malebolge inver la porta
del bassissimo pozzo tutta pende,
lo sito di ciascuna valle porta
che l'una costa surge e l'altra scende;
noi pur venimmo alfine in su la punta
42   onde l'ultima pietra si scoscende.
La lena m'era del polmon sì munta
quand'io fui su, ch'i' non potea più oltre,
anzi m'assisi ne la prima giunta.
«Omai convien che tu così ti spoltre»
disse 'l maestro; «ché, seggendo in piuma,
48   in fama non si vien, né sotto coltre;
sanza la qual chi sua vita consuma,
cotal vestigio in terra di sé lascia,
qual fummo in aere ed in acqua la schiuma.
E però leva su: vinci l'ambascia
con l'animo che vince ogni battaglia,
54   se col suo grave corpo non s'accascia.
Più lunga scala convien che si saglia;
non basta da costoro esser partito:
se tu m' intendi, or fa sì che ti vaglia.»
Leva' mi allor, mostrandomi fornito
meglio di lena ch' i' non mi sentia,
60   e dissi: «Va, ch' i' son forte e ardito.»
Su per lo scoglio prendemmo la via,
ch' era ronchioso, stretto e malagevole
ed erto più assai che quel di pria.
Parlando andava per non parer fievole;
onde una voce uscì de l' altro fosso,
66   a parole formar disconvenevole.
Non so che disse, ancor che sovra 'l dosso
fossi de l' arco già che varca quivi;
ma chi parlava ad ire parea mosso.

if it had not been that the height of this wall was less than that of the other, while I do not know about Virgil, I certainly should have been beaten. But because Malebolge as a whole slopes toward the mouth of the lowest pit, far down, the site of each valley requires its first wall to be high and its second lower. At last we did reach the place where the final stone was broken off. My breath was so milked from my lungs when I reached the top that I could go no farther, but sat down as soon as I got there.

[VIRGIL] "Now you must throw off laziness," said my teacher, "because by lying on feathers you don't get famous, nor under quilts. He who spends his life without fame leaves such a trace of himself on earth as smoke in the air and foam on water. Therefore rise up, overcome your weariness with the spirit that overcomes in every fight, if by its heavy body it is not crushed down. You must go up a longer stairway; it is not enough that you have left these here. If you understand me, now profit by it."

[DANTE] Then I stood up, pretending that I was better furnished with breath than I knew I was, and said: "Go on, for I am strong and eager."

CIRCLE EIGHT, BOLGIA SEVEN

[Darkness in the bolgia of thieves: 24.61–78]

[NARRATOR] We went on our way over the rock bridge, which was rugged, narrow and difficult, and much steeper than the one before it. I kept talking in order not to seem tired. Then[6] the sounds of a voice came from the next ravine, not such as could be formed into words. I do not know what it said, though by then I was on the summit of the arch that crosses there, but he who was

Io era volto in giù, ma li occhi vivi
non poteano ire al fondo per lo scuro;
72   per ch' io: «Maestro, fa che tu arrivi
da l' altro cinghio e dismontiam lo muro;
chè, com' i' odo quinci e non intendo,
così giù veggio e neente affiguro.»
«Altra risposta» disse «non ti rendo
se non lo far; chè la dimanda onesta
78   si de' seguir con l' opera tacendo.»
Noi discendemmo il ponte da la testa
dove s' aggiugne con l' ottava ripa;
e poi mi fu la bolgia manifesta:
e vidivi entro terribile stipa
di serpenti, e di sì diversa mena,
84   che la memoria il sangue ancor mi scipa.
Più non si vanti Libia con sua rena;
chè se chelidri, iaculi e faree
produce, e cencri con anfisibena,
nè tante pestilenzie, nè sì ree
mostrò già mai con tutta l' Etiopia,
90   nè con ciò che di sopra al Mar Rosso ee.
Tra questa cruda e tristissima copia
correan genti nude e spaventate,
sanza sperar pertugio o elitropia:
con serpi le man dietro avean legate;
quelle ficcavan per le ren la coda
96   e 'l capo, ed eran dinanzi aggroppate.
Ed ecco a un ch' era da nostra proda,
s' avventò un serpente che 'l trafisse
là dove 'l collo a le spalle s' annoda.
Nè *o* sì tosto mai nè *i* si scrisse,
com' el s' accese e arse, e cener tutto
102   convenne che cascando divenisse;
e poi che fu a terra sì distrutto,
la polver si raccolse per se stessa,
e 'n quel medesmo ritornò di butto.

speaking seemed to be moving on.[7] I was bending down, but my eager eyes could not reach the bottom because of the darkness.

[DANTE] Hence I said: "Teacher, please go on to the next boundary ridge, and then let us go down the wall, because, just as I am hearing sounds from below, but not understanding, I am looking down but making out nothing."

[VIRGIL] "I make you no other answer," he said, "than the doing; because a proper request should be followed by a deed, in silence."

[*The serpents of the seventh bolgia: 24.79–96*]

[NARRATOR] We went down from the bridge at the end where it joins the eighth bank, and the bolgia then was visible to me. I saw in it a frightening multitude of serpents, so horrible in kind that the memory still curdles my blood. Libya with her sand should boast no longer, because if she produces chelydri, jaculi and phareae, and cenchris as well as amphisbaena, never did she display so many plagues nor so dangerous, along with all Ethiopia and with the Red Sea coast. Among this cruel and evil abundance, people naked and horror-stricken were running, without hoping for hiding place or heliotrope. Their hands were tied behind them with serpents which fastened the head and the tail to their loins and were bunched in front of them.[8]

[*Vanni Fucci, who stole from a church: 24.97–151*]

[NARRATOR] And as I looked, upon one near our bank plunged a serpent that pierced him where the neck is joined to the back. Never was *o* or *i* written so fast as he took fire and burned. So then he dropped down entirely in ashes; and when he lay on the ground so destroyed, that dust gathered itself together and at once became

Così per li gran savi si confessa
   che la fenice more e poi rinasce,
108   quando al cinquecentesimo anno appressa:
erba nè biada in sua vita non pasce,
   ma sol d' incenso lacrime e d' amomo,
   e nardo e mirra son l' ultime fasce.
E qual è quel che cade, e non sa como,
   per forza di demon ch' a terra il tira,
114   o d' altra oppilazion che lega l' omo,
quando si leva, che 'ntorno si mira
   tutto smarrito de la grande angoscia
   ch' elli ha sofferta, e guardando sospira;
tal era il peccator levato poscia.
   Oh potenza di Dio, quant' è severa,
120   che cotai colpi per vendetta croscia!
Lo duca il domandò poi chi ello era;
   per ch' ei rispuose: «Io piovvi di Toscana,
   poco tempo è, in questa gola fiera.
Vita bestial mi piacque e non umana,
   sì come a mul ch' i' fui; son Vanni Fucci
126   bestia, e Pistoia mi fu degna tana.»
E io al duca: «Dilli che non mucci,
   e domanda che colpa qua giù 'l pinse;
   ch' io 'l vidi uomo di sangue e di crucci.»
E 'l peccator, che 'ntese, non s' infinse,
   ma drizzò verso me l' animo e 'l volto,
132   e di trista vergogna si dipinse;
poi disse: «Più mi duol che tu m' hai colto
   ne la miseria dove tu mi vedi,
   che quando fui de l'altra vita tolto.
Io non posso negar quel che tu chiedi:
   in giù son messo tanto, perch' io fui
138   ladro a la sagrestia de' belli arredi,
e falsamente già fu apposto altrui.
   Ma perché di tal vista tu non godi,
   se mai sarai di fuor da' luoghi bui,

the very same. So learned men assert that the phoenix dies and then is reborn when it reaches its five hundredth year. Grass or grain it does not eat in its whole life, but only drops of incense and of amomum; and nard and myrrh form its winding sheet. As it happens that a man falls—he knows not how—through the might of a devil that throws him to the ground, or through the force of some other constriction that grips him, and when he rises, he gazes about, wholly bewildered by the great distress he has endured, and he breathes heavily as he looks around, thus was the sinner when he stood up.

[POET] *Oh how severe is God's power, which showers such blows in punishment!*

[VANNI FUCCI] My guide then asked him who he was, to which he answered: "I fell from Tuscany, a little while ago, into this savage gorge. A bestial life pleased me, and not a human, as suited a bastard like me. I am Vanni Fucci the beast, and Pistoia was a fitting den for me."

[DANTE] And I said to my guide: "Tell him not to scamper off, and ask him what sin shoved him down here, for I knew him as a man of blood and of murders."

[NARRATOR] And the sinner, who understood, made no false pretense, but turned on me his attention and his face, with an expression of wretched shame.

[VANNI FUCCI] Then he said: "I am the more pained that you have caught me in the wretchedness where you see me than when I was taken from the other life. I cannot deny what you ask. I am placed so far down because I stole from the sacristy the fine furnishings, and falsely then it was charged to another. But that you may not rejoice in such a sight,[9] if ever you get out of these dark

apri li orecchi al mio annunzio, e odi:
Pistoia in pria de' Neri si dimagra;
144   poi Fiorenza rinova gente e modi.
Tragge Marte vapor di Val di Magra
ch'è di torbidi nuvoli involuto;
e con tempesta impetuosa e agra
sovra Campo Picen fia combattuto;
ond'ei repente spezzerà la nebbia,
150   sì ch'ogni Bianco ne sarà feruto.
E detto l'ho perché doler ti debbia!»

places, open your ears to my prophecy and hear. First, Pistoia, without the Neri, is shrunken; then Florence changes people and methods.[10] Mars will get from Val di Magra lightning surrounded with dark clouds; and in a tempest driving and bitter, a battle will be fought at Campo Piceno. Then the lightning will so split the clouds that every White will be wounded by it. This I have said to cause you pain."[11]

CANTO 25

Al fine de le sue parole il ladro
le mani alzò con amendue le fiche,
gridando: «Togli, Dio, ch'a te le squadro!»
Da indi in qua mi fuor le serpi amiche,
perch'una li s'avvolse allora al collo,
6   come dicesse 'Non vo' che più diche';
e un'altra a le braccia, e rilegollo,
ribadendo se stessa sì dinanzi,
che non potea con esse dare un crollo.
Ahi Pistoia, Pistoia, ché non stanzi
d'incenerarti sì che più non duri,
12   poi che in mal fare il seme tuo avanzi?
Per tutt'i cerchi de lo 'nferno scuri
non vidi spirto in Dio tanto superbo,
non quel che cadde a Tebe giù da' muri.
El si fuggì che non parlò più verbo;
e io vidi un centauro pien di rabbia
18   venir chiamando: «Ov'è, ov'è l'acerbo?»
Maremma non cred'io che tante n'abbia,
quante bisce elli avea su per la groppa
infino ove comincia nostra labbia.
Sovra le spalle, dietro da la coppa,
con l'ali aperte li giacea un draco;
24   e quello affuoca qualunque s'intoppa.
Lo mio maestro disse: «Questi è Caco,
che sotto il sasso di monte Aventino
di sangue fece spesse volte laco.
Non va co' suoi fratei per un cammino,
per lo furto che frodolente fece
30   del grande armento ch' elli ebbe a vicino;
onde cessar le sue opere biece
sotto la mazza d' Ercule, che forse
li ne diè cento, e non sentì le diece.»

CANTO 25

CIRCLE EIGHT, BOLGIA SEVEN, *cont.*

[Vanni Fucci's defiance of God: 25.1–16]

[VANNI FUCCI] At the end of his words the thief raised his hands, making *fiche* with both, and yelled: "Take them, God, because I fit them to your measure."[1]

[NARRATOR] After that the serpents acted as my friends, because one of them twisted itself around his neck, as though to say: "I am not letting you speak further"; and another around his arms and bound him fast, tightening itself in front until he could not wiggle them.

[POET] *O Pistoia, Pistoia, why do you not decree to burn yourself up, so you will last no longer, since in doing evil you surpass your ancestors?*

[NARRATOR] In all the dark circles of Hell I saw no spirit so proud against God, not that spirit which fell down from the walls of Thebes.[2] He rushed away without saying another word.

[Cacus the thievish centaur: 25.17–33]

[CACUS] And I saw a centaur full of wrath calling: "Where, where is the harsh man?"

[NARRATOR] In Maremma I believe there are not so many snakes as clung to him from his croup to the place where our form begins.[3] On his back behind the nape of his neck, with open wings was lying a dragon, and that sets on fire whatever it touches.

[VIRGIL] My teacher said: "That is Cacus, who beside the cliff of Mount Aventine again and again made a lake of blood. He is not in the company of his brothers,[4] because by fraud he stole the great herd nearby. For that, his knavish doings ceased under the club of Hercules, who hit him perhaps a hundred blows; yet he did not feel ten of them."

Mentre che sì parlava, ed el trascorse,
    e tre spiriti venner sotto noi,
36   de' quai nè io nè 'l duca mio s' accorse,
se non quando gridar: «Chi siete voi?»:
    per che nostra novella si ristette,
    e intendemmo pur ad essi poi.
Io non li conoscea; ma ei seguette,
    come suol seguitar per alcun caso,
42   che l' un nomar un altro convenette,
dicendo: «Cianfa dove fia rimaso?»:
    per ch' io, acciò che 'l duca stesse attento,
    mi puosi il dito su dal mento al naso.
Se tu se' or, lettore, a creder lento
    ciò ch' io dirò, non sarà maraviglia,
48   ché io che 'l vidi, a pena il mi consento.
Com' io tenea levate in lor le ciglia,
    e un serpente con sei piè si lancia
    dinanzi a l' uno, e tutto a lui s' appiglia.
Co' piè di mezzo li avvinse la pancia,
    e con li anterior le braccia prese;
54   poi li addentò e l' una e l' altra guancia;
li diretani a le cosce distese,
    e miseli la coda tra 'mbedue,
    e dietro per le ren su la ritese.
Ellera abbarbicata mai non fue
    ad alber sì, come l' orribil fiera
60   per l' altrui membra avviticchiò le sue.
Poi s'appiccar come di calda cera
    fossero stati, e mischiar lor colore;
    nè l' un nè l' altro già parea quel ch' era,
come procede innanzi da l' ardore,
    per lo papiro suso un color bruno
66   che non è nero ancora e 'l bianco more.
Li altri due il riguardavano, e ciascuno
    gridava: «Ohmè, Agnel, come ti muti!
    vedi che già non se' nè due nè uno.»

[NARRATOR] While that was being said, he too moved past.

*[Three Florentine thieves (Agnello, Buoso, Puccio).
Agnello blends with a serpent (the transformed
Cianfa): 24.34–78]*

[THE THREE THIEVES] And at the same time, three spirits came near us, whom neither my guide nor I noticed until they shouted: "Who are you?"

[NARRATOR] This stopped our conversation, and then we gave attention only to them. I did not recognize them.

[ONE OF THE THIEVES] Yet it came about, as by some chance it often does, that one of them needed to name another, saying: "What has become of Cianfa?"[5]

[NARRATOR] On hearing that, to make my guide attentive, I put my finger from my chin up to my nose. If now, reader, you are slow to believe what I write, I shall not be astonished, because I who saw it scarcely admit it to myself. While I was keeping my eyes fixed on them, suddenly a serpent with six feet threw itself upon the front of one of them, and fastened itself tight to him. With its middle feet, it clung to his belly; with those in front, it grasped his arms; then it set its teeth in both his cheeks; its rear legs it stretched along his thighs, and put its tail between the two and behind him stretched it up to his loins. Ivy never rooted itself in a tree so tight as the terrible beast fastened itself to the other's body. Then they stuck together as if they had been hot wax and mixed their colors, and neither of them now seemed what he had been, just as in front of fire on a piece of paper a dark color moves along which is not really black, though the white dies away.

[TWO FLORENTINE THIEVES] The other two watched it and each one shouted: "Oh, Agnello, how you are changing! See now how you are neither two nor one."

Già eran li due capi un divenuti,
    quando n'apparver due figure miste
72   in una faccia, ov'eran due perduti.
Fersi le braccia due di quattro liste;
    le cosce con le gambe e 'l ventre e 'l casso
    divenner membra che non fuor mai viste.
Ogni primaio aspetto ivi era casso:
    due e nessun l'imagine perversa
78   parea; e tal sen gio con lento passo.
Come 'l ramarro sotto la gran fersa
    dei dì canicular, cangiando siepe,
    folgore par se la via attraversa,
sì pareva, venendo verso l'epe
    de li altri due, un serpentello acceso,
84   livido e nero come gran di pepe;
e quella parte onde prima è preso
    nostro alimento, a l'un di lor trafisse;
    poi cadde giuso innanzi lui disteso.
Lo trafitto 'l mirò, ma nulla disse;
    anzi co' piè fermati sbadigliava
90   pur come sonno o febbre l'assalisse.
Elli 'l serpente, e quei lui riguardava;
    l'un per la piaga, e l'altro per la bocca
    fummavan forte, e 'l fummo si scontrava.
Taccia Lucano omai là dove tocca
    del misero Sabello e di Nassidio,
96   e attenda a udir quel ch'or si scocca.
Taccia di Cadmo e d'Aretusa Ovidio;
    ché se quello in serpente e quella in fonte
    converte poetando, io non lo 'nvidio;
ché due nature mai a fronte a fronte
    non trasmutò, sì ch'amendue le forme
102   a cambiar lor matera fosser pronte.
Insieme si rispuosero a tai norme,
    che 'l serpente la coda in forca fesse,
    e il feruto ristrinse insieme l'orme.

[NARRATOR] No sooner had the two heads become one than two mixed forms appeared in one face, where the two were lost. Two arms were made of four branches;[6] the thighs with the lower legs and the belly and the chest became bodily parts such as never before were seen. All earlier shapes were canceled there; the perverted figure resembled both and neither one; and it moved along at a slow pace.

[*Man (Buoso degli Abati) and serpent (Guercio de' Cavalcanti) exchange forms: 25.79–141*]

[NARRATOR] Just as under the heavy scourge of the dog days, the lizard, shifting from hedge to hedge, seems a lightning flash as it crosses the road, so seemed, as it came toward the bellies of the other two, a fiery little serpent,[7] purple and black as a peppercorn; and it pierced one of them at the place where we take our first nourishment, then fell flat in front of him. The pierced man looked at it, but said nothing. Instead, without moving his feet, he yawned just as though sleep or fever attacked him. He stared at the serpent and it at him. One at his wound and the other at its mouth was sending out heavy smoke, and smoke met smoke.

[POET] *Let Lucan now be silent rather than tell of the wretched Sabellus and of Nassidius, and attend to hearing what bursts out here.[8] Let Ovid be silent about Cadmus and Arethusa, because if he, writing his poem, changed one into a serpent and the other into a spring, I do not envy him,[9] because he never transshifted two natures, one for the other, so that both forms were quick to exchange their matter.*

[NARRATOR] They conformed with each other by such rules that the serpent divided his tail into a fork and the wounded man drew his feet together. His shanks

Le gambe con le cosce seco stesse
s'appiccar sì, che 'n poco la giuntura
108   non facea segno alcun che si paresse.
Togliea la coda fessa la figura
che si perdeva là, e la sua pelle
si facea molle, e quella di là dura.
Io vidi intrar le braccia per l' ascelle,
e i due piè de la fiera, ch' eran corti,
114   tanto allungar quanto accorciavan quelle.
Poscia li piè di rietro, insieme attorti,
diventaron lo membro che l' uom cela,
e 'l misero del suo n' avea due porti.
Mentre che 'l fummo l' uno e l' altro vela
di color novo, e genera il pel suso
120   per l' una parte e da l' altra il dipela,
l' un si levò e l' altro cadde giuso,
non torcendo però le lucerne empie,
sotto le quai ciascun cambiava muso.
Quel ch' era dritto il trasse ver le tempie,
e di troppa matera ch' in là venne
126   uscir li orecchi de le gote scempie:
ciò che non corse indietro e si ritenne
di quel soverchio, fè naso a la faccia,
e le labbra ingrossò quanto convenne.
Quel che giacea, il muso innanzi caccia,
e li orecchi ritira per la testa,
132   come face le corna la lumaccia;
e la lingua ch' avea unita e presta
prima a parlar, si fende, e la forcuta
ne l' altro si richiude; e 'l fummo resta.
L' anima ch' era fiera divenuta,
suffolando si fugge per la valle,
138   e l' altro dietro a lui parlando sputa.
Poscia li volse le novelle spalle,
e disse a l' altro: «I' vo' che Buoso corra,
com' ho fatt' io, carpon per questo calle.»

and his thighs were so fused into one that soon their juncture did not show. The divided tail took the shape lost there, and its skin grew soft and that of the other hard. I saw his arms entering into his armpits, and the two feet of the animal,[10] which were short, growing long as much as his were shortened. Then the hind feet, twisted together, became the member which man conceals, and that of the wretch lengthened as two. While the smoke covers both of them with new color, and produces hair in one spot and from its opposite removes it, one figure rises up and the other falls, yet not turning aside their wicked eyes, under which each one changed his muzzle. The one standing drew his back upon his temples, and from the too-much substance that came there, ears pushed out on his diminished cheeks. What did not run backward, but remained from that excess, made a nose on the face, and the lips grew to proportionate size. The one lying down shoved its snout forward and drew its ears back into its head as the snail does its horns; and its tongue, which earlier was united and ready for speech, was split, and the slit in the other's closed up; and the smoke ceased. The soul that had become an animal rushes hissing through the valley, and the other behind him spits as he speaks.

[GUERCIO] Then he turned on the snake his new back, and said to the other:[11] "Let Buoso[12] run on all fours along this path as I have done."

Così vid' io la settima zavorra
mutare e trasmutare; e qui mi scusi
144   la novità, se fior la penna abborra.
E avvegna che li occhi miei confusi
fossero alquanto, e l' animo smagato,
non poter quei fuggirsi tanto chiusi,
ch' i' non scorgessi ben Puccio Sciancato;
ed era quel che sol, de' tre compagni
150   che venner prima, non era mutato:
l' altr' era quel che tu, Gaville, piagni.

[*Pride in poetic originality. Curiosity about
unnamed sinners: 25.142–151*]

[NARRATOR] So I saw the seventh lot of rubbish[13] shift
and transshift.

[POET] *And here let the novelty excuse me if my pen
writes a bit confusedly.*

[NARRATOR]And though my eyes were somewhat bewildered and my courage lessened, those did not escape
so covertly that I did not fully recognize Puccio Sciancato. And he only of the three companions mentioned
earlier was not changed.[14] The other was he whom you,
Gaville, weep.[15]

CANTO 26

Godi, Fiorenza, poi che se' sì grande,
    che per mare e per terra batti l'ali,
    e per lo 'nferno tuo nome si spande!
Tra li ladron trovai cinque cotali
    tuoi cittadini onde mi ven vergogna,
6   e tu in grande orranza non ne sali.
Ma se presso al mattin del ver si sogna,
    tu sentirai di qua da picciol tempo
    di quel che Prato, non ch'altri, t'agogna.
E se già fosse, non saria per tempo:
    così foss'ei, da che pur esser dee!
12   ché più mi graverà, com più m'attempo.
Noi ci partimmo, e su per le scalee
    che n'avean fatte i borni a scender pria,
    rimontò il duca mio e trasse mee;
e proseguendo la solinga via,
    tra le schegge e tra' rocchi de lo scoglio
18   lo piè sanza la man non si spedia.
Allor mi dolsi, e ora mi ridoglio
    quando drizzo la mente a ciò ch'io vidi,
    e più lo 'ngegno affreno ch'i' non soglio,
perché non corra che virtù nol guidi;
    sì che, se stella bona o miglior cosa
24   m'ha dato 'l ben, ch'io stessi nol m'invidi.
Quante il villan ch'al poggio si riposa,
    nel tempo che colui che 'l mondo schiara
    la faccia sua a noi tien meno ascosa,

CANTO 26

CIRCLE EIGHT, BOLGIA SEVEN, *cont.*

[The infamy of Florence: 26.1–12]

[POET] *Rejoice, Florence, since you are so famous that you flap your wings over sea and land, and throughout Hell your name is spread! Among the thieves I found five such citizens of yours who cause me shame; and you do not rise to great renown through them. But if I dream truly when morning is near, in a little time you will know what Prato, as well as others, craves for you. And if already it had been, it would not be early. Oh that it had been, since it must be! because on me it will weigh the heavier the older I grow.*

[Movement to bolgia eight. Dante's grief at what he had seen: 26.13–24]

[NARRATOR]We turned away, and up the steps that the projecting rocks had made for our earlier descent,[1] my guide went and pulled me with him, and as we continued our lonely[2] way among the crags and among the boulders of the rocky bridge, the foot without the hand did not get on.

[POET] *Then I was pained, and now again I am pained when I bring to memory what I saw, and more than I am wont, I restrain my poetic power, to keep it from running where goodness and wisdom do not guide it, so that, if favoring star or better thing has given me what is good, I may not grudge it to myself.*

CIRCLE EIGHT, BOLGIA EIGHT

[The flames in the bolgia of tricksters: 26.25–45]

[NARRATOR] The farmer who is resting on a hill—in the season when he who brightens the world is least hiding

come la mosca cede a la zanzara,
vede lucciole giù per la vallea,
30   forse colà dove vendemmia e ara;
di tante fiamme tutta risplendea
l'ottava bolgia, sì com'io m'accorsi
tosto che fui là 've 'l fondo parea.
E qual colui che si vengiò con li orsi
vide 'l carro d'Elia al dipartire,
36   quando i cavalli al cielo erti levorsi,
che nol potea sì con li occhi seguire
ch'el vedesse altro che la fiamma sola,
sì come nuvoletta, in su salire;
tal si move ciascuna per la gola
del fosso, ché nessuna mostra il furto,
42   e ogni fiamma un peccatore invola.
Io stava sovra 'l ponte a veder surto,
sì che s'io non avessi un ronchion preso,
caduto sarei giù sanz'esser urto.
E 'l duca, che mi vide tanto atteso,
disse: «Dentro dai fuochi son li spirti;
48   ciascun si fascia di quel ch'egli è inceso.»
«Maestro mio,» rispuos'io, «per udirti
son io più certo; ma già m'era avviso
che così fosse, e già voleva dirti:
chi è in quel foco che vien sì diviso
di sopra, che par surger de la pira
54   dov' disse Eteòcle col fratel fu miso?»
Rispuose a me: «Là dentro si martira
Ulisse e Diomede, e così insieme
a la vendetta vanno come a l'ira;
e dentro da la lor fiamma si geme
l'agguato del caval che fé la porta
60   onde uscì de' Romani il gentil seme.
Piangevisi entro l'arte per che, morta,
Deidamia ancor si duol d'Achille,
e del Palladio pena vi si porta.»

his face from us, when the fly gives place to the mos-
quito—sees many fireflies down in the valley, right
down where he picks grapes and plows. With as many
flames the eighth bolgia was lighted up, as I saw the
very moment I reached a place where the bottom was
visible. And as he who revenged himself with the bears
saw the chariot of Elijah as it left the earth—when the
horses rose straight up to the sky, until he could not
follow them with his eyes enough to see more than the
flame only, like a little cloud, rising up—so each one is
moving in the depth of the gorge, in such a way that
none of them shows the spirit masked, yet every flame
is hiding a sinner.[3] I stood on the bridge, stretching so
far forward to look that if I had not held to a crag, I
should have fallen without being pushed.

[*Virgil explains the bolgia of the crafty:*[4] *26.46–84*]

[VIRGIL] My guide, seeing how intent I was, said:
"Within the flames are the spirits; each one is swathed
in what burns him."
[DANTE] "My teacher," I answered, "I am surer after
listening to you; but before you spoke, I thought it was
so, and I was just about to say to you: 'Who is in the
fire so divided at the top that it seems to rise from the
pyre where Eteocles was laid with his brother?' "
[VIRGIL] He replied to me: "There inside are suffering
Ulysses and Diomed; and they are together in punishment as in sin.[5] Within their flame they are groaning
for the stratagem of the horse, that opened the door
through which came the noble race of the Romans.
Within, they weep for the trick through which Deidamia, though dead, still mourns for Achilles; and for the
Palladium there they pay the penalty."

«S'ei posson dentro da quelle faville
    parlar» diss'io, «maestro, assai ten prego
66 e ripriego, che il priego vaglia mille,
che non mi facci de l'attender niego,
    fin che la fiamma cornuta qua vegna:
    vedi che del desio ver lei mi piego!»
Ed elli a me: «La tua preghiera è degna
    di molta loda, e io però l'accetto;
72 ma fa che la tua lingua si sostegna.
Lascia parlare a me, ch'i' ho concetto
    ciò che tu vuoi; ch'ei sarebbero schivi,
    perché fuor greci, forse del tuo detto.»
Poi che la fiamma fu venuta quivi
    dove parve al mio duca tempo e loco,
78 in questa forma lui parlare audivi:
«O voi che siete due dentro ad un foco,
    s'io meritai di voi, mentre ch'io vissi,
    s'io meritai di voi assai o poco
quando nel mondo li alti versi scrissi,
    non vi movete; ma l' un di voi dica
84 dove per lui perduto a morir gissi.»
Lo maggior corno de la fiamma antica
    cominciò a crollarsi mormorando
    pur come quella cui vento affatica;
indi la cima qua e là menando,
    come fosse la lingua che parlasse,
90 gittò voce di fuori, e disse: «Quando
mi diparti' da Circe, che sottrasse
    me più d' un anno là presso a Gaeta,
    prima che sì Enea la nomasse,
nè dolcezza di figlio, nè la pieta
    del vecchio padre, nè 'l debito amore
96 lo qual dovea Penelopè far lieta,
vincer poter dentro da me l' ardore
    ch' i' ebbi a divenir del mondo esperto,
    e de li vizi umani e del valore;

[DANTE] "If within those flares[6] they can speak," I said,
"Teacher, I earnestly pray you—and further I pray that
one prayer may count as a thousand—that you will not
prohibit my waiting until the horned flame gets here;
you see that in eagerness I bend toward it."
[VIRGIL] To this he replied: "Your prayer deserves great
praise; therefore I grant it. But keep your tongue quiet.
Leave the talking to me, for I apprehend what you want.
Because they were Greeks, they are sure to be annoyed
by your language."
   When the flame came where time and place seemed
right to my guide, in this way he spoke: "O you who
are two within one fire, if aught I deserved from you
when I was living, if I deserved from you much or little
when in the world I wrote my noble verses, do not pass
on, but one of you tell me where he died unknown."

[Ulysses describes his last voyage: 26.85–142]

[ULYSSES] The larger horn of the noble[7] flame shook as
it murmured, as though disturbed by the wind. Then
turning its tip to one side and the other, as though it
were the tongue that spoke, it brought forth voice and
said: "When I left Circe, who kept me hidden more
than a year close by Gaeta—before Aeneas so named
it—neither fondness for my son, nor filial piety toward
my aged father, nor the love due to Penelope, which
should have made her happy, could conquer my zeal to
gain experience with the world and with human vices

ma misi me per l' alto mare aperto
  sol con un legno, e con quella compagna
102 picciola da la qual non fui diserto.
L'un lito e l' altro vidi infin la Spagna,
  fin nel Morrocco, e l' isola de' Sardi,
  e l' altre che quel mare intorno bagna.
Io e' compagni eravam vecchi e tardi,
  quando venimmo a quella foce stretta
108 dove Ercule segnò li suoi riguardi,
acciò che l' uom più oltre non si metta:
  da la man destra mi lasciai Sibilia,
  da l' altra già m' avea lasciata Setta.
'O frati,' dissi 'che per cento milia
  perigli siete giunti a l'occidente,
114 a questa tanto picciola vigilia
de' nostri sensi ch' è del rimanente,
  non vogliate negar l' esperienza,
  diretro al sol, del mondo sanza gente.
Considerate la vostra semenza:
  fatti non foste a viver come bruti,
120 ma per seguir virtute e canoscenza.'
Li miei compagni fec' io sì aguti,
  con questa orazion picciola, al cammino,
  che a pena poscia li avrei ritenuti;
e volta nostra poppa nel mattino,
  dei remi facemmo ali al folle volo,
126 sempre acquistando dal lato mancino.
Tutte le stelle già de l' altro polo
  vedea la notte, e 'l nostro tanto basso,
  che non surgea fuor del marin suolo.
Cinque volte racceso e tante casso
  lo lume era di sotto da la luna,
132 poi che 'ntrati eravam ne l' alto passo,
quando n' apparve una montagna, bruna
  per la distanza, e parvemi alta tanto
  quanto veduta non avea alcuna.

and virtues. But I set out on the deep open sea with one ship only, and with that small crew which had not forsaken me. One shore and the other I saw as far as Spain, as far as Morocco and the island of the Sards, and the others which that sea washes. I and my comrades were old and slow when we came to that narrow passage where Hercules put his warning marks, so that no man should go farther. On the right hand, Seville was left behind me; on the other, Ceuta had already been left behind. 'O brothers,' I said, 'who after a hundred thousand dangers have reached the west, from this tiny wakefulness of our senses that is left, do not reject experience, behind the sun,[8] of the world without man. Think of your origin; you were not created to live like beasts, but to pursue manliness and knowledge.' My comrades I made, with this short speech, so eager for the journey that then I scarcely could have held them back. So in the morning,[9] having turned our poop,[10] we made our oars wings for our foolish flight, ever inclining to the left hand. After a time, I saw at night all the stars of the southern pole, and our pole so low that it did not rise above the sea's level. Five times kindled and five times put out was the light beneath the moon after we had entered upon that high adventure, when we saw a mountain, dark because so far away. I judged it higher

Noi ci allegrammo, e tosto tornò in pianto;
chè de la nova terra un turbo nacque,
138   e percosse del legno il primo canto.
Tre volte il fè girar con tutte l' acque;
a la quarta levar la poppa in suso
e la prora ire in giù, com' altrui piacque,
infin che 'l mar fu sopra noi richiuso.»

than any I had ever seen.[11] We rejoiced, but soon our joy was turned to weeping, because in that new land a whirlwind rose that struck the front end of the ship. Three times it whirled her in the mighty waters; at the fourth, it raised her stern high and drove her prow down, as He decreed, so far that the sea was closed above us."

CANTO 27

Già era dritta in su la fiamma e queta
   per non dir più, e già da noi sen gia
   con la licenza del dolce poeta,
quand' un' altra, che dietro a lei venia,
   ne fece volger li occhi a la sua cima
6   per un confuso suon che fuor n' uscia.
Come 'l bue cicilian che mugghiò prima
   col pianto di colui, e ciò fu dritto,
   che l' avea temperato con sua lima,
mugghiava con la voce dell' afflitto,
   sì che, con tutto che fosse di rame,
12   pur el parea dal dolor trafitto;
così, per non aver via nè forame
   dal principio nel foco, in suo linguaggio
   si convertian le parole grame.
Ma poscia ch' ebber colto lor viaggio
   su per la punta, dandole quel guizzo
18   che dato avea la lingua in lor passaggio,
udimmo dire: «O tu a cu' io drizzo
   la voce e che parlavi mo lombardo,
   dicendo 'Istra ten va; più non t'adizzo,'
perch'io sia giunto forse alquanto tardo,
   non t'incresca restare a parlar meco:
24   vedi che non incresce a me, e ardo!
Se tu pur mo in questo mondo cieco
   caduto se' di quella dolce terra
   latina ond'io mia colpa tutta reco,
dimmi se i Romagnuoli han pace o guerra;
   ch'io fui de' monti là intra Urbino
30   e 'l giogo di che Tever si diserra.»

CANTO 27

CIRCLE EIGHT, BOLGIA EIGHT, *cont.*

[Guido da Montefeltro asks about the Romagna:
27.1–30]

[NARRATOR] At last the flame stood straight up and quiet, because no longer speaking, and then it was turning away from us with the kind poet's permission, when another, which was coming behind it, drew our eyes to its peak with an indistinct sound which was coming from it. Just as the Sicilian bull, which bellowed first with the lament of him who shaped it with his file (and that was just), would bellow with the voice of the tortured, so that though made of bronze, it still seemed pierced with sorrow, so the sad words of the shade, having at first no way or passage in the fire, were transformed to its language.

[GUIDO DA MONTEFELTRO] But after they had made their way over the point,[1] giving it that vibration which the tongue had given them as they passed, it said to us: "O you whom I address—you who just now were speaking Lombard, saying: 'Now go on, for I urge you no further'—because I have, I know, come a little late, you should not be distressed by pausing to talk with me. I am not distressed, you see—and I am burning. If just now you have fallen into this dark world from that pleasant Italian land from which I bring all my iniquity, tell me whether the Romagnuols are in peace or at war, because I was from the mountains lying between Urbino and the ridge from which the Tiber flows."

Io era in giuso ancora attento e chino,
quando il mio duca mi tentò di costa,
dicendo: «Parla tu; questi è latino.»
E io, ch'avea già pronta la risposta,
sanza indugio a parlare incominciai:
36 «O anima che se' là giù nascosta,
Romagna tua non è, e non fu mai,
sanza guerra ne' cuor de' suoi tiranni;
ma 'n palese nessuna or vi lasciai.
Ravenna sta come stata è molt'anni:
l'aquila da Polenta la si cova,
42 sì che Cervia ricuopre coi suoi vanni.
La terra che fé già la lunga prova
e di Franceschi sanguinoso mucchio,
sotto le branche verdi si ritrova.
E 'l mastin vecchio e 'l nuovo da Verrucchio,
che fecer di Montagna il mal governo,
48 là dove soglion, fan de' denti succhio.
Le città di Lamone e di Santerno
conduce il leoncel dal nido bianco,
che muta parte da la state al verno.
E quella cu' il Savio bagna il fianco,
così com'ella sie' tra 'l piano e 'l monte,
54 tra tirannia si vive e stato franco.
Ora chi se', ti priego che ne conte:
non esser duro più ch'altri sia stato,
se 'l nome tuo nel mondo tegna fronte.»
Poscia che 'l foco alquanto ebbe rugghiato
al modo suo, l'aguta punta mosse
60 di qua, di là, e poi diè cotal fiato:
«S'i' credesse che mia risposta fosse
a persona che mai tornasse al mondo,
questa fiamma staria sanza più scosse;
ma però che già mai di questo fondo
non tornò vivo alcun, s'i' odo il vero,
66 sanza tema d'infamia ti rispondo.

[*Dante speaks on the ills of the Romagna and
asks who the inquirer is: 27.31–57*]

[VIRGIL] I was still intent on what was below, bending over, when my guide touched me on the side, saying: "You speak; this man is an Italian."

[DANTE] So I, already prepared with my answer, without hesitation spoke thus: "O spirit covered from view down there,[2] your Romagna is not and never was without war in the hearts of her tyrants, but I left there no open war just now. Ravenna remains as she has been for many years; the eagle of Polenta broods her, so that she covers Cervia with her wings. The city that once stood the long test and made of Frenchmen a bloody heap, is under the green paws. And the old mastiff and the new one from Verrucchio, which dealt so ill with Montagna, in the place where they long have done so, are making gimlets of their teeth. The cities of Lamone and of Santerno are ruled by the young lion with the white nest,[3] who shifts his party from summer to winter. And she whose flank Savio washes, as she lies between the lowland and the mountain, lives between tyranny and free government.

"Now who you are, I pray that you will tell; do not be harder than I have been, if you wish your name to hold its head high in the world."[4]

[*The fox, Guido da Montefeltro, deceived by
Pope Boniface VIII: 27.58–111*]

[GUIDO] After the fire had roared a little in its fashion, its sharp point moved this way and that, and then gave breath to these words: "If I believed I were replying to a person who would ever go back to the world, this flame would rest without further shaking, but since from this depth a man never returned alive, if I am told the truth, without fear of bad reputation I answer. I

Io fui uom d'arme, e poi fui cordigliero,
  credendomi, sì cinto, fare ammenda;
  e certo il creder mio venia intero,
se non fosse il gran prete, a cui mal prenda!,
  che mi rimise ne le prime colpe;
72   e come e quare, voglio che m'intenda.
Mentre ch'io forma fui d'ossa e di polpe
  che la madre mi diè, l'opere mie
  non furon leonine, ma di volpe.
Li accorgimenti e le coperte vie
  io seppi tutte, e sì menai lor arte,
78   ch'al fine de la terra il suono uscie.
Quando mi vidi giunto in quella parte
  di mia etade ove ciascun dovrebbe
  calar le vele e raccoglier le sarte,
ciò che pria mi piacea, allor m'increbbe,
  e pentuto e confesso mi rendei;
84   ahi miser lasso!, e giovato sarebbe.
Lo principe de' nuovi Farisei,
  avendo guerra presso a Laterano,
  e non con Saracin né con Giudei,
ché ciascun suo nimico era Cristiano,
  e nessun era stato a vincer Acri
90   né mercatante in terra di Soldano;
né sommo officio né ordini sacri
  guardò in sé, né in me quel capestro
  che solea fare i suoi cinti più macri.
Ma come Costantin chiese Silvestro
  dentro Siratti a guerir de la lebbre;
96   così mi chiese questi per maestro
a guerir de la sua superba febbre:
  domandommi consiglio, e io tacetti,
  perché le sue parole parver ebbre.
E' poi ridisse: 'Tuo cuor non sospetti;
  finor t'assolvo, e tu m'insegna fare
102   sì come Penestrino in terra getti.

was a man of the sword, and later I was a cord-wearer,[5] since I believed that, so girded, I should make atonement. And certainly my belief would have proved true, except for the Big Priest—curses on him—who put me back into my earlier sins. And how and why I am going to tell you. While I was form in bones and flesh—that which my mother gave me[6]—my doings were not lionlike, but foxy. Underhand methods I knew expertly, and so I used my skill in them that my fame was carried to the ends of the earth. When I saw that I had come to that part of my life when every man ought to lower his sails and coil his cables, then what had earlier pleased me pained me and, having repented and confessed, I became a monk—O miserable wretch—and it would have served me. The head man of the new Pharisees, carrying on war near the Lateran—and not with Saracens or Jews, because all his enemies were Christians, not one of whom had helped capture Acre, or been a merchant in the Soldan's country—respected for himself neither his exalted post nor his sacred vows, nor for me that cord which once made its wearers thinner. But as Constantine sent to Soracte for Sylvester to cure his leprosy,[7] so this hypocrite sent for me as a physician to cure his towering fever. He asked me for advice, and I stood silent, because I thought his words a drunkard's. Then he said: 'Have no fear in your heart. From this moment I absolve you. And you must teach me how I can lay Palestrina low. Heaven I have power to lock and

Lo ciel poss' io serrare e diserrare,
    come tu sai; però son due le chiavi
    che 'l mio antecessor non ebbe care.'
Allor mi pinser li argomenti gravi
    là 've 'l tacer mi fu avviso il peggio,
108   e dissi: 'Padre, da che tu mi lavi
di quel peccato ov' io mo cader deggio,
    lunga promessa con l' attender corto
    ti farà triunfar ne l' alto seggio.'
Francesco venne poi, com' io fu' morto,
    per me; ma un de' neri cherubini
114   li disse: 'Non portar: non mi far torto.
Venir se ne dee giù tra' miei meschini,
    perchè diede il consiglio frodolente,
    dal quale in qua stato li sono a' crini;
ch' assolver non si può chi non si pente,
    nè pentere e volere insieme puossi
120   per la contradizion che nol consente.'
Ohmè dolente!, come mi riscossi
    quando mi prese dicendomi: 'Forse
    tu non pensavi ch' io loico fossi'!
A Minòs mi portò; e quelli attorse
    otto volte la coda al dosso duro;
126   e poi che per gran rabbia la si morse,
disse: 'Questi è de' rei del foco furo';
    per ch' io là dove vedi son perduto,
    e sì vestito andando, mi rancuro.»
Quand' elli ebbe 'l suo dir così compiuto,
    la fiamma dolorando si partio,
132   torcendo e dibattendo il corno aguto.
Noi passamm' oltre, e io e 'l duca mio,
    su per lo scoglio infino in su l' altr' arco
    che cuopre il fosso in che si paga il fio
a quei che scommettendo acquistan carco.

unlock, as you know; therefore two are the keys which my foregoer did not value.' So then his weighty arguments drove me to a place where I judged silence the worse plan, and I said: 'Father, since you will wash me clean from the sin into which I now am falling, big promises and little fulfilment will make you rejoice on your lofty throne.' "

[*The black cherub takes Montefeltro's soul:*
27.112–136]

[GUIDO] "Later, when I was dead, Francis came for me, but one of the black cherubim[8] said to him: 'Do not take him; do not wrong me. He ought to go down among my wretches, because he advised defrauding, for which until now I have been in his hair. He cannot be absolved who does not repent, nor can he at one time repent and be wilful, because of the contradiction, which does not allow it.' O miserable me! How I came to my senses when he seized me, saying: 'You did not at all[9] imagine that I might be a logician.' To Minos he carried me; and that judge eight times twisted his tail around his rigid back and, after in great fury he himself had bitten it, he said: 'This fellow is for the guilty in the concealing fire.'[10] Hence I am lost where you see me and, so clad,[11] I grieve inwardly."

[NARRATOR] When he had finished his speech in this way, the flame, lamenting, departed, twisting and shaking its sharp horn.

We walked on, my guide and I, over the rock bridge to the next arch, which rises above the moat in which they pay their fee who by putting asunder get a burden.

CANTO 28

Chi poria mai pur con parole sciolte
  dicer del sangue e de le piaghe a pieno
  ch' i' ora vidi, per narrar più volte?
Ogne lingua per certo verria meno
  per lo nostro sermone e per la mente
6 c'hanno a tanto comprender poco seno.
S'el s'aunasse ancor tutta la gente
  che già in su la fortunata terra
  di Puglia fu del suo sangue dolente
per li Troiani e per la lunga guerra
  che de l'anella fé sì alte spoglie,
12 come Livio scrive, che non erra,
con quella che sentio di colpi doglie
  per contastare a Ruberto Guiscardo;
  e l'altra il cui ossame ancor s'accoglie
a Ceperan, là dove fu bugiardo
  ciascun pugliese, e là da Tagliacozzo,
18 dove sanz'arme vinse il vecchio Alardo;
e qual forato suo membro e qual mozzo
  mostrasse, d'aequar sarebbe nulla
  il modo de la nona bolgia sozzo.
Già veggia, per mezzul perdere o lulla,
  com'io vidi un, così non si pertugia,
24 rotto dal mento infin dove si trulla:
tra le gambe pendevan le minugia;
  la corata pareva e 'l tristo sacco
  che merda fa di quel che si trangugia.

CANTO 28

CIRCLE EIGHT, BOLGIA NINE

[The poet's difficult task: 28.1–6]

[POET] Who, even in words unbound,[1] could ever set forth to their full extent the blood and wounds I now saw, even though often telling of them? Of a certainty, every tongue would fail, what with our language and what with our minds, which have little space for holding so much.[2]

[Battlefields compared with the bolgia of dividers: 28.7–21]

[NARRATOR] If again should be brought together the multitude who long ago in the ill-favored land of Apulia in agony shed their blood at Trojan hands, and in the long war that made such noble spoil of the finger rings, as Livy writes, who never errs, along with all who felt the pain of wounds in fighting Robert Guiscard; and that multitude whose bones are still heaped up at Ceperan, where every Apulian was a traitor, and there at Tagliacozzo, where without weapons the old Alardo conquered; and one could show a limb pierced, and another a limb cut off—as nothing would it be beside the ninth bolgia's loathsome state.

[Mohammed as a divider of the Church: 28.22–63]

[NARRATOR] A cask, when it loses the middle piece of its head or one of its cants, by no means gapes so wide as one I saw, who was split from chin to farting place; between his legs were hanging his guts; I could see his heart and the nearby parts and the loathsome sack that makes turd of what we gobble down.

Mentre che tutto in lui veder m'attacco,
　　guardommi, e con le man s'aperse il petto,
30　　dicendo: «Or vedi com'io mi dilacco!
vedi come storpiato è Maometto!
　　Dinanzi a me sen va piangendo Alì,
　　fesso nel volto dal mento al ciuffetto.
E tutti li altri che tu vedi qui,
　　seminator di scandalo e di scisma
36　　fur vivi, e però son fessi così.
Un diavolo è qua dietro che n'accisma
　　sì crudelmente, al taglio de la spada
　　rimettendo ciascun di questa risma,
quand'avem volta la dolente strada;
　　però che le ferite son richiuse
42　　prima ch'altri dinanzi li rivada.
Ma tu chi se' che 'n su lo scoglio muse,
　　forse per indugiar d'ire a la pena
　　ch'è giudicata in su le tue accuse?»
«Nè morte 'l giunse ancor, nè colpa 'l mena»
　　rispuose 'l mio maestro «a tormentarlo;
48　　ma per dar lui esperienza piena,
a me, che morto son, convien menarlo
　　per lo 'nferno qua giù di giro in giro:
　　e quest' è ver così com' io ti parlo.»
Più fuor di cento che, quando l' udiro,
　　s' arrestaron nel fosso a riguardarmi
54　　per maraviglia, obliando il martiro.
«Or dì a fra Dolcin dunque che s' armi,
　　tu che forse vedrai il sole in breve,
　　s' ello non vuol qui tosto seguitarmi,
sì di vivanda, che stretta di neve
　　non rechi la vittoria al Noarese,
60　　ch' altrimenti acquistar non saria leve.»
Poi che l' un piè per girsene sospese,
　　Maometto mi disse esta parola;
　　indi a partirsi in terra lo distese.

[MOHAMMED] While I was intent only on seeing him, he looked at me, and with his hands opened his breast, saying: "Now see how I expose myself.³ See how Mohammed is mangled. In front of me Ali is weeping, his face split from chin to hairline. And all the others you see here were sowers of dissension when alive, and for that cause they are so split. Back there is a devil who arrays us so cruelly, again putting to the sword's edge each of this group, whenever we have made the circuit of this road of pain, because our wounds are healed before we get back to his station.

"But who are you who on the rock bridge pause to look, clearly to put off your going to the penalty assigned for the sins you have confessed?"⁴

[VIRGIL] "Death has not yet come to him, nor does his sin lead him to be tormented," said my teacher, "but to give him full experience, I who am dead am charged to lead him down through Hell from round to round. And this is true, just as I am telling you."

[NARRATOR] More than a hundred there were who, when they heard him, checked themselves in the ravine to look at me with wonder, forgetting their suffering.

[MOHAMMED] "Now tell Fra Dolcino—you who, it seems, shortly will see the sun—that if soon he does not want to follow me here, he must supply himself so well with food that a snow blockade cannot give to the Novarese the victory that otherwise will not be easy to gain." Keeping one foot ready to move off, Mohammed thus spoke to me; then he pressed it on the ground in order to leave.

Un altro, che forata avea la gola
e tronco il naso infin sotto le ciglia,
66 e non avea mai ch' una orecchia sola,
ristato a riguardar per maraviglia
con li altri, innanzi a li altri aprì la canna,
ch' era di fuor d'ogni parte vermiglia;
e disse: «O tu cui colpa non condanna
e cu' io vidi in su terra latina,
72 se troppa simiglianza non m' inganna,
rimembriti di Pier da Medicina,
se mai torni a veder lo dolce piano
che da Vercelli a Marcabò dichina.
E fa sapere a' due miglior da Fano,
a messer Guido ed anco ad Angiolello,
78 che se l' antiveder qui non è vano,
gittati saran fuor di lor vasello,
e mazzerati presso a la Cattolica,
per tradimento d' un tiranno fello.
Tra l' isola di Cipri e di Maiolica
non vide mai sì gran fallo Nettuno,
84 non da pirate, non da gente argolica.
Quel traditor che vede pur con l'uno,
e tien la terra che tale qui meco
vorrebbe di vedere esser digiuno,
farà venirli a parlamento seco;
poi farà sì, ch'al vento di Focara
90 non sarà lor mestier voto né preco.»
E io a lui: «Dimostrami e dichiara,
se vuo' ch'i' porti su di te novella,
chi è colui da la veduta amara.»
Allor puose la mano a la mascella
d'un suo compagno e la bocca li aperse,
96 gridando: «Questi è desso, e non favella.
Questi, scacciato, il dubitar sommerse
in Cesare, affermando che 'l fornito
sempre con danno l'attender sofferse.»

[*Causers of dissension: Pier da Medicina, Curio,
Mosca dei Lamberti: 28.64–111*]

[PIER DA MEDICINA] Another, whose throat was slit and
his nose cut off close under his eyebrows, and who had
just one ear, pausing with the rest to look in wonder,
before any other spoke, opened his windpipe, which on
its outside was everywhere red, and said: "O you whom
guilt does not doom, and whom I saw in the Italian land,
if close resemblance does not deceive me, remember Pier
da Medicina, if ever you go back to see the lovely plain
that slopes from Vercelli to Marcabo. And tell the two
chief men in Fano, Messer Guido and also Angiolello,
that if our foresight here is not false, they will be thrown
out of their ship and drowned near Cattolica, through
the treachery of a wicked tyrant. Between the islands of
Cyprus and Majorca, Neptune never saw so great a
crime, not even one by pirates, not by Greeks. That
traitor who sees with but one,[5] and rules the city that a
shade with me here must wish he had been deprived of
seeing, will get them to come to confer with him. Then
he will so act that against the wind of Focara, they will
need neither vow nor prayer."

[DANTE] And I replied: "Point out to me and explain,
if you want me to carry up news of you, him of that
bitter sight."[6]

[PIER DA MEDICINA] Then he put his hand on the jaw of
one of his companions and opened his mouth, exclaim-
ing: "This is he, and he does not speak. He, an exile,
drowned Caesar's doubting, by declaring that a man
prepared always to his hurt delays."[7]

Oh quanto mi parea sbigottito
con la lingua tagliata ne la strozza
102   Curio, ch'a dir fu così ardito!
E un ch'avea l'una e l'altra man mozza,
levando i moncherin per l'aura fosca,
sì che 'l sangue facea la faccia sozza,
gridò: «Ricordera' ti anche del Mosca,
che dissi, lasso!, 'Capo ha cosa fatta,'
108   che fu mal seme per la gente tosca.»
E io li aggiunsi: «E morte di tua schiatta»;
per ch'elli, accumulando duol con duolo,
sen gio come persona trista e matta.
Ma io rimasi a riguardar lo stuolo,
e vidi cosa, ch'io avrei paura
114   sanza più prova, di contarla solo;
se non che coscienza m'assicura,
la buona compagnia che l'uom francheggia
sotto l'asbergo del sentirsi pura.
Io vidi certo, ed ancor par ch'i' 'l veggia,
un busto sanza capo andar sì come
120   andavan li altri de la trista greggia;
e 'l capo tronco tenea per le chiome,
pesol con mano a guisa di lanterna;
e quel mirava noi, e dicea: «Oh me!»
Di sé facea a se stesso lucerna,
ed eran due in uno e uno in due:
126   com'esser può, quei sa che sì governa.
Quando diritto al piè del ponte fue,
levò 'l braccio alto con tutta la testa,
per appressarne le parole sue,
che fuoro: «Or vedi la pena molesta
tu che, spirando, vai veggendo i morti:
132   vedi s' alcuna è grande come questa.
E perchè tu di me novella porti,
sappi ch' i' son Bertram dal Bornio, quelli
che diedi al Re giovane i ma' conforti.

[NARRATOR] Oh how frightened, with his tongue cut in his throat, was Curio, who was so forward to speak! [MOSCA DEI LAMBERTI] And one with both his hands cut off, raising the stumps in the dark air, so that the blood made his face filthy, shrieked: "You will also remember Mosca, who said—alas!—'Deed done is ended.'⁸ That was the seed of evil for the Tuscan folk."
[DANTE] And I added: "And death for your party."
[NARRATOR] Thereupon he, heaping sorrow on sorrow, went off mad with grief.

*[The grotesque punishment of Bertrand
de Born: 28.112–142]*

[NARRATOR] But I stood still to look at the crowd, and I saw something which, without better proof, I should fear, alone,⁹ to relate, if Conscience did not give me assurance—that good companion who makes a man free when he wears the corselet of knowing he is blameless. I certainly saw—and still I seem to see it—a body without a head walking along quite as were walking the others of that wretched flock; and it held its cut-off head by the hair, with one hand dangling it like a lantern.
[BERTRAND DE BORN] And the head looked at us and said: "Oh, me!"
[NARRATOR] Of itself it made a lamp for itself, and they were two in one and one in two. How that can be, He knows who so decrees.
[BERTRAND DE BORN] When this body was as close as could be to the bridge, it lifted to the utmost the arm which carried the head,¹⁰ to bring near us its words, which were: "Now see my loathsome penalty, you who, though you breathe, are looking at the dead; see if any is as great as this one. And that you may carry news of me, I tell you that I am Bertrand de Born, he who gave

Io feci il padre e 'l figlio in sè ribelli:
Achitofèl non fe' più d'Absalone
138   e di Davìd coi malvagi punzelli.
Perch' io parti' così giunte persone,
partito porto il mio cerebro, lasso!,
dal suo principio ch' è in questo troncone.
Così s' osserva in me lo contrapasso.»

the young king wicked encouragement. I put the father and the son at enmity with one another. Achitophel did not do more for Absalom and David with malicious urging. Because I parted persons so connected, I carry my brain—alas!—parted from its beginning in this trunk. So I make proportionate recompense.[11]

CANTO 29

La molta gente e le diverse piaghe
avean le luci mie sì inebriate,
che de lo stare a piangere eran vaghe;
ma Virgilio mi disse: «Che pur guate?
perchè la vista tua pur si soffolge
6   là giù tra l' ombre triste smozzicate?
Tu non hai fatto sì a l' altre bolge:
pensa, se tu annoverar le credi,
che miglia ventidue la valle volge.
E già la luna è sotto i nostri piedi:
lo tempo è poco omai che n' è concesso,
12   e altro è da veder che tu non vedi.»
«Se tu avessi» rispuos' io appresso
«atteso a la cagion per ch' io guardava,
forse m' avresti ancor lo star dimesso.»
Parte sen giva, e io retro li andava,
lo duca, già faccendo la risposta,
18   e soggiugnendo: «Dentro a quella cava
dov' io teneva or gli occhi sì a posta,
credo ch' un spirto del mio sangue pianga
la colpa che là giù cotanto costa.»
Allor disse 'l maestro: «Non si franga
lo tuo pensier da qui innanzi sovr' ello:
24   attendi ad altro, ed ei là si rimanga;
ch' io vidi lui a piè del ponticello
mostrarti, e minacciar forte, col dito,
e udi' 'l nominar Geri del Bello.
Tu eri allor sì del tutto impedito
sovra colui che già tenne Altaforte,
30   che non guardasti in là, sì fu partito.»
«O duca mio, la violenta morte
che non li è vendicata ancor» diss' io
«per alcun che de l' onta sia consorte,

CANTO 29

CIRCLE EIGHT, BOLGIA NINE, cont.

[Virgil rebukes misplaced compassion;
Florentine revenge: 29.1—36]

[NARRATOR] The crowd and the horrible wounds had made my eyes so drunken that they longed to weep.[1] [VIRGIL] But Virgil said to me: "What are you still staring at? Why does your gaze still rest down there among the wretched mutilated shades? You have not done so in the other moats. Consider, if you hope to count them, that the ravine makes a circle of twenty-two miles. And the moon is already beneath our feet; the time allowed us is now short, and there is more to see than you are seeing." [DANTE] "If you had noticed," I then answered, "the cause for my looking, I am sure you would have pardoned my delaying a while." Meanwhile my guide was moving off and I was going behind him, at the same time replying, and adding: "In that hollow at which just now I was looking so intently, I believe a spirit of my family weeps for the sin that costs so much down there." [VIRGIL] Then my teacher said: "From now on, don't waste any thought on him; give your attention to something else and let him stay there. I saw him almost under the bridge gesture at you with his finger and menace vigorously, and he said his name was Geri del Bello.[2] You were then so fully taken up with him who once held Hautefort[3] that you did not look there until he had gone." [DANTE] "O my teacher, his violent death, which is not yet revenged," I said, "by anybody who shares in the

fece lui disdegnoso; ond' el sen gio
sanza parlarmi, sì com' io estimo:
36   ed in ciò m' ha el fatto a sè più pio.»
Così parlammo infino al luogo primo
che de lo scoglio l' altra valle mostra,
se più lume vi fosse, tutto ad imo.
Quando noi fummo sor l' ultima chiostra
di Malebolge, sì che i suoi conversi
42   potean parere a la veduta nostra,
lamenti saettaron me diversi,
che di pietà ferrati avean li strali;
ond' io li orecchi con le man copersi.
Qual dolor fora, se de li spedali
di Valdichiana tra 'l luglio e 'l settembre,
48   e di Maremma e di Sardigna i mali
fossero in una fossa tutti insembre;
tal era quivi, e tal puzzo n' usciva,
qual suol venir de le marcite membre.
Noi discendemmo in su l' ultima riva
del lungo scoglio, pur da man sinistra;
54   e allor fu la mia vista più viva
giù ver lo fondo, là 've la ministra
de l' alto sire infallibil giustizia
punisce i falsador che qui registra.
Non credo ch' a veder maggior tristizia
fosse in Egina il popol tutto infermo,
60   quando fu l' aere sì pien di malizia,
che li animali, infino al picciol vermo,
cascaron tutti, e poi le genti antiche,
secondo che i poeti hanno per fermo,
si ristorar di seme di formiche;
ch' era a veder per quella oscura valle
66   languir li spirti per diverse biche.
Qual sovra 'l ventre, e qual sovra le spalle
l'un de l'altro giacea, e qual carpone
si trasmutava per lo tristo calle.

disgrace, made him scornful; hence he went on without speaking to me, as I take it; and so he has made me pity him more."

[The tenth "cloister" of Malebolge: 29.37–72]

[NARRATOR] So we kept talking until we reached the first place where, from the rock bridge, the next ravine would be visible to the very bottom, if the light were better. When we were above the last cloister of Malebolge, so that we could get a view of its monks, frightful lamentations pierced me, whose arrows were pointed with compassion, so that I covered my ears with my hands. Such pained outcry as there would be if, from the hospitals of Valdichiana between July and September, and from the Maremma and Sardinia, the sicknesses were all together in one ravine—such was there, and a stench came from it such as comes from gangrened bodies. We went down from the long rock bridge to the last bank, to the left as always, and then I could see more clearly to the very bottom, where the agent of the lofty Ruler, infallible Justice, punishes the falsifiers whom here it records. I do not believe the populace all sick in Aegina were a sadder sight—when the air was so full of enmity that the animals, even to the little worms, fell dead, and then the earlier inhabitants, according to what the poets rely on, were restored from the seed of ants—than the sight in that dark ravine of the spirits lying sick in revolting heaps. One was lying on the belly and another on the back of some other, and another on all fours moved himself along that

Passo passo andavam sanza sermone,
   guardando e ascoltando li ammalati,
72   che non potean levar le lor persone.
Io vidi due sedere a sé poggiati,
   com'a scaldar si poggia tegghia a tegghia,
   dal capo al piè di schianze macolati;
e non vidi già mai menare stregghia
   a ragazzo aspettato dal segnorso,
78   né a colui che mal volentier vegghia,
come ciascun menava spesso il morso
   de l'unghie sopra sé per la gran rabbia
   del pizzicor, che non ha più soccorso;
e sì traevan giù l'unghie la scabbia,
   come coltel di scardova le scaglie
84   o d'altro pesce che più larghe l'abbia.
«O tu che con le dita ti dismaglie,»
   cominciò 'l duca mio a l'un di loro,
   «e che fai d'esse tal volta tanaglie,
dinne s'alcun latino è tra costoro
   che son quinc'entro, se l'unghia ti basti
90   etternalmente a cotesto lavoro.»
«Latin siam noi, che tu vedi sì guasti
   qui ambedue» rispuose l'un piangendo;
   «ma tu chi se' che di noi dimandasti?»
E 'l duca disse: «I' son un che discendo
   con questo vivo giù di balzo in balzo,
96   e di mostrar lo 'nferno a lui intendo.»
Allor si ruppe lo comun rincalzo;
   e tremando ciascuno a me si volse
   con altri che l'udiron di rimbalzo.
Lo buon maestro a me tutto s'accolse,
   dicendo: «Dì a lor ciò che tu vuoli»;
102   e io incominciai, poscia ch'ei volse:
«Se la vostra memoria non s'imboli
   nel primo mondo da l'umane menti,
   ma s'ella viva sotto molti soli,

wretched path. Slowly, slowly, on we went without speaking, listening to the sick who could not raise their bodies.

[*Griffolino of Arezzo, an alchemist: 29.73–120*]

[NARRATOR] I saw two who sat leaning against each other, as plate is leaned against plate to warm, spotted from head to foot with scabs. And never did a stable boy for whom his lord is waiting, or one who can hardly keep awake, drive a curry comb as fast as each one was driving over himself the bite of his nails, in the great fury of his itching, which has no other remedy. And their claws were tearing off the thickened skin as a knife does the scales from the scardova or any other fish on which they are very big.

[VIRGIL] "O you who are ripping off your scales with your fingers," said my guide to one of them, "and who sometimes are using your fingers for pincers, tell us if there is any Italian among those in here, as I hope your nails may be everlastingly sufficient for such work."

[GRIFFOLINO OF AREZZO] "Italians we both are, whom you see here so wasted away," answered one of them, weeping, "but who are you who are asking us questions?"

[VIRGIL] So my guide said: "I am one who with this living man am going down from terrace to terrace, and my purpose is to show him Hell."

[NARRATOR] Then they broke off supporting each other[4] and, trembling, both looked at me, with others who had overheard.[5]

[VIRGIL] My good teacher came close to me saying: "Tell them what you want."

[DANTE] So I said, since he approved: "As you hope that your memory may not disappear from human minds in the first world,[6] but that it may live under many suns,

ditemi chi voi siete e di che genti:
la vostra sconcia e fastidiosa pena
108   di palesarvi a me non vi spaventi.»
«Io fui d'Arezzo, e Albero da Siena»
rispuose l'un «mi fé mettere al foco;
ma quel per ch'io mori' qui non mi mena.
Vero è ch'i' dissi lui, parlando a gioco:
'I' mi saprei levar per l'aere a volo';
114   e quei, ch'avea vaghezza e senno poco,
volle ch'i' li mostrassi l'arte; e solo
perch'io nol feci Dedalo, mi fece
ardere a tal che l'avea per figliuolo.
Ma ne l'ultima bolgia de le diece
me per l'alchimia che nel mondo usai
120   dannò Minòs, a cui fallar non lece.»
E io dissi al poeta: «Or fu già mai
gente sì vana come la sanese?
Certo non la francesca sì d'assai!»
Onde l'altro lebbroso, che m'intese,
rispuose al detto mio: «Tra'mene Stricca
126   che seppe far le temperate spese,
e Niccolò che la costuma ricca
del garofano prima discoverse
ne l'orto dove tal seme s'appicca;
e tra'ne la brigata in che disperse
Caccia d'Ascian la vigna e la gran fonda,
132   e l'Abbagliato suo senno proferse.
Ma perché sappi chi sì ti seconda
contra i Sanesi, aguzza ver me l'occhio,
sì che la faccia mia ben ti risponda:
sì vedrai ch'io son l'ombra di Capocchio,
che falsai li metalli con alchimia:
138   e te dee ricordar, se ben t'adocchio,
com'io fui di natura buona scimia.»

tell me who you are and of what peoples. Do not let your filthy and disgusting penalty scare you off from revealing yourselves."

[GRIFFOLINO] "I came from Arezzo; and Albert of Siena," replied one of them, "had me put in the fire. But what I suffered death for did not bring me here. It is true that I said to him, jokingly: 'I can lift myself up in the air to fly.' Then he, who was eager for novelty and had no sense, urged me to show him the method. And merely because I did not make him Daedalus, he had me burned by that fellow who treated him as his son. But to the last bolgia of the ten, for the alchemy I practiced in the world, Minos, to whom error is not possible, condemned me."

[*Florentine contempt for the Sienese: 29.121–139*]

[DANTE] Whereupon I said to the poet: "Oh, have there ever been people so empty-headed as the Sienese? Certainly not the French, by a great deal."

[CAPOCCHIO] This led the other leper, who heard, to reply to my smart saying: "Leave out Stricca, who knew how to spend temperately, and Niccolò, who first learned the costly habit of using cloves in the garden where such seed takes root; and leave out the gang with which Caccia d'Ascian squandered his vineyard and his great purse,[7] and Abbagliato showed his brain. But that you may know who so seconds you against the Sienese, eye me sharply until my face comes back to you. Then you will see that I am the spirit of Capocchio, who produced false metals with alchemy; and you must remember, if my eye serves me well,[8] what a good ape of nature I was."

CANTO 30

Nel tempo che Iunone era crucciata
   per Semelè contra 'l sangue tebano,
   come mostrò una e altra fiata,
Atamante divenne tanto insano,
   che veggendo la moglie con due figli
6   andar carcata da ciascuna mano,
gridò: «Tendiam le reti, sì ch' io pigli
   la leonessa e' leoncini al varco»;
   e poi distese i dispietati artigli,
prendendo l' un ch' avea nome Learco,
   e rotollo e percosselo ad un sasso;
12   e quella s' annegò con l' altro carco.
E quando la fortuna volse in basso
   l' altezza de' Troian che tutto ardiva,
   sì che 'nsieme col regno il re fu casso,
Ecuba trista, misera e cattiva,
   poscia che vide Polissena morta,
18   e del suo Polidoro in su la riva
del mar si fu la dolorosa accorta,
   forsennata latrò sì come cane;
   tanto il dolor le fè la mente torta.
Ma nè di Tebe furie nè troiane
   si vider mai in alcun tanto crude,
24   non punger bestie, non che membra umane,
quant' io vidi in due ombre smorte e nude,
   che mordendo correvan di quel modo
   che 'l porco quando del porcil si schiude.
L' una giunse a Capocchio, ed in sul nodo
   del collo l' assannò, sì che, tirando,
30   grattar li fece il ventre al fondo sodo.
E l'Aretin, che rimase, tremando,
   mi disse: «Quel folletto è Gianni Schicchi,
   e va rabbioso altrui così conciando.»

CANTO 30

CIRCLE EIGHT, BOLGIA TEN, *cont.*

*[The poet illustrates with classical instances
of insanity: 30.1–21]*

[POET] *At the time when, because of Semele, Juno was
enraged against the Theban family, as she showed once
and again, Athamas went so completely out of his mind
that, seeing his wife holding their two sons, one on each
arm, he yelled: "Set the nets, so I can catch the lioness
and the young lions."[1] Then he stretched out his pitiless
claws, snatched one named Learchus and whirled him
around and struck him on a rock; and his wife drowned
herself with the other burden.[2]*

*And when Fortune brought low on her wheel the pride
of the Trojans, which dared without limit, until with
the kingdom the king was wiped out, the sad Hecuba,
wretched and enslaved, when she saw Polyxena dead,
and on the seashore made the sad discovery of her Poly-
dorus, in her insanity barked like a dog—so sorrow
wrung her mind.*

[Insane falsifiers: 30.22–45]

[NARRATOR] But no Furies, either Trojan or from Thebes,
were ever so cruel to anyone—not in wounding beasts
and much less in wounding human bodies—as were
two pale and naked shades I saw, which ran biting as
does the boar when it escapes from the pen. One of
them came upon Capocchio and set its teeth into the
nape of his neck in such a way that, pulling, he scraped
his belly on the hard ground.

[GRIFFOLINO] And the Aretine, who kept trembling, said
to me: "That imp is Gianni Schicchi; that's the way he
deals with us in his madness."

«Oh!» diss' io lui, «se l' altro non ti ficchi
li denti a dosso, non ti sia fatica
36   a dir chi è pria che di qui si spicchi.»
Ed elli a me: «Quell' è l' anima antica
di Mirra scellerata, che divenne
al padre fuor del dritto amore amica.
Questa a peccar con esso così venne,
falsificando sè in altrui forma,
42   come l' altro che là sen va, sostenne,
per guadagnar la donna de la torma,
falsificare in sè Buoso Donati,
testando e dando al testamento norma.»
E poi che i due rabbiosi fuor passati
sovra cu' io avea l' occhio tenuto,
48   rivolsilo a guardar li altri mal nati.
Io vidi un fatto a guisa di leuto,
pur ch' elli avesse avuta l' anguinaia
tronca da l' altro che l' uomo ha forcuto.
La grave idropisì, che sì dispaia
le membra con l' omor che mal converte,
54   che 'l viso non risponde a la ventraia,
faceva lui tener le labbra aperte
come l' etico fa, che per la sete
l' un verso il mento e l' altro in su rinverte.
«O voi che sanz' alcuna pena sete,
e non so io perchè, nel mondo gramo,»
60   diss'elli a noi, «guardate e attendete
a la miseria del maestro Adamo:
io ebbi vivo assai di quel ch' i' volli,
e ora, lasso!, un gocciol d' acqua bramo.
Li ruscelletti che de' verdi colli
del Casentin discendon giuso in Arno,
66   faccendo i lor canali freddi e molli,
sempre mi stanno innanzi, e non indarno,
chè l' imagine lor vie più m' asciuga
che 'l male ond' io nel volto mi discarno.

[DANTE] "Oh," I said to him, "as you hope the other will not set his teeth into you, won't you be so good as to tell me who he is, before he makes off from here?".

[GRIFFOLINO] He answered: "That is the accursed Myrrha's dishonored soul; she became her father's lover with more than lawful love. She managed to sin with him by falsely taking another's form, just as the other who is moving away there had the poise, that he might gain the mistress of the herd,[3] to falsify himself as Buoso Donati, making his will and giving it legal form."

[Master Adam of Brescia, the counterfeiter:
30.46–90]

[NARRATOR] When the two lunatics whom I had been eyeing had gone by, I shifted my gaze to other wretches. I saw one who would have had the shape of a lute, if only his groin had been cut away from man's forked part.[4] The weight-causing dropsy—which, with fluid not absorbed, so deforms the body that the face is not in proportion with the belly—made him keep his lips open as does a man with hectic fever, who in his thirst turns one lip down toward his chin and the other upward.

[MASTER ADAM] "O you, who without punishment—I do not know why—are in the dark world," he said to us, "look upon and consider Master Adam's misery. When I was alive, I had plenty of what I wanted, but now—alas!—I long for a tiny drop of water. The little streams that from the green hills of the Casentino run down into Arno, making their channels cold and wet, are always before me, and not without effect, because their remembrance dries me more than this disease

La rigida giustizia che mi fruga
tragge cagion del loco ov' io peccai
72   a metter più li miei sospiri in fuga.
Ivi è Romena, là dov' io falsai
la lega suggellata del Batista;
per ch' io il corpo su arso lasciai.
Ma s' io vedessi qui l' anima trista
di Guido o d'Alessandro o di lor frate,
78   per fonte Branda non darei la vista.
Dentro c' è l' una già, se l' arrabbiate
ombre che vanno intorno dicon vero;
ma che mi val, c' ho le membra legate?
S' io fossi pur di tanto ancor leggiero
ch' i' potessi in cent' anni andare un' oncia,
84   io sarei messo già per lo sentero,
cercando lui tra questa gente sconcia,
con tutto ch' ella volge undici miglia,
e men d' un mezzo di traverso non ci ha.
Io son per lor tra sì fatta famiglia:
e' m' indussero a batter li fiorini
90   ch' avevan tre carati di mondiglia.»
E io a lui: «Chi son li due tapini
che fumman come man bagnate 'l verno,
giacendo stretti a' tuoi destri confini?»
«Qui li trovai, e poi volta non dierno»
rispuose, «quando piovvi in questo greppo,
96   e non credo che dieno in sempiterno.
L'una è la falsa ch'accusò Giuseppo;
l'altr' è il falso Sinòn greco da Troia:
per febbre aguta gittan tanto leppo.»
E l'un di lor, che si recò a noia
forse d'esser nomato sì oscuro,
102   col pugno li percosse l'epa croia.
Quella sonò come fosse un tamburo;
e mastro Adamo li percosse il volto
col braccio suo, che non parve men duro,

which disfleshes my face. The strict justice which punishes me takes from the place where I sinned, means for
making my sighs fly faster. There lies Romena, where I
falsified the coinage stamped with the Baptist, for which
I left up there my body burned. But if I could see here
the wicked soul of Guido or of Alexander or of their
brother,[5] for the fountain of Branda I would not give
that sight. One of them now is here, if the maddened
shades that go around tell the truth, but what good does
that do me, whose limbs are fast bound? If I were only
still active enough to go an inch in a hundred years, I
would already be on the path, searching for him in this
misshapen multitude, even though the bolgia circles
eleven miles, and is not less than half a mile across.[6]
Because of them I am in this company here; they persuaded me to strike the coins having three carats of
trash."

[A quarrel in Hell, unfit for the ears of a
gentleman: 30.91–148]

[DANTE] I said to him: "Who are those two wretches
who steam like washed hands in winter, lying close to
your right-hand borders?"[7]
[MASTER ADAM] "Here I found them—and then they did
not move—" he answered, "when I fell into this chasm,
and I do not believe they will forever. The first is she
who falsely charged Joseph. The other is Sinon,[8] the
false Greek of Troy. In their high fever, they throw off
such stench."
[NARRATOR] And the latter, indeed offended because
called so debased, with his fist struck his rigid belly. It
resounded like a drum.
[MASTER ADAM] And Master Adam struck him in the face
with his arm, which did not seem less hard, saying to

dicendo a lui: «Ancor che mi sia tolto
lo muover per le membra che son gravi,
108   ho io il braccio a tal mestiere sciolto.»
Ond'ei rispuose: «Quando tu andavi
al fuoco, non l'avei tu così presto:
ma sì e più l'avei quando coniavi.»
E l'idropico: «Tu di' ver di questo;
ma tu non fosti sì ver testimonio
114   là 've del ver fosti a Troia richesto.»
«S'io dissi falso, e tu falsasti il conio»
disse Sinone; «e son qui per un fallo,
e tu per più ch'alcun altro demonio!»
«Ricorditi, spergiuro, del cavallo»
rispuose quel ch'avea infiata l'epa;
120   «e sieti reo che tutto il mondo sallo!»
«E te sia rea la sete onde ti criepa»
disse il greco «la lingua, e l'acqua marcia
che 'l ventre innanzi gli occhi sì t'assiepa!»
Allora il monetier: «Così si squarcia
la bocca tua per tuo mal come suole;
126   ché s'i' ho sete e umor mi rinfarcia,
tu hai l'arsura e 'l capo che ti duole;
e per leccar lo specchio di Narcisso,
non vorresti a 'nvitar molte parole.»
Ad ascoltarli er'io del tutto fisso,
quando 'l maestro mi disse: «Or pur mira
132   che per poco che teco non mi risso.»
Quand' io 'l senti' a me parlar con ira,
volsimi verso lui con tal vergogna,
ch'ancor per la memoria mi si gira.
Qual è colui che suo dannaggio sogna,
che sognando desidera sognare,
138   sì che quel ch'è, come non fosse, agogna,
tal mi fec'io, non possendo parlare,
che disiava scusarmi, e scusava
me tuttavia, e nol mi credea fare.

him: "Though my limbs are so heavy that they keep me from walking, my arm is agile for such need."

[SINON] And Sinon answered: "When you went to the fire, it was not so ready, but as much and more when you were counterfeiting."

[MASTER ADAM] And the hydroptic: "You speak true about that, but you were not so true a witness at Troy when you were asked for the true."

[SINON] "If I answered falsely, you were the one who falsified the coinage," said Sinon, "so I am here for one error, and you for more than any other devil."

[MASTER ADAM] "Remember, false swearer, the horse," he of the swollen belly replied, "and I hope it plagues you that the whole world knows it."

[SINON] "And I hope that the thirst that cracks your tongue plagues you," said the Greek, "and the rotten water that in front of your eyes makes your belly such a hedge."

[MASTER ADAM] Then the money-coiner: "Your mouth likewise through your disease⁹ is gashed as always, because if I am thirsty and moisture stuffs me full, you are burning with fever and your head aches, and to lick Narcissus' mirror you would not need many words inviting you."

[VIRGIL] I was all intent on listening to them, when my teacher said to me: "Now just notice that I'm close to quarreling with you."

[NARRATOR] When I heard him speak to me in anger, I moved toward him with such shame that still at the remembrance my head swims. As is he who dreams something harmful—who as he dreams, may hope that he is dreaming, so that for what is, he longs as though it were not—such was I, not able to speak, yet longing to excuse myself, and, for all that, I was excusing myself, but did not believe I was doing it.

«Maggior difetto men vergogna lava»
   disse 'l maestro, «che 'l tuo non è stato;
144   però d'ogne tristizia ti disgrava.
E fa ragion ch'io ti sia sempre a lato,
   se più avvien che fortuna t'accoglia
   dove sien genti in simigliante piato:
ché voler ciò udire è bassa voglia.»

[VIRGIL] "Less shame washes away a greater fault," said my teacher, "than yours has been. Get rid of all regret, then. But imagine that I am always at your side, if later it happens that Fortune puts you where people are in such a brawl;[10] because to like to hear such things is a vulgar liking."

CANTO 31

Una medesma lingua pria mi morse,
   sì che mi tinse l'una e l'altra guancia,
   e poi la medicina mi riporse:
così od'io che solea far la lancia
   d'Achille e del suo padre esser cagione
6   prima di trista e poi di buona mancia.
Noi demmo il dosso al misero vallone
   su per la ripa che 'l cinge dintorno,
   attraversando sanza alcun sermone.
Quiv'era men che notte e men che giorno,
   sì che 'l viso m'andava innanzi poco;
12   ma io senti' sonare un alto corno,
tanto ch'avrebbe ogne tuon fatto fioco,
   che, contra sé la sua via seguitando,
   dirizzò li occhi miei tutti ad un loco.
Dopo la dolorosa rotta, quando
   Carlo Magno perdé la santa gesta,
18   non sonò sì terribilmente Orlando.
Poco portai in là volta la testa,
   che me parve veder molte alte torri;
   ond'io: «Maestro, dì, che terra è questa?»
Ed elli a me: «Però che tu trascorri
   per le tenebre troppo da la lungi,
24   avvien che poi nel maginare abborri.
Tu vedrai ben, se tu là ti congiungi,
   quanto 'l senso s'inganna di lontano;
   però alquanto più te stesso pungi.»
Poi caramente mi prese per mano,
   e disse: «Pria che noi siam più avanti,
30   acciò che 'l fatto men ti paia strano,
sappi che non son torri, ma giganti,
   e son nel pozzo intorno da la ripa
   da l'umbilico in giuso tutti quanti.»

CANTO 31

Interlude between Circles Eight and Nine

[Virgil accepts Dante's penitence: 31.1–6]

[NARRATOR] The same tongue first wounded me until both my cheeks were red, then gave me medicine. So I have heard that Achilles' spear and that of his father would confer[1] first a bad and then a good reward.[2]

[Is that a town in the dim distance? 31.7–39]

[NARRATOR] We turned our backs on the wretched valley, crossing without speech over the bank which encircles it. In that place, there was less than night and less than day, so I could not see far ahead. But I heard a horn sounding so loud that it would have made any thunderclap feeble. It directed my eyes, which tracked the sound in a backward course, to one place only. After his melancholy defeat, when Charlemagne lost his holy company, Orlando did not blow so dreadfully. Not long did I keep my face turned that way, before I thought I saw many high towers.

[DANTE] I said: "Tell me, Teacher, what town is this?"

[VIRGIL] He replied: "Because you are peering through the mists from too far away, your fancy cannot but mislead you. You will find out, when you get there, how much your sight deceives you at a distance; so spur yourself on a little more." Then he took me kindly by the hand and said: "Before we get farther, so that the real will seem to you less strange, I am going to tell you that they are not towers but giants; and in a circle around the bank of the pit, they are in it up to their navels—all of them."

Come quando la nebbia si dissipa,
    lo sguardo a poco a poco raffigura
36   ciò che cela il vapor che l' aere stipa,
così forando l' aura grossa e scura,
    più e più appressando ver la sponda,
    fuggiemi errore e cresciemi paura;
però che come su la cerchia tonda
    Montereggion di torri si corona,
42   così la proda che 'l pozzo circonda
torreggiavan di mezza la persona
    li orribili giganti, cui minaccia
    Giove del cielo ancora quando tuona.
E io scorgeva già d' alcun la faccia,
    le spalle e 'l petto e del ventre gran parte,
48   e per le coste giù ambo le braccia.
Natura certo, quando lasciò l' arte
    di sì fatti animali, assai fè bene
    per torre tali essecutori a Marte.
E s' ella d' elefanti e di balene
    non si pente, chi guarda sottilmente,
54   più giusta e più discreta la ne tene;
chè dove l' argomento de la mente
    s' aggiugne al mal volere ed a la possa,
    nessun riparo vi può far la gente.
La faccia sua mi parea lunga e grossa
    come la pina di San Pietro a Roma,
60   e a sua proporzione eran l' altre ossa;
sì che la ripa, ch' era perizoma
    dal mezzo in giù, ne mostrava ben tanto
    di sopra, che di giungere a la chioma
tre Frison s'averien dato mal vanto;
    però ch'i' ne vedea trenta gran palmi
66   dal luogo in giù dov'uomo affibia 'l manto.
«Raphèl maÿ amèch zabì almì»
    cominciò a gridar la fiera bocca,
    cui non si convenian più dolci salmi.

[NARRATOR] As, when the fog clears, our vision little by little makes out what the haze which thickens the air is hiding, so, as my vision pierced the thick and murky atmosphere, while we were getting closer and closer to the edge of the pit, error left me and fear gained upon me.

[*The towering giants, guardians of*
Circle Nine: 31.40–111]

[NARRATOR] As above her round wall-circuit, Montereggioni is ringed with her towers, so, over the rim that encircles the pit,[3] from the middle of their bodies towered the horrid giants, whom Jove still threatens from the sky when he thunders. And then I was making out the face of one of them, his shoulders and his breast and much of his belly, and both his arms down by his sides. Certainly Nature, when she gave up the making of such creatures, was quite right in taking such warriors from Mars. And if she does not repent for elephants and whales, anybody who looks closely thinks her for that more observing and prudent, because when the power of the mind is added to malice and strength, man cannot defend himself. That giant's face I thought as long and broad as the pine cone of St. Peter's at Rome, and the rest of his body was in proportion, so that the bank which, from his middle down, was a cincture of modesty,[4] still showed above it so much of him that three Frisians could not have bragged that they reached his hair. Hence I saw thirty spans[5] of him below the place where a man pins his mantle.
[NIMROD] "Raphel mai amecche zabi almi,"[6] yelled his savage mouth, to which softer psalms were not suited.

E 'l duca mio ver lui: «Anima sciocca,
    tieni col corno, e con quel ti disfoga,
72   quand' ira o altra passion ti tocca!
Cercati al collo, e troverai la soga
    che 'l tien legato, o anima confusa,
    e vedi lui che 'l gran petto ti doga.»
Poi disse a me: «Elli stesso s'accusa;
    questi è Nembròt, per lo cui mal coto
78   pur un linguaggio nel mondo non s'usa.
Lasciamlo stare e non parliamo a voto;
    ché così è a lui ciascun linguaggio
    come 'l suo ad altrui, ch'a nullo è noto.»
Facemmo adunque più lungo viaggio,
    volti a sinistra; e al trar d'un balestro
84   trovammo l'altro assai più fero e maggio.
A cinger lui qual che fosse 'l maestro,
    non so io dir, ma el tenea soccinto
    dinanzi l'altro e dietro il braccio destro
d'una catena che 'l tenea avvinto
    dal collo in giù, sì che 'n su lo scoperto
90   si ravvolgea infino al giro quinto.
«Questo superbo volle essere sperto
    di sua potenza contro al sommo Giove»
    disse 'l mio duca, «ond'elli ha cotal merto.
Fialte ha nome; e fece le gran prove
    quando i giganti fer paura a' Dei:
96   le braccia ch'el menò, già mai non move.»
E io a lui: «S'esser puote, io vorrei
    che de lo smisurato Briareo
    esperienza avesser li occhi miei.»
Ond'ei rispuose: «Tu vedrai Anteo
    presso di qui, che parla ed è disciolto,
102   che ne porrà nel fondo d'ogni reo.
Quel che tu vuo' veder, più là è molto,
    ed è legato e fatto come questo,
    salvo che più feroce par nel volto.»

[VIRGIL] My guide shouted at him: "Absurd soul, stick to your horn, and with that get rid of anger or any emotion that molests you. Feel for it at your neck, and you will find the cord that holds it, O giddy soul, and you will see it hooping your big chest."

Then he said to me: "He accuses himself. This is Nimrod, through whose folly one language only is not now used in the world. We may as well let him alone and not talk uselessly, because every language is to him as his to us, which to no one is known."

[NARRATOR] We then went farther, bearing to the left, and a crossbow-shot away we reached the next giant, much more savage and larger. What skilled workman bound him, I cannot say, but his left arm was girt up in front, and his right arm behind, with a chain which fettered him from his neck down, so that on his visible part it was wound around him as far as the fifth turn.

[VIRGIL] "This proud giant tested his might against great Jove," said my guide, "and this is his reward. Ephialtes he is named, and he did great feats when the giants frightened the gods. The arms with which he struck, never more does he move."

[DANTE] And I said to him: "If it is possible, I should like my eyes to examine for themselves the measureless Briareus."

[VIRGIL] He answered: "You will see Antaeus nearby, who speaks and is loose; and he will put us down in the depths of all wickedness. The one you wish to see is much farther on; he is bound and quite like this one, except that his expression is more savage."

Non fu tremoto già tanto rubesto,
 che scotesse una torre così forte,
108 come Fialte a scuotersi fu presto.
Allor temett' io più che mai la morte,
 e non v' era mestier più che la dotta,
 s' io non avessi viste le ritorte.
Noi procedemmo più avante allotta,
 e venimmo ad Anteo, che ben cinqu' alle,
114 sanza la testa, uscìa fuor de la grotta.
«O tu che ne la fortunata valle
 che fece Scipion di gloria reda,
 quand'Annibàl co' suoi diede le spalle,
recasti già mille leon per preda,
 e che se fossi stato a l' alta guerra
120 de' tuoi fratelli, ancor par che si creda
ch' avrebber vinto i figli de la terra;
 mettine giù, e non ten vegna schifo,
 dove Cocito la freddura serra.
Non ci fare ire a Tizio nè a Tifo:
 questi può dar di quel che qui si brama;
126 però ti china, e non torcer lo grifo.
Ancor ti può nel mondo render fama,
 ch' el vive e lunga vita ancor aspetta,
 se innanzi tempo Grazia a sè nol chiama.»
Così disse 'l maestro; e quelli in fretta
 le man distese, e prese il duca mio,
132 ond' Ercule sentì già grande stretta.
Virgilio, quando prender si sentio,
 disse a me: «Fatti qua, sì ch' io ti prenda»;
 poi fece sì ch' un fascio era elli e io.
Qual pare a riguardar la Garisenda
 sotto 'l chinato, quando un nuvol vada
138 sovr' essa sì, che ella incontro penda;
tal parve Anteo a me che stava a bada
 di vederlo chinare, e fu tal ora
 ch' i' avrei voluto ir per altra strada.

[NARRATOR] Never, I am sure, was an earthquake so violent to shake a tower so hard as Ephialtes instantly shook himself. Then I feared death more than ever; and nothing more was needed than my panic, if I had not seen the twisted chains.

> *[Antaeus lifts the travelers into the*
> *Ninth Circle: 31.112–145]*

[NARRATOR] We still went forward and came to Antaeus, who at least five ells,[7] not counting his head, rose above the bank.

[VIRGIL] "You who in the valley of good fortune, which made Scipio heir of glory when Hannibal and his soldiers turned their backs,[8] once caught a thousand lions as your prey; you of whom I can believe also that if you had been in that famous war of your brothers, the Earth's sons would have conquered—put us down (and don't be fussy about it) where the cold makes Cocytus solid. Do not make us go to Tityos or to Typhon. This man can give you something that you want here. So stoop, and don't turn up your nose. He can still give you fame in the world, because he is alive and looks forward to long life if, ahead of time, grace does not summon him to itself." So my teacher spoke.

[NARRATOR] And the giant in a hurry stretched out his hands, from which Hercules long ago felt powerful squeezing, and picked up my guide.

[VIRGIL] Virgil, when he felt himself gripped, said to me: "Come here, so I can grip you." Then he made one bundle of himself and me.

[NARRATOR] Just as Garisenda appears, if you are beneath her overhang when a cloud so passes above her that she may tilt toward you,[9] such Antaeus seemed to me as I stood to watch him stoop—and that was a moment when I should have chosen to go by another road.[10] But

Ma lievemente al fondo che divora
Lucifero con Giuda, ci sposò;
144   nè, sì chinato, lì fece dimora,
e come albero in nave si levò.

softly on the very bottom,[11] which holds in torment Lucifer with Judas, he set us down. He did not remain so bent, but raised himself like a mast on a ship.

CANTO 32

S'io avessi le rime aspre e chiocce,
   come si converrebbe al tristo buco
   sovra 'l qual pontan tutte l'altre rocce,
io premerei di mio concetto il suco
   più pienamente; ma perch'io non l'abbo,
6   non sanza tema a dicer mi conduco;
ché non è impresa da pigliare a gabbo
   discriver fondo a tutto l'universo,
   né da lingua che chiami mamma o babbo:
ma quelle donne aiutino il mio verso
   ch'aiutaro Anfione a chiuder Tebe,
12   sì che dal fatto il dir non sia diverso.
Oh sovra tutte mal creata plebe
   che stai nel luogo onde parlare è duro,
   mei foste state qui pecore o zebe!
Come noi fummo giù nel pozzo scuro
   sotto i piè del gigante assai più bassi,
18   e io mirava ancora a l'alto muro,
dicere udimmi: «Guarda come passi:
   va sì che tu non calchi con le piante
   le teste de' fratei miseri lassi.»
Per ch'io mi volsi, e vidimi davante
   e sotto i piedi un lago, che per gelo
24   avea di vetro e non d'acqua sembiante.
Non fece al corso suo sì grosso velo
   di verno la Danoia in Osterlicchi
   né Tanaì là sotto il freddo cielo,
com'era quivi; che se Tambernicchi
   vi fosse su caduto, o Pietrapiana,
30   non avria pur da l'orlo fatto cricchi.
E come a gracidar si sta la rana
   col muso fuor de l'acqua, quando sogna
   di spigolar sovente la villana;

CANTO 32

CIRCLE NINE, ROUND ONE (CAINA)

[*The poet's hard task in describing the lowest Hell: 32.1–15*]

[POET] *If I had verses harsh and strident, such as would suit the sad pit upon which rest all the other rocks,*[1] *I would press out the juice of my concept more completely,*[2] *but since I do not have them, not without fear shall I write,*[3] *because to describe the lowest part of the whole universe is not a task to be joked about, nor is it for a tongue that shouts "Mama" and "Papa."*[4] *But those ladies must assist my poem who assisted Amphion in building the walls of Thebes, so that from the deed the word may not differ. O multitude wretched beyond all other souls, who live in the place of which to speak is hard, better you had here been sheep or goats!*

[*Traitors to their relatives, in Caina: 32.16–72*]

[VIRGIL] When we were down in the dark pit near the giant's feet, much lower down,[5] and I still was gazing at the high wall, he said to me: "Watch how you step. Walk so that you do not trample on the heads of the weary wretched brothers."[6]

[NARRATOR] On that, I turned and saw, in front of me and under my feet, a lake which, through the cold, resembled glass, not water. For its channel in winter, the Danube in Austria or the Don, under the cold skies, never made so thick a garment as I saw there, so that if Tambernicchi had fallen upon it, or Pietrapana, not even at the edge would they have cracked it. And as, in order to croak, the frog lies with its muzzle out of the water, when the peasant woman often dreams of glean-

livide, insin là dove appar vergogna
eran l'ombre dolenti ne la ghiaccia,
36   mettendo i denti in nota di cicogna.
Ognuna in giù tenea volta la faccia:
da bocca il freddo, e da li occhi il cor tristo
tra lor testimonianza si procaccia.
Quand' io m' ebbi dintorno alquanto visto,
volsimi a' piedi, e vidi due sì stretti,
42   che 'l pel del capo avieno insieme misto.
«Ditemi, voi che sì strignete i petti,»
diss' io, «chi siete?» E quei piegaro i colli;
e poi ch' ebber li visi a me eretti,
li occhi lor, ch' eran pria pur dentro molli,
gocciar su per le labbra, e 'l gelo strinse
48   le lacrime tra essi e riserrolli.
Con legno legno spranga mai non cinse
forte così; ond' ei come due becchi
cozzaro insieme, tanta ira li vinse.
E un ch' avea perduti ambo li orecchi
per la freddura, pur col viso in giue,
54   disse: «Perchè cotanto in noi ti specchi?
Se vuoi saper chi son cotesti due,
la valle onde Bisenzo si dichina
del padre loro Alberto e di lor fue.
D' un corpo usciro; e tutta la Caina
potrai cercare, e non troverai ombra
60   degna più d' esser fitta in gelatina;
non quelli a cui fu rotto il petto e l' ombra
con esso un colpo per la man d'Artù;
non Focaccia; non questi che m' ingombra
col capo sì, ch' i' non veggio oltre più,
e fu nomato Sassol Mascheroni:
66   se tosco se', ben sai omai chi fu.
E perchè non mi metti in più sermoni,
sappi ch' io fui 'l Camicion de' Pazzi;
e aspetto Carlin che mi scagioni.»

ing, so were the lamenting shades, livid, in the ice up to the place where shame shows itself,[7] gnashing their teeth as a stork chatters. Each one downward only was keeping its face. The cold is bringing its proof from their mouths, and their sad hearts bringing its proof from their eyes. After I had looked around a while, I walked along.[8] And I saw two so tight together that the hair of their heads was intermingled.

[DANTE] "Tell me, you who so press your breasts together, who you are," I said.

[NARRATOR] They bent their necks, and when they had raised their faces to me, their eyes, up till then wet inside only, poured drops over their lips, and the cold hardened the tears between them and fastened them together.[9] Wood with wood no clamps ever joined so firmly, so that like two goats they butted together; with such anger they were overcome.

[CAMICION DE' PAZZI] And one who had lost both ears through the cold, still with his face down, said: "Why, among us, do you so long look at your reflection?[10] If you wish to learn who these two are, the valley from which the Bisenzio flows down belonged to Albert their father and to them. From one body they came forth; and you can ransack all Caina without finding any shade more deserving to be set in frozen pudding;[11] not that one whose breast and shadow were broken by a single blow from Arthur's hand;[12] not Focaccia; not this one who so obstructs me with his head that I can see no farther, and who was named Sassol Mascheroni. If you are a Tuscan, you now know well who he was. And so that you will not make me talk any more, I tell you that I was Camicion de' Pazzi, and I am waiting for Carlino, who will free me from blame."[13]

Poscia vid' io mille visi cagnazzi
 fatti per freddo; onde mi vien riprezzo,
72 e verrà sempre, de' gelati guazzi.
E mentre ch' andavamo inver lo mezzo
 al quale ogni gravezza si rauna,
 e io tremava ne l' etterno rezzo;
se voler fu o destino o fortuna,
 non so; ma, passeggiando tra le teste,
78 forte percossi il piè nel viso ad una.
Piangendo mi sgridò: «Perchè mi peste?
 se tu non vieni a crescer la vendetta
 di Montaperti, perchè mi moleste?»
E io: «Maestro mio, or qui m'aspetta,
 sì ch'io esca d'un dubbio per costui;
84 poi mi farai, quantunque vorrai, fretta.»
Lo duca stette, e io dissi a colui
 che bestemmiava duramente ancora:
 «Qual se' tu che così rampogni altrui?»
«Or tu chi se' che vai per l'Antenora,
 percotendo» rispuose «altrui le gote,
90 sì che, se fossi vivo, troppo fora?»
«Vivo son io, e caro esser ti puote»
 fu mia risposta, «se dimandi fama,
 ch'io metta il nome tuo tra l'altre note.»
Ed elli a me: «Del contrario ho io brama;
 levati quinci e non mi dar più lagna,
96 ché mal sai lusingar per questa lama!»
Allor lo presi per la cuticagna,
 e dissi: «El converrà che tu ti nomi,
 o che capel qui su non ti rimagna.»
Ond'elli a me: «Perché tu mi dischiomi,
 né ti dirò ch'io sia, né mosterrolti,
102 se mille fiate in sul capo mi tomi.»

[NARRATOR] Then I saw a thousand faces made purple by the cold. Hence I shudder, and always shall, at frozen streams.

CIRCLE NINE, ROUND TWO (ANTENORA)

[Traitors to party and country: 32.73–123]

[NARRATOR] While we were going toward the center to which everything heavy is drawn, and I was trembling in the unceasing chill—whether will or fate or fortune caused it,[14] I do not know; at any rate, walking among the heads, with force I struck my foot against the face of one of them.

[BOCCA DEGLI ABATI] Weeping, he shrieked at me: "Why do you kick me? If you don't come to increase the vengeance for Montaperti, why do you torment me?"

[DANTE] And I said: "Teacher, now wait for me here, to let me get rid of a suspicion about this man. Then you can make me hurry as fast as you like."[15]

[DANTE] My guide stood still, and I said to the man, who still was cursing violently: "Who are you, who are so rating me?"

[BOCCA] "And who are you," he replied, "who go through Antenora whacking our cheeks so hard that if you were alive you couldn't do so much?"

[DANTE] "I am alive, and I can be of value to you," was my reply, "if you wish fame, because I can put your name in my notebook."

[BOCCA] And he replied: "The opposite is what I want. Get out of here, and do not vex me further. You cannot flatter in this marsh."[16]

[DANTE] Then I seized him by the hair at the nape of his neck and said: "You'll give your name or you'll not have a single hair left."

[BOCCA] Yet he answered: "Even if you do scalp me, I will not tell who I am, or show[17] it to you, if you come down on my head a thousand times."

Io avea già i capelli in mano avvolti,
   e tratti li n'avea più d'una ciocca,
   latrando lui con gli occhi in giù raccolti,
quando un altro gridò: «Che hai tu, Bocca?
   non ti basta sonar con le mascelle,
108   se tu non latri? qual diavol ti tocca?»
«Omai» diss'io «non vo' che più favelle,
   malvagio traditor; ch'a la tua onta
   io porterò di te vere novelle.»
«Va via» rispuose, «e ciò che tu vuoi, conta;
   ma non tacer, se tu di qua entro eschi,
114   di quel ch'ebbe or così la lingua pronta.
El piange qui l'argento de' Franceschi:
   'Io vidi' potrai dir 'quel da Duera
   là dove i peccatori stanno freschi.'
Se fossi domandato altri chi v'era,
   tu hai da lato quel di Beccheria
120   di cui segò Fiorenza la gorgiera.
Gianni de' Soldanier credo che sia
   più là con Ganellone e Tebaldello,
   ch'aprì Faenza quando si dormia.»
Noi eravam partiti già da ello,
   ch' io vidi due ghiacciati in una buca,
126   sì che l' un capo a l' altro era cappello;
e come 'l pan per fame si manduca,
   così 'l sovran li denti a l' altro pose
   là 've 'l cervel s' aggiugne con la nuca.
Non altrimenti Tideo si rose
   le tempie a Menalippo per disdegno,
132   che quei faceva il teschio e l' altre cose.
«O tu che mostri per sì bestial segno
   odio sovra colui che tu ti mangi,
   dimmi 'l perchè» diss' io, «per tal convegno,
che se tu a ragion di lui ti piangi,
   sappiendo chi voi siete e la sua pecca,
138   nel mondo suso ancora io te ne cangi,
se quella con ch' io parlo non si secca.»

[BUOSO DA DUERA] I already had his hair twisted in my hand and had pulled out more than one lock, as he barked with his eyes turned down, when another shade shouted: "What's wrong with you, Bocca? Isn't it enough for you to chatter with your jaws, without barking? What devil is stirring you up?"

[DANTE] "Now," I said, "I don't care about your talking further, wicked traitor, because to your disgrace I will carry true news about you."

[BOCCA] "Go ahead," he replied, and tell what you will, but don't keep still, as you hope to get out of here, about that fellow who just now had his tongue so ready. He weeps here for the Frenchmen's coin. 'I saw,' you can say, 'the man from Duera in the place where the sinners keep cool.' If you are asked: 'Who else was there?' you have beside you that Beccheria fellow whose throat the Florentines sawed. Gianni de' Soldanier is, I believe, farther over there with Ganelon and Tebaldello, who opened Faenza when the citizens were asleep."

[Ugolino, starved to death by the
Pisans: 32.124–139]

[NARRATOR] We had just got away from him, when I saw two frozen into one hole, so that one's head was the other's cap. And as a hungry man manducates[18] bread, so the uppermost put his teeth into the other just where the brain joins with the spine. In no other way did Tydeus gnaw the temples of Menalippus in anger, than this one did the skull and the rest.

[DANTE] "O you who by such a bestial sign show your hate for the one you are eating, tell me the reason," I said, "with the agreement that, if you justly complain of him, I, knowing who you are and his sin, in the world above will recompense you for it, if that with which I speak does not dry up."

CANTO 33

La bocca sollevò dal fiero pasto
  quel peccator, forbendola a' capelli
  del capo ch' elli avea di retro guasto.
Poi cominciò: «Tu vuo' ch' io rinovelli
  disperato dolor che 'l cor mi preme
6   già pur pensando, pria ch' io ne favelli.
Ma se le mie parole esser dien seme
  che frutti infamia al traditor ch' i' rodo,
  parlare e lacrimar vedrai insieme.
Io non so chi tu se' nè per che modo
  venuto se' qua giù; ma fiorentino
12   mi sembri veramente quand' io t' odo.
Tu dei saper ch' io fui conte Ugolino,
  e questi è l' arcivescovo Ruggieri:
  or ti dirò perché i son tal vicino.
Che per l' effetto de' suo' mai pensieri,
  fidandomi di lui, io fossi preso
18   e poscia morto, dir non è mestieri;
però quel che non puoi avere inteso,
  ciò è come la morte mia fu cruda,
  udirai, e saprai s' e' m' ha offeso.
Breve pertugio dentro da la Muda
  la qual per me ha il titol de la fame,
24   e che conviene ancor ch' altrui si chiuda,
m' avea mostrato per lo suo forame
  più lune già, quand' io feci 'l mal sonno
  che del futuro mi squarciò il velame.
Questi pareva a me maestro e donno,
  cacciando il lupo e i lupicini al monte
30   per che i Pisan veder Lucca non ponno.
Con cagne magre, studiose e conte,
  Gualandi con Sismondi e con Lanfranchi
  s' avea messi dinanzi da la fronte.

CANTO 33

CIRCLE NINE, ROUND TWO (ANTENORA), *cont.*

[Ugolino's hatred for Archbishop
Ruggieri: 33.1–21]

[NARRATOR] That sinner raised his mouth from his savage food, wiping it on the hair of the head whose back he had destroyed.

[UGOLINO] Then he said: "You ask me to renew hopeless grief, which crushes my heart when I only remember it, before I speak of it. But if my words can be seeds from which can grow disgrace for the traitor I am gnawing, you shall hear both speech and weeping.[1] I do not know who you are, or in what way you have come down here; yet at any rate, you seem to me a Florentine when I hear you speak. So then, I was Count Ugolino and this is the Archbishop Ruggieri. Now I shall tell you why I am such a neighbor to him. That as the result of his wicked plans, trusting in him, I was arrested and then killed, I do not need to say. However, what you cannot have learned, namely, how cruel my death was, I shall tell you, and you will know whether he has injured me.

[Ugolino tells of his death and that of
his children: 33.22–78]

[UGOLINO] "A small crevice in the wall of the Muda,[2] which from me gets the name of Hunger Tower, and in which others still must be shut up,[3] had already through its opening shown me many moons, when I had the bad dream that tore the covering off my future. This man here appeared to me as director and lord, hunting the wolf and his cubs on the mountain which keeps the Pisans from seeing Lucca. With lean dogs, eager and well trained, he had put Gualandi and Sismondi and Lanfranchi ahead of himself, at the front. After a short

In picciol corso mi parieno stanchi
　lo padre e i figli, e con l' agute scane
36　　mi parea lor veder fender li fianchi.
Quando fui desto innanzi la dimane,
　pianger senti' fra 'l sonno i miei figliuoli
　ch' eran con meco, e domandar del pane.
Ben se' crudel, se tu già non ti duoli,
　pensando ciò che 'l mio cor s' annunziava;
42　　e se non piangi, di che pianger suoli?
Già eran desti, e l' ora s' appressava
　che 'l cibo ne solea esser addotto,
　e per suo sogno ciascun dubitava;
e io senti' chiavar l' uscio di sotto
　a l' orribile torre; ond' io guardai
48　　nel viso a' mie' figliuoi sanza far motto.
Io non piangea, sì dentro impetrai:
　piangevan elli; e Anselmuccio mio
　disse: 'Tu guardi sì, padre! che hai?
Perciò non lacrimai nè rispuos' io
　tutto quel giorno nè la notte appresso,
54　　infin che l' altro sol nel mondo uscio.
Come un poco di raggio si fu messo
　nel doloroso carcere, e io scorsi
　per quattro visi il mio aspetto stesso,
ambo le man per lo dolor mi morsi;
　ed ei, pensando ch' i' 'l fessi per voglia
60　　di manicar, di subito levorsi,
e disser: 'Padre, assai ci fia men doglia,
　se tu mangi di noi: tu ne vestisti
　queste misere carni, e tu le spoglia.'
Queta'mi allor per non farli più tristi;
　lo dì e l'altro stemmo tutti muti:
66　　ahi dura terra, perché non t'apristi?
Poscia che fummo al quarto dì venuti,
　Gaddo mi si gettò disteso a' piedi,
　dicendo: 'Padre mio, ché non m'aiuti?'

run, the father and his sons seemed to me weary, and I dreamed I saw the dogs' sharp fangs tear their sides. When I awoke before morning, I heard my children who were with me weeping in their sleep and asking for bread. You are very cruel if you too do not grieve, imagining what my heart told me. If indeed you do not weep, what is there that makes you weep? They were already awake, and the hour was near when food was always brought us, and because of his dream,[4] each one was afraid. Then I heard below the door of the frightful tower nailed shut. At that I looked in the faces of my children without saying a word. I did not weep—I so turned to stone within. They did weep, and my little Anselmo said: 'You look so strange, father; what is the matter?' Still I did not weep, and I did not answer all that day, or the night after, until the next sun came to the world. When a ray of light came into our sad prison and I saw on four faces my own expression, I bit both my hands in sorrow. And they, thinking I did it because I wanted to eat, at once stood up and said: 'Father, we should be much less pained if you fed on us; you put on us these wretched garments of flesh, and it is for you to take them off.' I stilled myself then, not to make them sadder. That day and the next we all kept silent. O hard earth! why do you not open? When we had reached the fourth day, Gaddo threw himself full length at my feet, saying: 'Father, why do you not help me?' Then he died,

Quivi morì; e come tu mi vedi,
vid'io cascar li tre ad uno ad uno
72   tra 'l quinto dì e 'l sesto; ond'io mi diedi,
già cieco, a brancolar sovra ciascuno,
e due dì li chiamai, poi che fur morti:
poscia, più che 'l dolor, poté 'l digiuno.»
Quand'ebbe detto ciò, con gli occhi torti
riprese 'l teschio misero co' denti,
78   che furo a l'osso, come d'un can, forti.
Ahi Pisa, vituperio de le genti
del bel paese là dove 'l sì suona,
poi che i vicini a te punir son lenti,
muovasi la Capraia e la Gorgona,
e faccian siepe ad Arno in su la foce,
84   sì ch'elli annieghi in te ogni persona!
Che se 'l conte Ugolino aveva voce
d'aver tradita te de le castella,
non dovei tu i figliuoi porre a tal croce.
Innocenti facea l'età novella,
novella Tebe, Uguiccione e 'l Brigata
90   e li altri due che 'l canto suso appella.
Noi passammo oltre là 've la gelata
ruvidamente un'altra gente fascia,
non volta in giù, ma tutta riversata.
Lo pianto stesso lì pianger non lascia,
e 'l duol che truova in su li occhi rintoppo,
96   si volge in entro a far crescer l'ambascia;
ché le lagrime prime fanno groppo,
e sì come visiere di cristallo,
riempion sotto 'l ciglio tutto il coppo.
E avvegna che sì come d'un callo,
per la freddura ciascun sentimento
102   cessato avesse del mio viso stallo,
già mi parea sentire alquanto vento:
per ch'io: «Maestro mio, questo chi move?
non è qua giù ogne vapore spento?»

and as sure as you are looking at me, I saw the three fall one after another in the course of the fifth day and the sixth. Then, already blind, I kept groping over them, and two days I called upon them after they were dead. Then stronger than sorrow was starvation."

[NARRATOR] When he had spoken, with eyes askance he laid hold of that wretched skull with his teeth, which on the bone had the power of a dog's.

[*The poet's invective against Pisa: 33.79–90*]

[POET] *Oh, Pisa, disgrace to the people of the fair land where the word si is used, since your neighbors are slow to punish you, may Capraia and Gorgona be moved and make a hedge for Arno at her mouth, that she may drown in you every person! Because even though Count Ugolino was said to have betrayed some of your towns, you should not at all have put his children to such torture. O modern Thebes! their tender age made innocent Uguccione and Brigata and the other two whom my song names above.*

CIRCLE NINE, ROUND THREE (PTOLOMEA)

[*Traitors to Guests: 33.91–108*]

[NARRATOR] We went further, to a place where the ice harshly sheathes a second group, not bending down but looking straight up.[5] Their tears themselves do not let them shed tears, and their weeping, which strikes blockage at their eyes, turns inward to increase their agony, because the first tears form a bulk and, like a mask of glass, completely fill the cup under the brow. And even though, as from a callus, all feeling had left its abode in my face through the cold, I did feel a little wind.

[DANTE] So I said: "Teacher, what causes this? Is not every motion of the air exhausted down here?"

Ed elli a me: «Avaccio sarai dove
di ciò ti farà l'occhio la risposta,
108   veggendo la cagion che 'l fiato piove.»
E un de' tristi de la fredda crosta
gridò a noi: «O anime crudeli,
tanto che dato v'è l'ultima posta,
levatemi dal viso i duri veli,
sì ch'io sfoghi 'l duol che 'l cor m'impregna,
114   un poco, pria che il pianto si raggeli.»
Per ch'io a lui: «Se vuo' ch'i' ti sovvegna,
dimmi chi se', e s'io non ti disbrigo,
al fondo de la ghiaccia ir mi convegna.»
Rispuose adunque: «I' son frate Alberigo;
io son quel da le frutta del mal orto,
120   che qui riprendo dattero per figo.»
«Oh» diss'io lui, «or se' tu ancor morto?»
Ed elli a me: «Come 'l mio corpo stea
nel mondo su, nulla scienza porto.
Cotal vantaggio ha questa Tolomea,
che spesse volte l'anima ci cade
126   innanzi ch'Atropòs mossa le dea.
E perché tu più volentier mi rade
le 'nvetriate lacrime dal volto,
sappie che tosto che l'anima trade
come fec'io, il corpo suo l'è tolto
da un demonio, che poscia il governa
132   mentre che 'l tempo suo tutto sia volto.
Ella ruina in sì fatta cisterna;
e forse pare ancor lo corpo suso
de l'ombra che di qua dietro mi verna.
Tu 'l dei saper, se tu vien pur mo giuso:
egli è ser Branca d'Oria, e son più anni
138   poscia passati ch'el fu sì racchiuso.»
«Io credo» diss'io lui «che tu m'inganni;
ché Branca d'Oria non morì unquanche,
e mangia e bee e dorme e veste panni.»

[VIRGIL] And he answered: "You soon will be where the eye will answer your question, seeing the cause that throws out the breeze."

[Souls in Hell, with bodies in the world above:
33.109–150]

[FRATE ALBERIGO DEI MANFREDI] One of the wretches of the cold crust shrieked at us: "O souls so wicked that to you the last station is given, take from my face the hard veils, so I may pour out—a little—the suffering that swells my heart, before my tears are frozen again."
[DANTE] So I said to him: "If you want me to help you, tell me who you are, and if I do not disencumber you, may I have to go to the farthest point of the ice."
[FRATE ALBERIGO] Then he answered: "I am Frate Alberigo; I am he of the evil garden's fruit, who here get date for fig."[6]
[DANTE] "Oh," I said, "are you too now dead?"
[FRATE ALBERIGO] And he answered: "How my body is getting along in the world above, I have no notion. This Ptolomea is so privileged that often the soul falls down here before Atropos releases it. And so that you more willingly will clear the glasslike tears from my face, I now tell you that as soon as a soul commits betrayal, as I did, its body is taken from it by a demon, who then controls it until all its time on earth is gone. The soul falls into this cistern here. And actually still above[7] is the body belonging to the soul that here behind me is wintering. You must know him, if you have only just come down here; he is Ser Branca d'Oria, and many years have gone by since he was so frozen in."
[DANTE] "I believe," I said, "that you are lying to me, because Branca d'Oria has not died, but eats and drinks and sleeps and wears clothing."

«Nel fosso su» diss'el «de' Malebranche,
  là dove bolle la tenace pece,
144   non era giunto ancora Michel Zanche,
che questi lasciò il diavolo in sua vece
  nel corpo suo, ed un suo prossimano
  che 'l tradimento insieme con lui fece.
Ma distendi oggimai in qua la mano;
  aprimi gli occhi.» E io non glieli apersi;
150   e cortesia fu lui esser villano.
Ahi Genovesi, uomini diversi
  d' ogne costume e pien d' ogni magagna,
  perchè non siete voi del mondo spersi?
Chè col peggiore spirto di Romagna
  trovai di voi un tal, che per sua opra
156   in anima in Cocito già si bagna,
ed in corpo par vivo ancor di sopra.

[FRATE ALBERIGO] "To the ditch of the Badclaws above," he said, "the place where the sticky tar boils, Michael Zanche[8] had not yet come down when this fellow left the devil in his place in his body,[9] and so did one of his relatives who carried out the betrayal with him. But now reach your hand here; open my eyes for me."

[NARRATOR] But I did not open them for him; and courtesy it was to be boorish with him.

[*Invective against Genoa:*[10] *33.151–157*]

[POET] *O Genoese, you men who are strangers to every observance, and abound in every vice, why are you not erased from the world?*

[NARRATOR] Because with the Romagna's most wicked spirit,[11] I found one of you such that for his deeds already in soul he bathes in Cocytus, and in body he is yet alive in the world.

CANTO 34

«*Vexilla regis prodeunt inferni*
    verso di noi; però dinanzi mira»
    disse 'l maestro mio «se tu 'l discerni.»
Come quando una grossa nebbia spira,
    o quando l' emisperio nostro annotta,
6   par di lungi un molin che 'l vento gira,
veder mi parve un tal dificio allotta;
    poi per lo vento mi ristrinsi retro
    al duca mio; chè non li era altra grotta.
Già era, e con paura il metto in metro,
    là dove l' ombre tutte eran coperte,
12   e trasparien come festuca in vetro.
Altre sono a giacere; altre stanno erte,
    quella col capo e quella con le piante;
    altra, com' arco, il volto a' piè rinverte.
Quando noi fummo fatti tanto avante,
    ch' al mio maestro piacque di mostrarmi
18   la creatura ch' ebbe il bel sembiante,
dinanzi mi si tolse e fè restarmi,
    «Ecco Dite» dicendo, «ed ecco il loco
    ove convien che di fortezza t' armi.»
Com' io divenni allor gelato e fioco,
    nol dimandar, lettor, ch' i' non lo scrivo,
24   però ch' ogni parlar sarebbe poco.
Io non mori', e non rimasi vivo:
    pensa oggimai per te, s' hai fior d' ingegno,
    qual io divenni, d' uno e d' altro privo.
Lo 'mperador del doloroso regno
    da mezzo il petto uscia fuor de la ghiaccia;
30   e più con un gigante io mi convegno,
che i giganti non fan con le sue braccia:
    vedi oggimai quant' esser dee quel tutto
    ch' a così fatta parte si confaccia.

CANTO 34

CIRCLE NINE, ROUND FOUR (GIUDECCA)

[Traitors to all mankind: 34.1–15]

[VIRGIL] "The banners of the King of Hell appear to us.[1] Therefore gaze ahead," said my teacher, "to see if you make him out."[2]

[NARRATOR] Thereupon, as when a thick mist rises or when darkness comes over our hemisphere, in the distance a windmill appears, I thought I saw such a building. Then on account of the gale, I shrank behind my guide, for there I had no other windbreak.[3] Now I was (and with fear I put it in verse) in a place where the shades were wholly covered, and showed through like a bit of straw in glass. Some are lying down, others are erect, one having his head uppermost, another his soles; others like a bow bend their faces toward their feet.

[Dis, or Satan, the fallen archangel: 34.16–54]

[VIRGIL] When we had gone on so far that my teacher thought fit to show me the creature whose appearance was once so beautiful, he moved from before me and had me stand still, saying: "There stands Dis; and you are in the place where you need to put on armor of fortitude."

[NARRATOR] How cold and speechless I then became, do not ask, reader, because I am not writing it, since all speech would be too weak. I did not die and I did not keep alive. Imagine now for yourself, if you have a speck of intellect, what I became, lacking both.

[NARRATOR] The sovereign of the realm of pain rose out of the ice as far as mid-chest, and with a giant I am more nearly equal than are the giants with his arms. Now you see what must be the size of the whole which fits

S' el fu sì bello com' elli è or brutto,
e contra 'l suo fattore alzò le ciglia,
36   ben dee da lui proceder ogni lutto.
Oh quanto parve a me gran meraviglia
quand' io vidi tre facce a la sua testa!
L' una dinanzi, e quella era vermiglia;
l' altr' eran due, che s' aggiugnieno a questa
sovresso 'l mezzo di ciascuna spalla,
42   e sè giugnieno al luogo de la cresta:
e la destra parea tra bianca e gialla;
la sinistra a vedere era tal, quali
vegnon di là onde 'l Nilo s' avvalla.
Sotto ciascuna uscivan due grand' ali,
quanto si convenia a tanto uccello:
48   vele di mar non vid' io mai cotali.
Non avean penne, ma di vispistrello
era lor modo; e quelle svolazzava,
sì che tre venti si movean da ello,
quindi Cocito tutto s' aggelava.
Con sei occhi piangea, e per tre menti
54   gocciava 'l pianto e sanguinosa bava.
Da ogni bocca dirompea co' denti
un peccatore, a guisa di maciulla,
sì che tre ne facea così dolenti.
A quel dinanzi il mordere era nulla
verso 'l graffiar, che tal volta la schiena
60   rimanea de la pelle tutta brulla.
«Quell' anima là su c' ha maggior pena»
disse 'l maestro, «è Giuda Scariotto,
che 'l capo ha dentro e fuor le gambe mena.
De li altri due c' hanno il capo di sotto,
quel che pende dal nero ceffo è Bruto;
66   vedi come si storce e non fa motto;
e l' altro è Cassio che par sì membruto.
Ma la notte risurge, e oramai
è da partir, chè tutto avem veduto.»

with such parts. If he was as handsome as now he is ugly, and exalted his brows against his maker, all sorrow might indeed issue from him. Oh what a great prodigy it seemed to me when I saw three faces on his head! One in front, and it was bright red. Two others there were, adjoining the first, above the middle of each shoulder, and they joined at the place for the helmet plume. The one to the right was yellowish white; the one to the left looked like those who come from the land whence the Nile descends. Under each face, out jutted two huge wings, large enough to befit so big a bird. Sails for the sea I never saw like those. They did not have feathers, but were like a bat's, and them he was flapping, so that from him were driven three winds, which froze Cocytus hard. With six eyes he was weeping, and on three chins were dripping tears and bloody spittle.

[*Judas, Brutus, Cassius, the great
traitors: 34.55–67*]

[NARRATOR] In each mouth he champed a sinner with his teeth, just like a flax brake, so that three of them he thus made sufferers. For the one in front, the biting was nothing compared with the scratching, because sometimes his back lacked every bit of skin.
[VIRGIL] "The soul up there which has the greatest pain," my teacher said, "is Judas Iscariot, whose head is inside and who shakes his legs outside. Of the other two, whose heads are turned down, the one who hangs from the black snout is Brutus—you see how he twists himself, without saying a word—and the other is Cassius, who is so large-limbed."

[*The travelers leave the Inferno: 34.68–139*]

[VIRGIL] "But night is rising again,⁴ and now we must leave, because we have seen everything."

Com'a lui piacque, il collo li avvinghiai;
ed el prese di tempo e luogo poste;
72   e quando l'ali fuoro aperte assai,
appigliò sé a le vellute coste:
di vello in vello giù discese poscia
tra 'l folto pelo e le gelate croste.
Quando noi fummo là dove la coscia
si volge, a punto in sul grosso de l'anche,
78   lo duca, con fatica e con angoscia,
volse la testa ov'elli avea le zanche,
e aggrappossi al pel com'uom che sale,
sì che 'n inferno i' credea tornar anche.
«Attienti ben, ché per cotali scale»
disse 'l maestro, ansando com'uom lasso,
84   «conviensi dipartir da tanto male.»
Poi uscì fuor per lo foro d'un sasso,
e puose me in su l'orlo a sedere;
appresso porse a me l'accorto passo.
Io levai li occhi, e credetti vedere
Lucifero com'io l'avea lasciato;
90   e vidili le gambe in su tenere.
E s'io divenni allora travagliato,
la gente grossa il pensi, che non vede
qual è quel punto ch'io avea passato.
«Levati su» disse 'l maestro «in piede:
la via è lunga e 'l cammino è malvagio,
96   e già il sole a mezza terza riede.»
Non era camminata di palagio
là 'v'eravam, ma natural burella
ch'avea mal suolo e di lume disagio.
«Prima ch'io de l'abisso mi divella,
maestro mio,» diss'io quando fui dritto,
102   «a trarmi d'erro un poco mi favella.
Ov'è la ghiaccia? e questi com'è fitto
sì sottosopra? e come, in sì poc'ora,
da sera a mane ha fatto il sol tragitto?»

[NARRATOR] As he directed, I clung to his neck, and he took his chance from time and place, and when the wings were open enough, he seized the hairy sides. From tuft to tuft he then went down between the thick pelt and the frozen crusts. When we had reached the place just where the thigh is changed into the large part of the hips, my guide with effort and labored breath turned his head where his legs had been,[5] and gripped the hair as though he were climbing upward, so that I supposed he was going back to Hell again.

[VIRGIL] "Take care, since by these stairs," said my teacher, breathing as though he were tired, "we must go away from such great wickedness."

[NARRATOR] Then he got out through a fissure in a rock and placed me, seated, on the edge. And then, with his clever stride, he came to me. I lifted my eyes, and expected to see Lucifer as I had left him, and I saw his legs extending upward. If then I was bewildered by it, the ignorant multitude can imagine, which does not perceive what the point is that I had passed.[6]

[VIRGIL] "Get to your feet," said my teacher, "the way is long and the road is rough, and already the sun is getting back to mid-tierce."[7]

[NARRATOR] No palace gallery were we then in, but a natural cavern with a rough floor and faintly lighted.

[DANTE] "Before I pull my roots from the abyss,[8] my teacher," I said, when I was standing, "say a few words to relieve my confusion. Where is the ice? And this devil, how is he set so upside down? And how in so short a time has the sun traveled from evening to morning?"

Ed elli a me: «Tu imagini ancora
　　d'esser di là dal centro, ov'io mi presi
108　　al pel del vermo reo che 'l mondo fora.
Di là fosti cotanto quant'io scesi;
　　quand'io mi volsi, tu passasti 'l punto
　　al qual si traggon d'ogni parte i pesi.
E se' or sotto l' emisperio giunto
　　ch'è contraposto a quel che la gran secca
114　　coverchia, e sotto 'l cui colmo consunto
fu l' uom che nacque e visse sanza pecca:
　　tu hai i piedi in su picciola spera
　　che l' altra faccia fa de la Giudecca.
Qui è da man, quando di là è sera:
　　e questi, che ne fè scala col pelo,
120　　fitto è ancora sì come prim' era.
Da questa parte cadde giù dal cielo;
　　e la terra che pria di qua si sporse
　　per paura di lui fè del mar velo,
e venne a l' emisperio nostro; e forse
　　per fuggir lui lasciò qui luogo voto
126　　quella ch' appar di qua, e su ricorse.»
Luogo è là giù da Belzebù remoto
　　tanto quanto la tomba si distende,
　　che non per vista, ma per suono è noto
d' un ruscelletto che quivi discende
　　per la buca d' un sasso, ch' elli ha roso,
132　　col corso ch' elli avvolge, e poco pende.
Lo duca e io per quel cammino ascoso
　　intrammo a ritornar nel chiaro mondo;
　　e sanza cura aver d' alcun riposo,
salimmo su, el primo e io secondo,
　　tanto ch' i' vidi de le cose belle
138　　che porta 'l ciel, per un pertugio tondo;
e quindi uscimmo a riveder le stelle.

[VIRGIL] And he replied: "You are still supposing that you are on the other side of the center, where I grasped the hair of the evil serpent which pierces the world. You were on the other side as long as I was going down. When I reversed, you were passing the point to which weights are pulled from every direction. Now you are beneath the celestial hemisphere which is placed opposite that which covers the land, beneath whose zenith was killed the man who was born and lived without sin.[9] You have your feet on the little sphere which forms the other face of the Judecca. Here it is morning when over there it is evening. And Satan, whose hair was our ladder, is set in the ice as he was before. On this side he fell from Heaven, and the land which was spread out here before his fall, veiled itself with the sea in fear of him and went to our hemisphere, and indeed, to escape him, the land which now is on this side left the empty space here, and collected above."[10]

[NARRATOR] Down there is a place distant from Beelzebub as far as the cave extends, which is known not by sight but by the sound of a little stream that comes down there through a rocky tunnel which it has eaten out in its winding course, and which slopes but little.[11] My guide and I took that dark path in order to return to the world of light, and without thought of any rest we climbed,[12] he first and I second, until, through a round opening, I saw the beautiful things that the sky holds; and we came out from there to look again at the stars.[13]

NOTES

CANTO 1

1. Without introduction, the poem begins abruptly, in the midst of an unexplained action. We are to take it as the narrative of fictitious events told as though they were facts. If ever the poem was intended to relate an imagined dream, as many have supposed, no warning is here given.

2. Editors interpret this sentence in accord with their concept of the entire poem. I have chosen simplicity. Dante leaves us to guess the course of the right road.

3. The poem is for the most part a returned traveler's narrative. This traveler, named Dante, is not the historical Dante. Yet the historical Dante sometimes does appear, so mingled with the fictitious traveler that separation is impossible. Often the poet, abandoning his fiction, speaks directly. This tempts the reader to forget that he is perusing a made-up story, and to take poetry for fact. Throughout this volume the passages in which Dante speaks primarily as poet, or makes the returned traveler a poet, are in italics.

4. The sun.

5. Of this night no account is given.

6. As from a storm-tossed boat.

7. This danger is one of the unexplained references of this canto. Having escaped, Dante pauses in body, but his mind retains the feeling that he must strive to escape.

8. Later Dante says that he had planned to catch this animal (*Inf.* 16.108). In *De Vulgari Eloquentia* 1.16 he represents himself as hunting a panther which he hopes to take—a figure for his search for the Italian language at its best.

9. See also lines 94 ff. The wolf is a normal symbol of avarice. Plutus, the god of riches, is called "he-wolf" (7.8), and the she-wolf is cursed on the ledge of Purgatory where avarice is purified (*Purg.* 20.10). In his *Ars Poetica*, known to Dante, Horace makes greed inimical to poetry (324 ff.). Can Dante be thinking of avarice as damaging art, as well as doing more general injury?

10. Probably derived by Dante from Virgil's *Aeneid* 1.328, suggested by *Odyssey* 6.149.

Virgil is a shade, but why does Dante suppose so? We can hardly be content with Cristoforo Landino's comment that phantasms often appear in forests. The word *shade* is used as though Dante were already within the realm of the dead, where disembodied spirits would normally be encountered; he shows no astonishment on being told that Virgil is not now a man. The passage perhaps indicates the unfinished state of this canto.

11. For the mountain see *Inf.* 1.13; 2.120; 24.21. Can a mountain so described be other than important? In 2.120, the situation —if anything may be inferred from the brief reference—is not that the animals drive him back, but that they block the shortest way, the road of 1.3. The plan of the poem then might be that of a journey to the delightful mountain by an indirect road. It is difficult to take the mountain as a figure for Heaven, to which the traveler finally rises. So difficult is this reference that most commentators within my observation make no attempt to explain it. One detailed modern commentary has no note on lines 77–78. Can Virgil be thinking of Mount Parnassus and the poet's fame? Possibly here is a vestige of a plan for the *Commedia* unlike the present one. How completely did Dante revise this canto, to adapt it to the remainder of the poem?

Though Dante is in dire need, Virgil pauses to give some account of himself as a poet. Instead of protesting, Dante lays aside his terror for a suitable reply (1.79–87). Interest in poetry conquers dramatic probability.

12. Evidently the style used in Dante's *Canzoni*, written earlier than the *Commedia*, which as a comedy does not employ the elevated style of the epic. See *De vulgari eloquentia* 2.3.

13. In *Convivio* 4.12 Dante writes that desire for wealth is never satisfied.

14. Unexplained, after centuries of effort.

15. Quoted from *Aeneid* 3.522, where it applies to the seacoast. Dante may mean *humble* or *lowly*.

16. Beatrice.

17. We suppose the journey about to begin, but it is delayed for all of the next canto.

CANTO 2

1. The first canto, then, has occupied the time from morning until evening, yet the second requires no more than a few min-

utes, if the travelers entered Hell Gate that evening (2.1).

2. This invocation, according to Virgil's example in the *Aeneid*, is expected early in Canto 1. Virgil precedes it with a statement of his subject, which Dante dispenses with. Both were perhaps crowded out by the abrupt beginning of Canto 1.

3. The word *cominciare*, rendered *said*, literally means *begin*. In the *Commedia* its meaning often is as here. Perhaps this is an abbreviation of *cominciai a dir* (*Inf.* 2.56; 11.17, 21.119; *Purg.* 3.23; 26.139; etc.), with variations in person, etc. More often *dire* is lacking. *Cominciare* is also used with other verbs, as in *Par.* 30.5, where it is better untranslated. Once *togliere* instead of *cominciare* is used with *dire* (*Par.* 12.2). Dante's *cominciare* is apparently imitated from Virgil, *Aeneid* 1.325, etc.

4. Aeneas, the father of Silvius, visited the lower world, according to Book 6 of Virgil's *Aeneid*. Virgil is Dante's guide, presumably, because that book is the chief literary source of the *Inferno*. Dante had also a general debt to Virgil as an artist.

5. St. Paul, thought to indicate himself when he writes that he knew a man who visited the Third Heaven and Paradise (II Cor. 12:2–4).

6. Speaking of the moral effect of poetry, Dante writes: "What a spur (stimulus) to fortitude and magnanimity it was when Aeneas, alone with the Sibyl, was bold enough to go into Hell to visit the soul of his father Anchises, facing so many dangers, as is related in the sixth book of the *Aeneid*" (*Convivio* 4.26.9)!

7. In Limbo souls are in suspense in that they are in Hell, yet not fully so, since they are not actively punished. Cf. *Inf.* 4.45.

8. Beatrice. Since Canto 1 makes Dante ready to follow Virgil, the introduction of Beatrice is not necessary to account for the journey. Her presence here gives the poem a semblance of unity; otherwise so important a character would appear only when nearly two-thirds of the poem has been completed. The report of her conversation with Virgil is as though originally she was intended to appear in person; for example, Virgil reports word for word the compliments she paid him (lines 59, 60, 67, 114).

9. Here, the words *in sua favella*, which commentators call redundant, are absorbed into the translation. Boccaccio thought they meant *in her dialect*, that of Florence.

10. Dante is not befriended by Chance or Fortune.

11. This suggests Heaven as resembling an earthly court. The

Paradiso offers no such analogy. For gratitude, see Canto 22, note 3.

12. You by yourself are sufficient to make the human race superior to everything "beneath the moon," that is, on earth.

13. According to Dante's astronomy, the earth is at the center of the universe.

14. In Limbo, to which Beatrice descended, there is no torturing fire; Dante indeed makes use of fire only in some portions of Hell, but fire and Hell are conventionally associated.

15. The Virgin Mary.

16. In harmony with her name (from *lux, light*), she was especially concerned with the eyes. Her only other action in the poem is to carry the traveler from Antepurgatory to the gate of Purgatory (*Purg.* 9.55). She sits in the heavenly rose (*Par.* 32.137). Even Dante's sons in their commentaries say nothing of any devotion to her by the poet.

17. This passage is unexplained.

18. See Canto 1, note 11.

19. Cf. *Inf.* 1.136. The similarity emphasizes the complementary and partially duplicate character of Cantos 1 and 2. As also an expansion of Canto 1, the second canto is part of the introduction. Canto 3 begins the journey. Did Dante think these two cantos ready for the reading which he hoped would bring him fame, or did he plan to revise them further?

CANTO 3

1. The truth.

2. Unknown to mortals other than St. Paul and Aeneas (*Inf.* 2.32). Or, here are neutrals, unknown to fame (3.36, 49).

3. Sometimes thought to refer to crude dialects, such as Nimrod's (31.67). Virgil's "beauteous language" is his only specified qualification for rescuing the lost traveler (2.67). Was barbarous language one of the horrors of Hell? Consider Dante's work *On the Vulgar Tongue* (the Italian language).

4. They did not rebel against God with Satan.

5. See Canto 12, note 2. *Alcuna* is sometimes interpreted as negative here, making the meaning "so that the damned may not," etc.

6. Usually taken to mean that the banner, as though having volition, disdained any pause. With support from the fourteenth-

century commentator Buti, I suspect the meaning to be that repose was not allowed it by the laws of Hell, fixed by the Almighty.

7. Much ink has been spent on this character. Had Dante intended his name to be known, could he not at least have hinted it? He is one of those of whom Virgil said: "Let us not talk" (line 51). The world allows them no fame (line 49).

8. Strictly, all the sinners Dante sees in Hell, having shadowy bodies, are naked. Yet Dante seems to mention nakedness for some purpose, as to make the souls seem more abject. Though Virgil would be supposed naked, I suspect the illustrators are right who have given him robes befitting his dignity. When the lost traveler first sees him, he asks whether he is a shade or a man (1.66). He would hardly expect to meet a naked man in the forest. The poet has over the illustrator the advantage that he can leave the matter unsettled, and the reader may be wise not to ask or wonder about it. Cf. Canto 4, note 9.

For Dante's clothing, see 15.24; 16.8; 24.31. Shades are never represented as supposing that, being clothed, he must be alive.

9. According to the purpose of the moment, Dante avails himself of the local climate (here the murky air of Hell), or neglects it.

10. Evidently Charon knows that Virgil is a shade and Dante living; how, we are not told. Cf. 12.81; 23.88; etc.

11. *Purg.* 2.41.

12. Perhaps Dante has in mind the falcon summoned with an artificial bird, or the captive birds used by hunters as decoys.

13. Literally, "fell like a man who is overcome by sleep." Yet, as the beginning of the next canto shows, the traveler was himself overcome. Hence I have put the translation in its simplest form, as I have done in other instances, though the line dividing a mere form of expression from an actual comparison is not always clear. Cf. a passage, by no means unique, in Boccaccio: "Essendo già vicino al dì, morendosi egli sopra la quercia di freddo, sì come quegli che sempre da torno guardava, si vide innanzi forse un miglio un grandissimo fuoco" (*Decamerone* 5.3). Literally, "When it was almost day, and he was dying of cold up in the oak tree, like a man who was always gazing around, he saw about a mile away a huge fire." Though this seems a comparison, the meaning is that the man was himself looking around.

CANTO 4

1. Virgil later rebukes Dante for showing pity for the damned (*Inf.* 20.28).

2. For other instances in which Virgil hurries his pupil, see *Inf.* 11.112–115; 17.76; 29.11; *Purg.* 12.5; 15.79.

3. Between the Crucifixion and the Resurrection, Christ harrowed Hell, that is, defeated Satan and delivered from Hell spirits divinely chosen.

4. Usually rendered "honorable people occupied that place." On the analogy of *Inf.* 11.69, I have reversed subject and object. Even these great shades are in prison, as is said in 2.52; 4.44–45. Cf. also 11.38–39; 18.99. For similar reversals of direct order, see *Inf.* 8.6; 11.9.

5. The speaker is not revealed. See Canto 32, note 6.

6. The name of poet rather than Virgil personally is honored.

7. Epic poetry, the *Iliad* and the *Odyssey*.

8. The literal meaning of this statement seems never to have been explained.

9. This indicates that, if the matter is to be considered, all the shades in Limbo are clothed; Caesar would hardly be an exception. So we are to assume Virgil as suitably clad. For nakedness, see 3.100; 13.116; 14.19; 16.35; 23.118; 24.92; 30.25. For a possible exception, see 10.33 and the note.

CANTO 5

1. The word *orribilmente* has an adjectival sense. See Sapegno's edition of the *Commedia*, and Allan H. Gilbert, "Dante's Rimario," *Italica*, XLIV (1967), p. 423; cf. *Inf.* 2.15.

Minos is commonly said to come from Virgil, *Aeneid* 6.432. Closer is

> Arbiter hos dura versat Cortynius urna,
> vera minis poscens adigitque expromere vites
> usque retro et tandem poenarum lucra fateri.
> (Statius, *Thebaid* 4.530 ff.)

(The Cortynian judge shakes them in his rigid urn, with threats demanding the truth, and forces them to reveal their lives from the outset and to tell what they have gained from their toils.) Note the word *minis*, and with Dante's *confessa*, cf. *expromere*, *fateri*. The *arbiter Cortynius* is Minos.

2. What I have rendered *take the downward road* is sometimes

explained as meaning *fall* or *are hurled*, in harmony with 33.133, where a soul is said to *fall ruinously*. We also read that Minos *sends* a soul to the Seventh circle (13.96). For more on how souls reach their circles, see Canto 28, note 4. The sixteenth-century Landino says that devils lead the souls down from Minos' judgment seat.

3. The verb *entrare* often means *enter*, but here perhaps Dante has in mind the less obvious meaning of the Latin *ingredior*, *walk* or *go*, as in *Aeneid* 4.177. Cf. *Inf.* 2.142; 7.105; 13.16; *Purg.* 3.101 (Sapegno glosses *procedete*—*proceed*), 25.7; Boccaccio, *Decamerone* 5.7 (Bari, 1955), p. 384, line 21. Dante often combines *entrare* with a preposition meaning *into*, as in *Inf.* 9.26.

4. Lines 23–24 are repeated from the conversation with Charon (3.94 ff.). Virgil accuses Minos of shouting and blocking the journey, though the judge seems trying to be helpful. Perhaps Dante failed to revise the passage.

5. Literally, *mute of all light. Muto*, as a rime word, need not be rigidly defined. A little later, the darkness is not so great that shades cannot be made out at some distance (line 77).

6. By confusion with Latin *libido* and Italian *libidine*, the word *libito* often appears in English translations as *lust*. Perhaps there is also confusion with Chaucer's language, as, "His lustes were as lawe in his decree" (*Monkes Tale* 3667). To Chaucer, *lustes* meant *wishes, desires* of any sort, not unlawful sexual desires. Guido da Pisa comments: "By her laws she made permissible whatever is pleasing." Dante is playing with the similarity of *libito* and *licito*, which he found in his source, Paulus Orosius, *Hist.* 1.4.

7. Dictys says that Achilles fell in love with Polyxena (*Trojan War*, Book 3). Dares says "he loved her vehemently, and was so violently enamored and so tormented by his passion that he hated his own life." His application for her hand gave occasion for a Trojan plot against his life. Paris and other armed men concealed themselves in a temple of Apollo to which Achilles, with one companion, came under truce to negotiate the marriage. When attacked, the two Greeks defended themselves bravely but, without shields or armor, fell before the darts of the Trojans (*Destruction of Troy*).

8. Dante takes Virgil's advice, just given, to wait until the shifting winds (lines 31, 43, 75) bring the two souls near. The figure of the cranes (line 47) suggests regularity impossible to

the wind-driven shades of this circle. The illustrative part of the figure is that the cranes sing while in the air; the rest is non-illustrative, to fill out the epic simile without respect to the context. The notion of regularity in the movement of the two shades has been strengthened for English-speaking readers by translations of *van, vanno,* and *venir* (lines 46, 48, 74) as though they indicate motion. They are rather akin to such English expressions as *he goes badly dressed,* meaning *he usually is badly dressed.* These verbs are in the present passage also used of motion (lines 78, 81, 86), the regular movement possible for the shades when the wind drops (line 96). Cf. 27.129, and the note.

9. Possibly indicating the motion of the two lovers when the wind ceases. The *sweet nest* is a non-illustrative part of the epic simile, which is developed in its own right.

10. The word *perverso* (rendered *horrid*) has troubled commentators. For example, Scartazzini-Vandelli gloss it with the vague *grave, orribile* (*heavy, horrible*). Longfellow offers the literal *perverse.* But what does that mean? Dante's choice of the word seems affected by the rime. Another word seemingly so affected is *pugna* (6.30). The writer of the *Ottimo Commento* reports Dante as almost admitting that he sometimes defined rime words to suit himself (on *Inf.* 10.85). For other words suggesting concern with rime, see the Index (not a complete list). See also Gilbert, "Dante's Rimario," *Italica* XLIV (1967), 409–424.

11. I follow Sapegno's interpretation, naming supporters beginning with the fourteenth-century commentator Buti. The usual modern interpretation is that Francesca is afflicted by the manner of her death, so sudden as to preclude repentance.

12. As the commentator Francesco da Buti (1324–1406) says, Galeotto or Galehaut was the man through whose means Lancelot and Guinevere had carnal conjunction.

CANTO 6

1. Cerberus is traditionally a three-headed dog, yet Dante speaks of his hands (line 17), perhaps using the word for rime.

2. A strange substitute for the drugged honey-cake given to Cerberus by Virgil's Sibyl (*Aeneid* 6.420).

3. Usually interpreted: "they would like to be deaf." This is less vigorous and less probable than actual deafening. I interpret *vorrebber* (literally, *would wish*) as here used idiomatically, as often, with varied meaning, in the *Decameron,* as 3.3 (several

times); 3.10 (Bari, 1955, p. 261, line 31); 4.8; 7.9; 8.10; 9.1. For *volere* expressing necessity rather than wish, cf. *Inf.* 16.15; *Purg.* 13.18. The present passage, literally and fully expressed, would run: "They would have to be deaf" to be able to escape his barking. The statement lacks the reflexive pronoun, as does *Morgante* 27.61. "E non vorrebbe anche saperlo Orlando." This does not mean: "He would fain not recognize even Orlando"; but rather: "He could not recognize even Orlando," or simply: "He did not recognize even Orlando." Giovanni Fiorentino writes that Pope Boniface VIII (*Inf.* 19.53; *Purg.* 20.86; *Par.* 30.148), when seized at Alagna, said: "Da che per tradimento Cristo volle esser preso, così sia di me" (Since by treachery Christ was taken captive, so let me be) (*Il Pecorone* 14.21).

4. This well expresses the nature of the shades, yet the poet treats them like substantial bodies whenever the nature of his narrative requires it. For example, the traveler kicks a shade as something solid (*Inf.* 32.78). Most of the sufferings of Hell and Purgatory are inflicted on the body, however shadowy. In Purgatory, when the spirits desire food that they do not take, the shade becomes thin. Inquiring how this can be, the traveler receives an explanation of the efficacy of the spirit to modify the shade (*Purg.* 25.20 ff.). This is suggestive for Hell, though not fully applicable. The punishments of Hell more or less clearly represent the life the sinner deliberately lived on earth. Flattery, for example, is a filthy sin (*Inf.* 18.125–126). The spirit that moved in filth in the world is fittingly submerged in filth in Hell.

5. The history of Florence, as of other Italian cities, was largely a record of civil strife. See, for example, the preface of Machiavelli's *History of Florence.*

For knowledge of the future by the damned, see *Inf.* 10.97 ff.

6. Pope Boniface VIII. His interference in Florentine feuds was one cause of Dante's banishment from the city.

7. If Dante had specific men in view, the clue is now lost. Perhaps it means that such men are very few in Florence. Autobiographical interpreters like to fancy that Dante thought himself one of the two.

8. Lower down than Ciacco. See *Inf.* 10.32; 16.41, 44; 28.106.

9. For *diverse* (*diverse*) as *horrible*, see Tommaseo's *Dizionario*, and *Aspramonte* (Bologna, 1951) 3.36.8: "a horrible demon," according to Boni's glossary; cf. 3.135.32; 3.139.3; 3.143.30; Boccaccio, *Teseida* 1.65. See *Inf.* 3.25 (and Sapegno's

note); 6.13; 7.105; 29.1; etc. Latitude of interpretation is often possible. The meaning *terrible* does not occur in the *Purgatorio* or the *Paradiso*.

10. Their condemnation at the Last Judgment.

11. They expect to be more perfect after the Last Judgment.

CANTO 7

1. Literally, *who knew all*. Cf. 8.7 and 10.131, and the note. Virgil's knowledge is adequate in Hell. In Purgatory (as 2.63), his information fails.

2. The word *lacca* (which has caused difficulty), rendered *hollow*, is a synonym for circle, convenient as a rime word.

3. Though the cavity of Hell is a container, it is hardly a sack. Nevertheless perhaps Dante intended the figure in his verb *insacca* to be observed. Is he influenced by its riming capacity?

4. Here Dante has strained the meaning of his rime word, *bruni* (*black*). The avaricious have lived in such spiritual darkness that they are unrecognizable. Note the play on *recognize*.

5. Bitterly complained of. Dante elsewhere uses *cross* figuratively (*Inf.* 16.43; 23.125; 33.87).

6. Virgil frequently reminds his charge that this is not a leisurely journey, as in *Inf.* 10.115; 11.112; 14.139; 17.40, 76; 24.46; 29.11; 32.19, 84; *Purg.* 12.4.

7. The traveler's eagerness to see is often spoken of. See, for example, 26.43, and Allan H. Gilbert, *Dante and His Comedy* (New York, 1963), pp. 7 ff.

CANTO 8

1. Phlegyas, like Filippo Argenti a little later (line 33), assumes that the traveler is one of the damned moving down to his proper circle. See Canto 28, note 4.

2. According to medieval psychology the angry man injures himself. Cf. *Inf.* 12.14–15.

3. With grim comedy the damned are called "dignified citizens"; some of them, like the magnanimous Farinata, deserve the adjective. The army is made up of devils.

4. *Worried* renders *m'adiri*, which may be taken as meaning *be angry*, and was so interpreted by medieval commentators, who say that Virgil's color (9.1, 3) was the red of anger. Modern expositors (Scartazzini-Vandelli, Sapegno) explain it, with citation of parallels, as I have rendered it. This harmonizes with the

description of Virgil's manner (8.118–119). Commentators who soften *m'adiri* still, somewhat inconsistently, cling to the medieval view of Virgil's color as that of anger.

5. How Virgil learned this is not told.

CANTO 9

1. This sentence offers only my guess at the drift of lines 1–3, so difficult as to provoke Scartazzini into writing: "I shall speak honestly. The way in which Dante has expressed himself here seems to me to show too much brain-racking." Sapegno interprets: "The pallor which fear had brought to my face caused Virgil the more promptly to remove from his the new color which appeared there because of vexation and distress (see 8.118–120); that is, it induced him to curb his own distress and to return sooner to his natural appearance." In my interpretation I am in harmony with an obscure fourteenth-century commentator who, without mentioning Virgil's color, writes: "Seeing Virgil return, Dante was distressed and grew pale. Then Virgil, seeing that Dante was afraid and dismayed, tried to encourage him not to fear, because they would win the fight in the city" (*Chiose sopra Dante, Testo inedito*, ed. Lord Vernon, Florence, 1846, pp. 69–70). Line 3 may refer to the effect of Virgil's assurance in 8.121–130, covering his discouraged beginning in line 120.

To Petrarch, possibly echoing line 3, the "new color" is the pallor of death (*Ballata 5: Volgendo gli occhi al mio novo colore*).

2. These words continue Virgil's speech at the end of the preceding canto, after a pause for listening.

3. In lines 14–15 we are warned against completing the sentence in a way to indicate very serious anxiety on Virgil's part.

4. *Tal* (*such*) is sometimes taken to mean God, sometimes Beatrice, with reference to *Inf.* 2. *Tal* here is easily connected with *tal*, the deliverer of 8.130, and with *altri* (*he*) in 9.9. *Tal* without a noun usually has a personal reference; might it here mean *such a safe journey* as was promised to Dante (*Inf.* 2.124–126)? Perhaps it is enough to say that Virgil's speech is wavering, divided between uncertainty and confidence.

5. A Thessalian witch in Lucan's *Pharsalia* (6.507–827). Dante gives a heathen witch power over the Christian Inferno.

6. The flesh had been stripped from the soul, thought of as more especially the man himself. Cf. *Inf.* 13.90–108; 33.122–147.

7. Theseus assisted in an attempt to take Persephone from the

lower world. He was captured and kept prisoner until released by Hercules.

Here Dante identifies his Hell with the Greek lower world. Dante does not mention Theseus as a visitor in 2.13–32.

8. Commentators, followed by translators, observing that at his distance the traveler could not feel the pungency of the distant smoke, have gone through logical processes to make the word *acerbo* (*pungent, bitter, harsh*) mean *intense, thick,* etc. I have preferred to translate it as Dante, in his freedom with rime words, seems to have written it. In the preceding line, the word *antica* (*filthy*) probably strengthens *scum,* without reference to age. Cf. the note on *Inf.* 26.85.

9. I have kept Dante's verbal repetition. Sapegno speaks of rhetorical redundancy. I add search for a rime. *Passo* (or a compound) occurs in nineteen of the twenty-one rimes in *-asso* in the *Commedia. Grasso* appears in rime here only.

10. To the distress of allegorical interpreters, some of the fourteenth-century commentators identified this messenger with Mercury, god of eloquence (for example, Lord Vernon, ed., *Chiose sopra Dante,* pp. 71, 77).

11. Hercules, visiting Hell, chained Cerberus and led him off, or enabled Theseus to do so; the chain wore off Cerberus' hair. Dante, doubtless because Virgil did so, places Cerberus in Hell, in spite of Hercules' exploit. Hercules might also have been named as a visitor to Hell in 2.13–32. The classical hero is here made the executor of Christian fate (line 97).

12. Usually rendered "where the Rhone forms a lake" or about that. Buti explains it as I have translated it, as does Sapegno. Cf. 20.66, and Canto 11, note 11.

13. Literally, among the monuments, flames were scattered. One ms. reads *entra.* For *intra, tra, in,* see Rohlfs' *Histor. Grammatik der Italien. Sprache,* parr. 808, 816. The rendering *in the tombs* fits with line 131, which suggests internal heat. *Sparte* occurs in the *Commedia* seven times, always riming with *parte, arte,* except once with *parte, Marte;* rime affects meaning here. Guido da Pisa paraphrases: "The sepulchres are internally full of flames."

As some commentators have observed, the word *tra* in line 118 (*tra gli avelli*) cannot have the same meaning as in *tra le sepolture* (10.38), for the latter would then have Virgil push his pupil into the flames.

14. The word *martiri* is used also in 10.2. The accent requires the translation *sufferings*. I suspect, however, that in defiance of the accent or shifting it for the rime in 10.2, Dante intended *martyrs*, ironically, just as the tenth bolgia is called a cloister and its inhabitants monks (29.40 f.). Could he have meant that the Epicureans were martyrs for their mistaken faith? Guido da Pisa paraphrases "between the walls and the sepulchres."

CANTO 10

1. At the end of the world, after the Final Resurrection, all men will assemble for the Last Judgment in the Valley of Jehoshaphat at Jerusalem (Joel 3:2, 12). Thence the damned will return to Hell.

2. See 3.80; 9.87; 10.39; 17.40; 26.72. Virgil controls his pupil's speech.

3. The word *forse*, commonly *perhaps*, is for Dante frequently stronger than that. Cf., for varying assurance, *Inf.* 10.63; 12.16; 13.122; 23.79; 26.30, 75; 27.122; 28.56; 29.15; 30.101; 33.134; 34.124; Pulci, *Morgante* 4.87. In the *Morgante*, of Lorenzo the Magnificent's time, *forse* is often affirmative rather than doubtful.

4. It appears that Farinata is to be imagined as clothed, unlike the souls generally. See Canto 4, note 9.

5. The poet Guido Cavalcanti, called by Dante "the first of my friends" (*Vita Nuova* 3.99). For his poetical reputation see *Purg.* 11.97.

6. If this passage were easy, Pagliaro would not have given it eighteen pages (*Ulisse*, pp. 192–210). Sapegno calls it "one of the most discussed and most difficult in the poem." Admitting the difficulties and unable to explain them, I still incline to accept the tradition that line 63 indicates the nearby Virgil. Is either Beatrice or God, neither in the context, to be indicated by a mere *cui?* Perhaps Guido spoke against Virgil when talking with Dante about an opinion reported in *Vita Nuova* 31: "Conciossiacosachè le parole, che seguitano a quelle che sono allegate, sieno tutte latine, sarebbe fuori del mio intendimento se io le scrivessi. E simile intenzione so che ebbe questo primo mio amico, a cui ció scrivo, cioè ch' io gli scrivessi solamente in volgare" (Since the passages following those brought forward would all be Latin, it would be contrary to my plan to write them. And this first friend of mine, to whom I write this, I know had a similar wish, that is, that I should write to him in Italian only). The word

ebbe—which so affected Guido's father— is here used of the living Guido, as in *Inf.* 10.63. In the *Vita Nuova*, it seems to refer to an occasion when they discussed language; is some such reference to be assumed for the *Inferno*? Are we to suppose that the visitor to the heretics intended to continue speaking, and that Cavalcante suddenly interrupted him with his shouted questions, on hearing *ebbe*, a word in the past tense?

For *forse*, see note 3, above.

7. Boccaccio writes: "Since Cavalcante de' Cavalcanti held something of the opinion of the Epicures, it was said among the common people that the purpose of his speculations was to discover that there is no God" (*Decamerone* 6.9).

8. Why do you speak in the past tense, as of a dead man?

9. The battle of Montaperti, on the Arbia River, where the Guelfs were defeated.

10. According to Machiavelli's *History of Florence* (2.11), up to the year 1282 (twenty-two years after Farinata's death) the Florentine magistrates met in churches, of which the most obvious is San Giovanni. The word rendered *prayers* can also mean *orations*, such as might be made by the rulers of Florence. Perhaps Dante uses the word ironically, with its two meanings in mind. For discussion, see Antonino Pagliaro, *Ulisse*, pp. 39, 211, 677, 766.

11. Another instance of Virgil's wish to make the journey rapid.

12. The Emperor Frederick II, and, so it is supposed, Ottaviano degli Ubaldini, cardinal from 1245 to 1273.

13. Farinata's suggestion of Dante's banishment in lines 79 ff.

14. Beatrice. Literally, "whose fair eye sees all." Cf. 7.3. The meaning probably is "whose fair eye sees the whole voyage of your life." More extensive claims for Beatrice's knowledge would hardly be so briefly and incidentally expressed. In 15.90 Beatrice's powers are limited to explanation of Dante's future.

CANTO 11

1. I owe this suggestion for the meaning of *stipa* to Benvenuto da Imola, who says it means a coop or cage for poultry. Another meaning is *pigpen* (Tommaseo's *Dizionario*), suitable because of the stench from it (line 5). For the pit of Hell as a container, see *Inf.* 7.16–18. Many commentators prefer the meaning *mass* or *crowd*.

2. Virgil here gestures toward the chasm of lower Hell (Circles

Seven, Eight, and Nine), on the brink of which the travelers stand.

3. Not an animal vice, but requiring the use of reason.

4. Sodom indicates those indulging in sodomy. Cahors indicates the sin (in the Middle Ages) of taking interest on money. Apparently men from the French city of Cahors settled in various European cities as moneylenders. Relatively few such lenders were actually from that city; in fact, those whom Dante saw in Hell were all Florentines, with the exception of one Paduan (*Inf.* 17.70).

5. The man who defrauds is conscious of it and deliberate; the violent man acts before he thinks.

6. A figurative way, perhaps suggested by the rime of *imborsa*, *morsa*, *Caorsa*, of saying: "who does not trust him."

7. The general duty of man to any man, without special obligation or agreement.

In line 55, I accept *incida* (*cuts*), instead of the usual *uccida* (literally, *kills*), from Petrocchi. To his persuasive note I add that Benvenuto da Imola in his comment quotes the word as *incida*.

8. Satan. Sometimes explained as the city of Dis (8.68).

9. Literally, *fat swamp*. Commentators usually explain the adjective *pingue* by a process which approaches leaving its place blank and supplying a meaning suggested by earlier accounts of the Stygian Swamp (7.110, 121; 8.10; etc.); their result is a word meaning *muddy* or about that. Dante surely allows himself freedom in rime words, but perhaps not license. Yet *pinguis* in Latin and *pingue* in Italian mean not only *fat* but by a normal extension *rich, fertile, abundant*. The Styx is populous (7.118; 9.79). I have ventured, therefore, on a translation of *pingue* acceptable to lexicographers. Cf. the forest of spirits (4.65–66).

10. These four groups are the sinners of Circles Two to Five.

11. The Sixth Circle, immediately within the city wall, offers difficulties. In the exposition of Hell just preceding, Circles Seven, Eight, and Nine have been dealt with (lines 16–60), and Circles Two to Five will be treated (lines 70–90). Circle Six is omitted.

When the city of Dis is seen from a distance (8.70), its mosques are prominent. Can these be merely the towers of the walls? The view of a city always includes buildings within, seen over the walls. Dante's traveler is eager to see what is within the fortress (9.108), yet after entering mentions a great plain (9.110) but no buildings. The comparison with Arles suggests tombs outside the city. Benvenuto says that they are *near* (*iuxta*) Arles, Boccac-

cio *outside,* and Ariosto that they are *near (Orlando Furioso*
39.72). Somewhat similarly, within the strong fortress of 4.106
there is a meadow of fresh grass, nothing more. That fortress
seems to occupy only a small part of the First Circle. But interpreters often have made the wall of the city of Dis extend entirely around the Sixth Circle, perhaps a thousand miles, and
include in the city everything below, as the wide desert of the
sodomites (15.13–15), the cliff between Circles Seven and Eight,
Malebolge, and the final pit of Satan. If we think of a literal
city inclosed with a wall and entered through a gate, the word
city applied to all of lower Hell loses meaning.

The word *city* is, however, figuratively used, as in the inscription over the gate of Hell, the City of Pain (3.1). An analogy is
that of Heaven as the City of God (1.126, 128). The same words,
city of pain, are also applied to the city of Dis seen in the distance
(9.32). Do they there indicate only the literal city with its
"mosques" before the traveler's eyes (8.70; 9.32)? When Farinata, within the walls of Dis, addresses the traveler as one going
through the "city of fire," does he refer only to the space occupied by the burning tombs of the heretics, or to all Hell (10.22)?

When in the present passage (11.73) the traveler asks why
the shades of Circles Two to Five are not in the "fiery city," he
does not ask why they are not in the circle of the heretics, but
why they are not "within these rocks" (11.16), that is, in Circles
Seven, Eight, Nine. Observing that Virgil has not mentioned the
shades of the upper circles, Dante asks: why the distinction?

At least we need not be too literal in picturing all of lower Hell
as a walled city, and need not hold Dante to the utmost of consistency in using language or in imagining the parts of his Hell.

12. Aristotle's *Ethics,* well known to Dante.

13. Expositors have difficulty in finding bestiality in the *Ethics.*

14. Outside Circles Seven, Eight, Nine.

15. The souls in Circles Seven, Eight, Nine. Expositors have
been distressed by Dante's failure to mention in this context Circle
Six, that of the heretics.

16. Aristotle's *Physics.*

17. Gen. 2:15; 3:19.

CANTO 12

1. The Minotaur. See line 12.

2. Annotators debate whether *alcuna* means *some* or *no.* No

mortal has descended the slope (line 30), yet the travelers do get down. Guido da Pisa renders: "No way or path is found." Cf. 3.42, and the note. See Tommaseo's *Dizionario, s.v. alcuno,* sect. 10.

3. Cf. *Inf.* 8.63, and the note.

4. Theseus, Duke of Athens (as in Shakespeare's *Midsummer Night's Dream*) slew the Minotaur with the help of Ariadne, who, like the monster, was Pasiphae's child.

5. *Varco,* here rendered *opening,* is often difficult in verse. In the *Commedia,* it occurs only in rime. Petrarch and Ariosto use it as a rime word.

6. Never trodden by a living man. See 12.61 and the note.

7. Dante uses the abstract, rather than saying "angry and insane beast."

8. See *Inf.* 4.55–61.

9. Literally, *this old cliff.* But the word *old* probably has secondary, if any, suggestion of age, as in some colloquial English expressions. The same is probably true of *vecchio* in 18.79. Cf. Pulci, *Morgante* 5.38; 15.54; 19.30, 53; 20.51; 27.23.

10. In Phlegethon, the river of boiling blood.

11. This speech, with line 82, implies that the centaurs are accustomed to seeing the damned come down the slope on their journey to their assigned place lower down in Hell. For such movement, see 28.44 and the note.

12. Nessus does prove reliable, so perhaps the returned traveler, as he narrates his experience, is looking back on it. But how does he now know that Nessus is faithful? Hercules and Deianira, whom he attempted to carry off, did not find him so. Dante knew their story (line 68).

13. Dante amusingly emphasizes their immersion to their foreheads (line 103).

14. Since Dante calls Phlegethon a *fossa* (*ditch, pit, grave, den,* etc.), he possibly thought of it among the wonders of Hell as a circular pond hundreds of miles in circumference and having in its midst a huge island, the remainder of Hell. He calls it a river, classing it with the other rivers of Hell (14.116 ff.). A normal river, however, would hardly flow in a complete circle, without beginning or end. As to gravitation, Dante's rivers, however strange in other respects, behave normally. The words *tyrants* and *tyranny* (lines 104, 132) with the prefix *ra-* (line 131) have led to the assumption that the centaur is speaking of movement

around the enormous circle back to Alexander and the other tyrants. But he makes here no reference to those earlier tyrants; Attila and Pyrrhus are not in the strictest sense tyrants, and the two Rinieri are called highway robbers (lines 134–138). As the centaur speaks, he almost points at the deep place a short distance back which his charges have seen, and at the other not far ahead which they do not see; this is suggested by *da quest' altra* and *di qua* (lines 130, 133).

Raggiungere (line 131), if we trust Tommaseo's *Dizionario*, has as its primary meaning not *rejoin* but *join*. Seemingly, then, the centaur is speaking of a second deep place about as far beyond the ford as the distance along the river already covered by the travelers.

CANTO 13

1. Still usually explained, as by Buti in the fourteenth century: "If I should tell you, you would not believe." Yet the easier reference is not to something Virgil might say, yet does not say, but to the passage in the *Aeneid* (3.22–43) referred to below (13.46–50), which Dante is avowedly, as it were, imitating. The feeling that Virgil is here exhorting the traveler to have faith in the *Aeneid* appears in the reading, apparently an unwarranted emendation for the sake of meaning, of *daran* for *torrien*. It is a commonplace that *togliere* has other meanings than *take away* (e.g., *Inf.* 25.109; *Par.* 6.57). In Tommaseo's *Dizionario* (*togliere*, sec. 30) is indicated Dante's use of *togliere* as though it were the Latin *tollere* in *Par.* 22.79 (cf. also 15.98). Possibilities for the Latin word are *excite, beget, engender*. Guido da Pisa (a fourteenth-century commentator) translates the passage: "Et ideo bene respice, et sic videbis quasdam res que tollerent fidem credulam sermonibus meis" (And therefore look about, and in that way you will see certain things that will excite firm faith in my narrative).

For *tollere* in other than its frequent sense of *remove*, see Dante's *Second Eclogue* 33; *De Monarchia* 3.9.40. The last is a quotation from Luke 22:36, where *tollat* appears in the Authorized Version as *take*, in the sense of *furnish oneself with*. In the letter to Can Grande, attributed to Dante, is quoted from Horace, *vocem comoedia tollit*, that is, "comedy elevates her voice to the level of tragedy."

2. See note 1, above.

3. A figure taken from birdliming, that is, the catching of birds by means of a sticky substance holding them to the branches to which they have been enticed.

4. More literally, *my sleep and my pulses*. The text of this passage is sometimes given in a form to be rendered *veins and arteries*, like *Inf.* 1.90.

5. By breaking the bark, they enable the tree to give voice to its lament, as did the tree Dante broke a twig from.

6. The soul will get its body for the Resurrection and Last Judgment. See Canto 10, note 1; *Inf.* 6.97.

7. Since Lano ran too slowly, he was killed at the battle of the Pieve del Toppo (1287), with a grim jest here called *jousts* or *battle of the spurs*.

8. The god Mars, whose mutilated statue stood at the end of a bridge over Arno. His "art," or occupation, is warfare.

9. Sometimes the passage is interpreted: "Those citizens who rebuilt the city would have made the workmen labor uselessly." I take *fatto* (line 150) as pleonastic. See Canto 31, note 1; Siebzehner-Vivanti, *Dizionario della Divina Commedia, s.v. fare,* sect. 19; Tommaseo, *Dizionario, s.v. fare,* sect. 186.

CANTO 14

1. The word *ghirlanda*, possibly an instance of Dante's liberty with meaning in rime, obviously means *garland* or *crown*. When so taken, it implies that the fiery plain is encircled by the forest, and the forest in turn by the wretched river, the Phlegethon with its boiling blood. That is, the first round (*girone*) of the Seventh Circle surrounds the second, and the second round incloses the third. If the idea of surrounding or engarlanding is pressed, Dante is writing in terms of the diagrams of the *Inferno* rather than in terms of what is within the reach of his dramatic traveler's eyes. The circumference of the Seventh Circle is, according to modest computations by those who chart the Inferno, some 180 miles; those very generous with Hell raise the figure to thousands. At the lowest computation, the observer on the spot would get little effect of encircling but much of bounding. Dante earlier mentions the proximity of river to forest (12.139–13.2). He speaks also of the limit or boundary between the second round and the third round of this circle (14.4–5).

Any reader wishing to follow the conventional diagrams will render *ghirlanda* by *surrounds* instead of by *bounds*, and will translate *abbraccia* (12.53) by *encircles* or some word equally in harmony with the charts. See the discussion in the Introduction, p. xxi.

2. From Petrocchi's text I have accepted *marturi* (*torture*), replacing the usual *maturi* (*soften, ripen*). *Seems not to torture* reinforces line 46 (*seems not to heed*) and is carried on in line 65 (*no suffering could be a torture*). On the other hand, his pride is "not extinguished" (line 64). The difficult *torto* (*irate?*) seems a concession to rime. Wrath appears in Buti's comment. Cf. *rabbia, furor* in lines 65, 66.

3. Here, as in similar passages, I have not translated the word *par* (lines 69, 70), thinking it wholly rhetorical. If it does add to the meaning, it has no English equivalent; *as you see*, for example, is too emphatic. There are, however, passages in which *par* (or some other form of the verb *parere*) is essential to the meaning, and must be translated. See Canto 18, note 5. Cf. Pulci, *Morgante* 27.1.

4. *Forgotten* (literally, *like an ancient thing*). This meaning, though unconvincing, is generally accepted. So far as I have observed, no modern has taken up Buti's hesitating suggestion that the word *vieta* (*ancient*) comes from *vietare* and means *forbidden* (to inhabitants). It then would be a shortened form of the participle *vietata*. Porena suggests that it is the Latin *vieta*, meaning *dried*. Seemingly he thinks of it as associated with *guasto* (*laid waste*—line 94) and indicating that the water making Ida pleasant (line 98) had disappeared. Dante allowed himself liberties in rime words.

5. For *dentro*, see Canto 27, note 7.

6. A frequent explanation is that the statue of the old man is in a cave; the tears dripping from the statue, when collected, pierce a hole by which they escape from the cave. Yet how can a figure in a cave look toward Rome as its mirror? The situation requires a figure standing on the mountain (see note 5, above). In line 114 a variant reading is *questa* (*this*), which I translate. The word *grotta*, in Dante meaning *bank*, not *cave* (as in Ariosto), refers to the rocky mountain under his feet. See Canto 34, note 3.

7. *Margin* (*vivagno*): Sometimes explained as the margin of the forest. Sometimes said to be the margin of Circle Seven. But does Dante the traveler know yet that the margin of this circle overhangs the great pit of Malebolge? I suspect that—led partly by need for a rime—Dante is using the word as a synonym for *circle*.

8. From the tears dropping from the statue.

9. *Purg.* 28.128; 30.143; 31.102. Dante is submerged beneath Lethe's waves, but nothing is said of washing, only of drinking. Since the traveler is a living visitor to the world of the dead, we need not assume that his experience is like that of the dead.

CANTO 15

1. This passage emphasizes the magnitude of the plain. The reader is to forget the oft-mentioned darkness of Hell (e.g., 8.93). When it is invoked, visibility is diminished.

2. The text preferred by Petrocchi, and generally printed, requires "putting down my hand to his face." Yet arguments for that text, other than expertly technical, are not impressive. I have not observed that any commentator notices that the text I follow, that of Sapegno, is supported by lines 44–45. The passage is part of a sequence: The traveler stares at the unknown who addresses him (line 26), recognizes Brunetto (lines 27–28), bends in respect, not familiarity (line 29) (no other shade is addressed as *Ser*), continues his respectful attitude (lines 44–45, echoing with *chino* the *chinando* of line 29). Cf. 5.110: *chinai 'l viso*, and 10.34 for a similar use of the pronoun. For another instance of courteous bending by the traveler, expressed with the same words, see *Purg.* 11.73, 78.

Buti comments on *mia*, Benvenuto da Imola on *mano*. *Mia* appears in the 1474 text of Stefano Taliche Ricaldone (Milan, 1888).

3. For this formula, cf. *Inf.* 21.82; 32.76.

4. Commentators who make *Inf.* 1.1 factual autobiography explain this clause as "before I was thirty-five."

5. Usually understood as *straw* or *fodder*, but Benvenuto da Imola glosses as *sterquilinium et lectum* (*litter-heap and bed*). Pagliaro argues for such an interpretation. Possibly my rendering gives the sense of the line.

6. This figurative language apparently means "Let wicked Florentines (immigrants from Fiesole) associate with and honor only those as wicked as themselves, without heeding good men, who show the virtues attributed to the best of the Romans."

7. Be dead.

8. In the book of memory.

9. Cf. 10.131.

10. On Dante's interest in famous characters, see Canto 20, note 10.

11. An encyclopedic work in French, or possibly *The Little Treasure,* an Italian poem.

CANTO 16

1. The traveler, if not prevented by the fire, should show his respect by hurrying to meet them instead of letting them run after him.

2. In their eagerness, not being yet sure that Dante is heeding their request that he stop (to which he must pause to get Virgil's consent) they repeat it, as well as their belief—essentially a question—that they are addressing a Florentine.

The passage is sometimes interpreted that they resumed their lamentations (14.20, 27). This explanation was plausible for medieval commentators who interpreted the pronoun *ei* (16.19) as a cry of pain.

3. The text of this passage offers difficulties. It is often interpreted to mean that they move their necks and their feet in opposite directions. I follow what seems the simpler reading, not that printed by Petrocchi. To his discussion and that by Pagliaro (*Ulisse,* 709 ff.), I add that the words *tra loro* (*among them*) are unimportant, as in 32.39, where Sapegno glosses *in that place.* I trust that they are sufficiently indicated by my possessive *their.* In 16.23, 47, they are normal. With something of comedy, the three sinners both continue their obligatory rapid pace (14.24; 15.37) and remain near the visitor, at whom they courteously continue to look, as much as their necessary motion in a circle permits, by turning their necks. They strain their necks to the utmost; then, when the traveler is out of sight behind them, whirl their heads in the opposite direction.

Does Dante compare the three with boxers or with wrestlers, or has he combined two types of contest? The comparison applies to wrestlers, except that they do not strike.

4. They speak as though certain that they are addressing a Florentine (lines 8–9), though the poem records no answer by Dante assuring them that they are correct until line 58—perhaps to keep the action from dragging.

5. The Italian word here (*freghi*) is used for such actions as stroking a cat. Annotators often give the word a meaning derived from the context. I do not offer my translation as accurate. Perhaps this illustrates Dante's tendency to overstrain the meaning of rime words.

6. I have translated literally, though commentators often explain that the meaning is *descend*. Dante seems to have used *tomi* (*fall*) to get a rime.

7. To a person going south it was in Dante's time the first or most northerly river south of the Po which did not flow into that great river, but had an individual channel to the sea. In the low region near the sea, the relation of the rivers has since been modified.

8. *Inf.* 1.33.

CANTO 17

1. Earlier said to be merely of stone (14.83). *Marmi* allows rime here.

2. Further than in his appearance, Geryon is not developed as a symbol of fraud. As a means of transportation, he is wholly reliable. The Eighth Circle and below, of which he is in some sense the guardian, is the region of fraud.

3. Arms are implied by the mention of armpits. Doubtless we are to imagine them as very short, lizard-like.

4. A notoriously difficult passage. I have accepted the paraphrase by Buti in his commentary on the *Commedia*.

5. In the *Decameron* 6.10 appears a comic character, dirty and ragged: "Without thought of his hood, so very greasy that it would have befouled the great kettle of Altopascio, and of his torn patched jacket enameled with filth around his neck and under his armpits and showing more spots and more colors than Tartar or Indian rugs ever did, and of his shoes badly broken and his torn breeches." Geryon is also *filthy* (*sozza*) (17.7).

The inference is that such reference to Oriental fabrics was common or proverbial with comic suggestion; if so, Geryon's appearance is so much the more comic rather than dignified, to fit the tone of the episode. See the Introduction, p. xxx.

6. Literally, *near the diminished place*, explained by commentators as meaning near the edge of the precipice bounding the circle. The usurers are on the burning sand, removed from the brink by the width of the rocky path (lines 24, 32, 43–45). The adjective *scemo* occurs in the *Commedia* only in rime; that suggests that its meaning here may be unusual. Can it mean *near the edge* of Circle 7, Round 3 (lines 38, 43, 44)?

7. The riders now hear the water striking at the bottom of the fall. This passage fits with the tone of the context, such as the

comparison with the waterfall near San Benedetto (16.100), to suggest that the descent is not greater than that of an earthly waterfall. If so, the comparisons with Phaethon and Icarus (17.106 ff.) are comic exaggerations to emphasize the passenger's fear.

The poem does not indicate the course of the stream through or across Malebolge on its way to Cocytus (14.119), nor do I recall any chart showing a bold attempt to do so. Geographical probability is not the poet's first concern.

8. Literally, *like an arrownock*, that is, the notch in the end of the arrow that fits the string.

CANTO 18

1. Geometrical treatments of Malebolge show concentric wheels (banks) with spokes (lines of bridges) extending from the outer rim and ending in the well or pit as the hub. The bridges are sometimes seven, more often ten. Such an interpretation is not that of the early commentators. For example, Guido da Pisa writes: "Over each bolgia, so that it is possible to go from one to another is one (*unus*) iron-colored and rocky bridge. . . . Over each and every ditch is one bridge." Soon after 1500, Manetti published a plan showing one line of bridges, and the fourteenth-century commentators write as for one line only. The single reference to another (and only one other) line of bridges is by Malacoda or Badtail, a deliberate liar (21.111; 23.140–144). Since a fortress would have but one entrance bridge, the illustrative value of lines 10–18 disappears if some ten lines of bridges (only one of them to be used by the travelers) are imagined. Dante's use of the plural, *fortresses* (*castelli*), to indicate any fortress or all fortresses has contributed to the difficulty. He might have said *a castle*. But the plural is carried throughout for the sake of the rime, and sometimes is required, since there are ten "little bridges," one for each ditch. Only one bridge, crossing all the bolgias, is mentioned in 23.134–136.

The impression given by the later part of the poem is that the line of bridges ends at the inner bank of the tenth bolgia (29.52, 53). From that point there seems quite a distance to the edge of the pit where the giants stand (31.7–27, 38). There is also difficulty about the "well exceedingly wide and deep" (18.5). It is wide enough to contain all of the Ninth Circle. But its comparative depth is not great. A giant some seventy-five feet tall can transfer the travelers from the top to the bottom (31.143). Geryon's descent seems greater. One ingenious commentator imagines Antaeus carrying the travelers down a long slope.

Is Dante required to be consistent, and is his Hell a subject for mechanical drawing?

2. Scourged by the devils, the souls move faster than the travelers.

3. No clear explanation of these circles has been given. A suggestion is that the course of the travelers has up to now been in segments of the circles of Hell, always turning to the left (14.124–127), but now, in the Eighth Circle, they abandon any circular movement, to go directly across the circle, following the line of bridges, except for minor deviations, soon corrected. The word here is *cerchia*, nowhere, unless here, indicating the circles of Hell; it does, however, apply to one of the terraces of Purgatory (*Purg.* 22.33). *Cerchio* is usual.

4. This bolgia is deep and narrow, as are most of the others. See, for example, 19.42.

5. Literally, "seemed (*parea*) to be taken from." Further passages make evident that the ordure really was so taken (lines 116, 131). Hence I have translated here (and in similar instances of *parere*) as fact rather than appearance. Cf., for example, 14.69, 70, and the note; 18.84; 24.26; 31.105; 33.134; 34.43.

6. This old American word for *head* is equivalent to the Italian *zucca*. My spelling indicates the dialectal pronunciation.

7. This incident is supposed to come from Cicero's version of a passage in Terence's *Eunuchus*. The flattery consists in raising *grandi* (*high*) to *maravigliose* (*incredibly high*).

CANTO 19

1. One of Dante's synonyms for *bolgia*.

2. The simplest explanation of line 21 ("I trust this will be a seal," etc.) is that it gives the reason for telling that the narrator broke the font in San Giovanni, namely, that—in a way suited to comedy—he may convince readers that he is telling the truth about the holes in the third bolgia. His deliberately false logic runs thus: (1) I say that I saw holes in Hell. (2) I know such holes because I broke one in San Giovanni, as any visitor to the church can see. (3) Hence my statement about the holes in Hell is true.

Thus Aristotle observed poets telling lies convincingly, by supporting the false with the true (*Poetics* 24). So line 21 means: What I did proves it.

Elsewhere Dante—for the sake of his fiction—proves his comic narrative reliable. He swears by his *Comedy* that he saw the incredible Geryon (16.128), and he makes his fear of the Malebranche real by comparing it to what he asserts he saw at Caprona (21.94).

The verb *sganni* (19.21)—literally, *undeceive*—occurring here only in the *Commedia*, is a rime word, to be interpreted liberally. What does a seal (its subject) do? So I render it *assure*.

The comparison in lines 16–21 is apparently like that of a giant's face to a metal pine cone to be seen at St. Peter's in Dante's time, and still existing (31.59). Here the comparison is with pits or holes which some of Dante's readers had seen in the Florentine baptistery, and which still existed in the sixteenth century. The comparison is in shape and diameter only; Dante's further narrative is the normal development of an epic simile; there is no comparison of the function of the holes or of the position of those in them.

The fourteenth-century commentators who, by visiting the baptistery, could have seen the holes there, do not agree on their purpose. The matter is still debated; Pagliaro, in his *Ulisse*, gives it eighteen pages. From Guido da Pisa, who probably had seen in the Pisan baptistery a font which some suppose to resemble that in San Giovanni in Dante's time, I translate his Latin paraphrase of Dante's text and his comment:

> These holes were not wider [an error for *less wide*] nor larger than those in my beautiful church of Saint John, made as places for the baptizing priests. One of these holes, not many years ago, I broke for the sake of a boy who was being suffocated in it. . . . In this church are fonts in which, at Easter, children are baptized. In the circumference of these fonts are pits in which stand the priests and levites [i.e., assisting clergy] to whom has been assigned the duty of baptism.

Some of the fourteenth-century commentators were of a different opinion, namely, that the pits held water for the baptism of infants. This is the function of those in the Pisan font, according to the 1959 edition of the Italian Touring Club's *Toscana*,

p. 138. This is confirmed by the description of the font in the Cathedral at Massa Marittima (Sac. Curzio Breschi, *La voce di un monumento*, Massa Marittima, 1940).

Pagliaro says of the fourteenth-century commentators, including Dante's son Piero: "Their information appears a simple development of what each one believed he could draw from the poet's succinct account." The only commentator who says that the break (repaired?) was visible is the author of the *Ottimo Commento*; he does not say that he saw it. Pagliaro mentions no record independent of the *Commedia*. Yet every Florentine reader of the *Commedia* observed the passage, and every visitor to the city went to see San Giovanni. The Dantesque font stood there until 1577 (Scartazzini-Vandelli). Until some independent record of Dante's action appears, the student cannot avoid asking whether the brief narrative of breaking the font is partly or wholly fictitious, the work not of autobiographer-poet but of poet only.

The word *per* (line 18) is by Dante used with even greater variety of meaning than Tommaseo's *Dizionario* prepares a reader for. On the other hand, other prepositions are used when *per* is expected (e.g., 23.20, with Petrocchi's note); is Dante's feeling for euphony one reason? The article often does not appear after *per*, and *loco* frequently lacks one (for example, 1.114; 5.28).

For somewhat analogous circumlocutions with *place* or *place where*, see 1.114; 2.71, 84; 12.94; 17.36; 25.21; 26.30; 28.24; 31.66; 34.76; etc.

3. This is often interpreted that the simoniacs showed above ground their feet and the part of their legs from ankle to calf muscle, that is, some nine inches. Meanings of *gamba, grosso*, and *zanca* (19.23, 24, 45) make this possible. Yet there are other possibilities. *Grosso* may mean also the whole body (22.27). If the comparison with a post (19.47) means anything, nine inches is too little. Judas Iscariot has his head in Satan's mouth and "waves his legs (*gambe*) outside" (34.63); his back is also outside, clawed by Satan (34.59). A mention of joints (19.26) has been taken as referring to knees. The motion of the protruding parts of the simoniacs is vigorous enough to break ropes (19.27). Probably, then, *gambe* means the entire leg; the simoniacs, to be as ridiculous as possible, protrude from the ground from foot to hip.

So in the fourteenth century Guido da Pisa interpreted, writing that the sinners were thrusting out of their holes "their feet and their legs up to their buttocks (*nates*), and all the rest from the buttocks to the head was inside there." Thus they appear in fifteenth-century illustrations (Lamberto Donati, *Il Botticelli e le prime illustrazioni della* Divina Commedia, Florence, 1962, pp. 131, 146, and a 1487 illustration reproduced in Chimenz's edition, p. 169).

4. Perhaps vague, as though to say that prophecies deceived him. The "lawless shepherd" from the west is Pope Clement V.

5. From II Macc. 4:7–5:10 (an apocryphal book of the Old Testament). Jason was an "ungodly wretch" who bought the office of high priest.

6. Judas.

7. Charles (of Anjou) I of Naples and Sicily (1220–1285).

8. From Rev. 13 and 17. Not the woman but the beast on which she rides has the heads and horns. Is Dante's modification deliberate? The woman is the Church, and the husband the Pope, in Dante's time grown corrupt.

9. The Emperor Constantine, changing his capital from Rome to Constantinople, was supposed to have bestowed on the Pope wealth and temporal power. This is called the Donation of Constantine.

10. The fourth bank is the inside boundary of the third bolgia. The bridge crosses the fourth bolgia.

CANTO 20

1. Minos judges all who fall into Hell (5.4–12).

2. See the Introduction, chap. 5.

3. His beard.

4. The Italian *a tergo* (*at the back*) means *behind*. Playing on it, Dante writes *al ventre* (*at the belly*), though still meaning *behind*, as he expresses with the verb *s'atterga* (*is at his back*).

5. The word *ronca*, here only in the *Commedia*, like many of Dante's rime words, is subject to free interpretation. The passage is almost universally interpreted: "The Carrarese, who lives below, tills the ground." Farmers, however, are somewhat more likely to till ground below rather than above, as in Dante's simile in *Inf.* 26.25–30. So far as I have observed, only Caverni, as recorded by Scartazzini, is disturbed by the interpretation *tills* (more strictly, *clears away bushes*). He suggests that Dante has abbreviated *arronzare*, which can mean *labor* (see Battaglia's

Grande Dizionario). Petrocchi records the reading *arronca* in one manuscript. Guido da Pisa allows *cultivate* as a second alternative, but gives first "the Carrarese quarry marble," for "*roncare* means to quarry stones from the mountains." Note the "white marbles" of line 49.

6. A fortress near Merano.

7. *Pennino* refers not to the Apennines but to a part of the Pennine Alps.

8. Empty of the soul, the especially personal part of man, though body is recognized in the belief that souls would have their bodies back for the Last Judgment. See 13.103.

9. Did Dante make the obvious insertion of Manto's story because he liked it, for variety, or to give the canto its required length? Even with the forty-five lines on Manto it is still below the average length of 138.82 lines for the cantos of the *Inferno*.

10. On the traveler's interest in persons worth noting, see *Inf.* 15.102; 23.74; *Par.* 17.138. To the modern it often appears that he makes exceptions to this rule.

11. Cf. *Par.* 2.51. Cain is the man in the moon. For his murder of Abel he was transported there and compelled always to carry a bundle of thorns. Seville, in Spain, stands for the extreme west. Sapegno explains *sotto* here as *presso* (near). Cf. 32.17, and note.

CANTO 21

1. This bolgia, like the second (18.109–112), is so deep and narrow that the travelers must reach the top of the arch of the bridge before they see into it. In 22.149 it seems also imagined as narrow. Yet the scene of 21.29–45 requires space; the devil does not see the travelers, who are on the bridge with him.

2. A statement of what the traveler did, though in the form of a comparison. See *Inf.* 3.136 and the note.

3. *Bedaubed.* On this debated word, I have followed Sapegno.

4. My word *fleshhooks* comes from Chaucer, *Somnours Tale* 22. This devil's hook seems later to have become his pitchfork. In line 57, the fleshhook is a kitchen tool.

5. Guido da Pisa, so far as I have observed, is the only commentator who deals convincingly with this word *accaffi* (*play at odd and even*): "In Tuscany there is a child's game called *a caffo*. A boy shuts up in his hand coins or beans or something of the sort to an even or odd number, and says to his playmate: 'Guess.' The latter says either 'odd' or 'even.' This game is called, as I said, *a caffo*. In the same way the grafters in their proceedings

keep their hands closed, and what they appear to put in one box, they put in another." Lexicons do not give this meaning for *accaffare*.

6. This has traditionally been interpreted, because of *chiedere* (*ask*), that a beggar, attacked by dogs, asks alms where he stands. The word *poverello* (*poor little man*) does not generally mean beggar. This brief narrative implies a master of the dogs. Would a beggar attacked by them ask for protection or for food? The parallel between action and illustrative comparison is that the poor man and Virgil shout, the latter with some boldness. A narrative simile is not to be pushed into excessive parallels. Thus in lines 7–17, the parallel is only in lines 8 and 17, the boiling of the pitch.

7. Literally, *your defenses*. I accept Castelvetro's suggestion that this is a figure for *offenses*.

8. Virgil elsewhere says something like this to the guardians of Hell (3.95; 5.23; 7.11; 12.88). Why do all of them, including the false Badclaws, so easily believe that Virgil is telling the truth?

9. Fact or fiction? See Gilbert, *Dante and His Comedy*, p. 2.

10. In readiness to strike.

11. When Christ visited Hell immediately after the Crucifixion.

12. Such scatalogical jokes are not uncommon in the Middle Ages. See Sacchetti, *Trecento novelle* 54, 133, 145, 156; Chaucer, *Somnours Tale*.

CANTO 22

1. A Tuscan proverb.

2. Full of, expert in. A Biblical expression perverted. See Acts 9:15. Cf. *Morgante* 17.6: "a vessel of all knowledge and ability"; and *Aspramonte* 1.3; "arca d'invidia" (box of envy).

3. Some English versions say that the Frate's clients praise him. The translators forget that the grafters work under cover. So far as I have noted, Sapegno is the only one, among translators and commentators, who finds gratitude in this passage. Cf. Boccaccio, *Decamerone* 10.3; *Teseida* 3.56, rubric; 8.25; Pulci, *Morgante* 10.78; 15.61; 21.170. Cf. *Inf.* 2.74.

4. Cf. *a gran divizia lacciuoli* (*Decamerone* 8.7, near the end).

5. Flying is faster than running.

6. They retire to the brink of the next or sixth ravine or

bolgia, where they cannot be seen by grafters who raise their heads above the tar of bolgia five.

7. I follow an interpretation given by Buti in the fourteenth century. For similar use of the word *proposto*, see *Inf.* 2.138. The other interpretation is that the Navarrese slipped from the clutches of Curlybeard, who was still holding him (line 60). Against the latter is that the sinner's trick required the absence of visible Malebranche or Badclaws (line 100). Would sinners be supposed to disregard Curlybeard's presence? Earlier we are told that they flee from him (lines 29–30).

8. Cf. line 124. Calcabrina (Brinerubber) is angry at Alichino (Wildhunter) for having advised action that made the devils ridiculous.

9. See Canto 28, note 10.

10. The ditch is here made narrow enough to permit rescue with an implement possibly five feet long.

CANTO 23

1. The mouse wishes to cross the stream. The frog promises to carry her across. In the middle the frog tries to drown her. As they struggle a hawk seizes and eats both.

2. The two words meaning *now*, though alike in meaning, are not, as an early commentator remarks, alike in sound. Expositors either try hard to find the fable and the adventure parallel or remark that they are not much alike. Is Dante joking?

3. If I were a mirror.

4. Did Dante deliberately make this inconsistent with the devil's journeys to Lucca (21.39)?

5. Often rendered "a painted people."

6. He is said to have had criminals wrapped in lead for burning to death.

7. Cf. 15.102; 20.103–105; and probably 1.116.

8. On the narrow bolgia, see 19.42; 30.87.

9. The narrator, returned from his journey, has explained the nature of the mantles (23.64–65), but the traveler until now knows nothing of the lead.

10. In this strange figure of speech, the sinners with their weights are compared with scales or balances heavily weighted. Their lamentations are the squeakings of the balances.

11. The podesta, an important Florentine official, was not a Florentine, but brought from some other part of Italy.

12. A part of Florence ruined as the result of the corruption of these two men.

13. This bolgia is so narrow as to be blocked by one man's body. Evidently the travelers do not go beyond this point; we are not told that they pass beyond the body (in appearance) of Caiaphas, the high priest largely responsible for Christ's condemnation, and they are only told of, but do not see, his associates.

Normal order might be: "He must perceive, before anyone passes along, how much the passer weighs." I have tried to suggest Dante's contorted order, caused by desire for emphasis, and also, it seems, for rime. *Pria,* frequent in various positions in Dante's lines, is one of his resources for rime, though less frequent than *via,* with which it here rimes.

14. Those responsible for the execution of Jesus brought on Jerusalem the divine vengeance, with the Roman army led by Titus as its instrument.

15. Caiaphas is actually "crucified on the ground" (line 111). Yet when Jacopo Rusticucci speaks of himself as *posto in croce* (*put on the cross*), he means *tortured* (16.43; cf. 7.91; 33.87). The three words are applied to Christ, with literal meaning, by Petrarch (*Canzone* 2.23). It seems that the words here have a double meaning, *like a cross* and *in torment.* In all the instances referred to, *croce* is a rime word.

16. See *Inf.* 27.113.

17. This bolgia is unusually deep (23.53; 24.41); Virgil, carrying his pupil, ascends without difficulty from the third (19.126), the only other into which the travelers descend.

18. As though Virgil gestured toward the preceding bolgia. Badtail promised, falsely, another bridge (21.111). See Canto 18, note 1.

CANTO 24

1. A basket is a *gavagno,* included in the verb *ringavagna.* I have translated literally, thinking that Dante wished the colloquial effect. Cf. 7.18; 11.54.

2. Can Dante have supposed that a peasant would mistake hoarfrost for snow? Is this a city man's view of the country?

3. Virgil's pleasant expression at the mountain's base is not mentioned though perhaps implied (*Inf.* 1.92, 113). It is spoken of in 3.20.

Lines 16–21 imply Virgil's serious displeasure with his pupil, as when he listened to a vulgar dispute; a figure resembling that of the plaster for the wound is there used (30.133; 31.3). Can the lines here have been composed for such a scene rather than for one in which Virgil's anger is not against his charge but against the lying devils?

4. Sometimes referred to the gowns of the hypocrites, without need, for any gown is unsuited for climbing. If we are to be minute, Dante was wearing a gown when recognized by Brunetto Latini (15.24). Would he have been so clothed in preparation for the forest and mountain of Canto 1? Further in this strain, could the hypocrites with their weights have surmounted the ruins of the bridge in their progress around their circle? But there is a limit to the putting of poetry before the eye.

5. Suggesting that Virgil, as a spirit, had no body to lift.

6. The word rendered *Then* (*onde*) is often interpreted as causal; the speaker has heard Dante talking. Torraca says the voice has no relation to Dante, and Sapegno moves in the same direction. Hence my rendering.

7. Some of the sinners are running (line 92). A different text makes the voice that of a wrathful person. No further reference is made to the speaker. Is this a sign of unfinished work by the poet? For *mosso ad ire* (*going*) cf. *Purg.* 3.85; *Par.* 21.36; Petrarch, *Rime* 332.58.

8. This passage gave difficulty in the fourteenth century. Benvenuto da Imola rests one of his alternative explanations on the reading *dietro* (*behind*) rather than *dinanzi* (*before*) in line 96. Petrocchi does not list that variant. Grandgent comments: "The snakes that bound the hands behind had their heads and tails thrust right through the bodies (from back to front) and tied in front." Though I think my rendering probable, I do not insist on it. Cf. the binding serpent of 25.4–9, and the same words (*per le ren*) in 25.57, where *per* cannot mean *through*. On *per* see the last paragraph but one of Canto 19, note 2.

9. Vanni's party was opposed to Dante's.

10. The Blacks will gain control of Florence.

11. The Whites, Dante's party, will be defeated and Dante exiled.

CANTO 25

1. The *fica* is an obscene gesture of contempt. Vanni Fucci considers himself as giving God his deserts.

2. See 14.63–69.

3. The horse's form of the centaur ends and the human begins at the horse's shoulders.

4. The other centaurs who guard the river of blood (*Inf.* 12.55–100).

5. Commentators identify Cianfa dei Donati with the six-footed serpent which at once appears; at least, Dante gives nothing more on him.

6. The Italian word is *liste* (*stripes* or *strips*), here a rime word. In the *Ottimo Commento* (on *Inf.* 10.85) Dante is reported to have said that he could give new meaning to rime words; hence I have ventured the translation *branches* for the forelimbs of man and beast.

7. The transformed Guercio Cavalcanti. See line 151.

8. My achievement in poetry.

9. Apparently with some amusement, Dante does not compare himself with Lucan and Ovid in poetical achievement, but in the extravagance of his presentation of serpents and transformations, as compared with theirs. For the two poets, see 4.90.

10. The forelegs of the serpent are so short that Dante calls them feet.

11. Of the three mentioned in line 35.

12. Some call him Buoso degli Abati, others Buoso dei Donati, one of the three of line 35.

13. Commentators explain *zavorra* (*lot of rubbish*), the souls of the seventh bolgia, as ballast, which would be of little value. Though this seems unsatisfactory, I can offer nothing better.

14. See line 35.

15. Guercio Cavalcanti, the little serpent of line 83.

CANTO 26

1. A disputed passage. I follow a text and interpretation now general. According to Petrocchi, the descent made travelers pale. Buti's text makes them descend because of the darkness. For a similar reascent by the path of descent, see 19.126.

2. Why the word *lonely*? The two travelers do not meet other visitors to Hell, nor do they see souls moving down to appointed places. See *Inf.* 28.44 and the note.

3. Often explained as though *furto* and *invola* (lines 41, 42) have their usual meanings of *theft, steals*. Siebzehner-Vivanti (*Dizionario della Divina Commedia*) suggests that *furto* is a participle from *furare*, meaning *robbed*, or *taken from sight, invisi-*

ble. Guido da Pisa twice paraphrases with the word *continet* (*contains*), and explains the beginning of line 48: "spirits are concealed." Scartazzini and Pagliaro speak of concealment, in harmony with 27.36, where Montefeltro, one of those swathed in flames, is addressed as a soul "concealed." So, with additional justification from the fourteenth-century commentator Buti, I abandon the notion of theft. *Furto* occurs here only in the *Commedia* (except for a disputed reading in 25.29); it can claim the privilege of rime words.

The pertinent part of the comparison beginning in line 34 is that Elisha saw only the flame of the fiery chariot in which Elijah departed, as the traveler saw the flame containing the sinner, but not the sinner himself.

4. A remark by one of the "black cherubim" (27.116) has fastened on all the sufferers in this bolgia the appellation of Evil Counselors. The fourteenth-century commentator Benvenuto da Imola repeatedly calls them "very astute." Ulysses has not given bad advice; he is paying the penalty for his tricks. Montefeltro is generally fox, though in one instance adviser. Even he was honest with the Pope in telling him how to be successfully fraudulent.

5. The word *ira* (literally, *wrath*) has been often explained as *sin.* Castelvetro suggests that they brought down on themselves the wrath of God (Robert C. Melzi, *Castelvetro's Annotations to The Inferno,* The Hague, 1966, p. 42). Guido da Pisa uses the word *culpa.* Was Dante searching for a rime? Most *-ira* rimes in the *Inferno* use *ira.*

Anger appears in the story of Palamedes, whom Ulysses hated for revealing the trick by which the Ithacan was avoiding the expedition to Troy. He devised a scheme that caused the execution of the innocent Palamedes (Hyginus, *Fabulae* 95, 205). According to Dictys, Diomed and Ulysses, envying Palamedes, conspired against and murdered him (*Trojan War,* Book 2). This is anger and sin enough to explain the punishment of the two. Anger did not motivate Ulysses' stratagems against Troy, mentioned in the following lines.

In associating Ulysses and Diomed, perhaps Dante recalled that Ovid's Ajax refers to them as friends, declaring Ulysses worthless without Diomed (*Metam.* 13.69, 100). Ulysses himself asserts: "Diomed shares his deeds with me, commends me, and is confident with Ulysses as his companion" (*Metam.* 13.239). The two are associated by Dictys and Dares (*Trojan War,* Book

2; *Destruction of Troy*). Boccaccio resembles Ovid, writing that Ulysses "brought with him Diomed, whom he ever loved with friendly loyalty" (*Teseida* 6.44; cf. 7.17, 103, 220; 8.19, 26; 9.46).

In telling of this bolgia, Dante uses words which, if taken literally, express motion (26.52, 57, 68, 76; 27.2, 4, 129; see Canto 27, note 11). In various of the bolgias the sinners move around the circle. This is a device for bringing the damned to the traveler, instead of making him go to them, as he usually does in the earlier circles of Hell, and in the last circle. In several bolgias, however, the procession is abandoned, as in the third, where the simoniacs are planted in the ground. Motion is used in the punishment of the hypocrites, who must walk under their heavy burdens. The seducers in the first bolgia are hurried on by the whips of demons, but their suffering is in the scourging rather than in the motion. So considering the processions in Malebolge as a method for securing variety in narrative rather than for intensifying pain, I do not find motion in 26.52, 57, and 27.129. We may recall that modern Italian sometimes uses as auxiliaries verbs which literally express motion.

6. Literally, *sparks*. The liberalized meaning secures rime.

7. The flame is called *antica* (*noble*) in the Latin sense of superiority in dignity or worth. See Forcellini, *Lexicon Totius Latinitatis*, s.v. *antiquus*. Dante often uses the word in the Latin sense, as *Inf.* 1.116; 10.121. Here it rimes; a majority of the Commedia's rimes in -*ica*, -*iche*, -*ico* include *antico*.

8. In the Southern Hemisphere.

9. Following Pagliaro (*Ulisse*, pp. 411 f.), who cites Benvenuto da Imola and Torraca, I translate *mattino* as *morning* rather than *Orient*. Yet since there is no earlier reference to night, the word *morning* is unexpected. A partial explanation may be that the *Commedia* offers *mattino* only in rime, and always riming with *cammino*, as here.

10. *Poppa* means *ship*, by the figure of a part for the whole. Did Dante reject the more obvious *prora*, used several times in the *Commedia*, because of its similarity in sound to *nostra*, just preceding?

11. Some commentators infer that Ulysses saw the Mount of Purgatory in the hemisphere of water. Statius speaks of the lower part of that mountain as subject to earthquakes (*Purg.* 21.55 ff.), so perhaps it is subject to such tempests as destroyed Ulysses' ship. Earthquakes, as Statius says, were believed to be

caused by subterranean winds. Cf. Milton, *Paradise Lost* 1.230 ff.; 6.195 ff.

CANTO 27

1. The flame vibrates in harmony with the tongue, reproducing the words formed by the tongue. The poet suppresses the effect of the other vocal organs. English translators often agree with Longfellow's "up through the point" (line 17), as though the words escaped from a hole in the flame. Harry Morgan Ayres puts it "up to the tip." Buti explains that the flame moved just like a tongue in speaking. Benvenuto da Imola writes: "According to the motion of the tongue within the flame, the point of the exterior flame was moved, so that the movement of the flame that could be seen was in harmonious agreement with the movement of the hidden tongue." Cf. *shaking* (line 63). Lana, another commentator, is of the same opinion, using the words "reaching the point of the tongue." "Through the point" may be supported by a rigid interpretation of *uscire, go out of* (line 6), but the word can be vaguely used, as in 18.69 and 27.78. In these three instances it is in rime. *Su per*, frequent in Dante, does not mean *up through* alone; cf. line 134.

2. A strange anticipation of the *Paradiso*, where the blessed are often said to be concealed in light.

3. Maghinardo Pagani had in his coat of arms a blue lion in a white field. The word *nest*, strange for a lion, is perhaps a concession to rime.

4. Literally, *hold brow*, meaning *be famous*.

5. A Franciscan, girded with a cord.

6. That is, while I was alive. The soul, which is speaking, was form for the matter of the body. From this man whose life was spent in arms, we do not expect the language of philosophy.

7. Difficulty with this passage is apparent in Longfellow's "Constantine sought out Sylvester . . . within Soracte." Yet his note quotes from an English version of the *Legenda Aurea*: "Constantine sent his soldiers in search of Sylvester." In the fourteenth-century Italian version of the *Legenda* (Florence, 1924) and in Giovanni Fiorentino's *Il Pecorone* 17.2, Mount Soracte appears, but no cave. Sapegno and Petrocchi explain *d'entro* as implying a cave; some texts give *dentro*. Manuscripts do not use the distinguishing apostrophe. A parallel is *Par.* 6.12: "D'entro le leggi trassi il troppo e il vano" (I removed what was useless

and ineffective in the laws). At least no cave is suggested here. *Dentro (d'entro)* uncombined with other prepositions occurs elsewhere in the *Commedia*, as *Inf.* 9.106 and *Purg.* 30.28; the combinations often seem not to affect meaning. Sometimes *dentro* seems no more than a dissyllabic *in*, as in "dentro alla divina voglia" (*Par.* 3.80); cf. "in divina natura" (*Par.* 13.26) "nella tua voglia" (*Purg.* 33.99). In the *Legenda Aurea* and *Il Pecorone*, Sylvester is "nel Monte Soratte" (Siratte). In the latter, Constantine "mandò nel monte per Silvestro" (sent to the mountain for Sylvester). Guido da Pisa comments: "Just as Constantine sent soldiers to (Latin *ad*) Mount Sirapti to consult the holy Pope about the cure of his leprosy, so Boniface in turn sent to the place of the Minor Friars to consult the Count." Guido does not mention a cave; nor does Brunetto Latini in his *Trèsor*, 1.87, as quoted by Lord Vernon in his *Readings on the Inferno*. Cf. Canto 14, notes 5 and 6.

8. A devil or black angel (cf. 23.131). The cherubs (not the tiny winged children later so called) formed one of the nine orders of angels (*Par.* 28.98 ff.). Such of them as rebelled with Satan became devils.

9. I have taken *forse (not at all)* as strengthening the affirmation. Alternatives would be *I see that* or *perhaps*, as ironical. See Canto 10, note 3.

10. Cf. 26.41, 42, 47, 48.

11. In the Italian stands the word *andando* (literally, *going*). Editors' uncertainty about it appear in their varying punctuation: comma before and after; before but not after; after but not before; no comma. These sinners, like many in Malebolge, walk around their circle, but their punishment is not in their walking but in their burning garments. Montefeltro's words *si vestito* (*so clothed*) repeat Virgil's statement that these sinners are swathed in what burns them (26.48; cf. 27.36). A rejected textual variant for *andando* is *ardendo* (*burning*).

For the simplest interpretation, one comma is used, after *andando*. This makes the word an example of the idiomatic *go*, frequent in Italian, and also in Greek and English; it indicates no motion, but is equivalent to *be*; hence it can often be omitted in translation. See Battaglia and Pernicone's *Grammatica Italiana* (1960), p. 316, and Battaglia's *Grande Dizionario*, under *andare* 32. He gives as an instance, from Dante's *Vita Nuova* 33: *la donna ond'io vo sì dolente* (the lady because of whom I am so sorrowful). Cf., with a reference to clothing similar to Monte-feltro's, *andar cinto* (*Par.* 15.112), literally, *go belted*, but properly merely *belted*.

This simple explanation is that of the fourteenth-century commentator, Benvenuto da Imola. Less probable is the explanation of the fourteenth-century Buti (seemingly followed by the modern Momigliano), who finds continuance in the gerundive *going*. Cf. 5.46, 48, 74, and Canto 5, note 8; *Purg.* 23.104; Pulci, *Morgante* 27.2.

CANTO 28

1. Free from the restraint of verse, that is, in prose.

2. On the weakness of the poet's intellect and of the Italian language, see the *Convivio*, Canzone 2. 14–18 and the comment on it (3.4.4). Dante's use of the word *seno* (*bosom*, that is, the space between the chest and a garment where something can be put) to indicate capacity, potency (perhaps unique), seems an example of his willingness to enlarge meaning for the sake of rime.

3. *Expose myself* (*mi dilacco*). Students give these words a meaning deduced from the context, as indeed Dante, in his free use of the rime word, requires.

4. Cf. 8.18, 33; 33.110, 111 for other suppositions that the travelers are moving down through Hell to their assigned circle of punishment. By the word *lead* in his reply (lines 46, 49), Virgil seems to accept Mohammed's idea of the soul's downward journey. For rapid fall to the right circle, see 13.97; 27.26; 30.95; 33.133; for still another means of getting there see 21.34 ff. A downward journey is suggested by the centaur's words (12.61–62, 82) and by 5.15 (see the note there) and 13.96. In Hell the two travelers never see souls either journeying or falling; in Purgatory, Statius is moving upward. Apparently Dante did not seek consistency.

5. With but one eye. A ruler of Rimini called Malatestino "of the Eye."

6. The man who must wish he had never seen Rimini, mentioned just above. He is Curio, who prepared himself for the hell of the causers of division by giving, in that city, the advice to Caesar reported in the next speech.

7. From Lucan: *semper nocuit differre paratis* (*Pharsalia* 1.281), "delaying always injures the prepared." Dante quotes this

in his letter to the Emperor Henry VII (Epistle 7). It seems that *l'attender sofferse* may be rendered by the one word *delayed* (for the proverbial form, *delays*), though Longfellow, for example, translates: *allowed delay*.

8. By this speech Mosca brought about the murder of Buondelmonte dei Buondelmonti by the Amidei. This caused feud and civil war in Florence.

9. The word *only* (*solo*) is sometimes explained as meaning *on my own authority only*. This seems not more than a reinforcement of what is otherwise said. Can the need for a rime be invoked?

10. The words *con tutta la testa* have troubled translators. Cf. Boccaccio's story of Andreuola's attempt to dispose properly of her husband's body. When arrested by the police, "*con tutto il corpo* di Gabriotto n'andò in palagio" (4.6). Evidently this means "taking the body of Gabriotto with her, she went to the palace." See also *Aspramonte* 2.55.50: "Si gittò con tutto el cavallo nell' aqua" (literally, He threw himself into the water with all his horse). Striking is the address to Fortune by Boccaccio's Troilus: Why didn't you carry away "Paris con tutta Elena" (Paris with all Helen) (*Filostrato* 4.31)? Cf. *Inf.* 17.25; 19.64; 22.147; Sachetti, *Trecentonovelle* 86. See Blanc, *Grammatik der Italiänischen Sprache*, p. 234; Tommaseo, *Dizionario*, *s.v. tutto*, sect. 8.

11. Dante transliterates the word *contrapassum* (*countersuffering, counterpassion*), found in the medieval Latin of Aristotle's *Ethics*, meaning that a transgressor should suffer in accordance with his sin, as "an eye for an eye, a tooth for a tooth." Bertran' is divided because he divided, and to the same extent. For discussion, see Allan H. Gilbert, *Dante's Conception of Justice* (New York, 1965), the Index under *counterpassion*.

CANTO 29

1. One commentator suggests "to keep looking and to weep as a result." I have, however, translated as though Dante has used the word *stare* for *grazia* (*elegance of style*), as often in Italian, without adding to the meaning of the associated verb. See Tommaseo's *Dizionario*, *s.v. stare*, sec. 49.

2. Usually annotators assume that some of the damned name him. But perhaps this is an abbreviation of the formula of *Purg.* 26.97: *Io odo nomar se stesso il padre mio* (*I heard my father give his name*, or even, *My father gave his name*). See *Inf.* 32.19

and the note. The present line lacks *se stesso* (*himself*). Must Geri's otherwise unnoticed anonymous companions be brought in? Apparently all those who converse with the travelers have moved on (28.63, 111), but the crowd can pause (28.52–53).

3. Bertrand de Born's castle.

4. See *Inf.* 29.73 ff.

5. The travelers stand on the bank above the ditch, which they do not enter. They converse only with sinners near them. The bolgia seems as narrow as those preceding. See *Inf.* 30.87 and the note, and *calle* (path), in 29.69.

6. We speak of this world and the next one. Dante has his traveler in the next or second world speak of the first one.

7. I adopt Petrocchi's reading *fonda*, defined as *borsa* (*purse*) by the commentator Daniello (1568).

8. "If I am correct in thinking that I recognize you."

CANTO 30

1. The word *varco*, apparently part of a formula meaning *catch*, does not appear in the translation. Perhaps it might be rendered by *surprise*. It occurs in the *Commedia* nine times, always in rime.

2. With the child in her arms.

3. That is, to gain the best of the mares owned by Buoso.

4. That is, if his swollen body had been cut from his legs.

5. Explained at the end of the paragraph.

6. Virgil told his pupil that the preceding ravine had a circuit of twenty-two miles (29.9). Several are narrow; see, e.g., 18.109 and the note; 22.149 and the note; 23.84. There seems no reason —*long* (29.53) probably refers to the distance from the first bank—to think this bolgia exceptional in width until Master Adam speaks of the half-mile, though he has just used the word *sentiero* (*path*). Does the poet abandon consistency? Does a short distance seem half a mile to the immobile Master Adam? Hell is already so wonderful that a stone bridge half a mile long need not much trouble a reader. See Canto 29, note 5.

7. A grotesque reference to Master Adam's size and his inability to move.

8. By deceiving the Trojans, he induced them to take within their city the wooden horse in which Greek warriors were hidden. At night they opened the city gates to their comrades outside and captured the city. Thus Sinon was essential to the fall

of Troy. Dante's animus against him is seemingly because, as an enemy to the Trojans, he was an enemy to the Romans, who considered the Trojan Aeneas their founder (2.13–24). Dante, as appears in his *De Monarchia*, considered the Roman Empire divinely established. Odysseus, like Sinon, is put in Hell because of the stratagem of the wooden horse and other acts against the Trojans (26.58–63). Both the Greeks are political rather than personal falsifiers.

9. Accepted by some in the fourteenth century was the reading, instead of *tuo mal*, of *mal dire*, which has been rendered *evil words*. I follow the text according to which Master Adam says, as is frequent in such disputes: "You're another." Sinon's mouth, like Adam's, shows disease. Guido da Pisa renders the clause: "Dilatatur os tuum pro tuo malo" (Your mouth is held open because of your sickness).

10. An instance of the poet's belittling of his traveler named Dante. Virgil fears that he will again slip into vulgar conduct. Seemingly, Virgil has moved away to continue the journey, while his pupil stands listening.

CANTO 31

1. In line 4, I have accepted from Petrocchi the word *far* (literally, *to make*), which he finds in a few early texts. (I find it also in Buti's commentary.) He attributes its usual omission—now seemingly conventional—to "failure to understand the pleonastic and phraseological *far*." As a parallel, he offers the debated passage, *Par.* 11.78, which he thinks has been explained with "abnormal syntactical construction." Cf. 13.150, and the note. It may be rendered: "Concord . . . and pleasant expression are the cause." Boccaccio writes: "Tutti . . . fecero dire a Gigliuozzo" (They all said to Gigliuozzo) (*Decamerone* 5.3); such wording, variously clear as to actor, is frequent in the *Decameron* (for example, 5.3 a second time; 5.9; 5.10; 7.3; 8.10 (p. 180, line 35, ed. Bari 1955). Cf. Pulci, *Morgante* 6.4.2. So Dante's *far esser* may be taken as *esser*.

2. Literally, "to be the cause first of good and then of bad reward." The word *mancia* occurs in the *Commedia* only here and in *Par.* 5.66, where also it has troubled commentators. Rime seems partly to explain its appearance in both passages.

3. In praising this simile of the city wall with towers, Guido da

Pisa speaks of the wall (*murus*) of the pit as crowned with giants. Petrocchi rejects the conjectural emendation *così 'n* (line 42). Vandelli's assertion that Buti offers it is not in accord with the edition of 1858, in either text or comment. Benvenuto da Imola, on *torregiavan*, emphasizes the encircling effect of the towers, as do the *Chiose* edited by Lord Vernon. Tommaseo's and Battaglia's *Dizionarii* gloss the riming word *corona* (line 41) as *surround*, not *crown*. Cf. *Par.* 10.65, 23.95; Virgil, *Aeneid* 9.380; Boiardo, *Orl. Inn.* 1.5.60.

4. The word *perizoma*, from the Greek, is applied in Gen. 3:7 to the aprons of fig leaves with which Adam and Eve covered their nakedness after the Fall.

5. The distance from the end of the thumb to that of the little finger, when fully spread, about nine inches. Thus the giant is 22.5 feet from waist to shoulder, perhaps more than 70 feet high, if we take the measurements literally.

6. Perhaps intended to be nonsense; at least, still unexplained.

7. The ell was a north European measure, probably vague for Dante's early Italian readers. Whether the poet intended this giant to be a little larger or a little smaller or about equal to Nimrod is not clear. Had he wished to be exact he might have used a Florentine measure.

8. The fame lost by Hannibal came to Scipio at the battle of Zama.

9. Garisenda is a high leaning tower still standing in Bologna, though lowered after Dante's time. If a man stands near the base of the tower, on the side to which it inclines, it seems poised to topple over on him. If a cloud then moves from that side over the top of the tower, the cloud seems to stand still and the upper part of the tower seems to be moving as though to fall upon him.

10. Did Boccaccio imitate this comic formula when he wrote of the timid Maestro Simone, frightened by a black, horned beast, the disguised Buffalmacco: "Fu ora che egli vorebbe essere stato innanzi a casa sua che quivi" (It was a time when he wished he had been at home rather than here) (*Decamerone* 8.9).

11. The giant stands with his feet on the lowest surface in Hell, that of Circle Nine. When the travelers are in Circle Eight, they see the giant down to his waist (31.32–33, 43–48), since his hips and legs are in the pit of Circle Nine. The giant takes up the travelers, who are standing in the Eighth Circle, and sets them down, at the level of his own feet, in the Ninth Circle (32.16–18).

CANTO 32

1. Seemingly this means that above this pit are all the other circles of hell.

2. A figure from the wine press.

3. Literally, *I am conducted to say*; perhaps it may be put: *I gird my loins to write*. But *conduco* approaches at least the class of a word not adding to the meaning but used for elegance (and here for rime). To that extent it is not to be rendered in translation (cf. 2.10; 29.3, and notes); I have preferred, with this warning, not to express it here. Cf. Boccaccio, *Decamerone*, Introduction: "A scriverla mi conduco" (literally, I conduct myself to write it).

4. In *On the Vulgar Tongue* 2.7.4, Dante speaks of these two words as childish in their simplicity and not suited for the noble diction of tragedy.

5. Much lower than the Eighth Circle, so that the traveler stares at the high wall (line 18) down which Antaeus has lowered them. Commentators have trouble with the passage partly through misunderstanding the phrase *sotto i pie del gigante* (*near the giant's feet*, line 17) as *beneath the giant's feet; sotto i piedi* (line 23) does mean *beneath my feet*. For *sotto* as *near*, see *Inf.* 20.126 and note; 25.26, 35; Ariosto, *Orl. Fur.* 14.98; 36.49; 45.63; Tommaseo, *Dizionario*, s.v. *sotto*, sec. 2. The Latin *sub* can signify immediate proximity. One device for making *sotto* mean *under* or *beneath* is to have the ice which floors the entire Ninth Circle slope down like the side of a funnel. As Giovanni Agnelli says (*Topo-cronografia del viaggio dantesco*, p. 48), Cocytus is a lake, therefore level (line 23). It is also like a frozen river (lines 25–27). The giants stand on the icy floor of the Ninth Circle or pit, the lowest part of Hell, extending horizontally to the place where Satan rises from the ice.

Though we should never forget the setting of Dante's stage, there is always risk in attempting to turn his poetical descriptions into specifications for mechanical drawings.

6. Who spoke these words? There are many variations on the formula *dicere udi'* (*I heard said*), to be translated according to the context. Sometimes it is a graceful and variety-gaining or even metrically convenient way of putting *He said*. This appears in *Par.* 24.67, 79, 97; 26.46, where it alternates with a number of words meaning *said*: *spirava, spirò, soggiunse, uscì, risposto, fummi, ricominciò, dicendo, disse* (*Par.* 24.54, 82, 88, 103,

118; 26.4, 22). The speaker may be named later, as in *Purg.* 20.19–30, or may be left to inference, as in *Purg.* 31.98. Virgil, as guide, not long before gave his charge directions (31.134). The narrative is interrupted by fifteen lines of invocation (32.1–15); then Virgil, as the commentator Torraca suggests, seems to resume his function as guide by cautioning the visitor about his next movements. Here, as often (cf. 32.84, and the note), Virgil hurries the pupil who stands gazing too long. In 14.73 Virgil similarly cautions his pupil to watch where he sets his feet. See 29.27, and note 2.

My interpretation requires me to follow the commentators who make the word *brothers* refer to all the shades in the ice, not merely to the two brothers to whom Dante speaks (32.21, 58). Nowhere else are the damned referred to as brothers. See note 8, below.

7. Up to their faces.

8. Often interpreted: "I looked down at my feet," or even sometimes translated, amusingly: "I turned to my feet." If so, the clause repeats line 23, which makes the traveler see the lake under his feet. I find no precise parallel, though Dante refers to the feet when telling of movement, as in *Inf.* 9.104. Cf. *Purg.* 10.28, 70; *Par.* 3.33; 6.22; Virgil, *Aeneid* 2.756; Catullus 63.52; and *Purg.* 30.130: *volse i passi*, on which Sapegno comments: *s'incamminò.*

The action, it seems, is that after seeing the ice ahead and under his feet (line 23), the traveler observed the whole lake (line 40). He then moved forward until he reached the two shades to whom he spoke (lines 41–69). Proceeding, he saw others to whom he did not speak (line 73); one of them he struck in the face. Thereafter he again went on (line 124) to encounter Ugolino. After his narrative, the narrator says: "We went further" (33.91). Thus the traveler, after seeing the ice under his feet and looking at the lake (32.23, 40), went steadily forward; his first advance is that of line 41. His words there are comparable with the English: "I took to my heels."

Possibly interpretative is Petrocchi's variant *volsi li piedi* (literally, *I turned my feet*), akin to *I' mossi i piè* (*Purg.* 10.70).

9. A puzzling passage, discussed in Gilbert, "Dante's Rimario," in *Italica* XLIV (1967), p. 416. Porena emends with *li labbri*, a reading fitting with *essi* and *riserrolli* in line 48, but not to be found in any manuscript. Did Dante fail to revise the passage?

Yet though Porena's emendation is violent, I believe him right in holding that Dante wishes to explain why the brothers do not speak. Can he have divined what Dante wrote, and may the accepted text give the copyists' correction of *labbri* to the gender familiar to them?

I suppose that when the shades wept with their heads down (line 37), their tears fell to the ground (line 38), leaving their faces dry. When they raised their heads, the tears ran down to their lips (cf. *Inf.* 34.53–54), where they froze, sealing their lips tight. They alone among the damned do not reply to the traveler. A neighbor, careful to keep his head down (32.53, 97, 105; 33.93), answers for them. Thus Dante varies the formula of address and answer.

10. My rendering is influenced by the possibly fanciful suggestion—as old as Tommaseo's edition (1869) and repeated by Sapegno (seemingly without knowledge of Tommaseo's note) from Torraca and Vandelli—that the lake, appearing like glass (line 24), acts as a mirror, in which Camicion, looking only down (lines 37, 53), sees Dante's reflection. The passage is also prosaically interpreted: "Why do you stare at us?" Elasticity of meaning is frequent in Dante's rime words.

11. Commentators, who find something ironic or even comic here, refer to the last line of Camicion's speech, to lines 117–120, and to 33.120. Buti comments: like chickens in broth." Daniello in 1568 said that the ice is likened to gelatin that people make, and the spirits to the pieces of meat or of fish of which it is made. Those who take the passage in dead earnest make the word *gelatina* merely *ice.*

12. King Arthur's lance-thrust let light through the traitor Modred.

13. Relatively, because wickeder.

14. Whose will, Dante's (as a character in the poem) or God's? On destiny and God's will, cf. *Inf.* 15.46; 21.82. One commentator remarks that if Dante acted deliberately he could hardly go on to say: "I do not know." Against hitting any of the sinners, the traveler had been warned, perhaps by Virgil, his guide and director (32.19). Those thinking he was warned by some other than Virgil find no substitute for the Latin poet, who does not wish his charge to wait long anywhere, as here in staring at the wall (32.18). If warned by Virgil, the pupil would hardly have resolved to disobey. Possibly explanatory is the traveler's im-

mediately preceding statement that he trembles in the cold. Is it intended to explain that, being not quite in command of his shaking feet, he kicked the sinner? Contrast 6.35, 36.

15. The traveler knows that Virgil wishes the journey to meet its schedule. See 7.99; 10.115; 11.112; 14.139; 17.40, 76; 23.145; 24.46; 29.11; 34.94–96; *Purg.* 12.4.

16. These shades cannot be flattered by a promise of fame, since, as Bocca has just said, they prefer to be unknown, though glad to defame their enemies (32.113 ff.; 33.8). *Sapere* (here *sai*), commonly meaning *know*, may approach or even attain the meaning of *can*. Siebzehner-Vivanti's *Dizionario della Divina Commedia* (1958) gives as instances *Inf.* 1.10; 6.41; 12.24; 29.113. *Mal* may move toward or reach the meaning *not* (Tommaseo's *Dizionario, male, avv.*, sec. 3). My rendering might be softened to something like "You have little chance to flatter."

17. Some interpret this that he will not raise his face, which he holds steadily down (line 105), lest Dante recognize him. It is even said that he cannot know that the traveler never has seen him. Is the idea of *tell* repeated for emphasis? At least the form *mosterrolti*, riming here only, gives the poet variety in rime.

18. I have transliterated Dante's *manduca* (*eats*), as rare in Italian as in English. It occurs here only in the *Commedia*, apparently to provide a rime.

CANTO 33

1. *Vedere* may mean *hear* rather than *see*, as in *Par.* 7.5. Cf. Boccaccio, *Decamerone* 7.2: "Gianello, il quale stava con gli orecchi levati per vedere se d'alcuna cosa gli bisognasse temere," etc. (Johnnie, who had his ears open to see [literally] whether he needed to be afraid of anything). Perhaps the present passage may be "hear speech and see tears."

2. Petrocchi, with support from fourteenth-century commentators, takes *Muda* as the name of the tower.

3. An emendation now often printed makes the line begin *E 'n che*. Petrocchi finds the *'n (in)* or *in* in no early text. It does, however, appear in Buti, Benvenuto da Imola, Stefano Taliche Ricaldone (1474), and Daniello (Venice, 1568). Guido da Pisa twice writes Petrocchi's form.

Sapegno and Chimenz, a few words farther on, print *altrui*, explaining it as *altri*, a nominative. If so, it is the only nominative instance in the *Commedia* (according to Fay's *Concordance*;

he read *altri* in this line). For *altrui* as nominative, see Blanc's *Grammatik der Italiänischen Sprache*, p. 324, and Rohlfs's *Historische Grammatik*, sec. 506. Battaglia's *Grande Dizionario* says that *altrui* is never a subject; see Tommaseo's *Dizionario, altrui,* sec. 5. Guido da Pisa renders the passage: "Convenit quod adhuc alteri recludatur" (which still must be shut on others). His Latin dative, *alteri,* shows that he interpreted *altrui* as dative.

Early emenders did not realize that *che,* as Petrocchi says, is a "complement of place," equivalent to *in che.* I follow his text.

4. The word *sonno* (normally *sleep*) in line 26 is equivalent to *sogno* (*dream*). Though in the rime here, it occurs out of rime with the same meaning (*Par.* 12.65). In line 38, *sonno* is usually taken to mean *sleep.* Thus the words *suo sogno* (*his dream,* line 45) offer as though known to the reader a dream by the sons which has not been mentioned. Commentators, even with some confusion of the words, deduce explanations to save the poet's consistency. Apparently we must suppose a textual error or a slip by the poet.

5. The sinners in the preceding portion of the Ninth Circle were looking down (32.37).

6. The date is more valuable than the fig; his punishment is graver than his sin.

7. Above: on earth. For *actually* (*forse*), see Canto 10, note 3. By *is,* I render *par,* which might be *is to be seen.* See Canto 18, Note 5. Cf. Pulci, *Morgante* 4.73, 92.

8. See 22.88. Michael Zanche was betrayed and murdered by his son-in-law, Branca d'Oria.

9. Early texts of line 145 are divided between *un* (*a*) and *il* (*the*). Cf. *Inf.* 23.143. Yet translators and commentators—among them the fourteenth-century Buti—who print *il,* often explain the passage as though it read *un,* in accord with *un demonio* (*a demon*) of line 131. But Dante's son Pietro treats both lines—at unusual length—as though referring to Diabolus or Satan, with abundant scriptural citation, as Luke 22:3: "Then entered Satan into Judas." His interpretation harmonizes with his allegorical emphasis.

Is it possible that *il* is to be taken in the sense of *that,* referring to *un demonio* (131) (Tommaseo, *Dizionario, il, pronome,* sec. 8)? I accept Petrocchi's text.

10. Branca d'Oria was from Genoa.

11. Frate Alberigo was from Faenza in Romagna.

CANTO 34

1. Generally rendered: "The banners of the King of Hell advance toward us." *Prodeunt* commonly means *advance*, and *verso* often means *toward*. Yet, as at least one commentator says, Satan cannot advance, and the travelers walk toward him. In classical Latin, *prodeo* can mean *appear*. The fourteenth-century commentator Buti renders the passage: "In verso di noi si manifestano li gonfaloni del re" (To us are shown the standards of the king). The *Commento anonimo*, on a similar explanation, comments: "*Prodeo, prodis* mean *show*." The *Chiose sopra Dante* edited by Lord Vernon (Florence 1846) explain *prodeunt* as *sissi manifestano*. Guido da Pisa speaks of these banners as "placed" in that position when Christ harrowed Hell. Dante's *verso* often means *to*.

If we cling to the traditional translation, can Virgil be joking, saying that the banners of Hell advance because they cannot advance?

2. Benvenuto da Imola explains that such a standard indicates the presence of the king.

3. Literally, "there was no other bank [than Virgil]," as though the poet were combining two ideas: "There is no other shelter than Virgil" and "There is no sheltering wall." *Grotta* is used in the *Commedia* nine times, eight of them in rime; only three tercets in such rimes lack the word. As a sought-for rime word, it varies in meaning: *mountain* (*Inf.* 14.114), *bank* (21.110; 31.114), *cliff* (*Purg.* 1.48), *rocks* (22.65). Since *altro* is a flexible word, did Dante mean "no bank of any sort?" Cf. Canto 14, note 6.

4. Night is spoken of as though it were a heavenly body. Cf. *Purg.* 2.4; 25.3. Twenty-four hours have passed since the travelers entered Hell (*Inf.* 2.1).

5. Cf. *Inf.* 17.103 for a similar movement by Geryon.

6. Explained in lines 106 ff.

7. Half-past seven or later in the morning. In line 68 Virgil had said it was evening, being then in the eastern hemisphere. Having passed the earth's center, he is now in the western hemisphere. He speaks as though they were on the surface rather than at the center. Since they have gone halfway around the earth, they have changed their time by twelve hours.

8. The word *divellere* and its synonyms, meaning *uproot*, are used five times, in varying forms—*avelse* (*Purg.* 1.136), *disvelta*

(*Inf.* 13.95), *divelse* (*Par.* 27.98), *svelle* (*Inf.* 12.74)—always in rime; once it has its literal meaning (*Purg.* 1.136). In the present passage, it is strange, since the traveler has not fixed or rooted himself in Hell, and his departure is not violent. Partly because of its strangeness, I have translated literally here, hoping to give (I fear with exaggeration) something of the original effect. Obviously Dante welcomed these words as furnishing him rimes. The rime *-else* appears twice in the *Commedia*, and *-elta* once; *-ella* and *-elle* are frequent.

9. The hemisphere of water (opposite the land mass of the Old World, and composed of parts of the southern and western hemispheres of modern nomenclature) in which, though at the center of the globe of earth, the travelers now stand, was for Dante without land except the mountain of Purgatory or the mysterious land that Ulysses approached (26.133), sometimes identified with Purgatory. Jerusalem, where Christ died, is for Dante the center of the landmass formed by Europe, Asia, and Africa.

10. When Satan, having rebelled against God, was thrown from Heaven, he struck the earth on the side of the globe opposite the continents known in Dante's time. All the dry land on the side where he fell fled to the other hemisphere, presumably adding itself to the continents of Europe, Asia, and Africa. Also, material within the earth fled before him, leaving an empty space, and emerging to compose the mountain of Purgatory. Some take this empty space as merely the cave entered by the travelers on leaving Satan's side (lines 97 ff.). Others take it as all of Hell. Such a theory possibly does not conflict with the statement about the creation of Hell in the inscription on its gate (3.7 f.). At its utmost, it gives Purgatory a height of over 3,000 miles. Such extravagance has driven some topographers to content themselves with the material removed from the cave. I have not observed that they discuss the course by which this material emerged from the center to the surface in order to form the mount.

When making this removal of material a topographical fact, for the *Commedia*, they take Dante's *forse* (line 124) not as a doubting *perhaps*, but as affirmative. See Canto 10, note 3.

11. What seems to issue from debate on this passage is that into the natural cavern (line 98) where the travelers stand, at the point farthest from Satan, descends a stream to which the trav-

elers are guided by hearing rather than sight, in the dim light. Its course offers a path to the earth's surface. Dante is evidently little interested in the transition from Hell to Purgatory.

12. The vertical climb so casually mentioned is half the earth's diameter or, as Dante supposed, 3,250 miles. This is hardly to be covered without rest except in a dream or a miraculous journey, just as the other thousands of miles from Hell Gate to the center are hardly to be covered in a normal twenty-four hours, with however much aid from Geryon and others.

13. However much—and not with complete necessity in Dante —the partitive idea of lines 137–138 is emphasized, there is still repetition in line 139. In 1568 Daniello explained: "The stars, which were the beautiful things he had mentioned." The duplication seems to come largely from Dante's love for symmetry, determining him to end all three parts of his poem with the same word: *stars* (*stelle*). Also in 1.40, the stars are "beautiful things."

1215 Buondelmonte murdered in Florence (*Inf.* 28.104; *Par.* 16.136 ff.). Florentine factions are called Guelfs (usually opposed to the Roman—really German—Emperor and favoring the Pope) and Ghibellines (favoring the Emperor).

1248 Guelfs expelled from Florence (*Inf.* 10.48).

1251 Guelfs return to Florence (*Inf.* 10.49).
      Ghibellines expelled from Florence (*Par.* 16.154).

1260 Florentine Guelfs defeated by Florentine and Sienese Ghibellines at Montaperti (*Inf.* 10.85 f.).
      Farinata degli Uberti, a Ghibelline, prevents the destruction of Florence (*Inf.* 10.91 ff.).

1265 Dante's birth at Florence.
      King Manfred, a Ghibelline, defeated by Charles of Anjou (*Purg.* 7.113 ff.) and killed (*Purg.* 3.128) at Benevento.

1266 Gianni de' Soldanieri, a Ghibelline, betrays his party to the Guelfs (*Inf.* 32.121).
      Catalano, a Guelf, and Loderingo, a Ghibelline, chosen to hold jointly the office of podesta in Florence; they govern corruptly (*Inf.* 23.100 ff.).

1268 Conradin, a Ghibelline, the Emperor's son, defeated at Tagliacozzo (*Inf.* 28.17) by Charles of Anjou and put to death (*Purg.* 20.68).

1269 Ghibellines led by Provenzano Salvani and Guido Novello defeated at Colle by Florentine Guelfs (*Purg.* 11.121; 13.115).

1280 Tebaldello, a Ghibelline, treacherously admits hostile Guelfs into Faenza (*Inf.* 32.122).

1282 Guido da Montefeltro, a Ghibelline, defeats the Pope's army at Forlì (*Inf.* 27.43).

1288 Guelfs from Arezzo defeat Sienese Ghibellines at the Pieve del Toppo (*Inf.* 13.121).
      Count Ugolino, a Guelf, imprisoned in the Hunger Tower at Pisa (*Inf.* 32.124–33.90).

1289 Death of Count Ugolino (*Inf.* 33.75).
      Florentine Guelfs defeat Ghibellines from Arezzo at Campaldino (*Purg.* 5.92).

Florentine and Lucchese Guelfs capture Caprona from Ghibelline Pisans (*Inf.* 21.95).

1292 ? or soon after   Dante composes the *Vita Nuova*. Most of his short poems are usually assigned to his youth.

1293   Giano della Bella active, on the popular side, in reforming the government of Florence (*Par.* 16.131).

1295 or 1296   Dante enrols in the guild of Physicians and Apothecaries; thereafter he is active in Florentine politics.

1298 ? Dante perhaps begins the *Commedia*.

1300   The year attributed to Dante the traveler's fictitious journey in the *Commedia* (*Inf.* 21.113).

The Black (Neri) party, led by Corso Donati (*Purg.* 24.81 ff.), and the White (Bianchi) party, led by Vieri de' Cerchi, fight in Florence.

Dante goes on a governmental mission to the town of San Gimignano, where he addresses the people (May 7). Dante serves as one of the six Florentine priors, for the usual two months' term (*Purg.* 6.141 ff.), June 15–August 15. He and the other priors banish both the White and the Black leaders.

1301   Dante goes as one of an embassy to Pope Boniface VIII in Rome.

The Blacks gain control of Florence, with the aid of Pope Boniface VIII (*Inf.* 19.23; *Par.* 27.22; 30.148).

1302   Dante, as a leader of the White party, is by the Black party fined and banished two years for financial corruption in his office of prior. The charge is usually considered false, a political trick by his enemies.

The Black party sentences Dante to death by burning. During his exile from Florence, lasting for the rest of life, Dante visited almost all parts of Italy (*Convivio* 1.3). Fulcieri da Calboli, podesta at Florence, beheads several of the Bianchi (*Purg.* 14.55 ff.).

Dante attends a meeting of White exiles at San Godenzo, in Tuscany (June 8).

1303 ? Disgusted with the other Whites, Dante abandons them, to form a party by himself (*Par.* 17.61 ff.).

Dante in Forlì.

1304 ? Dante in Verona with Scaliger family (*Par.* 17.70 ff.).

1306   Dante in Padua.

Dante at Sarzana, in Lunigiana, as agent for the Malaspini (*Purg.* 8.128 ff.).

1307–1309 Dante perhaps composes the *Convivio*.

1311 Dante at Milan at the coronation of the Emperor Henry VII.

Dante's letter to the Princes and Peoples of Italy in support of the Emperor Henry VII (Epistle 5).

Dante's letter to the Florentines threatening the Emperor's vengeance (Epistle 6, March 31, written in the Casentino, probably at the Castle of Poppi).

Dante's letter urging the Emperor Henry VII to attack Florence (Epistle 7, April 16, also from the Casentino). Dante excluded by name from an amnesty granted to Florentine exiles.

1314 Dante in Lucca.

1315 Dante again condemned to death by the Florentines as a Ghibelline and a rebel.

1316 Dante again excluded from a Florentine amnesty to exiles.

1317 ? Dante again with the Scaligers in Verona.

1317 ? Invited to Ravenna by Guido Novello da Polenta.

1319, 1320 ? Dante's Latin eclogues to Giovanni del Virgilio. Dante visits Mantua.

1320 Dante's treatise *De aqua et terra* delivered as a public dissertation at Verona, January 20.

1321 One of an embassy from Ravenna to Venice. Dante's death at Ravenna.

The dates of Dante's work *On Monarchy* and his unfinished *On the Vulgar Tongue* (the Italian language) are not firmly established. For internal evidence on their dates, see Gilbert, "Did Dante dedicate the *Paradiso* to Can Grande della Scala?" in *Italica* XLIII (1966), 119–122.

OUTLINE OF THE *INFERNO*

SINS OF VIOLENCE

Circle 7, Round 1
Canto 12

The Minotaur. Descent to Circle 7. Christ's harrowing of Hell. The centaurs. Phlegethon, the river of boiling blood, punishing violence to other men.

Circle 7, Round 2
Canto 13

Trees containing the souls of those violent against themselves. Peter of Vinea on princely ingratitude. Violence to property punished by fierce dogs. A suicide's soul in a bush.

Circle 7, Round 3
14.1–16.89

The violent against God on the burning sands. Capaneo, defying God in words. (Virgil explains the rivers of Hell, flowing from a Cretan statue—14.76–15.12.) Brunetto Latini and three Florentine sodomites. Degenerate Florence. Usurers, Florentine and Paduan.

17.34–78

Descent on
Geryon's back
16.90–17.33
17.79–136

The abyss of lower Hell. The cord thrown into it. Geryon rises from the chasm. The travelers descend on Geryon's back.

SINS OF FRAUD AND MALICE AGAINST MEN GENERALLY

Circle 8, Bolgia 1
18.1–99

The plan of Malebolge, Circle 8. Panders and seducers scourged by devils. Venedico Caccianemico; Jason.

Circle 8, Bolgia 2
18.100–136

Flatterers in the filth of privies. Alessio Interminei; Thais.

Circle 8, Bolgia 3
Canto 19

Simoniacs upside down in holes. Popes Nicholas II, Boniface VIII, Clement V.

Circle 8, Bolgia 4
Canto 20

Virgil rebukes Dante for pitying the twisted bodies of the fortunetellers. Tiresias, Michael Scot, and some Italians. (Manto the founder of Mantua—20.58–102.)

Circle 8, Bolgia 5
21.1–57;
22.16–90

Boiling pitch like that of the Venetian navyyard submerges the grafters. A grafter brought from Lucca. A grafter tells his story. (The bridge broken when Christ harrowed Hell; the *Commedia* dated—21.112–114.)
Dante's fear of the demons. The Navarrese

and of bodies appearing alive but occupied by the devil. Dante's invective against Genoa.

Circle 9, Ring 4
34.1–69

Judecca, for betrayers of Redeemer and Emperor. Satan tortures Judas, Brutus, and Cassius.

Departure
from Hell
34.70–139

Lucifer's body as a ladder. Virgil explains the earth's center. The travelers climb up, to emerge on the island of Purgatory.

LIST OF PASSAGES NOTED

The list below will direct the reader to comments on or references to passages in the *Inferno* which appear elsewhere than in notes on the passages themselves, and to comments on or references to passages in the *Purgatorio* and the *Paradiso*. I hope that those using the *Commedia* as an exposition of itself—the best of commentaries—will consult this list when studying any passage.

INFERNO

PURGATORIO

PARADISO

INDEX

The index is designed to give the reader assistance beyond that furnished by a list of names. For example, under DANTE, Visitor to Hell, may be found entries suggesting the concept of the central character which seemingly the author intended to convey, such as *inquisitiveness*.

The reader is directed also to the List of Passages Noted which precedes the index.

289; swine, 63; tailor, 119; Tartar fabric, 135; thunder, 261; tinder, 113; tombs, 75; towers, 263, 267; traffic in Rome, 143; Trent, 93; trumpet, 175; Turkish textiles, 135; Tydeus, 277; Venetian navy yard, 167; water in race, 187; waterfall, 131; waves of sea, 53; wax, 207; windmill, 289; wings, 131; wounds, 233; writing, 199. *See also* Metaphor, Simile

tion. Intended to aid in the reading of the text, they give many references to other passages in the *Commedia*. Passages in which this translation departs from the usual are explained. Lack of historical notes is partly atoned for by a table of the events of Dante's life and times. A summary of the poem, indicating canto and line, is also provided.

A novel editorial feature of the translation is the indication of the various speakers. Lines not immediately dramatic are attributed either to the narrator who has returned from the journey or to the poet, when Dante speaks as such. Aided by this device, the reader does not forget that he is dealing with varied dialogue and drama instead of the uniform poetry suggested by the usual unbroken page.

Allan H. Gilbert, currently Visiting Professor of Literature at Drew University, is Professor Emeritus at Duke University, *Cavaliere nell' Ordine Al Merito della Repubblica Italiano*, and an Honored Scholar of the American Milton Society. He has been a Fulbright research fellow in Italy and a lecturer at the University of Florence. In addition to numerous articles, he is the author of *Dante's Conception of Justice, Dante and His Comedy*, and works dealing with Machiavelli, Milton, Shakespeare, Jonson, and literary criticism. He has translated Machiavelli's *Works* and Ariosto's *Orlando Furioso*.